Jordan

the Bradt Travel Guide

Carole French

edition

I

www.bradtguides.com

Bradt Travel Guides Ltd, UK
The Globe Pequot Press Inc, USA

LEBANON

Stroll among evergreen woodlands, Aleppo pines and strawberry trees in Ajloun Forest Reserve
page 168

Witness spectacular displays of music, dance and theatre among Greco-Roman remains at the Jerash International Fes
page 131

Join modern-day pilgrims at the Biblical sites of Baptism Valley
page 185

Float unaided in the Dead Sea, the lowest point on Earth
page 159

Marvel at the 'Rose City' of Petra, the former Nabatean capital carved painstakingly into the soaring rock face
page 201

Dive in the Gulf of Aqaba and discover coral reefs and kaleidoscopic marine life
page 235

Mingle with Bedouin tri in the Wadi Rum desert
page 223

Golan Heights

Lake Tiberias

Yarmouk

SYRIA

Umm Qays
Bayt Ras

RAMTHA (AR-RAMTHA)

Ajloun Forest Reserve

IRBID

Mafraq (Al-Mafraq)

Ajlun (Ajloun)

Jerash

Umm al-Jimal

Dibeen Forest Reserve

ZARQA (AZ-ZARQA)

Qasr al-Hallabat

Jordan

West Bank

SALT (AS-SALT)

AMMAN

Q Az

Bethany Beyond the Jordan

Qusayr 'Amra

Azra (Al-Azra

Mediterranean Sea

Madaba (Medaba)

Qasr al-Mushatta

Qasr al-Harrana

Sh W R

JERUSALEM

Dead Sea

Hammamat Ma'in

Umm Ar-Rasas

Majib Nature Reserve

Central Desert

Qasr al-Tuba

Gaza Strip

Qatraneh

ISRAEL

Salt pans

KARAK (AL-KARAK)

Qa'Al Hafira

Tafila (At-Tafila)

Dana Biosphere Reserve

EGYPT

Araba Valley

Shobak (Ash-Shawbak)

Petra (Al-Batra)

Wadi Musa

Ma'an

Qa'Al Jafr

Al-Mudawwara Desert

Rashidiyya (Ar-Rashidiyya)

Jabal Rum 1754m ▲

AQABA

Wadi Rum Protected Area

Gulf of Aqaba

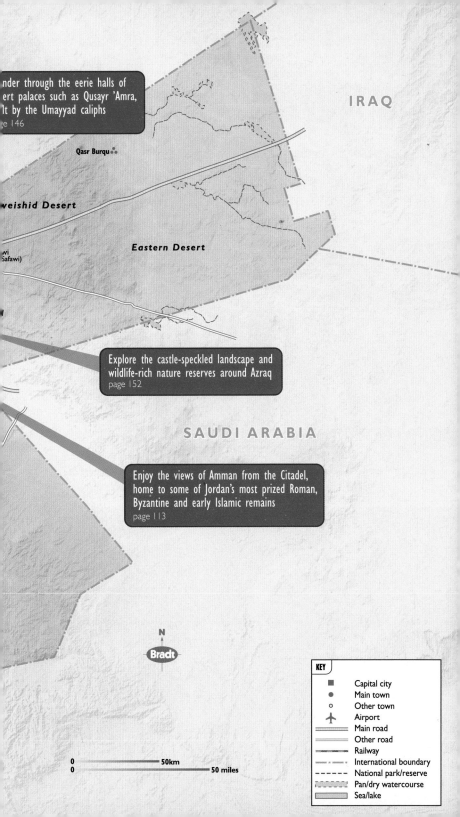

nder through the eerie halls of
ert palaces such as Qusayr 'Amra,
lt by the Umayyad caliphs
e 146

IRAQ

Qasr Burqu

weishid Desert

Eastern Desert

wi
Safawi)

Explore the castle-speckled landscape and
wildlife-rich nature reserves around Azraq
page 152

SAUDI ARABIA

Enjoy the views of Amman from the Citadel,
home to some of Jordan's most prized Roman,
Byzantine and early Islamic remains
page 113

N

Bradt

0   50km
0   50 miles

KEY

■ Capital city
● Main town
○ Other town
✈ Airport
━━━ Main road
━━━ Other road
┿┿┿ Railway
─·─·─ International boundary
─ ─ ─ National park/reserve
░░░░ Pan/dry watercourse
▨▨▨ Sea/lake

Jordan Don't miss...

Petra Marvel at the sheer height and colours of the Siq, and then get your first glimpse of the Al-Khazneh (The Treasury), appearing like a vision at the end of the gorge (AB) page 201

Wadi Rum
Sip herb tea with the Bedouin in the depths of the desert (SS) page 223

Dead Sea
Famous for its medicinal properties, the Dead Sea dominates the Jordan Valley and is the lowest point on Earth (SS) page 159

Amman
A monument to Jordan's ancient past, the Temple of Hercules in the Citadel rises above the honey-coloured houses of the capital, Amman
(H/A) page 114

Aqaba
The coral reefs and kaleidoscopic marine life make this tranquil harbour city a Mecca for divers
(MW/A) page 235

left No trip to the capital would be complete without sampling traditional Arabic coffee in one of its many coffee shops (SS) page 76

below Explore the archaeological wonders of the city among the extensive collections in the Jordan Archaeological Museum (CF) page 116

bottom With its bright blue dome and glittering mosaics, the Al-Abdullah mosque is a landmark on the Amman skyline (SS) page 121

right   Meticulously carved into the rock face, the imposing Roman Theatre is one of Amman's central locations for social gatherings, cultural performances and concerts (SS) page 118

below   Indulge in some bartering in the fragrant spice souks and bring back an authentic taste of the country (SS) page 110

bottom   The ruins of a 6th-century Byzantine church stand in the foreground of the Temple of Hercules in the Citadel (SS) page 118

right Experience true Bedouin hospitality over a cup of coffee (RM) page 223

below A camel race at Wadi Rum: although many of the Bedouin tribes have given up their nomadic existence and established permanent settlements, many in Wadi Rum still uphold the traditional ways of life (RM) page 223

AUTHOR

Carole French was first bitten by the travel bug as a child; one of her favourite activities was packing for family holidays, weeks in advance. In those days it was a beach holiday in the UK; now she travels the world as a freelance travel journalist and author in search of inspirational stories and lifestyles. Carole, a BBC-trained journalist who has worked and travelled extensively in the Middle East, as well as Europe, Asia and the Caribbean, divides her time between homes in the eastern Mediterranean and the UK. Along with Bradt Travel Guides, her clients include ABTA and the BBC.

AUTHOR'S STORY

I had long admired Jordan from afar, and even before I visited for the first time I knew instinctively it would make an impression on me. My imagination had already been captured by the city chic of Amman, awesome biblical sites and breathtaking natural beauty that I'd seen only in photos or read about, and I had become absorbed by the riveting history of Petra during my archaeology and architectural studies. The determined work for women's and children's rights by Jordan's first lady, Her Majesty Queen Rania of Jordan, and the kingdom's commitment to wildlife and habitat conservation, all subjects very dear to my heart, had reinforced my feelings about the country. So when my plane touched down in Amman for the very first time and I hopped in a jeep to begin exploring this fascinating country, it was a journey that would change my life. Friends would ask why I spoke so passionately about Jordan and I urged them to see it for themselves. Many did, and on their return thanked me for the motivation and advice I offered with utmost sincerity. This drove me to want to share my experiences of, and my passion for, this captivating country with others, and so the Bradt guide to Jordan was born. Along the way I have met many truly inspirational people, from Yaser who gave me a true insight into the life of a Bedouin over wild mint and cinnamon tea in the Rum Desert, Ali with his encyclopaedic knowledge of Jordan's archaeological sites, and Suleiman who taught me how to make a mean *mensaf*. While it may be my words that (I hope) bring Jordan to life for you on every page, this guide is a reflection of so many people's passion for this inspirational, vibrant and colourful kingdom.

PUBLISHER'S FOREWORD   *Adrian Phillips, Publishing Director*

You can't deny that Jordan has film-star good looks. The famous 'lost city' of Petra was the backdrop for *Indiana Jones and the Last Crusade*, while the Wadi Rum desert featured in *Lawrence of Arabia*. But the country has much to offer beyond the Hollywood stardust. There are the biblical sites of Christ's baptism and the beheading of John the Baptist, the diving opportunities on the Red Sea, the rejuvenating Dead Sea spa breaks and the trekking trails across the dunes. Jordan has also embraced eco-tourism, working to conserve the coral life in the Gulf of Aqaba and promoting initiatives to preserve Bedouin culture. Carole French is a vastly experienced travel writer who knows the Middle East like the back of her hand, and with this guide – researched with care and written with passion – she reveals how to get the most from your visit.

First edition published June 2012

Bradt Travel Guides Ltd, IDC House, The Vale, Chalfont St Peter, Bucks SL9 9RZ, England
www.bradtguides.com
Published in the USA by The Globe Pequot Press Inc, PO Box 480, Guilford, Connecticut
06437-0480

Text copyright © 2012 Carole French
Maps copyright © 2012 Bradt Travel Guides Ltd
Illustrations copyright © 2012 Individual photographers (see below)
Project manager: Elspeth Beidas

ISBN: 978 1 84162 398 6
British Library Cataloguing in Publication Data
A catalogue record for this book is available from the British Library

Photographs Alamy: blickwinkel (B/A), Michele Burgess (MB/A), Hemis (H/A), Y Levy (YL/A), Bill Lyons (BL/A), Michael McKee (MM/A), mediacolor's (M/A), Juergen Ritterbach (JR/A), Robert Harding Picture Library (RHPL/A), Maximilian Weinzierl (MW/A); Adam Balogh (AB); Dreamstime: Marta Mirecka (MM/DT); FLPA: David Hosking (DH/FLPA), Reinhard Dirscherl (RD/FLPA), Imagebroker, Norbert Eisele-Hei/Imagebroker/FLPA (IB/FLPA); Carole French (CF); Eric Lafforgue (EL); Radu Mendrea (RM); SuperStock (SS); Crispin Zeeman (CZ)
Front cover Petra (MM/DT)
Back cover The Treasury, Petra (EL); Traditional necklaces (CZ)
Title page The Treasury, Petra (RM); Arabic coffee making (SS); Traditional Bedouin carpet (SS)

Maps David McCutcheon
Colour map Relief map base by Nick Rowland FRGS
Some maps are based on source material provivided by kind permission of the Royal Jordanian Geographic Centre (RJGC).

Typeset from the author's disk by Wakewing, High Wycombe
Production managed by Jellyfish Print Solutions; printed in India

Acknowledgements

Knowing and having a passion for a country is only the beginning when starting out on the long road to producing a guide as informative as the Bradt guide to Jordan. Undertaking the painstaking research to ensure all the information is bang up-to-date is a massive task, and without the unstinting help of so many people to whom I will always be grateful the whole project could have remained in the 'ideas' tray for some time. My sincere thanks go to Ali Mousa Abu-Dayeh and Basel Ahmad, my guides on research trips whose astonishing knowledge of every corner of the country they are so clearly proud of proved an inspiration, and to our drivers Rami Rida Al-Remawi and George Tannous, without whom we would not have covered so much ground safely. I would like to thank Yaser M Zalabeh of Bedouin Life Camp for his kind hospitality and showing me how exciting life in the desert at Wadi Rum is, to Sulieman Kharman for sharing his expert knowledge of Petra and its treasures, and Husni Abu Gheida for sharing the secret of what makes Aqaba tick. Special thanks go to Anwar Atalia of Royal Jordanian, Suleiman Helalat, Giuseppe Ressa, Ziad Fostuq and Sewar Sawalha, Tarek Madanat, Ghada Najjar and Salem Batmani, Firas Al Bashir, Nabih S Riyal, Imad Malhas, Ahmad Ebdah, Ibtisam Abu Al Ezz, Arwa Mahadin, Hussein Tadros, Seif Saudi and Mohammad Sa'ed for all their help, hospitality and advice. Extra special thanks go to Nour Al Khalafat for her patience in proofreading my Arabic, and Milagros Hamoudeh and the team at the Royal Society for the Conservation of Nature and Wild Jordan, whose work I admire immensely. I would like to express my gratitude to Ahmad Al-Hmoud, David Symes, Juan Barros, Stephen Hurp, Steele Paulich and Lara Perez of the Jordan Tourism Board, to the team at Bradt Travel Guides, and my husband Edward French for their never-ending support, enthusiasm, encouragement and help. And finally, my thanks go to you, the readers. I hope you enjoy visiting Jordan and experiencing the warmth of its people, its remarkable heritage and seeing its fabulous sights as much as I do.

FEEDBACK REQUEST

If you have any comments, queries, grumbles, insights, news or other feedback, or would like to get in touch with the author, please contact us on ☏ 01753 893444 or e info@bradtguides.com. Alternatively you can add a review of the book to www.bradtguides.com or Amazon.

If you send an email to e info@bradtguides.com about changes to information in this book we will forward it to the author, who may include it in a 'one-off update' on the Bradt website at www.bradtguides.com/guidebook-updates. You can also visit this website for updates to information in this guide.

Contents

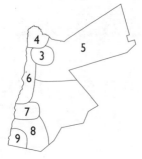

LIST OF MAPS

Introduction

Ahlan wa sahlan!

Jordan, officially the Hashemite Kingdom of Jordan, is an Arab country at the heart of the Middle East. Famously home to two of the world's greatest wonders – the Nabatean 'lost' city of Petra and the eerily calm Dead Sea – it is a mesmerising destination. It is a land of extraordinary contrasts and for visitors offers everything from sophisticated city life to nature reserves that are home to some of the world's rarest animals. The country's breathtaking canyons are a dream for hikers and climbers, desert and forest landscapes provide plentiful opportunities for exploration and world-class diving sites can be found off the coast. It is a country rich in history, natural beauty and charm, all of which the Jordanians are justifiably proud.

In the northern reaches of the country evergreen oak forests and rural villages blanket the countryside surrounding the spectacular remains of the Roman city of Jerash, while to the east and further south the landscape takes on the golden hue of a seemingly endless desert. In between are sites made famous in the Bible and the Quran, such as Bethany. Beyond is the Jordan, where Jesus is said to have been baptised by the prophet John the Baptist. There are also castles dating from the time of the Crusades perched high on mounds and palaces set deep in the eastern desert plains where Umayyad noblemen once relaxed in splendour.

The mighty Wadi Rum, a land of desert dotted with canyons and sand dunes where Bedouin tribes have lived for centuries dominates the southern stretches of Jordan, while the kingdom's only coastline is at Aqaba. This vibrant city looks out over the Gulf of Aqaba, which flows to the Red Sea and, as a result of its academically acclaimed marine work, offers a kaleidoscope of colour created by fish attracted to its offshore corals. Jordan's capital city is Amman and it is here that visitors will find gourmet restaurants, international hotels and shiny shopping malls that sit surprisingly well with its Roman and Islamic archaeological sites and bustling souks. Amman is a hub; a multicultural metropolis with a distinctly modern edge.

But Jordan's appeal stems as much from its people as its landscape. Inhabited by various settlers throughout history, from the Canaanites and Babylonians to the Byzantines and Ottomans, today Jordan is a progressive, stable country with a commitment to sustainable tourism. Visitors are warmly welcomed with the greeting *'ahlan wa sahlan'*. Roughly translated as 'welcome to my home', this phrase can be heard being spoken by the friendly and hospitable Jordanians to travellers many times a day with absolute sincerity. Its people, like Jordan itself, will leave an impression – one that could easily last a lifetime.

Part One

GENERAL INFORMATION

Full name The Hashemite Kingdom of Jordan

Location Middle East

Neighbouring countries Saudi Arabia, Iraq, Israel and Palestine, Syria

Size Approximately 96,200km^2

Climate Semi-arid

Status Constitutional Monarchy

Population 6.5 million (UN 2010)

Life expectancy 72 years (men), 75 years (women) (UN)

Capital Amman (population 2.2 million)

Other main towns Ajlun (Ajloun), Aqaba, Azraq (Al-Azraq), Petra (Al-Batra) at Wadi Musa, Irbid, Jerash, Karak (Al-Karak), Ma'an, Madaba, Mafraq (Al-Mafraq), Ramtha (Ar-Ramtha), Salt (As-Salt), Zarqa (Az-Zarqa)

Economy GNP JOD14,993 million; per head JOD3,653; inflation 3%

GDP 3.9%

Languages Arabic (official), English

Religion Sunni Muslim 92%, Christian 6%

Currency Jordanian dinar (JOD, unofficially known as the JD) = 10 dirham, 100 piastres and 1,000 fils, pegged to the US$.

Exchange rate US$1 = JD0.71, £1 = JD1.13, €1 = JD0.95 (March 2012)

National airline Royal Jordanian: www.rj.com

Main airports Queen Alia International Airport, Amman; King Hussein International Airport, Aqaba

International telephone code +962

Area telephone codes Ajlun 2; Aqaba 3; Azraq 5; Amman 6; Irbid 2; Jerash 2; Karak 3; Ma'an 3; Madaba 5; Mafraq 2; Petra 3; Ramtha 2; Salt 5; Wadi Rum 3; Zarqa 5

Time October to March: GMT +2 hours; April to September: GMT +3; US Eastern Time +7

Electrical voltage 220 AC volts, 50 cycles, requiring rounded two-prong wall plugs. US visitors will need a transformer.

Weights and measures Metric

Flag Black, white and green horizontal bands from top to bottom, red triangle to left side containing a white seven-pointed star

National anthem Al-salam Al-malaki Al-urdoni (Jordanian Royal Anthem)

National flower Black Iris (*Iris nigricans*)

National bird Sinai rosefinch

Public holidays New Year's Day: 1 January; His Majesty King Abdullah II's birthday: 30 January; Labour Day: 1 May; Independence Day: 25 May; Accession Day: 9 June; King Hussein I Remembrance Day: 14 November; Christmas Day: 25 December.

Variable religious holidays Mowlid an-Nabawi (Birthday of Prophet Muhammad); Easter; Eid al-Isra wal-Miraj (Night Journey to Heaven); Ramadan; Eid al-Fitr (a three-day or four-day feast to mark the end of Ramadan); Eid al-Adha (a four-day feast at the end of the Hajj month of pilgrimage to Makkah); First of Muharram (Islamic New Year)

Background Information

GEOGRAPHY

The Great Rift Valley, which runs from Syria down to Mozambique in eastern Africa, dominates the western border of the country. It passes through Jordan as the Jordan Rift Valley, formed by the Dead Sea and the Jordan and Araba rivers. Created millions of years ago when the region's tectonic plates are said to have realigned, the valley is a breathtaking sight. Jordan lies in an **earthquake zone** and occasional tremors are felt. One of the most recent was in January 2011 when the country experienced an earthquake measuring 4.5 on the Richter scale. Its epicentre was north of Amman. According to seismology experts at the University of Jordan, statistically the kingdom is prone to earthquakes measuring around 6.0 magnitude, but few have reached this strength in recent years.

Jordan is a **desert kingdom** that lies on the westernmost fringes of the Middle East. Saudi Arabia borders it to the east and south, while Israel and the West Bank lie to the west. Syria and Iraq are found to the north and northeast of Jordan. The spine-like Mountain Heights Plateau separates the western border from the deserts of the east. The country is almost landlocked, with only a short stretch of **coastline** around its southernmost city, Aqaba. The Gulf of Aqaba, which Aqaba overlooks, is famed for its extraordinary **coral reef ecosystem** and its abundance of multi-coloured marine life. For divers and snorkellers it's a must. Officially a protected area, the gulf flows to the Red Sea and follows a course along the coastlines of the Sinai region of Egypt and Saudi Arabia.

Aqaba is one of Jordan's main cities; others include its capital Amman, Zarqa (locally Az-Zarqa), Irbid and Jerash, Madaba and Karak (Al-Karak), Ajlun (Aljoun), Azraq (Al-Azraq), Ma'an and Salt (As-Salt), Mafraq (Al-Mafraq), Ramtha (Ar-Ramtha) and the community around Petra (Al-Batra) at Wadi Musa.

Jordan is a compact country of around 96,200km² (37,150 square miles) and yet the **diversity of its landscape** makes it unique. Along with its short coastline, Jordan has great expanses of desert, such as that found in the Wadi Rum region and the easternmost Badia territories. There are lush areas of forest teeming with flora and fauna, numerous species of which are endemic, and rocky valleys created over time in spectacular fashion by its rivers (*wadis*). Vast areas of arid terrain irrigated by streams and oasis, arable land with their uniform planting of crops, salt flats, high mountains and the eerily calm waters of the Dead Sea add to the remarkable landscape mix.

Essentially, the country is made up of **three main geographical areas**: the Mountain Heights Plateau in the centre, the Badia region to the east and the country's famous Jordan Rift Valley, which follows a route along its entire western border. **The Mountain Heights Plateau** stretches north to south in a spine-like fashion, with many of its peaks reaching well over 1,500m (4,920ft). The south of Jordan is dominated by the country's highest mountain landscape, which stretches south of the vast sandy and rocky terrain of the Wadi Rum to the Saudi Arabia border. Its peak, the Jabal Umm ad Dami, reaches a height of 1,854m (6,083ft) above sea level, and can often be seen covered with a brilliant white dusting of snow that glistens as the sun rises. In sharp contrast to the mountains is the **Dead Sea region**, which at -420m (-1,378ft) is the lowest point on dry earth. The landscape here is stark, yet the sea's still waters and its visible boulders covered with white crystal-like salt give it a sense of tranquillity.

The north of the country enjoys a largely Mediterranean climate and is characterised by great swathes of evergreen forest and a landscape of fruit trees. Apples, pears, plums, citrus fruits, grapes and olives thrive here, and are simply delicious. There are acres of arable land too, which is used for growing crops such as wheat, corn and cereals. Towards the northwest, vegetables like potatoes, cauliflowers and aubergine, that have for centuries provided the staple ingredients for many local dishes, dominate. Together, these areas produce more than half of all the fresh food products eaten by Jordanians today.

The **Badia region**, comprising five deserts including the Eastern Desert, Central Desert and to the south the Rum Desert, extends to the country's easternmost borders. It is a huge, arid, golden, desert-like plateau that stretches for miles, interspersed by the lush greenery of an odd oasis, areas of desert steppes, several seasonal streams and a handful of settlements, towering mountains and extraordinary rock formations.

JORDAN RIFT VALLEY Jordan's foremost creation of nature and an ecological Aladdin's Cave is the Jordan Rift Valley. It stretches from the north to the south of the country along its entire western boundary and is one of the most amazing, serene environments in the world. The valley in the north, known as the Ghor or the Jordan Valley after the Jordan River, is especially fertile and has streams flowing from the peaks of the Mountain Heights Plateau into the river that help to irrigate the landscape. The river rises from a number of sources, in particular the Anti-Lebanon Mountains in Syria, and makes its way in often spectacular fashion with waterfalls and gushing torrents to the Dead Sea.

If there was ever a place perfect for relaxation, the Dead Sea is it. Landlocked and fed by the Jordan River, along with lots of smaller *wadis*, it is a calm place of salt and mineral-rich waters that have drawn health-conscious visitors for centuries. The Dead Sea and its shoreline is a place of outstanding beauty. Everywhere there are deposits of salt that have turned stones, boulders and rock faces into glistening works of art. The reason for this is surprisingly simple; this expanse of water has no natural outlet to the sea so when the water evaporates with the heat of the sun its excessively high salt content – it is nine times saltier than the Mediterranean – is deposited on its shore. The most dramatic salt creations can be seen on a plain, known as the southern Ghor, which lies on the southern shores of the Dead Sea near Safi.

The Jordan Rift Valley continues south of the Dead Sea through the dry, barren landscape of the Wadi Araba gorge, also known as the Araba Valley and in biblical times as the Arabah Desert. You will find yourself travelling for mile after mile with spectacular mountains on one side and a panoramic view over, firstly, salt flats, and then a starkly rocky terrain on the other. Israel can be seen in the distance.

Rising from the Dead Sea, the gorge ascends to a height of around 230m (750ft) before falling again to sea level. Here, the highest temperatures of the Jordan Rift Valley are felt, making a challenging environment for both human and wildlife inhabitation. The valley completes its journey just northwest of Aqaba, at the point where it reaches the coastline of the Gulf of Aqaba.

MOUNTAIN HEIGHTS PLATEAU Extending from Umm Qays (also Qais) at one of the country's northernmost points to the town of Ras-an-Naqab to the south, the Mountain Heights Plateau is a terrain of rugged mountains and highlands that separate western Jordan from the arid deserts of the Badia region. The north receives the highest levels of rainfall. As such, it is a region of often fast-flowing rivers that provide water for irrigation.

The rivers of Wadi Musa, Wadi Hassa, Wadi Zarqa and the great Wadi Mujib all flow through this part of the plateau region. Vast areas of fertile land ripe for agriculture lie either side of the *wadis*, and because they yield crops for consumption they have attracted habitation for millennia. Amman and the major settlement areas of Karak, Irbid, Madaba and Zarqa are located in this part of the Mountain Heights Plateau region. Here, too, can be found the remains of the ancient Greco-Roman city of Jerash to the north of Amman, and the Nabatean city of Petra in the south, suggesting the area has been populated and provided sustenance for the people since the times of antiquity.

The southern areas of the plateau, south of the northern highlands, are characterised by a mix of steppes lying at different elevations. While the lower steppes around Madaba receive rainfall and, in turn, are blanketed with lush vegetation, the higher and southernmost steppes towards Ras an-Naqab are, in contrast, more barren. Little greenery interrupts the rugged mountains in shades ranging from gold to the warmest oranges and reds, and at times sliced by the green-grey of granite.

BADIA REGION Sparsely populated and yet accounting for well over two-thirds of the landmass of Jordan, the Badia region, known locally as Al-Badia, is a vast area of desert that lies to the east. Syria borders it to the north, while Iraq runs along its eastern boundary and Saudi Arabia lies to the south.

The Badia region has distinct geographical territories and is formed by five deserts. The Eastern Desert, where unusual volcanic rock formations rise alarmingly from the sandy floor, and the Rweishid Desert, which comprises a series of limestone plateaus irrigated by *wadis* and covered in vegetation, are to the north. Further south is the vast expanse of the Central Desert, where gentler sand dunes are crossed by *wadis* and provide a tempting terrain for 4x4 or camel excursions; the Al-Mudawwara Desert, which is rockier; and perhaps the most famous of all, the Rum Desert, location of the Wadi Rum protected area. The Rum Desert's landscape of massive mountains in shades of burnt orange and endless sand dunes, plus its serene atmosphere, has been described as moon-like. It is an extraordinary desert where many Bedouins still live a nomadic life under goat-hair tents (albeit these days with a concrete house nearby and jeeps outside replacing camels or donkeys as transport), where rare plants still thrive and where camel caravans can be seen in the distance on their way to a spring.

CLIMATE

The Jordan Rift Valley's lush and temperate environment is in marked contrast to the Badia desert territories. Between 6500BC and 5500BC there was, according to scientific analysis, a significant change in weather patterns across the region that is now the Middle East, which had a marked impact on the communities that lived here and the natural habitats where many species of wildlife and birdlife had long thrived. One of the most monumental changes was that the deserts of the region became hotter and drier. In Jordan, the whole of the desert region, known today as Badia, was affected. This new environment began to see a change in wildlife species to those more adept at desert habitats, while the Neolithic human communities that had begun to develop here started to seek alternative places to live. The harsher temperatures and lack of water meant it was difficult to cultivate crops and keep livestock. The communities moved towards the western boundaries of the country.

Today, Jordan has a climate similar to that of the Mediterranean, with subtropical hot, semi-dry summers and cool, often wet winters. However, the desert areas to the south and east, and the highest mountainous regions, can see significant variations in temperature to those found elsewhere; the deserts are generally much hotter and the highlands and mountains cooler.

August sees the hottest temperatures, which will often reach in excess of 36°C, whilst in the Badia region's desert areas, summer days are often scorching hot with temperatures reaching in excess of 40°C. During summer evenings and in winter, temperatures in the desert fall significantly. January is the coldest month, when it is quite common to see snowfall, particularly on the higher elevations of the highlands and mountains. On average, winter temperatures are around 14°C. Wear lightweight cottons and linens when touring the country in summer, but take a jacket or jumper for the cooler evenings. In winter, take warmer clothing and rainwear. (See also *What to take*, page 66.)

The desert region is particularly prone to strong, often gale-force, sirocco-style winds coming from the south in late spring and early autumn. It can be a hazardous time. Huge sand storms and dust clouds can change the landscape over several days. Sand is whipped up to create dunes and covers everything in the wind's path with a reddy-golden dusting. It can make driving or even walking difficult and potentially dangerous. Always take special care and listen to the expert advice of your tour or trek guide if you are planning excursions into the desert at this time.

The north and the west of the country, along the Jordan Valley and in the Mountain Heights Plateau, see the highest levels of rainfall. This is especially so from autumn through to mid-March, which when combined with the usual mild temperatures can result in the air feeling humid. In summer, the Dead Sea region at an elevation of below sea level can get extremely hot, with few, if any, periods of respite.

For more information on climate, see *When to visit*, page 37.

NATURAL HISTORY AND CONSERVATION

Jordan is home to some fine nature reserves and protected areas, each packed with wildlife. Its landscape of deserts and their oases, mountains blanketed with pine trees, wetlands, rich green valleys created by a network of *wadis*, and the remarkable coral reef ecosystem and its abundance of vividly coloured fish in the Gulf of Aqaba provide one of the most varied combinations of natural wildlife habitat in the world. Add to this list the Dead Sea and you could be forgiven for thinking that Jordan has it all.

NATURE RESERVES There are seven nature and wildlife reserves, along with the Dead Sea and the Aqaba Protected Area, at least six more sites being considered for reserve status and more areas being studied for their biodiversity. This is a country that recognises the importance of its fabulous flora and fauna, and takes the necessary steps to protect it.

The two most northerly official nature reserves are the **Ajloun Forest Reserve** and Dibeen Forest. Located about 90 minutes by road north from Amman near

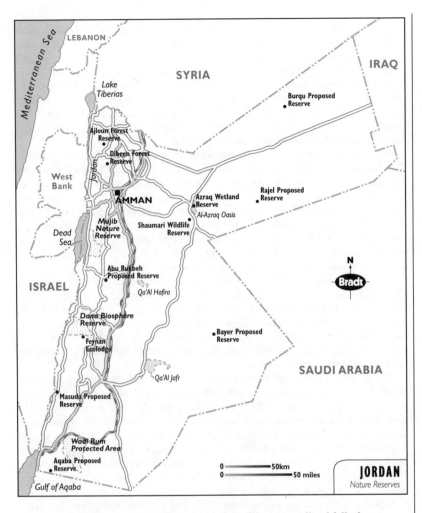

Ajlun, the Ajloun Forest Reserve is a wilderness of dense woodland full of evergreen oak (*Quercus calliprinos*) and Aleppo pine trees, along with wild pistachio (*Pistacia palaestina*) and carob (*Ceratonia siliqua*). You'll also see wild strawberry trees (*Arbutus andrachne*). Trees and plants flourish here due to the temperate climate and richly fertile soil. In spring it becomes a rainbow of colour as anemones and rockroses cover the forest floor. There are numerous birds and mammals, and if you are lucky, you might catch sight of the red fox (*Vulpes vulpes*) or the striped hyena (*Hyaena hyaena*).

Nearby is the **Dibeen Forest**, Jordan's newest reserve and home to more than 17 endangered wildlife species. The forest is made up of ancient Aleppo pines and evergreen oaks. In fact, it is considered one of the finest pine-oak forests in the Middle East. Here, if you are especially lucky, you could glimpse the endemic Persian red squirrel (*Sciurus anomalus*), which thrives in the forest habitat, or the stone marten (*Martes foina*). The grey wolf (*Canis lupus*) is known to roam in the forest too. Both the Ajloun Forest Reserve and the Dibeen Forest offer visitor information and nearby accommodation.

In the desert to the east are two excellent reserves: the **Azraq Wetland Reserve** and the Shaumari Wildlife Reserve, both of which have eco-lodges or campsites nearby. Managed by the Royal Society for the Conservation of Nature (RSCN) (see *Conservation*, page 11), the Azraq Wetland Reserve is one of the best places in Jordan to see migrating, breeding and wintering birds, including the country's national bird, the delicately grey and pink coloured Sinai rosefinch (*Carpodacus synoicus*). You may also catch sight of the Temmink's horned lark (*Eremophila bilopha*), the trumpet finch (*Rhodopechys githaginea*) or in winter the mighty Bonelli's eagle (*Aquila fasciatus*) soaring overhead.

Lying in the heart of the semi-arid desert landscape, the **Shaumari Wildlife Reserve** is a few kilometres southwest of the Azraq Wetland Reserve. Covering an area of 22km^2, it was founded with the specific purpose of breeding species of animal that were extinct in the local region and those that were endangered. On a visit look out for the magnificent Arabian oryx (*Oryx leucoryx*), a white antelope that was all but extinct in the 1970s and only survived because of a small protected herd in the US from which a new world breeding and reintroduction programme originated. Today, the Shaumari Wildlife Reserve works with zoos in other countries on a variety of breeding programmes.

The **Mujib Nature Reserve** is further south and is a dramatic place of contrasting terrains. To the north and south of the reserve are mountain ranges, which in places reach a height of around 900m (2,952ft). The reserve hugs the mountainside before falling sharply along the Wadi Mujib gorge with its impossibly sheer rock faces, to the Dead Sea. At -420m (-1,378ft) below sea level in part, the reserve is the lowest on earth. It has canyons, rivers and natural pools that prove a magnet for adventurous hikers and abseilers.

The 1,320m (4,330ft) variation between the highest and the lowest areas of the Mujib Nature Reserve ensure the diversity of landscapes and wildlife habitats is vast. Here, you can experience the thrill of hiking trails that follow routes over rocks and along rivers, and see a large number of plants, birds and wildlife. In fact, there have been more then 300 species of plant recorded in the reserve, 102 species of migratory bird and around a dozen species of carnivore. The figure is increasing as more are being discovered in the remote mountain areas and valleys, and recorded. Ibex mountain goats (*Capra ibex nubiana*) and numerous rare cat breeds are just some of the species being studied.

Heading south past Karak and Tafila you'll find the **Dana Biosphere Reserve**, a sprawling, silent place of rocky mountains, *wadis*, wooded forests, sand dunes and desert. The biodiversity here is extraordinary. You'll see an amazing number of birds – such as the Bonelli's eagle (*Aquila fasciatus*), Barbary falcon (*Falco pelegrinoides*), bulbuls and chukars – without even trying, along with mammals and plants. Recent records list over 700 different species of plant and 38 species of mammal. Half the reserve is off-limits to goat herders and the other half is controlled so wildlife here is thriving. A visitors' centre just inside the main entrance to the reserve has suggested hiking routes and comprehensive information about the reserve's various conservation projects.

'Moon-like' is a term often used to describe **Wadi Rum**, and as you stand gazing at its desert sand speckled with rock formations and blazing orange mountains it is difficult, if not impossible, to find any other word that captures its tranquil beauty. The **Wadi Rum Protected Area**'s complex ecosystem supports over 2,000 different plants and wildflowers, including poppies and Jordan's national flower, the Black Iris (*Iris nigricans*), along with more than 120 different species of birds and animals, many endemic, ensuring its importance in the fabric of Jordan.

The city of Aqaba hosts the country's southernmost protected area. Measuring some 25km in width, with a length of around 180km, the **Aqaba Protected Area** in the Gulf of Aqaba is home to around 230 species of coral, more than 1,200 species of fish and mammals, and a seemingly endless number of molluscs and crustaceans. Among the coral species is archelia, an extremely rare specimen resembling a black spindly tree, which is found at great depths. It is said to have been discovered by King Hussein I, the father of the present king of Jordan, himself on a diving expedition.

Today, the Gulf of Aqaba and its waters is a magnet for divers and snorkellers. However, because Jordan carefully controls tourism in the area, the coral reef ecosystem that begins close to the beach in the shallows and extends way out into the Red Sea, with its astonishing kaleidoscope of marine life, remains one of the finest and most well preserved in the world.

FLORA While the Dead Sea waters cannot support any form of animal or plant life because of their high mineral and salt composition, the surrounding area (and indeed the rest of Jordan's topography), helped by its climate, has an eco-system well refined so as to support a diversity of flora and fauna.

Spring is an especially colourful time in Jordan. From February through to May, the landscape becomes carpeted with more than 2,000 different species of plants and wildflowers, many of them endemic. It is a time when the soil and sand, still damp from the winter rains, begin to heat with the springtime warmth and this promotes plants' natural growth. Poppies and anemones turn the landscape red, while Jordan's national flower the Black Iris (*Iris nigricans*) can be seen in fields, on hillsides and on the edge of the forests. Madaba, especially, is known for having field after field of Black Iris.

The subtle blue-green of the olive tree leaf creates a hue over the landscape of the Jordan Valley throughout the year, with the pale pink flower of the almond tree dusting it in spring. The region hosts spectacular trees from the cedar family as well as eucalyptus. In the highlands and forests, evergreen oak (*Quercus calliprinos*) and Aleppo pine trees thrive, along with wild pistachio (*Pistacia palaestina*), carob (*Ceratonia siliqua*), strawberry trees (*Arbutus andrachne*), and a wealth of woodland flowers. In the deserts, cacti and trees of the acacia family – *Acacia albida*, *Acacia tortilis* and *Acacia iraqensis* – thrive in the hot climate.

WILDLIFE

Mammals The habitat of Jordan supports a whole host of mammals. The Arabian oryx (*Oryx leucoryx*) is one of the most celebrated. This impressive white antelope with its long, pointed horns and elegant stance became extinct in Jordan in the 1920s. By the 1970s it was extinct worldwide in the wild and would have been lost had it not been for an international rescue initiative launched by the World Wildlife Fund. Through careful breeding and attention, this wonderful mammal was reintroduced to the wild. Jordan's Shaumari Wildlife Reserve received 11 in 1978, and continues the work to save it from extinction to this day. It is still endangered, but in Jordan, at least, it is thriving and now there are over 200 in the reserve.

In the Mujib Nature Reserve more than ten species of carnivore thrive, including the red fox (*Vulpes vulpes*), the caracal (*Caracal caracal*) from the lynx family, and the Arabian leopard (*Panthera pardus nimr*). While in the Ajloun Forest Reserve you will see foxes, wolves and herds of wild boar. The park is an important breeding ground of the roe deer (*Capreolus capreolus*), which almost became extinct in the wild through excessive hunting. It is now the subject of a protect-and-release programme in order to reintroduce it back to the wild. The Dana Nature Reserve is one of the few breeding places of the striped hyena (*Hyaena hyaena*), one of the true hyenas of the Middle East and one that is classified as Near Threatened.

Other mammals you may encounter include rabbits and hares, bats, shrews and hedgehogs, including the smallest of the family, the desert hedgehog (*Paraechinus aethiopicus*). The rocky terrain and semi-desert climate provide a natural habitat for members of the ungulates family. The elegant Dorcas gazelle (*Gazella dorcas*) is often seen in large numbers, and you may chance upon a herd of the nimble-footed but endangered Nubian ibex (*Capra ibex nubiana*). The largest sector of mammals by far is rodents; squirrels, such as the beautiful red-grey Caucasian squirrel (*Sciurus anomalus*), rats, mice, voles and hamsters all live and thrive here. In the deserts, sand cats and desert foxes live, and there is evidence of the rare grey wolf (*Canis lupus*).

Birds The biodiversity of birdlife found in Jordan's wetland, its evergreen forests, desert steppes and mountainous habitats is extensive. Each ecosystem provides the perfect habitat for many species. Some live and thrive here all year round. In fact, records suggest there are around 150 different species indigenous to Jordan. In addition to this, the country lies on a major migration route between Europe, Asia and Africa, and as such there are several hundred more migratory species seen here at any one time. Birdwatchers can head for the nature reserves, all of which have been declared Important Bird Areas, known as IBAs. This international initiative was launched to recognise and protect bird habitats. A further 17 IBA sites have also been declared across the country.

In the IBA regions around the Dead Sea, in the Mujib Nature Reserve, the Dana Nature Reserve and along the length of the Wadi Araba near Jordan's southwestern boundary the species you are most likely to see are the sand partridge (*Ammoperdix heyi*), Dunn's lark (*Eremalauda dunni*), the green bee-eater (*Merops orientalis*), the Arabian babbler (*Turdoides squamiceps*), blackstart (*Cercomela melanura*) and the bar-tailed lark (*Ammomanes cincturus*).

In the western highlands and the wooded areas of the Dana Nature Reserve, the Dibeen Forest, and the lush landscape around Ajlun lives the Sardinian warbler (*Sylvia melanocephala*) and the Palestine sunbird (*Cinnyris oseus*). The woodchat shrike (*Lanius senator*), linnet (*Carduelis cannabina*), the spectacled warbler (*Sylvia conspicillata*) and the long-billed pipit (Anthus similis) prefer the open steppe habitats, as does the black-eared wheatear (*Oenanthe hispanica*).

In the Wadi Rum desert and other rocky IBA environments such as that found in Petra, Bonelli's eagle (*Aquila fasciatus*), Hume's tawny owl (*Strix butleri*), the griffin vulture (*Gyps fulvous*) and the fan-tailed raven (*Corvus rhipidurus*) have all been seen flying majestically in the skies. If you are lucky you may chance upon the beautiful rose-pink and grey Sinai rosefinch (*Carpodacus synoicus*), which is Jordan's national bird. Other species living in this rocky desert environment are the tawny owl (*Strix aluco*), blackstart (*Cercomela melanura*) and Tristram's grackle (*Onychognathus tristramii*).

The white-throated kingfisher (*Halcyon smyrnensis*) prefers the habitat created by water flows, so is often seen around the *wadi* valleys, while the red-rumped wheatear (*Oenanthe hispanica*) and the thick-billed lark (*Rhamphocoris clotbey*) are two of the most common species to be seen in the great expanse of the Eastern Desert and the Central Desert. The Azraq Wetland Reserve in the Eastern Desert hosts a dazzling array of species. Some thrive here throughout the year, while others are migratory. You may see the trumpeter finch (*Rhodopechys githaginea*), the desert wheatear (*Oenanthe deserti*), the Temmink's horned lark (*Eremophila bilopha*) or the desert lark (*Ammomanes deserti*). Imperial eagles and common cranes are a familiar sight in winter.

Other species you may encounter include the purple heron (*Ardea purpurea*), the great and little egret (*Ardea alba* and *Egretta garzetta*), the sooty shearwater (*Puffinus griseus*), the Cory's shearwater (*Calonectris diomedea*), the great crested grebe (*Podiceps cristatus*), and the great white pelican (*Pelecanus onocrotalus*). In the coastal region of Aqaba you may see the osprey (*Pandion haliaetus*). Two species of cormorants exist in Jordan: the great cormorant (*Phalacrocorax carbo*) and the pygmy cormorant (*Phalacrocorax pygmaeus*).

Flamingos and storks always provide an arresting sight, and in Jordan you may encounter the greater flamingo (*Phoenicopterus roseus*), the white stork (*Ciconia ciconia*) and the black stork (*Ciconia nigra*), plus many species of sandpipers, gulls, terns, falcons, hawks and eagles, crakes, coots, ducks, swans and geese, larks, swallows and martins, wagtails, nightjars, thrushes, swifts, oystercatchers and plovers.

Marine life Despite having only a short coastline, Jordan's marine life is one of the best in the world. This is all thanks to an amazing coral reef system in the Gulf of Aqaba, which lies northeast of the Red Sea. Here, more than 230 different species of soft and hard coral exists, each a living organism. One particularly rare species of coral is the archelia, which is found here at great depths. It is said to have been discovered by King Hussein I, a keen diver. There are thousands of species of fish, crustaceans, mammals, crabs, shrimps and lobsters, as well as marine plants and grasses that live on or around the coral reef system.

Of the fish, damsels, groupers, batfish, angelfish and parrotfish all swim in the waters off Aqaba, while turtles, dolphins and sea cows are visitors. In the spring you may catch sight of a manta ray (*Manta birostris*), or in June and July a harmless whale shark (*Rhincodon typus*). In the coral reef itself, when diving you may see the beautiful yellow masked butterfly fish (*Chaetodon semilarvatus*), the orange-coloured coral grouper (*Plectropomus pessuliferus*) or twin spot snapper (*Lutjanus bohar*), the delightful orange, black and white clownfish from the *Pomacentrides* family, or one of the odd, and dangerous, moray eel species like the giant moray (*Gymnothorax javanicus*). There's octopus too, and the venomous lion fish (*Pterois antennata*), around which you should take great care.

However, it isn't only the coral reef system that teems with life. In the grasses of the sea you may be fortunate enough to see a seahorse or two, or along the seabed, partially buried in sand, a starfish, lizard fish, a Red Sea moses sole (*Pardachirus marmoratus*), and crabs or sea urchins. All these species live and thrive in this environment, aided by a temperate climate and few sea currents.

In the waters off Aqaba you may catch sight of the distinctive pale grid-like markings on the back of a harmless whale shark (*Rhincodon typus*). As the largest fish to swim in the world's oceans (it can reach over 40ft in length) and a painfully slow swimmer, it makes a spectacular sight if diving or viewed from the deck of a boat. The best time to see a whale shark is in June or July, when its migration route takes it through the Gulf of Aqaba. It is a docile fish and, despite its imposing size, is considered no threat to humans. Equally worthy of whipping out the camera are the playful bottlenose dolphins (*Tursiops truncatus*) and species of porpoises that inhabit the waters.

CONSERVATION Jordan's diverse landscape and the biodiversity it hosts have long been recognised by the authorities and steps taken to preserve the environment.

One of the key initiatives in recent times was the founding of the **Royal Society for the Conservation of Nature** (RSCN) (✆ *06 461 6523;* f *06 463 3657;* e *tourism@rscn. org.jo; www.rscn.org.jo*) in the 1960s. A non-government organisation committed to environmental issues and conservation projects, it was the first such group in the Arab world and pioneered eco-thinking in the region.

Most of Jordan's nature reserves and parks, including the Dana Biosphere Reserve south of Karak, and the Mujib Nature Reserve near the Dead Sea, are run by the RSCN. A good place to learn more about the society's work is at the **Dead Sea Panoramic complex** (✆ *05 349 1133*), which can be found at Mujib Bridge on the coastal road entrance to the Mujib Nature Reserve. It is well signposted. Here you can visit its museum where displays show the ecology, geology and conservation efforts of the region, along with information on the ancient civilisations that once lived here. Its shop sells gifts crafted by local artisans, plus there's a super restaurant specialising in organic dishes. With all of this and the great view over the Dead Sea you can see why so many travellers on their way from Amman to Aqaba, or those exploring the Dead Sea region, make this a stop on their itinerary.

A separate division of the society, **Wild Jordan** (✆ *06 463 3589*), controls its ecotourism and rural handicraft initiatives. In Amman, the Wild Jordan Café is a great place to dine on organic food, view the handicrafts and pick up information about the group's work. Find it off Abu Bakr As Siddeeq Street (better known as Al-Rainbow Street or simply Rainbow Street), which is a main thoroughfare through Amman's 1st Circle district.

By visiting the reserves or purchasing handicraft items you are helping to protect the environment of Jordan, the vast collection of flora and fauna it supports and the programmes that protect endangered species. On top of this, your contributions help provide jobs for local rural communities (see also *Travelling positively*, page 84).

HISTORY

IN THE BEGINNING The land east of the river Jordan that was to become the Hashemite Kingdom of Jordan in more modern times, has been inhabited since the prehistoric period. Primitive axes, knives and scrapers made from materials such as basalt, chalcedony and flint that would have been fashioned and used by the Palaeolithic people who lived here around two million years ago have been discovered during a series of excavations. Archaeological evidence suggests communities continued to live here during the Mesolithic era, or Epipalaeolithic Middle Stone Age, and through to the Neolithic period of around 10000–4300BC.

The Neolithic period is said to have been a progressive time for the region. Farming was becoming more widespread, the use of clay to produce household receptacles was being pioneered and the introduction towards the end of the era and into the Chalcolithic (4300–3300BC), Bronze Ages (3200–1200BC) and Iron Age (1200–586BC) of metal tools, such as axes, hooks and arrowheads, was emerging.

Communities that until now had lived a more nomadic existence began to settle and live in primitive villages. They cultivated the land with cereals such as barley and wheat, chickpeas and legumes (lentils, beans and peas), aided by the use of clay pots and tools. This new sustainable food source from the land – which complemented hunting animals for their meat, fishing and living off fruit, olive and nut trees – meant that the population of the region not only became healthier but increased in number. It was largely during this era that the people began to see the merits of keeping goats and sheep too.

Although there are believed to be few, if any, archaeological remains from the Palaeolithic and Mesolithic periods in Jordan today, other than in museums, you can see the remains of Neolithic homes, thoroughfares and areas probably used to market products at Ain Ghazal, located just northwest of central Amman. Discovered in 1974, the site is believed to have been a settlement hosting several thousand people between 7250BC and 5000BC. Covering an area of around 15ha, it is considered one of the largest known archaeological sites from the period in the world. Artefacts discovered here include skulls, tools and plaster statues that have been dated to around 6000BC, which are now housed in the Jordan Archaeological Museum in Amman. The statues, particularly, are striking and friendly looking; standing about 90cm (3ft) tall, you are immediately drawn to their eyes, which are made from shells with detailing probably applied with a black tar-like substance, rather like bitumen.

CHALCOLITHIC (4500–3300BC) AND BRONZE AGES (3300–1200BC)

Jordan, and in particular the Jordan Valley region, continued to develop throughout the Chalcolithic era and the early, middle and late Bronze Ages. Transjordan, as the region was then known, began to develop trading links with Egypt and Mesopotamia, the latter being an area covering parts of modern-day Iraq, Syria, Turkey and Iran. Jordan traded with the countries of Arabia and Canaan, which in history was the name given to the region covering most of present-day Israel, Palestine, Lebanon and western Syria.

The main commodities were bronze tools forged out of tin and copper, which through the development of techniques and enhanced quality were now much sought-after. Most of the trading towns were concentrated in the north and northwest of the country, and its central plains, and as such the areas became wealthy. New towns were built and existing communities were rewarded with infrastructures of the like never before seen. In present-day Amman and Irbid, then two communities that became centres of trade, huge fortifications were built to protect the now wealthy communities from attack. In the nearby ancient town of Tabaqat Fahl, known as Pella, the bastions were said to be some of the most formidable ever seen in the region at the time. While all this activity was going on in north and central Jordan however, the south remained largely untouched by the new wave of commercialism. Its people, the Shasu, continued to live a nomadic existence.

Remains from Chalcolithic and Bronze Age periods are still visible today. Two of the best are at Tulaylat al-Ghassul, near the Dead Sea, and at nearby Bab adh Dhra. At Tulaylat al-Ghassul you can visit the Chalcolithic archaeological site just outside town, and clearly see how homes made of mud bricks dried by the sun would have been positioned around courtyards. At Bab adh Dhra, thousands of tombs dated to the era and containing personal items like jewellery and, of course, bones were unearthed during excavation works. The site is still being excavated today and more finds are expected. Amman, Irbid and Pella also all have remains from the era.

IRON AGE (1200–539BC)

As the Late Bronze Age became the Iron Age so some of the most important city-kingdoms in the region were founded. The kingdoms of Ammon, Moab and Edom and their people, the Ammonites, the Moabites and the Edomites, are mentioned in the Old Testament, and became key communities of the period. Lot, one of the foremost biblical characters of the Bible's Book of Genesis, is described in Genesis 19:37–38 as having produced the children, Ammon and Moab, by his daughters, while Edom is mentioned as a place inhabited by the Edomites in Genesis 36.

Ammon – which according to the Old Testament lay east of the Jordan River, the hill of Gilead and the Dead Sea – centered on its capital, Rabbah Ammon. It was a thriving city, so much so that it was coveted by King David (circa b1040BC, d970BC), the ruler of the Kingdom of Israel, who attacked and conquered the city, thereby adding it to his then kingdom. The battle of Rabbah Ammon and its conquest is referred to in the Bible in Amos 1:14, Jeremiah 49:2 and 3, and Ezekiel 21:20 and 25:5. Jordan's present-day capital, Amman, was built on the site of the ancient Rabbah Ammon.

The Moabites, meanwhile, founded their capital city as Kir of Moab, which records indicate was on the site of present-day Karak. The kingdom was south of Ammon and stretched from the Dead Sea and the southern section of the Jordan River across often mountainous terrain to the Arabian Desert. Mount Nebo, famous according to Jewish and Christian thinking as being the burial place of the Hebrew prophet Moses, lay in the kingdom's territory.

Although little is really known about the Moabites, with only biblical stories and archaeological remains giving a clue to their lifestyle, it is considered accurate that they shared common descent with their Israelite neighbours through the line of Terah, a biblical character from the Book of Genesis. Moab is believed to have had a period of Israeli rule, interspersed with times of independence, and out of the three kingdoms, Ammon, Moab and Edom, ranked as probably the richest through trading of its natural limestone and salt from the Dead Sea resources.

Edom, the other major kingdom to have been founded around the start of the Iron Age, lay south of Moab. The Edomites, too, traded in their natural resources that probably included copper. It brought wealth to this strategic kingdom on the main trade caravan route from Egypt. Bozrah was its capital city. It is mentioned several times in the Hebrew Bible, including its destruction in Amos 1:12. The remains of Bozrah can be found at Bosayra, a few kilometres from the city of Tafila.

Moab and Edom were subsequently conquered when the Neo-Assyrian Empire, one of the most powerful empires in the history of the world, and which controlled Mesopotamia for more than 320 years, expanded into what is now Jordan. The Ammonites, however, managed to resist the advances of the Neo-Assyrians and retained independence for a while, but its position was challenged when the whole region attracted the attention of the Babylonians from Iraq.

A period of furious battles ensued between these arch rivals, the Neo-Assyrians and the Babylonians, which were later joined by allied forces the Medes, Scythians and Susianians from Iran. The culmination of the battles was that the Babylonians took control of much of what had become known as the Levant region, or Holy Land, comprising most of the territory of present-day Israel, Palestine, Jordan and Lebanon. The power of the Transjordanian kingdoms diminished sharply as a result. Babylonian power was short-lived, however. The mighty force of the Persian Empire, keen to expand its territory, advanced on the region and both the Babylonian and Neo-Assyrian empires came under its control as separate provinces.

Persian rule brought a period of calm to the region, but it was a period not without problems. Because of the empire's vast size, records suggest that central control was often difficult and the king's authority was undermined. The empire included countries in Asia and the Middle East, Turkey, Macedonia, parts of Egypt and as far east as Libya. There were frequent localised periods of unrest that had the effect of weakening the empire, a fact that didn't go unnoticed by the king of Macedonia, Alexander the Great (b356BC, d323BC), a member of the ancient Greek royal Argead Dynasty.

ALEXANDER THE GREAT, THE PERSIANS AND THE GREEKS (539–63BC) Upon the death of his father, Philip II of Macedon, in 336BC, Alexander not only succeeded him, but inherited a solid, stable kingdom and a strong army with which to expand. His plans to establish one of the greatest empires the world had seen – not unlike the Persian Empire established under Cyrus the Great (b576BC, d530BC), a leader who he much admired for his heroism, politics and human rights achievements – were ambitious.

The Persian Empire, which bordered Alexander the Great's kingdom, was to become his target. Jordan and its empire neighbours were strong communities with solid transport and communication infrastructures introduced by the Persians. It made them attractive. In 333BC, Alexander the Great launched an invasion and defeated the Persian army in the Battle of Issus in southern Turkey. It was a stronghold area for the Persian Empire, ruled at that time by King Darius III (b380BC, d330BC), and severely dented its power.

Alexander, buoyed by his success, went on to conquer the whole of the Persian Empire over the next few years, as well as invading and conquering the remaining areas of Egypt that were outside the empire. For Jordan, it signalled the beginning of its Hellenistic period of rule. Alexander the Great died in 323BC at the age of 32. His accomplishments were enormous. He had built an empire that stretched from the Adriatic and Ionian Sea off the Greek mainland to India in just a little over ten years. He was succeeded by his son, Alexander IV of Macedon (b323BC, d309BC).

The story of Alexander IV is tragic. Born to Roxana of Bactria, an Asian princess and wife of Alexander the Great, the young Alexander IV was effectively denied the royal title and power by Greece's military after his father's death. Instead, the military placed the general, Perdiccas (circa b355BC, d320BC), in charge of the country as regent with Alexander's brother, Philip III (b359BC, d317BC), as ruler in name only. Alexander IV and Philip III would later be declared joint kings, although still had little power.

Perdiccas was assassinated around two years after taking power when mutiny flared in his army. Control of the empire now fell to his successor, the general and friend of Alexander the Great and Philip III, Antipater (b397BC, d319BC). When Antipater died in 319BC he left control of the empire, not to his son Cassander (b350BC, d297BC) as had been expected, but to his friend General Polyperchon (b394BC, d303BC). Cassander, furious at the rejection, launched his own bid for control of the empire.

After a series of battles that severely weakened the empire created by Alexander the Great, Cassander declared himself king. In a bid to secure his reign, however, he ordered that Alexander IV, now 13 years old, and his mother should die. Thus the mother and son were poisoned by Cassander's men. This series of events brought an end to the Argead Dynasty royal house and caused the break up of the empire. The empire now comprised four main divisions: the Pergamon Kingdom in Asia Minor, the Ptolemaic Kingdom in Egypt, the Kingdom of Macedon in Greece and, significantly for Transjordan, the Seleucid Empire. The Seleucid Empire, although retaining much of its Hellenistic heritage, covered land from southern Turkey through to India. This new period of rule was a troubling time for Transjordan. It lost strength and was increasingly being seen as a target for new invaders. The most significant of these were the Nabateans in the south and the Romans to whom they were allied.

JESUS AND THE NABATEANS (312BC–AD106) The Nabateans, an Arab ethnic group from a kingdom that covered great areas of Arabia, arrived in southern Transjordan around 312BC. At its zenith the kingdom stretched from the Arabian

Peninsula (known today as the Middle East) across the northern territories of Ptolemaic Egypt to the Kingdom of Judea of ancient Israel to the east. At its heart was its capital Petra.

Today one of the Seven Wonders of the World and Jordan's most famous tourist attraction, Petra was in antiquity a major city-state. Its wealth during the Nabatean era was legendary. Strategically, it was located at the point where several trade routes met, including two of the greatest routes – India to Egypt and Arabia to Damascus – which crossed at the exact spot where Petra lay. Merchants from Levant, Arabia, India, Egypt and East Asia traded in elaborate silks and textiles, gems, animal skins, feathers and spices.

What afforded the Nabateans their greatest wealth was revenue from the trading of incense, frankincense, myrrh and gold. The famed Incense Route of the 3rd and 2nd centuries BC ran partially through Transjordan, and it was the Nabateans who were recognised as having the control over its use along this stretch. It brought fabulous wealth. The Nabateans were a major force in the Middle East and the Levant in biblical times.

Petra grew from being a small settlement to one of the most magnificent cities of the ancient world with palaces and dwellings, tombs and even a theatre hewn into the rose-coloured sandstone rock face. The Nabatean kingdom and its city-states of Petra and Saltus (present day Salt, or locally As-Salt), which had long been allied with the Roman Empire, eventually became absorbed into its hegemony in 103AD.

The Nabatean and early Roman period saw the birth of Jesus of Nazareth in Bethlehem in present-day Israel. Although details of his life are difficult to establish with any certainty, most of the events chronicled in the gospels Matthew, Mark, Luke and John are generally regarded as being the most accurate. They tell of his virgin conception and his nativity in Bethlehem to Mary and Joseph, of the Three Wise Men bearing gifts and of King Herod who, on hearing of the King of Jews' birth, demanded all boys under two should be killed.

The Gospels recount Jesus's baptism by John the Baptist, talk of his teachings and disciples, and of his crucifixion, resurrection and ascension. Throughout present-day Jordan there are sites credited with being those referred to in the Bible as having been visited by Jesus. Perhaps the most famous is Bethany Beyond the Jordan, where Jesus was baptised and where he gathered his disciples Peter, Simon, Philip, Nathaneal and Andrew.

THE ROMANS (63BC–AD324) As Greek culture merged with the start of the country's Roman period there was much change in Transjordan. On the orders of Gnaeus Pompeius Magnus (b106BC, d48BC), the Roman general known as Pompey who sought to expand his empire, forces were sent to the north of the region. The result was that the officers identified a number of the region's historic towns as being strategic to the empire. The Decapolis cities as they became known – Decapolis literally meaning Ten Cities: *deca* being 'ten' in Greek and *polis* meaning 'city' – straddled the territory of present-day Jordan and Israel. Mentioned in the New Testament gospels of Matthew, Mark and Luke as having been visited by Jesus, they had been important places under Hellenistic times but had fallen into ruins when later occupied by Jewish communities.

Pompey, recognising their potential as key cities, planned to restore and improve their ruinous infrastructure, and declared them to be semi-independent city-states. The initiative remains one of the biggest achievements of the period. In Jordan the Greco-Nabatean-Roman city-states comprised Philadelphia, Gerasa and Gadara, present-day Amman, Jerash and Umm Qays respectively, along with Pella at

Tabaqat Fahl or Fihil, Arabella which is now Irbid, Al Husn, Capitolias known today as Bayt Ras and the ancient city of Raphana.

Under Roman rule the city-kingdoms were given considerable power and a degree of autonomy. As such, they retained their independence. They traded with each other and the world, growing wealthy as a result, and paid their taxes to the Romans. Great palaces and temples were built, along with roadways, marketplaces and buildings of worship. They were magnificent cities and although in ruins today are regarded as a symbol of Roman Jordan at its finest.

THE BYZANTINES (AD324–635) Transjordan came under the auspices of the Byzantine Empire from AD324. This new-found empire emerged after the collapse of the Western Roman Empire, a division of the Roman Empire that encompassed Greece and its regions. It was led by Emperor Constantine I (b272, d337), who enjoyed a direct succession from the ancient Roman emperors. The capital of the new empire, and inspiration for its name, was declared as being the ancient Greek colony of Byzantium, which the emperor subsequently renamed Constantinople. Lying on the Bosphorus, a strait between Europe and Asia, Constantinople is the present-day city of Istanbul in Turkey.

The Byzantine Empire era brought much development to Transjordan, in terms of infrastructure and an enhanced lifestyle for its growing populace. Significantly, it was also around this time that Christianity was accepted and the persecution of Christians came to an end. Emperor Constantine was a passionate follower and convert of the new Christian faith and, appalled by the atrocities of one of his predecessors, the Emperor Diocletian (b244, d311), who believed Christians to have no rights, had instigated a new law a few years previously calling for religious tolerance throughout the Roman Empire. The new law, known as the Edict of Milan, was signed by himself as ruler of the then Western Roman Empire that was to become the Byzantine Empire, and his counterpart the Emperor Licinius (b263, d325) who ruled the east. It became law in AD313, and remained so during Transjordan's Byzantine period.

It was during this period that churches were built to replace Roman temples as places of worship. One of the first, and today believed to be the oldest purpose-built church in the world, was built in the Byzantine town of Ayla, present-day Aqaba in southern Jordan. Also around this time, a small church was built on Mount Nebo to commemorate the end of Moses's life. Some of the stones can still be seen today in the wall around the apse.

Mount Nebo, and the nearby town of Madaba, became the focal point for Christian pilgrimages, and new churches were built in the ensuing years. Many of these churches, especially those around Madaba, were adorned with elaborate mosaics. In fact, Madaba became a celebrated centre for mosaicists and was dubbed 'The City of Mosaics'. The town's Orthodox Church of Saint George is famous for its 1,500-year old mosaic showing a map of Jerusalem and the Holy Land, which is believed to be the earliest surviving map of the region.

Transjordan's Byzantine era drew to a close during the reign of Emperor Heraclius (b575, d641) amid battles between Byzantium and invading Persian forces that had been fought for decades. The end came, however, not through submission to Persia as might have been expected, but from a new army comprising followers of the Prophet Muhammad (b570, d632).

EARLY ARAB RULE (AD636–661) Muhammad ibn Abdullah was born in AD570 in the city of Makkah (Mecca), in present-day Saudi Arabia. Records tell us that at just eight years of age he was orphaned, and brought up firstly by his grandfather and then his uncle, the wealthy Abu Talib. As the head of one of the country's most noble families, the Bani Hashim, and owner of a successful business, Abu Talib is said to have had the status and means to ensure his nephew was educated to the highest standards of the day. Muhammad was able to follow his own direction and worked for many years as a successful merchant. When he was 40 it is said he received his first revelation from God and went on to found the religion of Islam.

Over the next few years followers of the prophet grew in number. They became known as Muslims. Gradually the new religion took form and its power spread across the region until Muhammad's followers arrived in Transjordan. Despite defeat at one of their first battles with the ruling Byzantine Christians at Mu'ta near Karak in AD629, they went on to victory at the Battle of Yarmouk some seven years later. It was the beginning of Arab rule in Transjordan.

The Battle of Yarmouk was one of the most famous in the region's history between Muslim forces and the East Roman-Byzantine Empire. The Prophet Muhammad had died in AD632 and it was his successor, officially the first caliph or head of state, Abu Bakr (circa b573, d634), who led the Muslim army to victory. The battle took place on the banks of the Yarmouk river, which lies on the border of what is today Jordan and Syria. With the Byzantine armies defeated, the Muslim army took control of the region and over the next few years launched a series of victorious battles that resulted in their rule expanding at a considerable speed.

This early period of rule in Transjordan is referred to by followers of Sunni Islam as the time of the Righteous Caliphs, referring to the four caliphs who established the first caliphate, known as the Rashidun Caliphate, in AD632. The first caliph, Abu Bakr, who was also known as Abdullah ibn Abi Qahafa, was succeeded by Umar ibn al-Khattab (circa b586, d644) in AD634. Umar ibn al-Khattab held office for ten years. It was during this time that the Muslim armies conquered great swathes of Persia, Egypt and north Africa, Syria and Palestine, and Armenia and Mesopotamia, an area covering present-day Iraq and parts of Turkey and Iran. Umar ibn al-Khattub was succeeded by Uthman ibn Affan, also known as Othman (circa b579, d656), in AD644 and, finally, Ali ibn Abi Talib (circa b598, d661) who headed the caliphate from AD656 until his death in AD661.

Ali ibn Abi Talib's leadership was instrumental in Transjordan's history. When he took office as caliph in AD656 he appointed several trusted officers, replacing others who had served Othman. Among Othman's men was Muawiyah (b602, d680), the governor of Syria. Around this time the civil war, known as Fitna, was beginning to erupt. When the Caliph Ali ibn Abi Talib was assassinated in the culmination of a battle, it was Muawiyah who assumed power. The year was AD661, and with Muawiyah's leadership came the start of the Umayyad Caliphate.

THE UMAYYADS, ABBASIDS AND THE FATIMIDS (AD661–1171) From AD661 Transjordan experienced highs as the centre of the Islamic empire and then lows when it was replaced and fell into decline during the 435 years of rule by the next three caliphates. The Umayyads who hailed from Makkah, the Abbasids from Harran in southeast Turkey and the Fatimids from Tunisia, who it is said concentrated much of their efforts on their countries and cities of origin, brought mixed blessings for Transjordan.

The Umayyads (AD661–750) The second caliphate (although some scholars do not regard the early Arabs to have formed a caliphate and consider the Umayyads the first) revolved around its newly-appointed capital Damascus in Syria. This

change of capital was significant for Transjordan because it placed the region at the very heart of an empire that at its height was one of the largest ever seen in the world. It stretched from the furthermost borders of the Middle East right across north Africa and the southern areas of Turkey, and as far west as Spain in the Mediterranean. It covered in excess of five million square miles.

The town that is present-day Amman became the seat of the provincial governor in a district of Damascus known as Jund Dimashq. It was the military sector of the capital city. Keen to stamp their mark, the Umayyads built palaces, fortifications and monuments during their reign, including the impressive collection of well-preserved castles that can be visited today in Jordan's Eastern Desert. Here, caliphs would escape city life, race their horses and hunt.

The Qusair Amra, a regal palace full of frescoes that has been awarded UNESCO World Heritage Site status, the mighty Qasr al-Harrana with its fortress-like appearance and stone walls several metres thick, and the largest of all the Umayyad palaces, the impressive Qasr at-Tuba, are three of many dotted in the desert landscape.

The Abbasid Caliphate (AD750–969) The Umayyads were eventually overthrown by the next caliphate, the Abbasids, which was founded in AD750 by descendants of the Prophet Muhammad's uncle, Abbas ibn Abd al-Muttalib (circa b566, circa d653). When they took power the Abbasids moved their capital city from Damascus to Kufa and then to nearby Baghdad, which for Transjordan meant a period of relative obscurity. The country fell into decline. Although the Abbasids ruled the Transjordan region for over 200 years, there is little material evidence remaining of their power in Jordan today.

The beginning of the end for the Abbasids came when they began losing provinces to the resilient Umayyads, along with the Aghlabids (who ruled a territory known as Ifriqiya, today the northern coastal regions of Algeria, Tunisia and Libya) and a powerful new dynasty from Tunisia, the Fatimids. Transjordan, along with Syria, Sicily and parts of Italy, Palestine and Lebanon, came under the rule of the Fatimid Caliphate after it took control of Egypt in AD969, founding its new capital al-Qahira on the site of present-day Cairo.

The Fatimid Caliphate (AD969–1171) The Fatimid Caliphate was a time of growth for Transjordan and its neighbouring countries. The caliphate established prosperous trading routes with countries around the Mediterranean and the Indian Ocean, and forged links with powerful far eastern dynasties, most notably the Song Dynasty that ruled China for over 300 years.

While in many ways the Fatimids was one of the most progressive caliphates, its thinking also led eventually to its downfall. Its military comprised several ethnic groups that were divided by race into units. Kutama Berber tribesmen from Algeria who helped the Fatimids take Egypt in the first instance were considered the light cavalry sector, with other units being made up of soldiers from Egypt itself, Syrians, Black Africans and Armenians. Significantly, a strong element of its military was Turkish troops, which became the heavy cavalry sector of the army.

The set-up worked for a time, but then internal politics, different religious beliefs, an imbalance of power and a series of skirmishes amongst the ethnic groups turned to riots. The result was that the Fatimid's ideal army collapsed, its power was severely diminished and with it the region was thrown into disarray. Around this time the Turkish army's power grew. Known as the Seljuk Turks, the emerging dynasty sought to return the region to pure Islam and, with the region now in a weakened state, saw the opportunity to conquer its neighbouring countries that were under Fatimid, and also Byzantine, rule. The unstable region also caught the eye of the Mongols from China whose views on leadership were vastly different from those the area had previously seen, and their advances were often brutal. Additionally, to add to the confusion, the Abbasids saw the chance to regain their crown of power.

With so many conflicting nations vying for control the region was under the threat of complete disintegration. Perhaps unbeknown to all the participants of this chaotic unrest was the fact that another powerful nation was keeping a close eye on the state of affairs and itself saw an opportunity. The Crusaders wanted to restore order and Christian rule to the Holy Lands.

THE CRUSADERS, SALADIN AND THE AYYUBID DYNASTY (1096–1263) Aghast at
events in the Holy Lands and the threat to Christians from firstly the Fatimids and the Byzantines, and then the Mongols and the Seljuk Turks, the Roman Catholic Church vowed to intervene and restore order. A synod instigated to address the problem of the Holy Lands held in Piacenza, Italy in March 1095 that became known as the Council of Piacenza, was attended by over 4,000 bishops and senior officials of the church and around 30,000 laymen. Among them were the Byzantine Emperor Alexius I Komnenus (circa b1056, d1118) who sought to protect his empire from the invading Seljuk Turks, and representatives of the King of France, Philip I (b1052, d 1108). It was one of the largest synods ever held in the history of the church.

A few months later, supporters were reconvened at the Council of Clermont held in Clermont, France, where plans were put in place for the first of a series of crusades. Head of the church, Pope Urban II (circa b1035, d1099), called for unity amongst all European forces to regain control of the Holy Lands. His agenda was to free the sacred city of Jerusalem that was now under Seljuk rule. He called for forces to assist Emperor Alexius I Komnenus to repel the Turks from the region and restore Christianity. It met with massive support.

The Crusaders (1096–1250) The First Crusade ran from 1096 to 1099 and
comprised warrior knights and ordinary working class people from western European countries, including France, Italy and Germany, who travelled first to Constantinople, present-day Istanbul, and then southeast to Jerusalem. An assault was made on reaching Jerusalem, and the sacred city was captured in July 1099. The knights created four crusader states: the Kingdom of Jerusalem, which covered most of the territory of present-day Israel, Lebanon and Palestine; the state of the County of Tripoli, which expanded to western Syria and northern Lebanon; the Principality of Antioch, which was a state that covered parts of present-day Turkey and eastern Syria; and, finally, the County of Edessa, which reached to the easternmost areas of modern Turkey and beyond. A series of subsequent crusades in which the Knights Templars and the Knights Hospitallers played significant roles resulted in the states increasing in status and becoming centres of trade.

Saladin and the Ayyubids (1187–1263) The states, which included much of
present-day Jordan with strongholds at Shobak and Karak, survived largely intact well into the 13th century. However, there were threats, with the most challenging and successful being from Muslim forces led by Salah ad-Din Yusuf ibn Ayyub, better known as Saladin (circa b1138, d1193). A Kurdish Muslim officer who had already expelled the Fatimid Caliphate from Cairo, and had assumed the role of the Ayyubid Sultan of Egypt, Saladin called for battle against the Crusaders.

In 1187, in a ferocious battle that became known as the Battle of Hattin, Saladin's army fought and slew most of the Crusaders' Kingdom of Jerusalem forces to gain control of the sacred city, and great swathes of Palestine and Transjordan. It was a significant period in Jordan's history for it meant that Islamic power was again dominant in the Levant. The battles and the loss of Jerusalem prompted the Crusaders to launch the Third Crusade, also known as the King's Crusade, which ran from 1189 until 1192. Although the Crusaders regained parts of the region, most notably the Palestinian coast in the 1190s, they failed to recapture Jerusalem. On Saladin's death in 1193 his powerful Ayyubid dynasty continued to rule for another 57 years, despite ongoing battles with Crusaders when the hands of power shifted.

MAMLUK DYNASTY AND THE OTTOMANS (1250–1917)
The beginning of the Mamluk dynasty and the subsequent rule by the Ottomans in the Levant came about through the weakening of the Ayyubids' power and the uprising of its powerful band of slave soldiers; the word Mamluk meaning 'a soldier of slave origin'. Most of its army comprised soldiers from Turkish or Russian ethnic groups that had been purchased at market and forced to fight. In return for their loyalty they were given food and shelter. However, the perceived promise of power grew strong, until when in 1250 with the Ayyubids in turmoil as their sultan lay dying the Mamluks assembled their forces and assumed power.

Mamluk Sultanate (1250–1516)
The beginning of the Islamic Mamluk Sultanate heralded a period of relative calm in the Levant, other than on-going battles with the Crusaders who were eventually expelled entirely from the region, and a ferocious battle fought with the Mongols. Led by Hulagu Khan (circa b1217, d1265), the grandson of the Mongol Empire's founder Genghis Khan, the Mongol army sought to expand its empire that stretched westwards from southwest Asia. In 1258 it targeted and destroyed Baghdad and moved through Transjordan to the Levant where it targeted Damascus. It was, however, stopped in its tracks and beaten back by the Mamluk warriors.

Transjordan flourished during the Mamluk period. Much of the organisation of the dynasty was centered on Cairo in Egypt where its army of slave soldiers were based and trained with much precision. The sultans established strong trading and political links between Transjordan and Egypt via the Red Sea, and some ten years later with Syria. It initiated a mail route between the countries and fortified their cities. The unity and strength of the Mamluk warriors and the region's brand new strongholds ensured invaders could be defeated. Indeed, the Mamluks fought the Mongols a number of times over the next few years and succeeded in preventing them achieving power. However, a new threat was emerging from the north: the Ottomans from Turkey.

The Ottoman Empire (1516–1917)
The Ottoman rule of Transjordan began after this long-established dynasty had captured the Byzantine city of Constantinople, declared it its capital and renamed it Istanbul, and then sought to expand its empire southwards. Under Selim I (circa b1465, d1520), who was the sultan of the empire from 1512 to 1520 and assumed the title Caliph of Islam, the Ottomans captured Damascus, Transjordan and Jerusalem before moving on to countries around the eastern Mediterranean and north Africa. In just a few years Selim had more than doubled the size of the empire.

Selim I's passion for expansion was continued by Suleiman the Magnificent (b1494, d1566), who became sultan of the empire from 1520 to 1566, and indeed by his successors for almost 400 more years. For Transjordan, however, the Ottoman period was largely one of decline as much of the empire's wealth was spent on its major cities of Istanbul, Jerusalem and Damascus, Algiers and Tripoli in north Africa and Baku on the edge of the Caspian Sea. Salt, however, was declared the regional capital of the empire and enjoyed a level of prosperity unseen previously. Elsewhere, the people continued their lives, pausing only to welcome passing pilgrims on their journey along the recognised pilgrimage route between Makkah and Damascus that passed through the country.

By the end of 1917 the Ottoman Empire was weak. A combination of unrest amongst its own diverse ethnic groups and the fact that World War I had ravaged great swathes of the empire's territories since 1914 had taken its toll. This, coupled with the effect of the Arab Revolt of 1916–18, which was led by Sharif Hussein bin Ali of Makkah (b1853, d1931) in his bid for independence from the Ottomans, and

LAWRENCE OF ARABIA

Lieutenant Colonel Thomas Edward Lawrence (b1888, d1935) was a British Army officer who had an in-depth knowledge of the Ottoman Empire's then provinces of Transjordan and Palestine due to his passion for archaeology. He had travelled extensively throughout the Levant. This knowledge became known to the British Army, which recruited him to the Intelligence Staff of the GOC (General Officer Commanding) Middle East in Cairo during World War I. It was from here he was sent to work with the Arabs in a liaison role during the Arab Revolt of 1916–18. His orders, it is said, were to persuade the Arab Army to unite with the British and work with its army on their strategy for exiting the Ottomans from the region.

The Arabs, keen for independence from the ruling Ottoman Turks themselves and spurred on by stories of ally troops succeeding in other areas controlled by the Ottoman Empire, were receptive to Lawrence's proposals for independence. The plan worked and the Arabs regained control of large areas of the Levant as the Ottoman Empire crumbled. Lawrence was seen by the Arabs as something of a hero. However, as records have revealed, throughout this time the British had secured crucial intelligence. It transpired that Britain had been in talks with the French, and together had drawn up a plan to divide the territories now under Arab rule. The Sykes-Picot Agreement saw Jordan, along with Palestine, come under the British mandate, while Syria and Lebanon formed part of the French mandate. A sense of betrayal was felt by the Arabs and, according to some reports, by Lawrence himself.

Lawrence went on to work with the British Army until his enlistment came to an end in 1935. Just two months after leaving service he was involved in a motorcycle accident in England, and died from his injuries. It is said that the neurosurgeon, Hugh Cairns, who treated him in the immediate hours after the accident, was so moved by the accident that he went on to pioneer the use of crash helmets by all motorcyclists. During his lifetime Lawrence found fame through newspaper clippings, books – including his own 1922 autobiography *Seven Pillars of Wisdom* – and the later publication of just some of the numerous letters he wrote to great names such as Winston Churchill, the actor Noel Coward and playwright George Bernard Shaw. In modern culture, Lawrence is probably best known for his portrayal by actor Peter O'Toole in the 1962 film, *Lawrence of Arabia*.

famously involved the British Army officer TE Lawrence, later known as Lawrence of Arabia, compounded the empire's disintegration. For Transjordan it was the beginning of a vibrant new era in its history.

EMIRATE TO HASHEMITE KINGDOM OF JORDAN (1921–51) The 1920s signalled a period of change for Transjordan. In effect, it began at the Paris Peace Conference of 1919, held as World War I reached its conclusion. It was a major meeting attended by more than 29 world leaders, many of whom were victorious in World War I. Its agenda was to agree peace terms for the defeated nations of the war, most notably Germany. Negotiations lasted for months but eventually a mandate was agreed. Significantly for Transjordan, the League of Nations was also created.

Designed as an international security organisation whose charter was to keep world peace through the prevention of war, and to handle disputes amongst countries through negotiation, the League of Nations was the forerunner to the United Nations, or UN, of today. One of its first tasks was to establish the boundaries of the Middle Eastern countries, which at the time were in considerable disarray following the disintegration of the Ottoman Empire.

At the time, an agreement between the British and the French, known as the Sykes-Picot Agreement, was already in place. The agreement had been negotiated a few years previously to decide who would control which areas, should the Ottoman Empire collapse. As had been expected it did, and the agreement now came into play. In accordance with what had been agreed, the French assumed control of Syria and Lebanon with clearly defined boundaries, while the British took Palestinian territories. Around 70% of the territories under what became known as the British Mandate for Palestine lay to the east of the Jordan River in the area known as Transjordan, or present-day Jordan.

In 1921, Transjordan was officially separated from Palestine to become an autonomous political protectorate with control given to Sharif Abdullah bin al-Hussein (b1882, d1951), a long-standing ally of the British. The Emirate of Transjordan was officially created. Abdullah, a member of the Hashemite dynasty of the Hejaz region of Arabia, was declared the Emir of Transjordan. The country flourished as Abdullah set about building its political and social infrastructure and increasing its stature on the world platform. The population was mainly made up of Bedouin tribesmen who were loyal to Abdullah, himself of the same ancestry.

Abdullah, while instigating reforms for his country, was at the same time keen for the emirate to achieve independence and embarked on lengthy negotiations with the British to this end. The Emirate of Transjordan was officially declared independent on 25 May 1946, amidst much jubilation. The emirate became known as the Hashemite Kingdom of Transjordan, later shortened to the Hashemite Kingdom of Jordan in 1950, with Abdullah becoming king of the new independent state.

The new kingdom continued to grow strong, despite periods of unrest with neighbouring Palestine and the newly created state of Israel during which King Abdullah I successfully conquered the West Bank and parts of Jerusalem. These territories were later annexed to Israel and their Palestinian Arab residents offered sanctuary in Jordan and full Jordanian citizenship. The two largest influxes of Palestinians to Jordan were in 1948 following the Arab–Israeli War and in 1967 as a result of the Six-Day War. Today, Palestinian refugees, who have passports and IDs, and work and study in the country, outnumber the original Bedouin inhabitants of Jordan.

King Abdullah I ruled Jordan until his assassination by a gunman on a visit to the Al-Aqsa Mosque in Jerusalem on 20 July 1951, amid speculation that he had

23

entered into peace talks with Israel. He was accompanied by his grandson, Hussein bin Talal (b1935, d1999), who is said to have been hit but survived when a medal he was wearing deflected the bullet. Hussein went on to become King of Jordan a little over a year later.

MODERN HISTORY (1951–PRESENT)
Talal bin Abdullah (b1909, d1972), the son of Abdullah I, became King Talal I of Jordan upon his father's death. King Talal I, however, was reported to be suffering ill health. Amid concerns amongst his family and colleagues, he abdicated in favour of his son, Hussein bin Talal, in 1952. Nonetheless, during his short reign King Talal I was seen to forge stronger relations with Jordan's neighbours Saudi Arabia and Egypt, and is credited with introducing a more defined constitution that saw the government and its ministers having a clear line of responsibility to the Jordanian Parliament.

King Talal I's son Hussein bin Talal ascended to the throne as King Hussein I of Jordan on 11 August 1952. He was 16 years of age. King Hussein I's reign saw local unrest and wars, including the Six-Day War involving Egypt and Israel in 1967, and the Arab–Israeli War of 1973, however, he is credited and much-admired for successfully negotiating the landmark Israel–Jordan Treaty of Peace. Negotiations concluded on 26 October 1994 with a handshake between King Hussein I and the President of Israel Ezer Weizman in the presence of the then US President Bill Clinton. It brought an end to 46 years of war. Borders between the two countries were opened to much fanfare and two years later the two countries signed a Trade Treaty, which afforded them mutual respect to trade.

In July 1998 it was announced that King Hussein I was receiving treatment for lymphatic cancer and he died in the following February having been one of the all-time longest-serving leaders in the international political arena. He had held office for over 46 years and was seen as the voice of reason in an area of the world that was often turbulent. Hundreds of thousands of Jordanians lined the streets of Amman in an outpouring of grief as his funeral cortege passed.

The funeral of King Hussein I was attended by dignitaries from around the world. Among them were England's Prince of Wales, the US President Bill Clinton and three of his predecessors, Gerald Ford, George Bush Snr and Jimmy Carter, the Russian President Boris Yeltsin, and leaders from the Middle East and north Africa, including the President of the Palestinian National Authority Yasser Arafat, Egypt's President Hosni Mubarak, President of Syria Hafez al-Assad and Israeli Prime Minister Binyamin Natanyahu and former prime minister Yitzhak Sharmir. The funeral and the fact that it brought together so many former adversaries was seen as a major point in not only Jordan's history but the world's.

King Hussein I married four times. His second wife, Antoinette Avril Gardiner (b1941), known as Her Royal Highness Princess Muna al-Hussein during her marriage, is the mother of the present king of Jordan, His Majesty King Abdullah II (b1962). Born in Suffolk, England, she met King Hussein I when she was working in the administrative office on the set of the film *Lawrence of Arabia* when the desert scenes were being filmed in Jordan. Her son, Abdullah bin al-Hussein, ascended to the throne on 7 February 1999. At the time it was reported that the new king faced economic and political challenges in Jordan, but as he had already forged good relationships with many of the Gulf rulers, and indeed leaders from around the world, it was felt the transition from one king to the next was likely to be smooth.

His Majesty King Abdullah II, together with his wife Her Majesty Queen Rania of Jordan whom he married in 1993, and with whom he has four children – Crown Prince Hussein (b1994), Princess Iman (b1996), Princess Salma (b2000) and Prince

Hashem (b2005) – is seen as a modern monarch and is much-loved by his people. He enjoys scuba diving and many other sports, is a keen user of the internet and is a passionate fan of the television series *Star Trek* in which he once acted as an extra. Significant for Jordan and its people too, is that the king is seen as a strong leader and one committed to maintaining good relations with neighbouring countries.

During his reign the country's economic growth has been considerable, largely due to his initiatives to increase foreign investment from the Middle East countries and the West, and forge greater business links with countries, notably the US, through the creation of free trade zones. He has also been credited with introducing social reforms that have had a positive effect on providing better quality housing, health services and education, and has been instrumental in an Israeli–Jordanian project to pipe water from the Red Sea to the dwindling Dead Sea, and a Syrian–Jordanian project to build a multi-million-pound dam on the Yarmuk River.

JORDAN TIMELINE

Pre–c20,000BC	Paleolithic period
c20,000–10,000BC	Mesolithic period
c10,000–4500BC	Neolithic period and the start of agriculture in the Jordan Valley
c4500–3300BC	Chalcolithic period
c3300–1900BC	Early Bronze Age
c1900–1550BC	Middle Bronze Age
c1550–1200BC	Late Bronze Age
c1200–539BC	Iron Age: Transjordanian kingdoms of Ammon, Moab and Edom founded
539–332BC	Persian period and Christianity becomes official religion
333BC	Alexander the Great conquers the Persians
332–63BC	Hellenistic period
323BC	Death of Alexander the Great
312BC–AD106	Nabatean period and the founding of Petra
63BC–AD324	Roman period and the founding of the Decapolis cities
0	Birth of Jesus of Nazareth in Bethlehem
AD324–635	Byzantine period
AD570	Birth of Prophet Muhammad
AD629	Battle between Muslims and Christians at Mu'ta near Karak
AD632	Death of Prophet Muhammad
AD632–661	Early Islamic Rule
AD636	Battle of Yarmouk with Muslims' victory against Byzantine troops
AD636	Jordan converts to Islam
AD661–750	Umayyad Dynasty of Muslim caliphs; Damascus declared the capital city
AD750–969	Abbasid Dynasty assume power from the Umayyads
AD969–1171	Fatimid Dynasty rules Jordan
1096	Beginning of the Crusades
1099	Jerusalem captured by the Crusaders
1171–1263	Ayyubid Dynasty assumes power
1187	Battle of Hattin and victory of Saladin against the Crusaders
1250–1516	Mamluk Dynasty rules Jordan
1516–1917	Ottoman period under several sultans, including Suleiman the Magnificent

1912	Nabatean city of Petra rediscovered
1916	Beginning of the Arab Revolt inspired by Colonel Lawrence of Arabia
1918	End of the World War I; Ottoman Empire collapses
1920	Transjordan and Palestine come under British mandate
1921	Creation of the Emirate of Transjordan
1921	Abdullah I becomes Emir of Transjordan
1946	Country becomes the independent Hashemite Kingdom of Transjordan
1946	Abdullah I becomes king of the new independent state
1950	Renamed Hashemite Kingdom of Jordan
1950	West Bank and East Jerusalem annexed from Jordan; refugees flee
1951	King Abdullah I assassinated
1951	Talal bin Abdullah becomes King Talal of Jordan but abdicates in 1952
1952	Hussein bin Talal becomes King Hussein of Jordan at the age of 16
1967	Six-Day War that sees Israel seize the West Bank and Jerusalem
1973	Arab-Israeli War
1994	Israel–Jordan Treaty of Peace signed
1999	King Hussein I dies
1999	Abdullah bin al-Hussein becomes His Majesty King Abdullah II of Jordan.
2001	His Majesty King Abdullah II inaugurates a joint electricity link with Egypt and Syria
2002	Israel–Jordan project unveiled to pipe water from the Red Sea to the Dead Sea
2003	Local elections show support for His Majesty King Abdullah II
2004	Syria–Jordan Wahdah Dam project unveiled
2007	Petra is named as one of UNESCO's New Seven Wonders of the World
2009	His Majesty King Abdullah II announces new economic reforms
2011	Protests in Amman over economic reforms
2011	Awn al-Khasawneh appointed new prime minister

GOVERNMENT AND POLITICS

The Hashemite Kingdom of Jordan is a constitutional monarchy headed by His Majesty King Abdullah II. The king, who ascended the throne on the death of his father, King Hussein I, is seen as a modern thinker who believes in peace, progress and economic stability. One of the first announcements he made after being crowned was to pledge his support for the peace treaty Jordan had shared with Israel since 1994, along with a commitment to the relations it enjoyed with the US. These two issues have not always been popular with Jordanians, however.

His Majesty King Abdullah II also pledged a commitment to increasing foreign investment, establishing a more open political arena for the people of Jordan, and, significantly, to refocus his government's thinking on economic reform, a subject that was, and still is, an issue with many Jordanians. A ten-year programme of political, social and economic reform was announced, and although it has had its critics it has had considerable success. The country has seen the emergence of independent parties that play their part in local politics and the founding of free trade zones that have helped the growth of the economy and an increase in its foreign investment.

Although the king is the ultimate figure of authority, and has the power to appoint and dissolve governments, declare war, approve new laws and legislation, and commands the country's military, Jordan's representative government is an important entity in its own right. It has a prime minister and a cabinet, known as the Council of Ministers, through which the king exerts his power. The prime minister is Awn al-Khasawneh, an International Court of Justice judge and former chief of the royal court, who took office in October 2011.

The Council of Ministers is responsible to the Chamber of Deputies, one of two parliamentary chambers under the country's constitution. Comprising 120 democratically elected members from local constituencies, including female

members and those from different religious and ethnic groups, the Chamber of Deputies, or the House of Representatives, is the lower house of the parliamentary National Assembly of Jordan. It is the legislative branch of the government.

The legislative responsibility of the chamber is shared with the Chamber of Notables, the upper house of the National Assembly, otherwise known as the Assembly of Senators or the Senate. Its members are key public political or military figures and appointed to the Senate by the king. They hold a four-year term, after which they may step down or be reappointed. The current President of the Senate is a former prime minister Taher Nashat al-Masri. The judicial branch is an independent branch of the government.

At local level, Jordan is divided into 12 governorates, including the Capital Governorate that centres on Amman, the Aqaba Governorate to the south and the Irbid Governorate to the north. Other governorates are Ajlun, Mafraq, Amman and Zarqa, Balqa, Madaba, Karak, Tafila and Ma'an. Each is headed by a governor appointed by the king, who is responsible for all the departments totalling 52 within the governorate.

Jordan has around 30 different political parties that have emerged since the political reforms instigated by King Hussein I and then those of His Majesty King Abdullah II that legalised opposition parties. Most could be said to be Islamists, Arab nationalists, leftists or liberals, and include the Jordanian Ba'th Arab Socialist Party, the Jordanian Communist Party and the Jordanian People's Democratic Party. The opposition party credited with the most power in Jordan is the Islamic Action Front (IAF).

ECONOMY

The economy had suffered significantly from political instability in the region, but when His Majesty King Abdullah II came to the throne in 1999 he immediately announced his intention to refocus his government's plans on economic reforms and has monitored and instigated new measures when necessary ever since. This has included dissolving and appointing governments and replacing prime ministers. The king has had some considerable success, and has been credited with developing Jordan to such an extent that it is attracting increasing foreign investment and is now seen as a major player in the Levant and Middle East.

The country's economic growth rate was at one time around 7% per annum, more than double the figure before the present king's reign, although in the past couple of years it has settled at around 3.2%. The World Bank classifies Jordan as an upper-middle-income country, with a per capita GDP of US$4,390 quoted for 2010. Unemployment amongst its population, which is high, stood at around 14%, although officially this has dropped to around 12%. Jordan has implemented initiatives for better standards of housing, education and health services for everyone with considerable success, but calls for reform are staged periodically, with living near or under the poverty line being the main issue for the population demanding change. The most recent street protests were in 2011, sparked by similar protests in Tunisia and Egypt.

Inflation has been kept under control, largely thanks to the Jordanian dinar's exchange rate being fixed to the US dollar since 1995. Key to the success of low inflation and the economic reforms so far has been a business infrastructure that provides for competitiveness and sustainability, and a modern banking system that greatly helped it avoid becoming a victim of the global financial crisis of recent years. His Majesty King Abdullah II is also reported to have urged the government to lower internet charges in a bid to increase usage amongst Jordanians for business as well as leisure.

Free trade zones have played their part too. Aqaba is an important one, and there are zones in Irbid, Ajlun, Mafraq, the Dead Sea and at Ma'an, all of which have seen unparalleled investment in their infrastructures. Significantly, the king also negotiated a free trade zone agreement with the US, which was followed by similar agreements with the European Union, Canada, Singapore and Malaysia, and many of its eastern Mediterranean and north African business partners, including Turkey, Syria and Iraq. Jordan now has more free trade agreements in place than any other Arab country and is being viewed by world companies as a viable business centre.

Unlike its neighbouring oil-rich Middle Eastern countries, Jordan has few natural resources, including water, which in many ways hinders its economic growth, so it relies heavily on trade and foreign aid, which mostly comes from the US. What it does have is a strong phosphates industry. In fact, it is one of the largest producers and exporters of the mineral, which is used as a fertiliser in agriculture, in animal feeds, cosmetics, ceramics, water treatment and food preservatives.

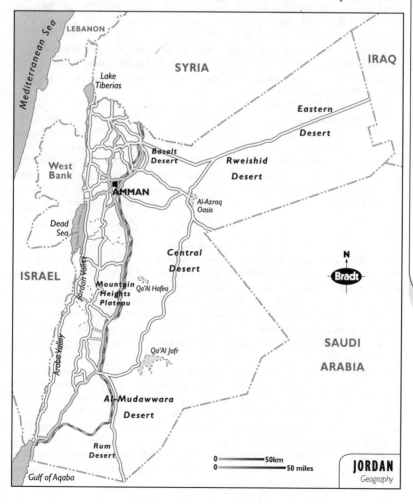

Jordan has resources of oil shale, which it exports for use in resins, cement, glues and for heating, along with uranium. Tourism – particularly in the areas of religious tours, activities, spas and wellbeing, nature and health – is a key area in which the country, under the king, plans to expand.

PEOPLE

The people of Jordan are generally well educated, have good literacy levels and enjoy a quality of life that is higher than in some other countries in the region. Social reforms have long been on the political agenda, and as a result there has been investment in town and city infrastructures to create homes, jobs, better educational opportunities and enhanced leisure opportunities. Millions have been invested in the country's healthcare system, to the point that it is now seen as one of the finest in the region.

In the main, Jordanians are polite and friendly, and you will be greeted with a smile and the offer of help. They are a conservative people who appreciate good manners, smart dress and modesty. Most live very well, although there are still several thousand who live below the poverty line. In 2008, His Majesty King Abdullah II launched a five-billion-dinar Decent Housing for a Decent Living initiative that aimed to give all poorer families, including refugees, the chance of owning their own home. A total of 100,000 affordable homes costing around 24,000 dinar each are currently being built throughout the country, with provision for a further 100,000 if demand requires.

The country's 6.5 million population, which has grown rapidly over the past 50 years, is made up almost entirely of Sunni Muslim and Christian Arabs who equate to 98% of the total. Many hail from Palestine and fled during the 1948 Palestine War and the Six-Day War in 1967. The remaining 2% of the population are either Circassian, from the territory that includes Turkey, parts of Russia, Syria and Iraq, or Armenian from the Republic of Armenia in the Caucasus region of Eurasia. Most Jordanians live in rural areas; in fact, a total of around 80% of the population. The remainder, around 2.2 million, live in the country's capital Amman.

LANGUAGE

The official language of Jordan is Arabic, which takes three forms: classical, the ancient version used in the Holy Koran; the modern standard form, which is accepted for public address and scholarly writings; and colloquial, the most commonly spoken version. The latter has no real written equivalent, and when written using the Latin alphabet the spelling used is English. However, the interpretation of how a word is spelt can vary enormously, so be prepared for variations of spellings of the same word. Street addresses can be particularly problematic for visitors.

English is widely spoken throughout Jordan. In fact, most Jordanians are fluent English speakers, but as a visitor it is always appreciated if you can converse in just a little Arabic. You may only feel confident giving a basic greeting like *marhaba* ('hello'), *sabahl al-khayr* ('good morning'), *masa al-khayr* ('good afternoon'), *kayf halak* ('how are you?' [to a man]) and *kayf halik* ('how are you?' [to a woman]) or *assalaamu alaykum* ('peace be with you'), but you are sure to be rewarded with a beaming smile of gratitude. Jordanians are often well travelled themselves, or have been educated overseas, and as a result French, Italian, Spanish and German are also widely spoken languages.

RELIGION

Jordan values its ethnically and religiously diverse population and is seen as a model of tolerance. It is this tolerance that has afforded Jordan a peaceful and stable climate, which its people and visitors can enjoy. The country's constitution allows for all to have the freedom to practise one's chosen religious beliefs, providing they are in accordance with the law and moral customs of the kingdom.

Islam is the predominant religion amongst both Arabs and non-Arabs, and is the state religion. In fact, around 92% of the total population is Muslim, and in particular follow the Sunni branch of the faith. Christianity is practised by around 6% of the population, many of whom are indigenous Jordanian Christians belonging to the Greek Orthodox Church of Jerusalem. Most are of Arab descent, but of those that originate from other lands, Armenians make up the largest number. Other minority religions include the Baháï faith that can trace its routes back to 19th-century Persia, and Druze, which originated in Lebanon, Israel and Syria around 1,000 years ago. Jordan's Druze communities live mainly in the eastern desert regions.

All religious beliefs are respected and representatives from different faiths form part of the government's structure, the parliamentary National Assembly of Jordan and the military. While Islamic teachings are offered to all students, it is not mandatory for non-Muslims to study. What is not acceptable, however, is to attempt to convert a Muslim follower to Christianity. The government bans such actions, and while it is not forbidden to attempt to convert a Christian to Islam it is not looked upon favourably.

SUNNI MUSLIM The Sunni branch of Islam followed by the majority of Jordan's Muslims is an ancient faith based on the words and beliefs of the Prophet Muhammad (b570, d632), to whom God, or Allah as he is known in Arabic, revealed his message to mankind. Sunni Muslims follow the words of *hadiths*, which are scriptures detailing Muhammad's words and actions that work in conjunction with the teachings of the Islamic holy book, the Holy Koran. The sovereignty of Allah is undisputed, with the unity of Muslims before Allah as one of the main principals of Islam.

There are four schools of law to the Ahlus-Sunnah Wa al-Jama'ah branch, or Sunnah, Sunni for short, which literally means People of the Tradition and the Congregation. These are the Shafi'i School (followed by most Jordanian Sunni Muslims), the Hanafi School, the Maliki School and the Hanbali School. Muslims come together five times a day for prayers facing the holy city of Makkah, and celebrate festivals together, including Ramadan.

Festivals The main religious festivals celebrated by Sunni Muslims in Jordan are:

Mowlid an-Nabawi A variable day held to celebrate the birthday of the Prophet Muhammad, founder of Islam.

Eid al-Isra wal-Miraj Meaning Night Journey to Heaven, this festival marks the Prophet Muhammad's journey and ascension.

Ramadan Variable according to the Islamic Lunar calendar, Ramadan is the holy month of fasting.

Eid al-Fitr A three- or four-day feast to mark the end of Ramadan.

Eid al-Adha This four-day feast is held to mark the end of the Hajj, the month of pilgrimage to Makkah.

First of Muharram The Islamic New Year.

CHRISTIANS Jordan has an indigenous Christian population that is Arab by descent, with most being Holy Land Levantine Arabs. Most Jordanian Christians belong to the Greek Orthodox Church of Jerusalem, which follows the Julian calendar that runs 13 days after the Gregorian calendar used in the west. Christians' beliefs focus on the birth of Jesus Christ at Christmas, his crucifixion and resurrection celebrated at Easter every year, and the descent of the Holy Spirit upon the apostles of Christ in Jerusalem according to the New Testament Acts of the Apostles 2:1–31 in the celebration known as Pentecost. It is believed the day of Pentecost marked the founding of the Church, and that the Gospel of Christ spread from Jerusalem.

There are other Christian churches followed by Jordanian Christians, including the Syriac Orthodox Church and the Syrian Catholic Church, which share many of the same beliefs. The latter is one of the oldest churches in the world, founded in Asia by, it is believed, St Peter the Apostle. The Roman Catholic Church regards this noted Christian leader, born around the same time as Christ, as its first Pope. Other churches include the Latin Rite Catholic Church, the largest in the Catholic faith and currently headed by Pope Benedict XVI; the Ancient Church of the East; the Anglian Communion; the relatively modern 16th-century Assyrian Church of the East; and the Melkite Greek Catholic Church, which is followed by Middle Eastern and Greek Christians.

Non-Arab Christians are mostly comprised of Armenians, who follow the Armenian Apostle Church or the Armenian Catholic Church, with the remainder being expatriates from Europe, Sri Lanka, the Philippines and, in more recent times, from Iraq.

Festivals The main religious festivals celebrated by Christians in Jordan are:

Epiphany A celebration of the God appearing as Jesus Christ, which is held on 19 January according to the Julian calendar.

Lent A period of fasting held for 40 days before Easter, which recognises Jesus's fast before he began his teachings, known as the *first coming* according to the Gospels of Matthew, Mark and Luke.

Easter Focusing on Good Friday and Easter Sunday, Easter marks Jesus's resurrection. It is followed 40 days later by **Ascension Day**, the day he rose to heaven.

Christmas A religious celebration marking the birth of Jesus Christ. It has been accepted as a public holiday for all in Jordan.

RELIGIOUS SITES Jordan is blessed with many sites mentioned in the Bible and the Holy Koran, to which pilgrims are drawn. Umm Qays was one of the major cities of Roman times and mentioned in the New Testament, and it was here that Jesus Christ is said to have performed one of his miracles. Pella, site of many stories involving biblical patriarch Isaac's sons Jacob and Esau is another of the main religious sites of Jordan; along with Salt, where there are ancient tombs of biblical characters; and the city of Jerash and Umm Ar-Rasas. Also, the present-day cities of Amman; Madaba, which is referred to extensively in the Old Testament as Medeba, home of the Moabites; Aqaba in the south; and the Nabatean city of Petra, which in biblical times was an important trading centre.

The King's Highway, which today partially links the southern towns and cities with the highway to Amman, is mentioned several times in the bible, the first instance being in Genesis 20:17 when Moses sought to lead his people on their journey through the ancient kingdom of Edom to Canaan (ancient Levant). This ancient highway was an important trade route that linked Egypt to Jordan via the Sinai Peninsula, and northwards to Syria, and is considered to be the earliest known road in the world to have been in continuous use. For more information see *The King's Highway*, page 161.

PILGRIMAGE SITES Bethany Beyond the Jordan is one of the foremost sites of pilgrimage. According to the Bible and numerous ancient texts, it is here that Jesus Christ was baptised by the preacher John the Baptist and anointed by God. It is said that during his stay in Bethany Beyond the Jordan he first prayed to God and gathered the first of his disciples, Nathanael, Peter, Simon, Andrew and Philip. Nearby, a cave has been identified as being that where John the Baptist lived. In Byzantine times the cave was transformed into a church. Throughout this area are the remains of many other churches and monasteries, including one believed to be an early Christian prayer hall. You can still see some remarkably well-preserved mosaics that would have adorned the floor of its central hall. Located on Elijah's Hill and dating from around the 3rd century, it is believed to be one of the earliest examples of a religious building used for prayer.

Bethany Beyond the Jordan lies in the Jordan Valley as it approaches the Dead Sea from Amman. In the Bible's Old Testament Book of Genesis, God is credited with describing the Jordan Valley created by the Jordan River as the 'Garden of the Lord'. Many scholars believe this to be the Garden of Eden, home to the first man and woman created by God, namely Adam and Eve.

Southeast of here lies Mount Nebo, a place of pilgrimage where texts tell us the Hebrew prophet Moses saw the Promised Land and where he is now buried. Further south is the town of Mukawir, known as Machaerus in biblical times, which is best known for being where Roman ruler Herod Antipatros (circa b20BC, dAD39) had John the Baptist beheaded in around AD36.

EDUCATION

The United Nations Educational, Social and Cultural Organisation (UNESCO) ranks the education system in Jordan for men, women and children as being the 18th highest in the world, and the best amongst all Arab countries. The Jordanian authority made education one of its top priorities some years ago, investing over 20% of its total annual expenditure into providing teachers, schools and universities. It was seen as a way to provide enhanced social interaction, as well as having an impact on the development of Jordan as a country. The policy paid off, for now well over 90% of the population is regarded as being well educated, with higher than average mathematic, science and literacy skills. In turn, these same people have driven trade and industry, and helped the country to grow its economy.

There is almost a 100% attendance rate for primary school children, with the total number of secondary and high-school students increasing year on year. Most students attend state school, but the country has a growing number of

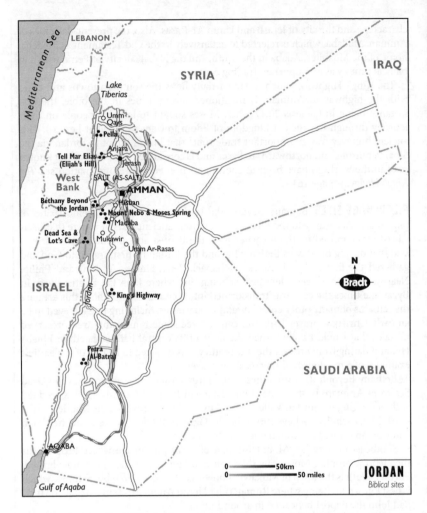

JORDAN
Biblical sites

private schools offering basic through to higher vocational curriculums. The vast majority, around 83%, go on to higher education. Jordan has many public, private and affiliated universities, such as the University of Jordan in Amman, the Jordan University of Science and Technology in Irbid, the Yarmouk University in Irbid and the Hashemite University in Zarqa. Of the subjects studied, mathematics is seen as the leader in terms of skill level, closely followed by the sciences. The country also has one of the region's highest numbers of university graduates in technology and engineering.

CULTURE

Jordan has a vibrant cultural scene that in many ways reflects the personality of its modern monarchy. A passionate follower of the arts and sports, and well travelled, His Majesty King Abdullah II is committed to promoting cultural activities for his people to enjoy and has introduced programmes designed to preserve the country's archaeological, artistic and historical heritage. Amman is the cultural hub of the country, and it is here you will find most of the artistic and performing arts venues and sports facilities, but other towns, such as Aqaba, are seeing an increase in the number of venues opening (see *Arts and entertainment* in the *Practical Information* chapter, page 37). The 'Life' section of the *Jordan Times* and *Go Magazine* are two of the best publications that give comprehensive information on all the major arts and cultural events taking place in Amman and around the country. Jordanians are enthusiastic when it comes to festivals. Some of the many festivals that appear in the annual calendar are religious, while others are cultural (see *Public holidays and festivals* in the *Practical Information* chapter, page 77).

HERITAGE The cultural and creative heritage of Jordan is especially prolific in the country's many museums, craft centres and souks. You'll see tapestries produced with bold patterns or delicately woven scenes showing stories. Goat-hair rugs and tents are still made by hand, as are ceramics and pottery, and leatherwork. Jordan's heritage is evident, too, in stories, songs and ballads that have been handed down through the generations, and are a key part of a traditional Bedouin family's evening. Although more and more Bedouins now live in buildings rather than tents, these age-old stories and songs still play a vital part of everyday life. Villages have their own dances and songs for births, weddings and funerals, and host festivals to mark the start of the agricultural growing season and the subsequent harvesting of crops that have their origins set deep in tradition. Jordan is a modern country that celebrates its history in a grand style.

The art of relaxation.

You stretch out and relax as you comfortably lay in your bed. There's nothing like a good night's sleep before an eventful day and with Royal Jordanian's Crown Class flatbeds, that is exactly what you will get.

Royal Jordanian. Turning every journey into a masterpiece.

www.rj.com

ROYAL JORDANIAN
The art of flying.

2

Practical Information

WHEN TO VISIT

Jordan is a diverse country and one that appeals to many different types of travellers. If you like exploring cities and ancient sites then it is best to avoid the hot temperatures of summer, unless you are a sun-lover. Conversely, if you're planning an activity trip into the mountains, then it's best to avoid the winter months when snowfall can block roadways and hinder your journey. With all that in mind, the best months to visit are March through to June and then from mid-September through to late November.

SPRING The rich green countryside and golden desert areas like Wadi Rum are outstanding in spring. From the beginning of March the landscape becomes dotted with all manner of wild flowers. The hues are amazing, ranging in colour from the deep colour of the Black Iris (*Iris nigricans*), Jordan's national flower, to the bright reds of poppies and anemones. Temperatures are pleasantly warm. In Amman and Petra, which lies around 1,000m above sea level, you can expect highs of around 28–30°C, while further south in Aqaba and around the Dead Sea region the temperature can be a few degrees higher.

SUMMER The Jordan Valley, Wadi Rum and the easterly desert areas experience their hottest temperatures in summer and can become quite oppressive, making many forms of exercise something of a trial. Highs can peak at around 45°C. Aqaba, which enjoys a Mediterranean climate, will be hot too, with average maximum daily temperatures reaching around 38°C. The north and cities like Amman are generally a few degrees cooler, although still well into the 30°Cs.

AUTUMN Visiting from mid-September through to November, when the temperatures fall and become pleasantly fresh, opens up the possibility for more energetic activities. It's a great time to come if you're planning a hiking expedition for example, or simply want to spend a week or so floating in the Dead Sea. The landscape, too, takes on a greener look and wildflowers begin to reappear, prompted by the first rainfalls of the winter season.

WINTER With average highs of 20°C and little rainfall, Aqaba remains welcoming even in winter, but the rest of the country can feel quite chilly most days and downright cold in the evenings. You can expect a fair amount of rainfall in the north of the country, and frequent dustings or even heavy falls of snow in the higher mountainous areas right through to around the end of February.

Jordan has many highlights, but you may want to build your trip around some of the following.

PETRA Dubbed the Rose City because of the remarkable hues in the rocky landscape that dominates this region, the UNESCO World Heritage Site of Petra at Wadi Musa must surely top the list of Jordan's highlights. Once the capital city of the Nabateans who settled in Jordan some 2,500 years ago, it is today Jordan's most visited landmark. Petra is an overwhelming space where the architectural skills of these ancient people fuse, in spectacular fashion, with an area of incredible natural beauty. There are hundreds of different monuments to see here, each painstakingly carved into the rock face. You'll pass through the narrow gorge known as the Siq (As-Siq) with its soaring walls, see the Al-Khazneh (the Treasury) and Urn Tomb, the Ad-Deir monastery and the Obelisk Tomb and Bab As-Siq Triclinium.

AMMAN Amman, the capital city, combines ancient sites with modern buildings that house government offices, art galleries, trendy restaurants and cafés, craft workshops and designer fashion shops. Its Citadel, nestled on a hill high above the city, is where some of the country's most prized Roman, Byzantine and early Islamic remains and artefacts have been found during a series of excavation projects. See the splendid Temple of Hercules, built around AD161–66 in Jordan's Roman era, and the Umayyad Palace, dated to around AD730. In the grounds lie the remains of a small Byzantine church with its distinctive Corinthian capitals. It is one of the earliest known religious structures in the country. At the foot of the Citadel is one of the major landmarks of Amman, its spectacular Roman Theatre, and if you are lucky enough to be in town when an operatic or theatrical performance is being performed here, be sure to visit and enjoy the atmosphere.

JERASH North of Amman lies Jerash, where some of the most impressive Greco-Roman remains to be seen anywhere in the world can be explored. For centuries this ancient city – then known as Gerasa and one of the ten eastern cities (Decapolis) of the Roman Empire – lay buried in sand, but extensive excavations have revealed the remains of homes, arches, a hippodrome and even a cathedral.

Jerash covers a massive area with a network of what were once pristine colonnaded walkways. There are the remains of temples and churches to explore, many with mosaic floors, plus two remarkably well-preserved theatres, one capable of seating around 3,000 spectators. The south theatre is still a focal point of the city and regularly hosts cultural events and musical concerts today.

UMM QAYS AND AJLUN Around 50km further north, towards the Syrian border, is Umm Qays where the remains of the Roman city of Gadara can be visited. With its well-preserved remains of a colonnaded main street and theatre, it is an extraordinary site. Nearby is Ajlun (also spelt Ajloun), a bustling city that is surrounded by the pine forests of Ajlun-Dibbine. It revolves around a mound topped by the impressive remains of a 12th-century fortress, known as Ajlun Castle, or Qal'at Ar-Rabad. Cross its bridge to see its well-preserved inner architecture and mosaic floors. The views out towards the Ajloun Forest Reserve are worth the climb up narrow, well-worn stone steps.

DEAD SEA The Dead Sea is without doubt a creation of nature worthy of a prime spot in the highlights of Jordan list. This great expanse of water that dominates the

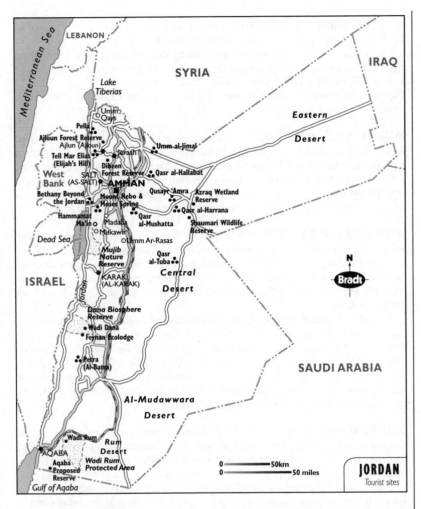

Jordan Valley is the lowest point on earth. The high temperatures, low humidity and high atmospheric pressure at this low depth combine to oxygenate the air, and since antiquity it has been one of the most visited places on Earth by people seeking curative powers.

The Dead Sea has few, if any, pollutants in the air, and being below sea level it receives a reduced penetration of the sun's UV rays. The high mineral content of its waters and its thick brown mud, which when applied to the skin draws out impurities and leaves you feeling clean and silky soft, makes this one of the world's most popular relaxation and wellness spots. Hotels offer spa packages and a viewing complex provides a panoramic vista of the sea.

MOUNT NEBO Nearby, another highlight of Jordan is Mount Nebo. It is where Moses, the character portrayed so vividly in the Bible, is buried, and today is a place of pilgrimage. The view of the Holy Land from its peak, including Jerusalem and Jericho, as well as the Jordan Valley and the Dead Sea itself, is truly awesome. The Jordan Valley is one of the most sacred sites, almost in its entirety, in the world. It is widely believed to have been the location of five cities mentioned in the Bible: Adman, Zeboim, Sodom, Gomorrah and Zoar.

The Jordan Valley is the location of Bethany Beyond the Jordan. Excavations there have unearthed the remains of small towns dating from the 1st century. The area, which includes Tell al-Kharrar, also known as Elijah's Hill, is where John the Baptist is said to have lived and where he baptised Jesus Christ. This area is an important site of religious pilgrimage.

MADABA A little further south is Madaba, an ancient city that was mentioned in the Bible in Numbers 21:30 and Joshua 13:9. It is home to one of the most remarkable collections of Byzantine and Umayyad mosaics in the world, including a 6th-century mosaic depicting a map of Jerusalem. The map gives a rare insight into the layout of the city in ancient times. Today, Madaba is considered the centre of modern mosaics in the country, and mosaicists can be seen at work.

WADI DANA AND WADI RUM While the southern half of Jordan might in many ways be dominated by Petra, there are two other natural attractions that shouldn't be missed in this part of the country. Wadi Dana, and its great expanse of wilderness that has been transformed into one of Jordan's foremost nature reserves, is the first, joined by the seemingly endless terrain of untouched desert that is the Wadi Rum Protected Area.

Dotted with monolithic rock formations and surrounded by rugged mountains, the 720 km² Wadi Rum desert is one of the most famous sites in Jordan. Here, in the red and orange hue of the mountains that surround Wadi Rum, and its soft golden sands dotted with greenery, you can mingle with Bedouin tribes who will almost always extend you a welcome into their homes to drink herbal tea. You can observe rare flora and fauna, take a camel trek or hike in this huge wilderness by day, or spend a night under the stars in a Bedouin camp.

GULF OF AQABA The most southerly of Jordan's treasures is its Gulf of Aqaba. Revolving around the sprawling, naturally green resort metropolis of Aqaba, Jordan's only coastal city, the region offers some of the best diving and snorkelling opportunities in the Middle East. The area is protected and a major ongoing eco-project. Just off its coast is the world's northernmost coral reef eco-system, teeming with brightly coloured marine life. There are over 500 different species of coral in these waters, including the rare archelia.

Moderate currents and warm waters have provided an ideal environment for crabs and lobsters, sea turtles, whales, thousands of crustaceans and molluscs, and over 1,000 different varieties of fish here. On the shoreline itself, excavations are being carried out to find what is believed to be the ancient city of Ayla, in antiquity probably the port referred to in the Hebrew Bible's Books of Kings 9:26.

SUGGESTED ITINERARIES

TOUR OF JORDAN
Weekend
Day 1 Amman City Tour & Jerash.
Overnight in Amman.
Day 2 Petra & Wadi Rum.
Overnight Petra.

One week
Day 1 Amman City Tour, Jordan Archaeological Museum.
Overnight Amman.
Day 2 Jerash, Ajlun & Umm Qays.
Overnight in Amman.

Day 3 Karak & the Dana Biosphere Reserve.
Overnight at Dana.
Day 4 Petra.
Overnight Petra.
Day 5 Wadi Rum & Aqaba City Tour.
Overnight Aqaba.
Day 6 Madaba, Mount Nebo & Mukawir.
Overnight Dead Sea.
Day 7 Dead Sea, Bethany Beyond the Jordan.
Overnight Dead Sea.

Two weeks
Day 1 Amman City Tour, Citadel & Jordan Archaeological Museum in Amman.
Overnight Amman.
Day 2 Desert Castles, including Qasr Azraq, Qsar al-Harrana & Qusayr 'Amra.
Overnight Amman.
Day 3 Jerash, Ajlun & Umm Qays.
Overnight in Amman.
Day 4 Mujib Nature Reserve.
Overnight in Madaba.
Day 5 Karak & the Dana Biosphere Reserve.
Overnight at Dana.
Day 6 Petra.
Overnight Petra.
Day 7 Petra & Wadi Rum.
Overnight Wadi Rum.
Day 8 Wadi Rum.
Overnight Wadi Rum.
Day 9 Aqaba City Tour, Aqaba Archaeological Museum.
Overnight Aqaba.
Day 10 Aqaba at leisure.
Overnight Aqaba.
Day 11 Madaba, Mount Nebo & Mukawir & Hammamat Ma'in.
Overnight Dead Sea.
Day 12 Dead Sea, Bethany Beyond the Jordan.
Overnight Dead Sea.
Day 13 Dead Sea at leisure.
Overnight Dead Sea.
Day 14 Jordan National Gallery of Fine Arts & the Haya Centre in Amman.
Overnight Amman.

Three weeks
Day 1 Arrive Amman & City Tour.
Overnight Amman.
Day 2 Citadel, Jordan Archaeological Museum & Roman Theatre in Amman.
Overnight Amman.

Day 3 Shopping in Downtown Amman souk, Gold Souk & malls.
Overnight Amman.
Day 4 Desert Castles: Qasr al-Mushatta, Qasr al-Harrana, Qusayr 'Amra.
Overnight Azraq.
Day 5 Azraq Wetl& Reserve.
Overnight Azraq.
Day 6 Desert Castles: Qasr Azraq & Qasr al-Hallabat.
Overnight Amman.
Day 7 Jerash.
Overnight Jerash.
Day 8 Salt, Pella & Umm Qays.
Overnight Jerash.
Day 9 Ajloun Forest Reserve & Dibeen Forest.
Overnight in Jerash.
Day 10 Bethany Beyond the Jordan, Mount Nebo & Moses Springs.
Overnight Madaba.
Day 11 Madaba, Umm Ar-Rasas, Mukawir & Hammamat Ma'in.
Overnight Dead Sea.
Day 12 Dead Sea at leisure.
Overnight Dead Sea.
Day 13 Dead Sea at leisure.
Overnight Dead Sea.
Day 14 Mujib Nature Reserve.
Overnight in Dead Sea.
Day 15 Karak & the Dana Biosphere Reserve.
Overnight at Dana.
Day 16 Petra.
Overnight Petra.
Day 17 Petra .
Overnight Petra.
Day 18 Wadi Rum.
Overnight Wadi Rum.
Day 19 Arrive Aqaba, Aqaba City Tour, Aqaba Castle & Aqaba Archaeological Museum.
Overnight Aqaba.
Day 20 Aqaba at leisure.
Overnight Aqaba.
Day 21 Aqaba at leisure.
Overnight Aqaba or Amman via internal flight.

ECO, FLORA AND FAUNA
Weekend
Day 1 Dana Nature Reserve.
Overnight Dana.
Day 2 Wadi Rum.
Overnight Wadi Rum.

One week

Day 1 Ajlun Nature Reserve & Dibeen Forest.
Overnight Ajlun.
Day 2 Azraq Wetl& Reserve & Shaumari Wildlife Reserve.
Overnight Amman.
Day 3 Dead Sea.
Overnight Dead Sea.
Day 4 Mujib Nature Reserve.
Overnight Madaba.
Day 5 Abu Rukeh Reserve*, Fifa Reserve* & Dana Biosphere Reserve.
Overnight Dana.
Day 6 Dana Biosphere Reserve & Wadi Rum.
Overnight Wadi Rum.
Day 7 Wadi Rum.
Overnight Wadi Rum.
* Proposed reserves

SPAS AND WELLBEING
Weekend

Day 1 Dead Sea Spas.
Overnight Dead Sea.
Day 2 Hammamat Ma'in Hot Springs & Amman.
Overnight Amman.

One week

Day 1 Amman Spas.
Overnight Amman.
Day 2 Dead Sea Spas.
Overnight Dead Sea.
Day 3 Dead Sea Spas.
Overnight Dead Sea.
Day 4 Hammamat Ma'in Hot Springs.
Overnight Ma'in.
Day 5 Excursion to Petra & Wadi Rum.
Overnight Wadi Rum.
Day 6 Aqaba Spas.
Overnight Aqaba.
Day 7 Aqaba Spas.
Overnight Aqaba.

ACTIVITIES AND FITNESS
Weekend

Day 1 Hiking, walking & relaxing in the Jordan Valley.
Overnight Dead Sea.
Day 2 Balloon trip at Wadi Rum & diving at Aqaba.
Overnight Aqaba.

One week

Day 1 Horseriding, golf, sports & museum visits in Amman.
Overnight Amman.
Day 2 Birdwatching in the Azraq Wetland Reserve.
Overnight Amman.
Day 3 Relaxing in the Dead Sea Spas.
Overnight Dead Sea.
Day 4 Hiking Wadi Mujib gorge in the Mujib Nature Reserve.
Overnight Al-Karak.
Day 5 Mountain climb to the shrine of Prophet Aaron at Petra.
Overnight Petra.
Day 6 Cycle & a balloon trip at Wadi Rum.
Overnight Wadi Rum.
Day 7 Snorkel & dive at Aqaba.
Overnight Aqaba.

HISTORY AND ARCHAEOLOGY
Weekend

Day 1 Jerash, Ajlun & Umm Qays.
Overnight Amman.
Day 2 Bethany Beyond the Jordan, Mount Nebo & Petra.
Overnight Petra.

One week

Day 1 Amman.
Overnight Amman.
Day 2 Jerash & Ajlun.
Overnight Amman.
Day 3 Umm Qays.
Overnight Amman.
Day 4 Desert Castles, including Qasr Asraq, Qsar al-Harrana & Qusayr 'Amra.
Overnight Amman.
Day 5 Bethany Beyond the Jordan & Mount Nebo.
Overnight Madaba.
Day 6 Madaba, Karak & Petra.
Overnight Petra.
Day 7 Petra.
Overnight Petra.

BIBLE AND RELIGION
Weekend

Day 1 Pella, As-Salt & Umm Qays.
Overnight Amman.
Day 2 Bethany Beyond the Jordan, Madaba, Mukawir & Mount Nebo.
Overnight Madaba.

One week

Day 1 Pella & Umm Qays.
Overnight Amman.
Day 2 As-Salt, Ajlun & Jerash.
Overnight Amman.
Day 3 Hisban, Bethany Beyond the Jordan, Mount Nebo & Moses Springs.
Overnight Dead Sea.
Day 4 Dead Sea, Lot's Cave, Hammamat Ma'in & Mukawir.
Overnight Madaba.

Day 5 Madaba, Umm Ar-Rasas & Karak.
Overnight Petra.
Day 6 Petra.
Overnight Petra.
Day 7 Aqaba & along the King's Highway to Amman.
Overnight Amman.

TOUR OPERATORS

Companies and tour operators around the world offer trips to Jordan. Below is a small selection of specialists that provide travel, accommodation and ancillary holidays or tailor-made packages for travellers. For a much wider choice visit the websites of ABTA The Travel Association (*www.abta.com*), AITO Association of Independent Tour Operators (*www.aito.com*), the US Tour Operators Association (www.ustoa. com), Canadian Tour Operators Association (*www.cato.ca*), Council of Australian Tour Operators CATO (*www.accc.gov.au*), European Tour Operators Association (*www.etoa.org*) and the World Tour Operators (*www.worldtouroperators.com*).

UK

Calverley Travel Limited Bayham Hse, 12–16 Grosvenor Rd, Tunbridge Wells, Kent TN1 2AB, UK; +44 (0)1892 515966; e pettitts@btconnect. com; www.pettitts.co.uk

Cox & Kings Travel Limited 6th Floor, 30 Millbank, London SW1P 4DU; +44 (0)20 7873 5014; e cox.kings@coxandkings.co.uk; www. coxandkings.co.uk

Go Travelling Limited 68 North End Rd, London W14 9EP; +44 (0)20 7371 1113; e sales@ onthegotours.com; www.onthegotours.com

Hadler Tours Limited 36 Coldharbour Rd, Redland, Bristol, Avon BS6 7NA, UK; +44 (0)117 973 2120; e info@hadlertours.ltd.uk; www.hadlertours.ltd.uk

Kuoni Travel Limited Kuoni Hse, Dorking, Surrey RH5 4AZ; +44 (0)1306 744541; e fareast.sales@kuoni.co.uk; www.kuoni.co.uk

McCabe Travel Limited 11 Hillgate Pl, Balham Hill, London SW12 9ER; +44 (0)20 8675 6828; e info@mccabe-travel.co.uk; www.maccabe-travel.co.uk

Page & Moy Travel Group Air Holidays Limited Compass Hse, Rockingham Rd, Market Harborough, Leics LE16 7QD; +44 (0)844 567 6633; e info@pageandmoy.co.uk; www. pageandmoy.co.uk

Ramblers Holidays Limited Lemsford Mill, Lemsford Village, Welwyn Garden City, Herts AL8 7TR; +44 (0)1707 331133; e info@ ramblersholidays.co.uk; www.ramblersholidays. co.uk

Travelbag Limited Glendale Hse, Glendale Business Park, Sandycroft, Deeside, Clwyd CH5 2DL; +44 (0)844 846 8658; e sales@travelbag. co.uk; www.travelbag.co.uk

USA

Abercrombie & Kent USA 1411 Opus Pl, Executive Towers West II, Downers Grove, Il 60515-1182; +1 630 725 3400; e info@ abercrombiekent.com; www.abercrombiekent.com

Adventures Incorporated 400 North Brand Blvd Suite 920, Glendale, CA 91203; +1 416 322 1034; e info@goway.com; www.goway.com/ adventure

AHI Travel 6400 Shafer Court Suite 200, Rosemont, IL 60018; +1 847 384 4500; e info@ahitravel.com; www.ahitravel.com

Collette Vacations 162 Middle St, Pawtucket, RI 02860; +1 401 727 9000; e info@ collettevacations.com; www.collecttevacations. com

Explorations 162 Middle St, Pawtucket, RI 02860, USA; +1 401 727 9000;

2

e web@explorationstouring.com; www.
explorationstouring.com

Gate 1 Travel 455 Maryland Rd, Fort
Washington, PA 19034; +1 215 572 7676;
e info@gate1travel.com; www.gate1travel.com

General Tours World Traveler 53 Summer St,
Keene, NH 03431; +1 603 357 5033; e info@
generaltours.com; www.generaltours.com

Globus 5301 S Federal Circle, Littleton, CO
80123-8934; +1 303 703 7000; e info@
globusjourneys.com; www.globusjourneys.com

Go Ahead Tours One Education St, Cambridge,
MA 02141; +1 617 619 1000; e info@
goaheadtours.com; www.goaheadtours.com

Homeric Tours 55 E 59th St, New York,
NY 10022; +1 212 753 1100; e info@
homerictours.com; www.homerictours.com

Insight Vacations 555 Theodore Frend Ave
Suite C204, Rye, NY 10580; +1 714 937
4990; e info@insightvacations.com; www.
insightvacations.com

SITA World Tours 16250 Ventura Bd Suite 300,
Encino, CA 91436; +1 800 421 5643; e info@
sitatours.com; www.sitatours.com

Tauck World Discovery 10 Norden Pl, Norwalk,
CT 06855-1445; +1 203 899 6500;
e info@tauck.com; www.tauck.com

Travcoa 100 North Sepulveda Bd Suite 1700, El
Segundo, CA 90245; +1 310 649 7104; e info@
travcoa.com; www.travcoa.com

Travel Bound 5 Penn Plaza 5th Floor, New York,
NY 10001; +1 212 334 1350; e fit.nyc@gta-
travel.com; www.booktravelbound.com

CANADA

Goway Travel 3284 Yonge St, Toronto, ON M4N
3M7; +1 416 322 1034; e info@goway.com;
www.goway.com.

AUSTRALIA

Goway Travel 350 Kent St, 8th Floor, Sydney,
NSW 1230; +61 (0)2 9262 4755;
e info@goway.com.au; www.goway.com.au

IN JORDAN Most of the companies in Jordan offering tours of the country's main sites and attractions are located in Amman, although a few can be found in the larger towns or within easy reach of Petra. The quality of tours can vary. The best option is to select a company that is a member or an affiliate of the Jordan Tourist Board; visit www.visitjordan.com.

Abercrombie & Kent Jordan Shmeisani-
Abdullah Bin Abbas St, 11183 Amman; 06 566
5465; e info@abercrombiekent.com.jo; www.
akdmc.com. A division of the Abercrombie & Kent
group, this Amman-based company specialises in
bespoke tours of all major sights for business &
leisure travellers.

Adonis for Travel & Tourism Ismail Hijazi St,
Amman; 06 562 7875; e jordan@adonistravel.
com; www.adonistravel.com. Tours throughout
the country are themed, & include classical tours,
which take in such sights as Mount Nebo, & a
range of 4x4 tours over desert & rugged terrain.

Adviser Travel & Tourism Tala'a Al Ali,
Wasfi al-Tal St, Amman; 06 553 8325; e
management@advisertours.com; www.
advisertours.com. Based in central Amman,
the company provides services to individuals &
companies. Tours include Romans & Nabateans in
English, French, Spanish, German & Italian.

Al Alia Travel & Tourism Company
Abdelrahim Haj Mohammad St, Amman;

06 582 9494; e aliatours@nets.com.jo; www.
aliatours.com.jo. A choice of tours from 2 to 13
days duration, include transfers & visits to all the
main sights of Jordan, plus Syria & the Holy Land,
Lebanon & Egypt.

Al Hani Travel & Tourism Al Abdali- King
Hussein St, Amman; 06 569 5701; e alhani@
nets.com.jo; www.alhanitravel.com. Specialising
in excursions throughout Jordan & beyond, along
with organising transfers, accommodation &
car hire. Daily tours include Wadi Rum, Jerash &
Ajlun.

Creative Tours Emmar Tower, Zahran St;
Amman; 06 555 0555; e info@creative-
tour.com; www.creative-tour.com. With a
multilingual team & a programme of tours
devised for business as well as leisure travellers,
this company organises tours of holy sites &
attractions. Conferencing & team buildings are
among its packages.

Dead Sea Beach Tours Ahmad al-Safi al-Najfi
St, Shmeisani, Amman; 06 566 1871; e info@

dsbt.com; www.dsbt.com. A range of tours, including its 7-day Treasures of Jordan, the 12-day Life of Jesus & the 7-day Arabian Nights tours are offered by this excursion & conferencing specialist.

Gaia Tours Shat al-Arab St, Amman; ☎06 552 9776; f 06 552 9776; e info@gaia-tours.com; www.gaia-tours.com. Take a jeep tour through the desert, enrol on a dive program in the Red Sea or opt for one of this company's 1-day & multi-day tours that visit all the country's highlights, including the Dead Sea, Wadi Rum & Aqaba.

Jordan Inspirational Tours Al Saad Bldg, 106 Petra; ☎03 215 7317; e info@jitours.com; www. jitours.com. A company that feels passionate about responsible tourism, Jordan Inspirational Tours offers a wide range of excursions from those on horseback & off-road vehicles to themed educational, photographic & nature tours.

Jordan Tours & Travel Wadi Musa, 71810 Petra; ☎03 215 4666; e eid@jordantours-travel. com; www.jordantours-travel.com. Petra by Night, cuisine & eco tours, & excursions on horseback, camel or by cycle are some of the tours available from this company.

Karma House Jordan Prince Mohammad St, Amman; ☎06 463 1654; e info@karma.com.jo; www.karmahousejordan.com. Organiser of tours that include its Adventure Enthused tour of the King's Highway, its Soul Searcher that features a visit to the desert castles & its Serenity Seeker tour with a float in the Dead Sea its highlight.

Nyazi ECO Tours Abdullah Ghosheh St, Aqaba; ☎06 581 5910; f 06 581 5902; e info@nyazi.

com.jo; www.nyazi.com.jo. Run by an antiquities & archaeology specialist, this company focuses on eco-themed tours but tailors itineraries to individuals' requirements.

Pan East Tours Abdul Rahim al-Waked St, Amman; ☎06 560 6420; e imad.malhas@ paneast.com.jo; www.paneast.com.jo. Along with biblical, trekking & incentive tours of Jordan's main attractions, Pan East also organises trips for travellers to Syria & Lebanon.

Petra Moon Tourism Services Wadi Musa 129, Petra; ☎03 215 6665; e info@petramoon. com; www.petramoon.com. Among the options offered by Petra Moon are tours of archaeological sites, eco programs, cuisine & handicrafts trips, with accommodation in tents through to luxury hotels.

Stars Desert Tour & Travel Madina Al-Munawara St, 11245 Amman; ☎06 551 6869; e info@starsdesert.com; www.starsdesert.com. Along with biblical & wellness programmes & tours of Jordan's most popular attractions, Stars Desert organises trips that combine Jordan with other destinations like Jerusalem in Israel, Damascus in Syria & Beirut in Lebanon.

United Travel Agency Abdul Hameed Sharaf St, Amman; ☎06 566 0490; e info@uta.com.jo; www.uta.com.jo. Also in Hamamat al-Tunisia St, Aqaba, & Taybet Zaman, Wadi Musa, near Petra. An agency that offers a host of tours from wellness & eco-themed itineraries to desert trekking, religious tours, hiking & educational programmes, plus international travel & conferences.

RED TAPE

PASSPORTS AND VISAS All visitors to Jordan need a **passport** with at least **six-month** validity remaining on arrival, and an **entry visa**, which can be obtained before departure at any Jordanian embassy, or on arrival into Jordan at any port of entry, except if entering via the King Hussein Bridge (Allenby Bridge) on the Jordan/Israel border (see page 54).

Obtaining a visa at an airport or port is a straightforward procedure. **Single-entry visas**, which cost JD20, are valid for 30 days. If you are entering the kingdom via Aqaba – Aqaba Special Economic Zone, see box, page 244 – then the 30-day single-entry visa is free. If you plan to stay longer you can easily extend the validity of your visa for up to three months, to a maximum of six months, at any police station after your arrival. It is advisable to register with the police a few days prior to the expiry of your single-entry visa if wishing to extend it. Visas, when purchased in Jordan, should be paid for in local currency. Visa charges are not applicable if you are arriving with a group of five or more people through an official Jordanian tour operator. If your visit involves crossing into Jordan from Israel via the King Hussein Bridge (Allenby Bridge) you must have purchased a visa in advance. **Multiple-entry visas** are available at JD60 and valid for six months, but these are only available from Jordanian embassies and consulates. Multiple-entry visas are ideal if you plan to cross borders and re-enter Jordan a number of times during your visit. Apply for a multiple-entry visa from your local embassy before your initial day of departure.

Exit tax is no longer applicable when you leave Jordan, other than with a vehicle. An exit service fee of JD5 per vehicle and JD8 per passenger is applicable at all land and sea border points.

Visas are granted to visitors from the following countries, but do check with your embassy prior to departure as requirements can change. Citizens of all other countries should contact their local Jordanian consulate or embassy prior to departure for up-to-date advice on requirements and whether a visa must be obtained before travel. Failure to have the correct documentation can result in you not being allowed entry into the kingdom.

Europe and Russia Andorra, Armenia, Austria, Azerbaijan, Belarus, Belgium, Bosnia and Herzegovina, Bulgaria, Croatia, Cyprus, Czech Republic, Denmark, Estonia, Finland, France, Georgia, Germany, Gibraltar, Greece, Holland, Hungary, Iceland, Ireland, Italy, Kosovo, Latvia, Lichtenstein, Lithuania, Luxembourg, Malta, Monaco, Montenegro, Norway, Poland, Portugal, Romania, Russia, San Marino, Slovak Republic, Slovenia, Spain, Sweden, Switzerland, Ukraine, United Kingdom and Vatican City.

Asia and Australasia Australia, Bhutan, China, Fiji, India, Indonesia, Hong Kong, Japan, Kazakhstan, Kiribati, Kyrgyzstan, Macau, Malaysia, Maldives, Marshall Islands, Micronesia, New Zealand, North Korea, Samoa, Singapore, Solomon Islands, South Korea, Taiwan, Tajikistan, Thailand, Tonga, Turkey, Turkmenistan, Tuvalu and Vanuatu.

Africa Algeria, Cape Verde, Egypt, Libya, Lesotho, Malawi, Mauritius, Namibia, São Tomé and Príncipe, Seychelles, South Africa, Swaziland, Tunisia and Zimbabwe.

Middle East Bahrain, Brunei, Israel, Kurdistan, Kuwait, Lebanon, Oman, Palestine/PNA Passport Holders, Qatar, Saudi Arabia, Syria, United Arab Emirates and Yemen.

The Americas Antigua and Barbuda, Argentina, Bahamas, Barbados, Bolivia, Brazil, Canada, Chile, Costa Rica, Dominica, Ecuador, El Salvador, Grenada, Guatemala, Guyana, Haiti, Honduras, Jamaica, Mexico, Nicaragua, Panama,

AQABA SPECIAL ECONOMIC ZONE

The Aqaba Special Economic Zone (ASEZ), which comprises the southern city of Aqaba and its surrounding towns inland and on the Gulf of Aqaba coastline, has a different set of entry regulations. If you are arriving at the port or airport at Aqaba, or across the border crossing from Saudi Arabia or the Wadi Araba (South Border) crossing from Israel then you will be granted an ASEZ visa. See *Visas and customs* in the Aqaba chapter, page 244.

Paraguay, Peru, St Kitts and Nevis, St Lucia, St Vincent, Suriname, Trinidad and Tobago, United States, Uruguay and Venezuela.

BORDER CROSSINGS You should observe rules applicable to land border crossings, and as they can change you should always check the most up-to-date information before and during your stay. Do not attempt to cross Jordan's border with Syria, Israel, Iraq and Saudi Arabia anywhere other than at official crossing points.

Syria The points of entry from Syria are at Jaber, which lies around 80km (50 miles) from Amman, and at Ramtha, around 90km (56 miles) from the capital.

Israel From Israel you can cross at three points. The King Hussein Bridge (Allenby Bridge) is to the south of the Jordan Valley and you must already have a visa to enter Jordan at this crossing. Tour buses or cars cannot cross at this border crossing. The two other crossings from Israel are the Sheikh Hussein crossing, also known as the North Border crossing, located near Lake Tiberias (Sea of Galilee), and the South Border crossing, which is also known as the Wadi Araba or the Arava crossing. This connects the Red Sea resorts of Eilat and Aqaba. There are no restrictions for vehicles at this crossing.

Iraq If you are travelling from Iraq you should cross at the Al-Karamah Border Crossing, which lies around 330km (205 miles) from Amman.

Saudi Arabia There are three points of entry from Saudi Arabia: cross at the Umari Border Crossing, which is the closest to Amman; the Mudawara Border Crossing; or the Durra Border Crossing. For more information and opening times, see page 54.

ANIMALS You should carry a certificate of health for your pet from your veterinary surgery to show if requested. However, there are currently no regulations that stipulate that pets will need to be vaccinated or quarantined.

CUSTOMS You should observe customs rules when arriving in Jordan, and, of course, when you depart. Being in possession of illegal drugs is unacceptable, and you may face a heavy fine, or at worst a long prison sentence. Personal items like cameras, digital music devices and clothing are exempt from duty, plus you are permitted to carry 200 cigarettes, 200g of tobacco, one litre of spirit and two litres of wine for private use. The Queen Alia International Airport has a well-stocked duty-free shop (⊕ 08.00–24.00), from which both visitors arriving and departing can make purchases. Keep your boarding card/stub as proof of flying to show if required, and your passport. Electrical items, personal computers and household items are subject to duty, but customs officials can make a note about such items in your passport and providing you have them with you when you depart you may be excused paying duty tax.

Customs rules in the Aqaba – Aqaba Special Economic Zone – which has lower taxation, are different. On the highway as you approach Aqaba you will go through a custom checkpoint and should declare any item that may be subject to tax on your departure. On departure you will go through a similar checkpoint, which will have Red and Green channels much like you see at airports. The duty-free allowance is 200 cigarettes and one litre of alcohol purchased in the zone, and anything above this should be declared.

2

EMBASSIES

FOREIGN EMBASSIES IN JORDAN

E Australia 41 Kayed al-Armouti St, Abdoun, Amman; ☎06 580 7000; f 06 580 7001; www.jordan.embassy.gov.au; ⏰ 08.30–16.30 Sun–Thu

E Austria Mithqal al-Fayez St 36, Amman; ☎06 460 1101; f 06 461 2725; e amman-ob@bmaa.gv.at; ⏰ 08.00–16.00 Sun–Thu

E Belgium Saad Juma St 17, 4th Circle, Jabal Amman, Amman; ☎06 465 5730; f 06 465 5740; e amman@diplobel.fed.be; www.diplomatie.be/amman (in English); ⏰ 08.00–16.00 Sun–Thu

E Canada Pearl of Shmeisani Bldg, Abdal Hameed Shoman St, Shmeisani, 11180 Amman; ☎06 520 3300; f 06 520 3396; e amman@international.gc.ca; www.jordan.gc.ca; ⏰ 08.00–16.30 Sun–Wed, 08.00–13.30 Thu

E Germany Bengasi St 31, Amman; ☎06 593 0351; f 06 593 2887; e germaemb@go.com.jo; www.germanembassy-amman.org; ⏰ 08.00–16.00 Sun–Thu

E India PO Box 2168, 1st Circle, Jabal Amman, Amman; ☎06 462 2098; f 06 465 9540; e amb.amman@mea.gov.in; www.indembassy.org.jo; ⏰ 08.00–15.00 Sun–Thu

E Netherlands 3 Abubakr al-Sarag St, Abdoun al-Shamal, Amman; ☎06 590 2200; f 06 593 0161; e amm-info@minbuza.nl; www.jordan.nlembassy.org; ⏰ 09.00–16.00 Sun–Thu

E Spain Zahran St, Amman; ☎06 461 4166; f 06 461 4173; e embespjo@mail.mae.es; ⏰ 08.30–15.30 Sun–Thu

E Switzerland 19 Ibrahim Ayoub St, Amman; ☎06 593 1416; f 06 593 0685; e amm.vertretung@eda.admin.ch; www.eda.admin.ch; ⏰ 08.00–15.00 Sun–Thu

E United Kingdom PO Box 87, Abdoun, Amman; ☎06 590 9200; f 06 590 9279; e amman.enquiries@fco.gov.uk; www.ukinjordan.fco.gov.uk; ⏰ 08.00–15.30 Sun–Wed, 08.00–15.00 Thu

JORDANIAN EMBASSIES ABROAD

E Australia 17 Cobbadah St, O'Malley, Act 2606, Australia; ☎+61 (02) 6295 9951; f +61 (02) 6239 7236; e jordan@jordanembassy.org.au; www.jordanembassy.org.au; ⏰ 09.00–15.00 Mon–Fri

E Austria Rennweg 17/4, A-1030 Vienna, Austria; ☎+43 (1) 4051025; f +43 (1) 4051031, e info@jordanembassy.at; www.jordanembassy.at; ⏰ 09.00–17.00 Mon–Fri

E Belgium Av FD Roosevelt 104, 1050 Brussels, Belgium; ☎+32 02 6407755; f +32 02 6402796; e jordan.embassy@skynet.be; www.jordanembassy.be; ⏰ 09.00–15.00 Mon–Fri

E Canada 100 Bronson Ave, Suite 701, Ottawa, Ontario K1R 6G8, Canada; ☎+1 613 238 8090; f +1 613 232 3341; e ottawa@fm.gov.jo; www.embassyofjordan.ca; ⏰ 09.00–15.00 Mon–Fri

E Germany Heerstrasse 201, D-13595 Berlin, Germany; ☎+49 30 36 99 600; f +49 30 36 99 60 11; e jordan@jordanembassy.de; www.jordanembassy.de; ⏰ 09.00–15.00 Mon–Fri

E India 30 Golf Links, New Delhi 110003, India; ☎+91 11 24653318; f +91 11 24653353; e jordan@jordanembassyindia.org; www.jordanembassyindia.org; ⏰ 09.00–15.30 Mon–Fri

E Netherlands Badhuisweg 79, 2587 CD The Hague, Netherlands; ☎+31 70 4167200; f +31 70 4167209; e info@jordanembassy.nl; www.jordanembassy.nl; ⏰ 09.00–15.00 Mon–Fri

E Spain Pº General Martínez Campos 41, 28010 Madrid, Spain; ☎+34 913191100; f +34 913082536; e consular@telefonica.net; www.embjordaniaes.org; ⏰ 09.00–15.00 Mon–Fri

E Switzerland Thorackerstrasse 3, 3074 Berne, Switzerland; ☎+41 31 384 04 04; f +41 31 384 04 05; e info@jordanembassy.ch; www.jordanembassy.ch; ⏰ 09.00–15.00 Mon–Fri

E United Kingdom 6 Upper Phillimore Gardens, London W8 7HB, UK; ☎+44 (0)207 937 3685; f +44 (0)207 937 8795; e info@jordanembassyuk.org; www.jordanembassyuk.org; ⏰ 09.00–15.00 Mon–Fri

E United States of America 3504 International Drive NW, Washington DC 20008, USA; ☎+1 (202) 966 2664; f +1 (202) 966 3110; e HKJEmbassyDC@jordanembassyus.org; www.jordanembassyus.org; ⏰ 09.00–15.00 Mon–Fri

GETTING THERE AND AWAY

BY AIR The Queen Alia International Airport in Amman is the main airport of Jordan and the home of its national airline, Royal Jordanian Airlines. It is also a major hub for Jordan Aviation, a private-owned Amman-based airline that serves the Middle East, Africa and Europe, along with providing transportation for the UN peacekeeping forces. VIP flight specialist and charter company Royal Falcon Airlines and a former subsidiary of Royal Jordanian Airlines, Arab Wings, fly from the airport too. The airport lies around 32km south of Amman city centre on the edge of the desert, and is easily reached via the country's main highway linking the south with Amman.

Tickets **Royal Jordanian** operates direct flights from major cities around the world, all of which can be booked easily online. New York, Detroit and Chicago in the USA, Montreal in Canada, Hong Kong and Bangkok in the Far East and Mumbai and Delhi in India are just some of the far-reaching routes that fly into Amman. It links most of the Middle Eastern cities, including Muscat, Abu Dhabi, Jeddah and Kuwait. Mediterranean and European destinations are served via flights to Larnaca in Cyprus, Athens, Rome, Milan, Zurich, Geneva, Madrid, Paris, Brussels, Frankfurt and London. It flies directly from Moscow, and serves north Africa via Tunis in Tunisia, Tripoli and Benghazi in Libya, Alexandria, Cairo and Sharm el Sheikh in Egypt and Khartoum in Sudan. Many other cities are served through code share arrangements with other airlines. If you're travelling with Royal Jordanian a big plus is that you can avoid lengthy queues at check-in by heading for the dedicated desks for self check-in.

More than 30 other airlines fly regularly into the Queen Alia International Airport, and most offer the option to book online. These include **American Airlines**, **Air France** (whose hub is the Charles de Gaulle airport in northern Paris) and **Air Baltic**, which serves passengers from in and around Riga in Latvia. **Austrian Airlines** flies to and from Vienna, **bmi** from the UK, and **Lufthansa** serves primarily German destinations in and around Frankfurt.

Travellers from the Middle East and north Africa are well catered for. Among the many airlines offering direct routes into Amman are **Bahrain Air**, **Egypt Air**, **Emirates**, **Jazeera Airways**, **Qatar Airways** and **Saudi Arabian Airlines**. **Turkish Airlines** links Istanbul with the city, as does **Petra Airlines**, which also serves the southern Turkish cities of Dalaman, Bodrum and Antalya. One of the most recent airlines to recognise Jordan's growing appeal as a business and holiday destination is British-based **easyJet**. In March 2011 it launched a direct route from London Gatwick to Amman, with a journey time of around five hours. More and more airlines are viewing Jordan as a desirable destination, making travel by air an increasingly easy and convenient option.

Airline contacts

✈ **American Airlines** ☏+1 800 433 7300; www.aa.com

✈ **Air Baltic** ☏+371 (0) 67006006; www.airbaltic.com

✈ **Air France** ☏+33 09 69 39 01 04; www.airfrance.fr

✈ **Arab Wings** ☏+962 06 489 9791; www.arabwings.com.jo

✈ **Austrian Airlines** ☏+43 5 1766 1061; www.austrian.com

✈ **Bahrain Air** ☏+973 1722 5757; www.bahrainair.net

✈ **bmi** ☏+44 (0) 1332 648181; www.flybmi.com

✈ **easyJet** ☏+44 (0) 843 104 5000; www.easyjet.com

✈ **Egypt Air** ☏+20 (2) 24830888; www.egyptair.com

✈ **Emirates** ☏+600 55 55 55; www.emirates.com

✈ **Etihad Airways** ☏+971 2 511 0000; www.etihadairways.com

✈ **Flydubai** ☏+971 4 301 0800; www.flydubai.com

QUEEN ALIA INTERNATIONAL AIRPORT

A modern, shiny airport with two passenger terminals and one cargo, the Queen Alia International Airport (AMM), known locally as Matar al-Malikah Alya ad-Dowaly, has undergone an exhaustive expansion programme in the past few years. Originally built in the late 1980s, the airport opened to much fanfare. It is named after King Hussein's first daughter Alia, but is often referred to having been named after the king's third wife, Alia Baha ad-Din Touqan, Queen consort of Jordan, who sadly died in a helicopter crash on 9 February 1977. The airport's expansion has seen it emerge as one of the major hubs of international travel in this part of the world, and it seems that no matter what time of day you arrive it bustles with activity.

Central to the airport's improvements is a brand new terminal designed by the British architect Norman Foster. Set to be a huge space that will rival some of the largest airports in the world, the new airport has long sweeps of glass frontage, a massive car parking area, lots of passenger facilities planned and the latest technology for companies' and travellers' use. Completion is expected around late 2012 to early 2013. When complete it is envisaged the airport will handle around 13 million passengers a year.

The airport, nonetheless, has a host of amenities, which will be enhanced even further when the brand new terminal opens. There are shopping outlets where you can buy souvenirs, confectionary, duty- and tax-free goods and the essentials, such as newspapers, books and bottled water. Travellers on the move are likely to appreciate the choice of restaurants and cafés serving most things from a quick cappuccino and muffin to a fast pizza or burger meal, while business travellers, and indeed techo leisure holidaymakers, can take advantage of the Wi-Fi available throughout the airports. Wi-Fi cards can be obtained from the World News cafés that are dotted around both terminals.

The airport has banks and currency exchange facilities, ATMs, a medical centre and executive lounges, plus wheelchairs, specially designed toilets and lifts, and assistance personnel to make the time spent in the terminals for travellers with restricted mobility or other disablements that much easier.

For more information visit www.amman-airport.com.

✈ **Gulf Air** ☎+973 17335777; www.gulfair.com

✈ **Iberia** ☎+34 902 400 500; www.iberia.com

✈ **Jazeera Airways** ☎+965 222 48940; www.jazeeraairways.com

✈ **Lufthansa** ☎+49 (0) 18 05 59 59; www.lufthansa.com

✈ **Oman Air** ☎+968 2453 1111; www.omanair.com

✈ **Petra Airlines** ☎+962 06 567 6212; www.petraairlines.com

✈ **Qatar Airways** ☎+974 4449 6000; www.qatarairways.com

✈ **Royal Falcon** ☎+962 06 5538538; www.rf.jo

✈ **Royal Jordanian** ☎06 520 2000; www.rj.com

✈ **Saudi Arabia Airlines** ☎+966 2 6860308; www.saudiairlines.com

✈ **Turkish Airlines** ☎+90 212 444 0 849; www.turkishairlines.com

Airport transport There are several options for getting from Queen Alia International Airport to Amman city centre. An **express bus** service that operates 24 hours daily is an easy and convenient option. Buses leave from outside the terminals every 30 minutes from 06.00 to 16.30, and every 60 minutes 17.00–03.00, for the journey into Amman's Abdali bus station. Cost is around JD3 per passenger.

There are car-hire facilities, including cars from local respected companies and from big international names (see page 72), inside the terminal, along with plenty of taxis parked in the ranks outside. The cost of a local taxi from the airport to

ROYAL JORDANIAN AIRLINES

National carrier Royal Jordanian Airlines flies to four continents with more than 500 flights every week to over 55 destinations. Its fleet includes the Airbus A340 for long-haul flights, along with the A310, A321, A319 and A320, which fly to destinations in the Middle East, Europe, the Gulf and north Africa. The fleet has recently been joined by the Embrear 195 and the Embraer 175, Brazilian-built aircrafts with just 100 and 72 passenger seats respectively, which are ideal for short flights around the Levant region. Royal Jordanian has offices in Jordan, including its advance check-in City Terminal (*7th Circle, Amman; ⊕ summer 07.30–21.30 daily, winter 07.30–21.00 daily*), plus almost every major capital city in the world.

ROYAL JORDANIAN IN JORDAN:
Abdoun, Amman Royal Jordanian Bldg, Mohammad Ali Janah St, Abdoun (near 5th Circle); ✆ 06 510 0000
Baghdad St Irbid; ✆ 05 100 000; f 05 100 000; e qirzzrj@rj.com; www.rj.com
King Hussein International Airport Aqaba; ✆ 03 201 8633; f 03 201 6555; e aqjtbrj@rj.com; www.rj.com
Queen Alia International Airport Amman; ✆ 06 445 3052; f 06 445 3053; e ammkzrj@rj.com; www.rj.com

ROYAL JORDANIAN AROUND THE WORLD, INCLUDING:
Australia Level 10 HCF Hse, 403 George St, Sydney NSW 2000, Australia; ✆ +61 (02) 92442701; f +61 (02) 92903306; e sydgarj@rh.com; www.rj.com
Belgium Rue Vilain XIIII 53–55 B-1000 Brussels, Belgium; ✆ +32 2 512 70 70; f +32 2 514 21 67; e brutrrj@rj.com; www.rj.com
Canada 2085 Union St, Montreal, Qc H3A2C3, Canada; ✆ +1 514 842 3300; f +1 514 288 7572; e yultorj@rj.com; www.rj.com
Egypt Zamalek Sporting Club Bldg, 26 July St, Mohandeseen, Cairo, Egypt; ✆ +20 2 3346 7540; f +20 2 3346 2446; e caitbrj@rj.com; www.rj.com
France 38 Av des Champs Elysées Paris, 75008 Paris, France; ✆ +33 01 42 65 99 91; f +33 01 42 65 99 91; e partbrj@rj.com; www.rj.com
India G-56 Connaught Circus, New Delhi 110 001, India; ✆ +91 11 23327667; f +91 11 23318356; e deltbrj@rj.com; www.rj.com
Kingdom of Saudi Arabia Ground Floor, Abraj Attawuneya, King Fahad Rd, Olaya, Riyadh, Kingdom of Saudi Arabia; ✆ +966 1 2180850; f +966 1 2180851' e ruhtorj@rj.com; www.rj.com
United Arab Emirates Shaikh Khalifa St, PO Box 4163, Omeir Travel Agency Bldg, 1st Floor, Abu Dhabi, UAE; ✆ +971 2 6225335; f +971 2 6224209; e auhtbrj@rj.com; www.rj.com
United Kingdom Space one, 1 Beadon Rd, 6th Floor, Hammersmith, London W6 0EA, UK: ✆ +44 (0) 8719 112 112; f +44 (0) 20 8748 5251; e lontbrh@rj.com; www.rj.com
United States of America 6 East 43rd St, 27th Floor, New York, NY 10017, USA; ✆ +1 212 949 0060; f +1 212 949 0488; e nyctbrj@rj.com; www.rj.com

central Amman is around JD5 and can be booked in advance (✆ 06 445 1302). Don't forget to add the international dialling code and country code, +962, if calling from abroad. Journey time into the city centre by road is around 50 minutes, although allow a little more in times of heavy traffic.

Regional airports Jordan's other main airport is the **King Hussein International Airport** in Aqaba, which handles flights from the nearby Red Sea region countries of Egypt, Israel and Saudi Arabia. Flights from international destinations are few but increasing in number, although some of them are seasonal. There is, however, considerable traffic from the Middle Eastern cities of Dubai, Doha and Bahrain. Daily flights between the airport and Amman provide a fast link between southern Jordan and the north, and take only around 45 minutes. There are usually more flights scheduled to serve the cruise ships that arrive periodically in Aqaba. The airport is compact and there are few amenities other than a couple of souvenir shops and a kiosk. Jordan also has a handful of smaller airports that handle military or domestic flights located in Azraq, Dafyanah and Mafraq.

BY SEA Jordan has a short coastline and a port and ferry terminal where cruise ships and passenger vessels from Egypt dock. Independent travellers can use a car-ferry service operated by **Arab Bridge Maritime Company** (✆ 03 209 2000; f 03 209 2001; www.abmaritime.com.jo) that plies a route between Nuweiba in Egypt and Aqaba in southern Jordan. Fast ferry departures from Nuweiba are at 11.00 and 17.00 and return departures from Aqaba are at 08.00 and 13.00, Sunday to Friday but times can and do vary so check the current timetable at least a day before your planned trip. The journey takes roughly one hour and costs around JD60 one way per person. The slow ferry departs from Nuweiba at 14.30, returning from Aqaba at midnight; both daily, but again subject to change. The slow ferry takes around three hours and costs around JD50. Vehicles on all crossings are charged separately, from around JD40 for a motorcycle and JD140 for a car. It is advisable to purchase your ferry ticket in advance if you can, as the passenger terminal in both Nuweiba and Aqaba can be busy prior to departures. Allow yourself plenty of time before your departure. **Sindbad Xpress** (Maysloon St, Aqaba; ✆ 03 205 0077; e reservation1@sindbadjo.com; www.sindbadjo. com) also operates fast passenger catamaran crossings from Egypt's Taba Heights Marina in Taba, South Sinai, to Aqaba's marina in Tala Bay, South Beach (variable departure times; duration 25mins; from around JD70). The Tala Bay marina is located a ten-minute drive south of the city centre. To enter Jordan by sea you will need a visa (see Passports and visas, page 45). If, during your holiday in Jordan, you intend to travel to Egypt, you will need to obtain an Egyptian visa, which can be purchased onboard both the fast and slower vessels. If you are planning to return to Jordan after your trip to Egypt and have a multiple-entry visa obtained when you first arrived then your arrival back in Aqaba should be straightforward.

BY TRAIN The only route into Jordan by train is from Syria, but at the time of publication this service is suspended because of unrest in and around Damascus. Normally, the **Hejaz Railway** (tickets available from the railway station on the day of departure only; JD2.50) trains run between Damascus and Amman once a week for the journey through often-spectacular countryside. The trip takes around nine hours. On a Sunday the train leaves Damascus at 07.30 and arrives in Amman at 17.00. It leaves Amman on Mondays at 08.00, arriving in Damascus at 17.00. Although there is a single-track railway line between Amman and Aqaba, there is no passenger service.

Construction began on the famous Hejaz Railway in 1900 under the direction of Sultan Abdul Hamid II (b1842, d1918) who wanted to eventually link the Ottoman Empire's capital, Constantinople (present-day Istanbul) with the holy city of Makkah. His aim was to provide a more convenient means of travel for Hajj pilgrims making the then long and arduous journey through the formidable wilderness of the Midian region and the Hejaz Mountains. In fact, the railway was never completed, and ran only from Damascus, which was then part of the Ottoman Empire and is now the capital of Syria, to Medina. The railway covered some 1,300km. Over time, and in particular during the world wars, much of it fell into disrepair. Today, there are only sections in operation, including Damascus to Amman for passengers, and a single track used for moving phosphate between Amman and Aqaba in southern Jordan. Some of the old locomotives have been restored and now ply these routes; if you are lucky you might see one as you drive to Wadi Rum from the Dead Sea region, or on approach to Aqaba. Bright orange in colour, they are a moving sight.

BY BUS Air-conditioned buses operated by the **Jordan Express Tourist Transportation Company** (JETT) in Amman (📞 06 585 4679; f 06 585 4176; www. jett.com) and **Syria**'s state-owned bus company, **Karnak**, run between Damascus and Amman twice daily (be sure to check the bus schedule before your planned journey as at the time of publication this service is subject to cancellations due to unrest in Syria). Buses generally arrive and depart from Abdali Bus Station in Amman to the Karnak bus station in Damascus. Journey time is around five hours, including the time it takes to complete formalities at the border crossing. A one-way ticket costs JD8 for adults and JD5 for children. This is a popular route so it is advisable to book several days in advance. Tickets are available from JETT, the Karnak offices at Karnak bus station and the Syrian Agency (📞 +963 118126238).

JETT and local operator, the **Saudi Public Transport Company** (SAPTCO) (📞 +966 (01) 2884400; f +966 (01) 2884411; e info@saptco.com.sa; www.saptco.com), operate daily bus services between Riyad, Jeddah and Dammam in Saudi Arabia to the Abdali bus station in Amman. The journey time from Riyad is approximately 17 hours, from Jeddah 18 hours and from Dammam around 21 hours. The companies also run a three-times-a-week service between the Saudi Arabia cities of Qaseem and Medina to Amman. Tickets are available from JETT and SAPTCO.

JETT services between Baghdad in Iraq and Amman run three times a week with a journey time of around 15 hours, while four times a week it operates a service between Beirut in Lebanon, in conjunction with the **Transport & Tourist Services Company of Lebanon** (S Solh Av, Badaro, Beirut; 📞 +961 1 399 777; f +961 1 399 780; e info@ttsbuses.com; www.ttsbuses.com). Journey time is around six hours. JETT, in conjunction with local operator **Egyptian Super Jet of the Arab Unity Company** (📞 +202 2 290 9013; e superjet@post.com) provides a service between Cairo in Egypt and Amman four times a week. Journey time is around 22 hours.

If you are planning to visit Jordan from Israel or the Palestinian Territories, you will find local buses or taxis from Damascus Gate in East Jerusalem that will drive you to the crossing point at the King Hussein Bridge (Allenby Bridge). Here your passport, visa and luggage will be checked, you will pay an exit tax, and then be escorted to a shuttle bus to the Jordanian terminal. From here you can take a service taxi for onward travel to Amman.

BY CAR Driving a car into Jordan is relatively straightforward through most of the border crossing points. There will be no duty to pay for up to one year unless you sell the vehicle to a local resident. To drive in Jordan you must have a full picture driving licence valid in your country of origin which you have held for at least one year. Be sure to take full insurance documents with you to show if asked to do so. For peace of mind you may wish to purchase added insurance in Jordan, which is generally inexpensive. Among the companies offering motor insurance are the **Jordan International Insurance Company** (*www.jiig.com*), the **Jordan French Insurance Company** (*www.jofico.com*) and the **Jordan Insurance Company** (*www.jicjo.com*). All travel over land into Jordan is subject to border crossing controls, not all of which are open 24 hours.

For more on border crossings, see page 47.

From Syria Cross at Jaber, the most convenient crossing at around 80km from Amman, or at Ramtha. Both are open 24 hours daily. There are no restrictions for vehicles and visas can be obtained here.

From Israel You can cross at any of the three points on the Jordanian–Israeli border. The King Hussein Bridge (Allenby Bridge) (⊕ *08.00–20.00 Sun–Thu for arrivals into Jordan & 08.00–14.00 for departures, 08.00–13.00 Fri–Sat*) lies to the south of the Jordan Valley at almost 60km from Amman. To cross here you must already have a visa to enter Jordan. Tour buses, taxis or cars cannot cross at this border crossing, and you will be required to disembark from your mode of transport in Israel, cross the bridge and take onward transport once in Jordan.

The Sheikh Hussein crossing, also known as the North Border crossing, is located near Lake Tiberias (Sea of Galilee), around 90km from Amman. It is open 24 hours daily. The South Border crossing, or the Wadi Araba crossing (⊕ *06.30–22.00 Sun–Thu & 08.00–20.00 Fri–Sat, except on the Islamic New Year & Yom Kippur when it is closed*), connects the Red Sea resorts of Eilat and Aqaba in the south. There are no restrictions for vehicles at either of these crossings and visas can be purchased for entry into Jordan.

From Iraq Cross at the Al-Karamah Border Crossing into Jordan from Iraq, which is open daily throughout the year. It can be found about 330km from Amman. Visas into Jordan are available at the terminal.

From Saudi Arabia Three border crossing points allow movement between Saudi Arabia and Jordan. The closest to Amman is the Umari Border Crossing, which is open 24 hours daily. It lies around 155 km from the capital. The two other points of entry are the Mudawara Border Crossing located around 322km from Amman, and the furthermost crossing, the Durra Border Crossing. Both are open 24 hours throughout the year and visas into Jordan are available.

ISRAELI PASSPORT STAMP

When crossing the King Hussein Bridge (Allenby Bridge) from Israel to Jordan your passport will be stamped by officials on both sides. If your plan is for onward travel to Syria, Lebanon or any other country that has not signed a peace treaty with Israel, ask that a separate piece of paper be stamped and not your passport.

BY TAXI Private taxis and service taxis, known as *serveeces* (pronounced *servees*) operate to and from the Abdali bus station in Amman to most cities of the neighbouring countries and from the King Hussein Bridge at the Israeli border. Private metered taxis are comfortable and not overly expensive; as a guide expect to pay around JD60 for a trip from Damascus to Amman, and about JD30 from the King Hussein Bridge to Amman. Service taxis are cheaper; for the same journeys expect to pay around JD12 and JD7 per person respectively. If you want the taxi to yourself you can negotiate a rate.

HEALTH *with Dr Felicity Nicholson*

People new to exotic travel often worry about tropical diseases, but it is accidents that are the biggest risk. Road accidents are very common in many parts of Jordan, so be aware and do what you can to reduce the risks. Try to travel during daylight hours, always wear a seatbelt and refuse to be driven by anyone who has been drinking. Listen to local advice about areas where violent crime is rife.

PREPARATIONS Preparations to ensure a healthy trip to Jordan require checks on your immunisation status: it is wise to be up to date on tetanus, polio and diphtheria (now given as an all-in-one vaccine, Revaxis, that lasts for ten years), typhoid and hepatitis A. Immunisations against hepatitis B and rabies may also be recommended.

Proof of vaccination against yellow fever is needed for entry into Jordan if you are coming from another yellow fever endemic area. (Visit the National Travel Health Network and Centre's website at www.nathnac.org for more information on affected countries.) If the vaccine is not suitable for you then obtain an exemption certificate from your GP or a travel clinic, although this is not an absolute guarantee that they will accept the waiver. Immunisation against cholera is not usually required for Jordan unless there are known to be current outbreaks – though as the climate is dry this is rare. Hepatitis A vaccine is recommended for those aged one and above (Havrix Monodose or Avaxim) and comprises two injections given about a year apart. The course costs about £100, but may be available on the NHS. It protects for 25 years and can be administered even close to the time of departure. Hepatitis B vaccination should be considered for longer trips (two months or more) or for those working with children or in situations where contact with blood is likely. Three injections are needed for the best protection and can be given over a three-week period if time is short for those aged 16 or over. Longer schedules give more sustained protection and are therefore preferred if time allows and for those under 16. Hepatitis A vaccine can also be given as a combination with hepatitis B as 'Twinrix', though two doses are needed at least seven days apart to be effective for the hepatitis A component, and three doses are needed for the hepatitis B. The timing is age dependent as for the hepatitis B.

The newer injectable typhoid vaccines (eg: Typhim Vi) last for three years and are about 85% effective. Oral capsules (Vivotif) may also be available for those aged six and over. Three capsules over five days lasts for approximately three years but may be less effective than the injectable forms. They should be encouraged unless the traveller is leaving within a few days for a trip of a week or less, when the vaccine would not be effective in time. Vaccinations for rabies are ideally advised for everyone, but are especially important for travellers visiting more remote areas, especially if you are more than 24 hours from medical help and definitely if you will be working with animals. Experts differ over whether a BCG vaccination against tuberculosis (TB) is useful in adults: discuss this with your travel clinic.

Protection from the sun
Give some thought to packing suncream. The incidence of skin cancer is rocketing as people are travelling more and spending more time exposing themselves to the sun. Keep out of the sun during the middle of the day and, if you must expose yourself to the sun, build up gradually from 20 minutes per day. Be especially careful of exposure between 11.00 and 16.00 and of sun reflected off water, and wear a T-shirt and lots of waterproof suncream (at least SPF15) when swimming. Sun exposure ages the skin, makes people prematurely wrinkly, and increases the risk of skin cancer. Cover up with long, loose clothes and wear a hat when you can. The glare and the dust can be hard on the eyes, too, so bring UV-protecting sunglasses and, perhaps, a soothing eyebath.

Summer temperatures in Jordan can exceed 40°C, so be sure to drink plenty of water to avoid dehydration. Tap water, while generally safe to drink, particularly in higher standard hotels, is usually heavily chlorinated and therefore not at all pleasant. You may find drinking bottled water the wiser option. It is widely available from supermarkets and kiosks. See also page 59.

Travel clinics and health information
A full list of current travel clinic websites worldwide is available on www.istm.org/. For other journey preparation information, consult www.nathnac.org/ds/map_world.aspx. Information about various medications may be found on www.netdoctor.co.uk/travel.

UK

✚ **Berkeley Travel Clinic** 32 Berkeley St, London W1J 8EL (near Green Park tube station); ☎ 020 7629 6233; ⏱ 10.00–18.00 Mon–Fri, 10.00–15.00 Sat

✚ **Edinburgh Travel Health Clinic** 14 East Preston St, Newington, Edinburgh EH8 9QA; ☎ 0131 667 1030; www. edinburghtravelhealthclinic.co.uk; ⏱ 09.00–19.00 Mon–Wed, 09.00–18.00 Thu & Fri. Travel vaccinations & advice.

✚ **Fleet Street Travel Clinic** 29 Fleet St, London EC4Y 1AA; ☎ 020 7353 5678; e info@fleetstreetclinic.com; www.fleetstreetclinic.com; ⏱ 08.45–17.30 Mon–Fri. Injections, travel products & latest advice.

✚ **Hospital for Tropical Diseases Travel Clinic** Mortimer Market Bldg, Capper St (off Tottenham Ct Rd), London WC1E 6AU; ☎ 020 7387 4411; www.thehtd.org; ⏱ 13.00–17.00 Wed & 09.00–13.00 Fri. Consultations are by appointment only & are only offered to those with more complex problems. Check the website for inclusions. Runs a Travellers' Healthline Advisory Service (☎ 020 7950 7799) for country-specific information & health hazards. Also

stocks nets, water purification equipment & personal protection measures. Travellers who have returned from the tropics & are unwell, with fever or bloody diarrhoea, can attend the walk-in emergency clinic at the hospital without an appointment.

✚ **InterHealth Travel Clinic** 111 Westminster Bridge Rd, London SE1 7HR; ☎ 020 7902 9000; e info@interhealth.org.uk; www.interhealth.org.uk; ⏱ 08.30–17.30 Mon–Fri. Competitively priced, one-stop travel health service by appointment only.

✚ **MASTA** (Medical Advisory Service for Travellers Abroad) At the London School of Hygiene & Tropical Medicine, Keppel St, London WC1E 7HT; ☎ 09068 224100 (premium-line number, charged at 60p/min); e enquiries@masta.org; www.masta-travel-health.com. For a fee, they will provide an individually tailored health brief, with up-to-date information on how to stay healthy, inoculations & what to take.

✚ **MASTA pre-travel clinics** ☎ 01276 685040; www.masta-travel-health.com/travel-clinic.aspx. Call or check the website for the nearest;

there are currently 50 in Britain. They also sell memory cards, treatment kits, bednets, net treatment kits, etc.

✚ **NHS travel websites** www.fitfortravel. nhs.uk or www.fitfortravel.scot.nhs.uk . Provide country-by-country advice on immunisation, plus details of recent developments, & a list of relevant health organisations.

✚ **Nomad Travel Clinics** Flagship store: 3–4 Wellington Terrace, Turnpike Lane, London N8 0PX; ☎ 020 8889 7014; e turnpike@ nomadtravel.co.uk; www.nomadtravel.co.uk; walk in or appointments ⏲ 09.15–17.00 daily, late night Thu. See website for clinics in west & central London, Bristol, Southampton & Manchester. As well as dispensing health advice, Nomad stocks mosquito nets & other anti-bug devices, & an excellent range of adventure travel gear. Runs a Travel Health Advice line on ☎ 0906 863 3414.

✚ **The Travel Clinic Ltd, Cambridge** 41 Hills Rd, Cambridge CB2 1NT; ☎ 01223 367362; e enquiries@travelclinic.ltd.uk; www. travelcliniccambridge.co.uk; ⏲ 10.00–16.00 Mon, Tue & Fri, 12.00–16.30 Wed & Thu, 10.00–15.30 Sat

✚ **The Travel Clinic Ltd, Ipswich** Gilmour Piper, 10 Fonnereau Rd, Ipswich IP1 3JP; ☎ 01223 367362; ⏲ 09.30–16.30 Mon, 09.00–19.00 Wed, 09.00–13.00 Sat

✚ **Trailfinders Immunisation Centre** 194 Kensington High St, London W8 7RG; ☎ 020 7938 3999; www.trailfinders.com/travelessentials/ travelclinic.htm; ⏲ 09.00–17.00 Mon, Tue, Wed & Fri, 09.00–18.00 Thu, 10.00–17.15 Sat. No appointment necessary.

✚ **Travelpharm** www.travelpharm.com. The Travelpharm website offers up-to-date guidance on travel-related health & has a range of medications available through their online mini-pharmacy.

Irish Republic

✚ **Tropical Medical Bureau** 54 Grafton St, Dublin 2; ☎ 01 2715200; e graftonstreet@tmb. ie; www.tmb.ie; ⏲ until 20.00 Mon–Fri & Sat mornings. For other clinic locations, & useful information specific to tropical destinations, check their website.

USA

✚ **Centers for Disease Control** 1600 Clifton Rd, Atlanta, GA 30333; ☎ 800 232 4636 or 800 232 6348; e cdcinfo@cdc.gov; www.cdc.gov/ travel. The central source of travel information in the USA. Each summer they publish the invaluable *Health Information for International Travel*.

✚ **IAMAT** (International Association for Medical Assistance to Travelers) 1623 Military Rd #279, Niagara Falls, NY 14304-1745; ☎ 716 754 4883; e info@iamat.org; www.iamat.org. A non-profit organisation with free membership that provides lists of English-speaking doctors abroad.

Canada

✚ **IAMAT** Suite 10, 1287 St Clair Street West, Toronto, ON M6E 1B8; ☎ 416 652 0137; www. iamat.org

✚ **TMVC** Suite 314, 1030 W Georgia St, Vancouver, BC V6E 2Y3; ☎ 604 681 5656; e vancouver@tmvc.com; www.tmvc.com. One-stop medical clinic for all your international travel health & vaccination needs.

Australia and New Zealand

✚ **IAMAT** 206 Papanui Rd, Christchurch 5, New Zealand; www.iamat.org

✚ **TMVC** (Travel Doctors Group) ☎ 1300 65 88 44; www.tmvc.com.au. 30 clinics in Australia & New Zealand, including: *Auckland* Canterbury Arcade, 174 Queen St, 1010; ☎ (64) 9 373 3531; e auckland@traveldoctor.co.nz; *Brisbane* 75a Astor Terrace, Spring Hill, QLD 4000; ☎ 07 3815 6900; e brisbane@traveldoctor.com.au; *Melbourne* 393 Little Bourke St, Vic 3000; ☎ (03) 9935 8100; e melbourne@traveldoctor.com. au; *Sydney* 428 George St, NSW 2000; ☎ (2) 9221 7133; e sydney@traveldoctor.com.au

South Africa

✚ **SAA-Netcare Travel Clinics** ☎ 011 802 0059; e travelinfo@netcare.co.za; www. travelclinic.co.za. 11 clinics throughout South Africa.

✚ **TMVC** NHC Health Centre, cnr Beyers Naude & Waugh Northcliff; ☎ 0861 300 911; e info@ traveldoctor.co.za; www.traveldoctor.co.za. Consult the website for clinic locations.

Personal first-aid kit A minimal kit contains:

- A good drying antiseptic, eg: iodine or potassium permanganate (don't take antiseptic cream)
- A few small dressings (Band-Aids)
- Suncream
- Insect repellent; impregnated bed-net or permethrin spray
- Aspirin or paracetamol
- Antifungal cream (eg: Canesten)
- Ciprofloxacin or norfloxacin, for severe diarrhoea
- Tinidazole for giardia or amoebic dysentery
- Antibiotic eye drops, for sore, 'gritty', stuck-together eyes (conjunctivitis)
- A pair of fine pointed tweezers (to remove hairy caterpillar hairs, thorns, splinters, coral, etc)

LONG-HAUL FLIGHTS, CLOTS AND DVT   *Dr Felicity Nicholson*

Any prolonged immobility, including travel by land or air, can result in deep-vein thrombosis (DVT) with the risk of embolus to the lungs. Certain factors can increase the risk and these include:

- Having a previous clot or a close relative with a history
- People over 40, with increased risk in over 80s
- Recent major operation or varicose-veins surgery
- Cancer
- Stroke
- Heart disease
- Obesity
- Pregnancy
- Hormone therapy
- Heavy smokers
- Severe varicose veins
- People who are tall (over 6ft/1.8m) or short (under 5ft/1.5m)

A deep-vein thrombosis causes painful swelling and redness of the calf or sometimes the thigh. It is only dangerous if a clot travels to the lungs (pulmonary embolus). Symptoms of a pulmonary embolus (PE) – which commonly start three to ten days after a long flight – include chest pain, shortness of breath, and sometimes coughing up small amounts of blood. Anyone who thinks that they might have a DVT needs to see a doctor immediately.

PREVENTION OF DVT
- Keep mobile before and during the flight; move around every couple of hours
- Drink plenty of fluids during the flight
- Avoid taking sleeping pills and drinking excessive tea, coffee and alcohol
- Consider wearing flight socks or support stockings

If you think you are at increased risk of a clot, ask your doctor if it is safe to travel.

- Alcohol-based hand rub or bar of soap in plastic box
- Condoms or femidoms

MEDICAL FACILITIES IN JORDAN Most hospitals in Amman are modern and well equipped, and you should find doctors speak English. In Aqaba, in southern Jordan, hospitals are generally of a high standard too, although if you are seeking medical help for a serious matter you will probably be referred without hesitation to Amman. Outside these locations, hospitals are few and far between, and those that are available may only offer fairly basic treatments. It is wise to avoid using them if at all possible, and seek medical help in Amman or Aqaba, or in larger towns such as Madaba and Irbid.

Amman

✚ **Al-Essra Hospital** Queen Rania al-Abdullah St (by Jordan University); ✆06 530 0300; f 06 534 7888; www.essrahospital.com

✚ **Al-Khalidi Medical Center** 30 Bin Khaldoun St; ✆06 464 4281; f 06 461 6801; www.kmc.jo

✚ **Al-Jazeera Hospital** Shmeisani; ✆06 565 7581; f 06 568 1261; www.aljazeerahospital.com

✚ **Arab Medical Center** ✆06 592 1199; www. amc-hospital.com

✚ **Jordan Hospital** Queen Noor St, Shmeisani; ✆06 560 8080; f 06 560 7575; www.jordan-hospital.com

✚ **Palestine Hospital** 11 Queen Alia St, Shmeisani; ✆06 560 7071; f 06 568 6406; www. palestinehospital.org.jo

Aqaba

✚ **Aqaba Modern Hospital** Tariq Bin Ziyad; ✆03 201 6677; f 03 201 3609

✚ **Islamic Hospital** Al Sharif Shakir Bin Zayd; ✆03 210 8444

✚ **Princess Haya Hospital** Princess Haya Circle; ✆03 201 4111/5; f 03 201 4117

Irbid

Al Najah Hospital Iscan Al Atiba; ✆02 710 0170; f 02 710 0171; www.alnajah-hospital.com

✚ **Irbid Specialty Hospital** ✆02 710 3100; f 02 710 1383; www.irbids-hospital.com

Madaba

✚ **Al Mahabba Hospital** Petra St; ✆05 324 5541

✚ **Government Hospital** City Centre; ✆05 324 1700

✚ **Madaba Nadim Hospital** City Centre; ✆05 324 1701

Petra

✚ **Ma'an Government Hospital** Town Centre; ✆03 213102/222

✚ **Wadi Musa Medical Center** Wadi Musa; ✆03 215 6434

Salt

✚ **Salt Government Hospital** City Centre; ✆05 355 2957/8

Zarqa

✚ **Zarqa Military Hospital** City Centre; ✆05 355 2957/8

WATER STERILISATION You can fall ill from drinking contaminated water so try to drink from safe sources, specifically bottled water where available. If you are away from shops, such as in the desert, and your bottled water runs out, make tea, pour the remaining boiled water into a clean container and use it for drinking. Alternatively, water should be passed through a good bacteriological filter or purified with chlorine dioxide.

COMMON MEDICAL PROBLEMS

Travellers' diarrhoea Travelling in Jordan carries a fairly high risk of getting a dose of travellers' diarrhoea; perhaps half of all visitors will suffer and the newer you are to exotic travel, the more likely you will be affected. By taking precautions

It is dehydration that makes you feel awful during a bout of diarrhoea and the most important part of treatment is drinking lots of clear fluids. Sachets of oral rehydration salts give the perfect biochemical mix to replace all the fluids you are losing in the diarrhea, but other recipes may taste nicer. Any dilute mixture of sugar and salt in water will do you good: try Coke or orange squash with a three-finger pinch of salt added to each glass (if you are salt-depleted you won't taste the salt). Otherwise make a solution of a four-finger scoop of sugar with a three-finger pinch of salt in a 500ml glass. Or add eight level teaspoons of sugar (18g) and one level teaspoon of salt (3g) to one litre (five cups) of safe water. A squeeze of lemon or orange juice improves the taste and adds potassium, which is also lost in diarrhoea. Drink two large glasses after every bowel action, and more if you are thirsty. These solutions are still absorbed well if you are vomiting, but you will need to take small sips. If you are not eating you need to drink three litres a day plus whatever is pouring into the toilet. If you feel like eating, take a bland, high-carbohydrate diet. Heavy, greasy foods will probably give you cramps. There is now good evidence that taking a single dose of ciprofloxacin (500mg) together with two stopping agents (such as Imodium) will be successful in stopping the diarrhoea in about 80% of cases. A second dose can be taken ten to 12 hours later if symptoms persist.

If the diarrhoea is bad, or you are passing blood or slime, or you have a fever, you will almost certainly need antibiotics in addition to fluid replacement. A dose of norfloxacin or ciprofloxacin repeated twice a day until better may be appropriate (if you are planning to take an antibiotic with you, note that both norfloxacin and ciprofloxacin are available only on prescription in the UK). If the diarrhoea is greasy and bulky and is accompanied by sulphurous, eggy burps, one likely cause is giardia. This is best treated with tinidazole (four x 500mg in one dose, repeated seven days later if symptoms persist) although a week of metronidazole is the next best thing. However, in both the above cases it is best to seek medical advice before commencing treatment unless you are not near help (in which case starting the antibiotics could be life saving).

against travellers' diarrhoea you will also avoid typhoid, paratyphoid, cholera, hepatitis, dysentery, worms, etc. Travellers' diarrhoea and the other faecal-oral diseases come from getting other peoples' faeces in your mouth. This most often happens from cooks not washing their hands after a trip to the toilet, but even if the restaurant cook does not understand basic hygiene you will be safe if your food has been properly cooked and arrives piping hot. The most important prevention strategy is to wash your hands before eating anything. You can pick up salmonella and shigella from toilet door handles and possibly bank notes. The maxim to remind you what you can safely eat is:

PEEL IT, BOIL IT, COOK IT OR FORGET IT.

This means that fruit you have washed and peeled yourself, and hot foods, should be safe, but raw foods, cold cooked foods, salads, fruit salads that have been prepared by others, ice cream and ice are all risky, and foods kept lukewarm in hotel buffets are often dangerous. That said, plenty of travellers and expatriates enjoy fruit and vegetables, so do keep a sense of perspective: food served in a fairly decent hotel in a large town or a place regularly frequented by expatriates is likely to be safe. If you are struck, see the box above for treatment.

Eye problems Bacterial conjunctivitis (pink eye) is a common infection; people who wear contact lenses are most open to this irritating problem. The eyes feel sore and gritty and they will often be stuck together in the mornings. They will need treatment with antibiotic drops or ointment. Lesser eye irritation should settle with bathing in salt water and keeping the eyes shaded. If an insect flies into your eye, extract it with great care, ensuring you do not crush or damage it otherwise you may get a nastily inflamed eye from toxins secreted by the creature. Small elongated red-and-black blister beetles carry warning colouration to tell you not to crush them anywhere against your skin.

Prickly heat A fine pimply rash on the trunk is likely to be heat rash; cool showers, dabbing dry and talc will help. Treat the problem by slowing down to a relaxed schedule, wearing only loose, 100%-cotton clothes and sleeping naked under a fan; you may need to check into an air-conditioned hotel room for a while.

Skin infections Any mosquito bite or small nick in the skin gives an opportunity for bacteria to foil the body's usually excellent defences; although this is less likely in the hot dry climate of Jordan than in other areas that are humid. It is essential to clean and cover even the slightest wound. Creams are not as effective as a good drying antiseptic such as a dry iodine spray (eg. Savlon Dry Spray). If the wound starts to throb, or becomes red and the redness starts to spread, or the wound oozes, and especially if you develop a fever, antibiotics will probably be needed: flucloxacillin (250mg four times a day) or cloxacillin (500mg four times a day).

For those allergic to penicillin, erythromycin (500mg twice a day) for five days should help. See a doctor if the symptoms do not start to improve within 48 hours. Fungal infections also get a hold easily in hot, moist climates so wear 100%-cotton underwear and shower often. An itchy rash in the groin or flaking between the toes is likely to be a fungal infection. This needs treatment with an antifungal cream such as Canesten (clotrimazole); if this is not available try Whitfield's ointment (compound benzoic acid ointment) or crystal violet (although this will turn you purple!).

INSECT-BORNE DISEASES Malaria does not exist in Jordan, but there are other insect-borne diseases. Dengue fever is not common but there are other similar arboviruses. These mosquito-borne diseases may mimic the high fevers and flu-like symptoms of malaria, but there is no prophylactic medication against them. The mosquitoes that carry dengue fever viruses bite during the day, so apply repellent if you see any. Symptoms include headaches, rashes, excruciating joint and muscle pains and fever. Viral fevers usually last about a week and are not usually fatal. Complete rest and paracetamol are the usual treatment; plenty of fluids also help. Some patients are given an intravenous drip to keep them from dehydrating. It is especially important to protect yourself if you have had dengue fever before, since a second infection with a different strain can result in the potentially fatal dengue haemorrhagic fever.

BILHARZIA OR SCHISTOSOMIASIS with thanks to Dr Vaughan Southgate of the Natural History Museum, London
Bilharzia or schistosomiasis is a disease caused by *Schistosoma haematobium* that may afflict parts of Jordan. It is an unpleasant problem that is worth avoiding, though can be treated if you do get it.

As the sun is going down, don long clothes and apply repellent on any exposed flesh. Pack a DEET-based insect repellent (roll-ons or stick are the least messy preparations for travelling). You also need either a permethrin-impregnated bed net or a permethrin spray so that you can treat bed nets in hotels. Permethrin treatment makes even very tatty nets protective and prevents mosquitoes from biting through the impregnated net when you roll against it; it also deters other biters. Otherwise, retire to an air-conditioned room or burn mosquito coils (which are widely available and cheap in Jordan) or sleep under a fan. Coils and fans reduce rather than eliminate bites. Travel clinics usually sell a good range of nets, treatment kits and repellents.

Mosquitoes and many other insects are attracted to light. If you are camping, never put a lamp near the opening of your tent, or you will have a swarm of biters waiting to join you when you retire. In hotel rooms, be aware that the longer your light is on, the greater the number of insects will be sharing your accommodation.

Leishmaniasis is caused by a protozoan parasite (Leishmania donovani species). It is spread by the bite of infected sandflies. These bite mainly at night and are most common in forested areas. It can cause skin or organ (visceral) disease but is rare in travellers unless trekking or living in jungle areas.

It is easier to understand how to diagnose it, treat it and prevent it if you know a little about the life cycle. Contaminated faeces are washed into a lake, the eggs hatch and the larva infects certain species of snail. The parasites can digest their way through your skin when you wade or bathe in infested fresh water.

Winds disperse the snails and cercariae. The snails in particular can drift a long way, especially on windblown weed, so nowhere is really safe. However, deep water and running water are safer, while shallow water presents the greatest risk. The cercariae penetrate intact skin, and find their way to the liver and breed. *Schistosoma haematobium* then, goes mostly to the bladder.

Although the adults do not cause any harm in themselves, after about four to six weeks they start to lay eggs, which cause an intense but usually ineffective immune reaction, including fever, cough, abdominal pain, and a fleeting, itching rash. The absence of early symptoms does not necessarily mean there is no infection. Later symptoms can be more localised and more severe, but the general symptoms settle down fairly quickly and eventually you are just tired. 'Tired all the time' is one of the most common symptoms among expats, and bilharzia, giardia, amoeba and intestinal yeast are the most common culprits.

Although bilharzia is difficult to diagnose, it can be tested for at specialist travel clinics. Ideally tests need to be done at least six weeks after likely exposure and will determine whether you need treatment. Fortunately it is easy to treat at present.

Avoiding bilharzia

- If you are bathing, swimming, paddling or wading in fresh water that you think may carry a bilharzia risk, try to get out of the water within ten minutes.
- Avoid bathing or paddling on shores within 200m of villages or places where people use the water a great deal, especially reedy shores or where there is lots of water weed.

- Dry off thoroughly with a towel; rub vigorously.
- If your bathing water comes from a risky source try to ensure that the water is taken from the lake in the early morning and stored snail-free, otherwise it should be filtered, or Dettol or Cresol should be added.
- Bathing early in the morning is safer than bathing in the last half of the day.
- Cover yourself with DEET insect repellent before swimming: it may offer some protection.

TICKBITE FEVER Middle Eastern ticks are not the rampant disease transmitters they are in the Americas, but they may spread tickbite fever and a few dangerous rare illnesses in Jordan. Tickbite fever is a flu-like illness that can easily be treated with doxycycline, but as there can be some serious complications it is important to visit a doctor.

Ticks should ideally be removed as soon as possible, as leaving them on the body increases the chance of infection. They should be removed with special tick tweezers that can be bought in good travel shops. Failing that you can use your finger nails: grasp the tick as close to your body as possible and pull steadily and firmly away at right angles to your skin. The tick will then come away complete, as long as you do not jerk or twist. If possible douse the wound with alcohol (any spirit will do) or iodine. Irritants (eg: Olbas oil) or lit cigarettes are to be discouraged since they can cause the ticks to regurgitate and therefore increase the risk of disease. It is best to get a travelling companion to check you for ticks; if you are travelling with small children, remember to check their heads, and particularly behind the ears.

Spreading redness around the bite and/or fever and/or aching joints following a tick bite imply that you have an infection that requires antibiotic treatment, so seek advice.

HIV/AIDS The risks of sexually transmitted infection are high in Jordan, whether you sleep with fellow travellers or locals. About 80% of HIV infections in British heterosexuals are acquired abroad. If you must indulge, use condoms or femidoms, which help reduce the risk of transmission. If you notice any genital ulcers or discharge, get treatment promptly since these increase the risk of acquiring HIV. If you do have unprotected sex, visit a clinic as soon as possible; this should be within 24 hours, or no later than 72 hours, for post-exposure prophylaxis.

RABIES Rabies is carried by warm-blooded mammals and is passed on to man through a bite, scratch or a lick of an open wound. It can also be spread by saliva getting into your mouth or eyes. You must always assume any animal is rabid even if it looks well, and seek medical help as soon as possible. Meanwhile scrub the wound with soap under a running tap or while pouring water from a jug. Find a reasonably clear-looking source of water (but at this stage the quality of the water is not important), then pour on a strong iodine or alcohol solution of gin, whisky or rum. This helps stop the rabies virus entering the body and will guard against wound infections, including tetanus.

Pre-exposure vaccinations for rabies are ideally advised for everyone, but they are particularly important if you intend to have contact with animals and/or are likely to be more than 24 hours away from medical help. Ideally, three doses should be taken over a minimum of 21 days. Contrary to popular belief these vaccinations are relatively painless.

If you are bitten, scratched or licked over an open wound by a sick animal, then post-exposure prophylaxis should be given as soon as possible, though it is never too late to seek help, as the incubation period for rabies can be very long. Those who have not been immunised will need a blood product called rabies immunoglobulin (RIG) – ideally human but horse (Equine) will do – and a full course of rabies injections. RIG is very expensive and hard to come by, but without it those who have not had the rabies vaccine beforehand run the risk of succumbing to the disease. However, if you've had three doses of vaccine before travel then you no longer need RIG and just two further doses of vaccine given three days apart is adequate. This is another reason why pre-exposure vaccination should be encouraged.

Tell the doctor if you have had any pre-exposure vaccines, as this will change the treatment you receive. And remember that, if you do contract rabies, mortality is 100% and death from rabies is probably one of the worst ways to go.

SNAKEBITE Snakes rarely attack unless provoked, and bites in travellers are unusual. You are less likely to get bitten if you wear stout shoes and long trousers when in the bush. Most snakes are harmless and even venomous species will dispense venom in only about half of their bites. If bitten, then, you are unlikely to have received venom; keeping this fact in mind may help you to stay calm.

Many so-called first-aid techniques do more harm than good: cutting into the wound is harmful; tourniquets are dangerous; suction and electrical inactivation devices do not work. The only treatment is antivenom. In case of a bite that you fear may have been from a venomous snake:

- Try to keep calm – it is likely that no venom has been dispensed
- Prevent movement of the bitten limb by applying a splint
- Keep the bitten limb *below* heart height to slow the spread of any venom
- If you have a crepe bandage, wrap it around the whole limb (eg: all the way from the toes to the thigh), as tight as you would for a sprained ankle or a muscle pull
- Evacuate to a hospital that has antivenom. It is held by the Al-Essra Hospital, Queen Rania al-Abdullah Street in Amman, and the Jordan Hospital, Queen Noor Street, Sheisani in Amman, see above for contact details.
- Never give aspirin; you may take paracetamol, which is safe. Never cut or suck the wound.
- Do not apply ice packs
- Do not apply potassium permanganate
- If the offending snake can be captured without risk of someone else being bitten, take this to show the doctor – but beware, since even a decapitated head is able to bite.

SAFETY

Jordan is generally a safe place to visit and if you venture out after about 19.00 in the evening you will probably find the main towns and cities almost deserted. Having said that, there are incidents of crime and you should be vigilant against pickpockets and petty thieves, especially in busier places.

EMERGENCY NUMBERS		
Police ☎191		**Fire** ☎199
Ambulance ☎199		**Traffic accidents** ☎190

As in many other countries in the world, there is a threat of terrorism and the occasional outburst of politically inspired unrest. You should be vigilant. The most recent period of unrest was in 2011 when street protests in Downtown Amman, fuelled by uprisings in Tunisia and Egypt, and incidents along the Jordan–Syria border resulted in a small number of injuries and reports of deaths. If you happen upon political rallies or demonstrations, whether organised or spontaneous, it is wise to avoid them for your own safety.

WOMEN TRAVELLERS

Women travelling alone should exercise the usual caution against crimes of a sexual nature, and in particular decline any offer, of a lift from strangers. Jordanians are a modest people and consider women dressing in a provocative manner unpleasant. If you dress is such a way, there is every possibility that you might be harassed by men thinking that you may be available. The wisest option is to dress modestly, for which you will be respected. You should cover your shoulders and arms, and never wear miniskirts or shorts.

If you are harassed, either verbally or more unlikely physically, then shout angrily and you will almost certainly embarrass your harasser. It is unacceptable for men to touch a woman, except possibly in a business situation where colleagues shake hands, and even then the woman would instigate the gesture.

It is also inappropriate for women to sit next to a male driver if travelling in, for example, a taxi. It is best to sit in the back to avoid any misunderstanding. On buses, it is generally accepted amongst Jordanians that you do not sit next to someone of the opposite sex unless you are married. A woman travelling alone should find another woman to sit next to. Wearing a ring to suggest you are a married woman even if you are not is also often a good deterrent against unwanted male attention. The Jordanian police advise that should you find yourself a victim of harassment, or become lost or stranded always call the emergency number (✎ 191 or 192) for assistance.

DISABLED TRAVELLERS

Travellers with disabilities may find exploring Jordan hard going and it might be advisable to stay with a group of people who are aware of any restriction you may have and who can assist if required. The terrain in places can be rough and as many of the major towns and cities are built on steep hills it can be difficult to get around and may potentially be unsafe for wheelchair users or visitors with restricted mobility. Jordan hasn't really addressed travellers with disabilities as well as it might, but things are changing and now a few more public buildings, hotels and restaurants are providing wheelchair access. The vast majority still do not, however.

The exception is some of the nature reserves operated by the Royal Society for the Conservation of Nature (RSCN) (✎ 06 533 7931; e adminrscn@rscn.org.jo; www.rscn.org.jo) where transportation can be arranged; and the Petra Archaeological Park, where visitors can take a horse and carriage ride through parts of the complex and, by arrangement, take a car back – telephone the Ministry of Tourism and Antiquities (✎ 06 460 3360; e tourism@mota.gov.jo), or arrange transport through your own tour or taxi company. Vehicles are available at the Wadi Rum Protected Area; telephone to make arrangements ahead of your visit (✎ 03 209 0600; www.wadirum.jo). Shuttle buses are available at the Baptism Site of Jesus Christ, which include Bethany Beyond the Jordan, Elijah's Hill and St Mary's Church (m *077 760 7036;* e *promotionunit@baptismsite.com; www.baptismsite.com*).

Literature and guidebooks for visitors with restricted hearing or sight, again, are not really available, so it's best to purchase a guidebook suitable for your needs before you depart for your visit.

GAY AND LESBIAN TRAVELLERS

Homosexuality is illegal in Jordan, although it is widely known that Amman has a small, circumspect underground gay and lesbian scene. If you were to happen upon the areas frequented by gay and lesbian couples you probably wouldn't even be aware of it, such is its discretion. However, public shows of affection between same sex couples, such as holding hands or kissing as a greeting, is all part of the social scene.

TRAVELLING WITH CHILDREN

You should exercise the usual care when visiting Jordan with children and not let them out of your sight. Particular hazards include the risk of falling in places like Petra, so hold on to them and don't let them near sheer cliffs. Care should also be taken around hotel swimming pools. Kids can be particularly vulnerable to stomach upsets, dehydration and sunburn too, so always have plenty of rehydration salts with you. It is advisable to keep your children out of the sun, which at times can be extremely strong, and ensure you cover their skin with a high-factor sun-cream. Take bottles of water and soft drinks, and snacks such as crisps and fruit that won't spoil or melt in the hot temperatures.

Jordanians love kids; they are a pivotal part of Jordanian culture and you will almost always see whole families, including babies and several toddlers, out shopping together, playing in the parks or dining in a restaurant until quite late into the evening. To a Western eye the latter may seen somewhat indulgent, but then Jordanians, or at least those that can afford it, love to spoil their children and buying them lots of goodies or allowing them to stay up late in a restaurant is all part of everyday life. Lower-income families spoil their children too, of course, but in ways that don't always involve spending lots of money on luxuries. But whether a child comes from a wealthy or a less well-off family you will rarely see one misbehaving in public.

You will find that most hotels and restaurants welcome them and provide amenities to keep babies, toddlers and teens well fed and entertained. Most have buffets, so even fussy eaters should find plenty of food they like. Venues that don't do buffets will almost always have a children's menu from which your youngsters can choose. Baby food, as well as items like nappies, is widely available, although if your baby takes a particular type of formula milk then pack plenty as brands may vary. Juices are always available and can be diluted easily with mineral or bottled water.

WHAT TO TAKE

Packing for your trip to Jordan depends largely on how you intend to spend your time. If you're planning to do lots of sightseeing interspersed with hours floating in the Dead Sea or relaxing on its shores, then you'll need to pack quite different things than if you're looking forward to taking full advantage of Jordan's fabulous hiking trails and mountains.

CLOTHING Comfortable light clothing, a hat or shawl to cover your head, swimwear and beach clothing like a sarong, comfy walking shoes and sandals are ideal if sightseeing and relaxing. As temperatures can often be hot, full-length linen trousers and long skirts are a good idea, worn with light T-shirts and tops (that cover shoulders and arms) to minimise dehydration. These will also be helpful to cover up your skin when in the towns and villages. The dress code in most hotels is smart casual; smart jeans are acceptable. You should also take a shawl, jacket, fleece or jumper for when evenings are cooler or to wear if visiting in the winter months. If taking an action-packed break then you should pack light, easy-to-wear clothing suitable for your activity.

You are almost certain to spend lengths of time in the sun visiting archaeological sites, simply exploring the towns or markets or enjoying your chosen activity. With this in mind, be sure to pack a hat, shawl or bandana to protect you from the sun's rays and also from the dust. Take good sunglasses and comfortable shoes. Good trainers are ideal for day-to-day exploring, or take specialist walking, riding or climbing boots if you plan more adventurous activities.

While Muslim women wear clothing that covers their arms, legs and hair, it is acceptable that Western women may not. However, men and, in particular, women should always dress conservatively in clothes that cover legs and shoulders. In fact, in the older Downtown areas of Amman and in the rural areas of Jordan, it would be highly inappropriate to wear revealing clothing, and you may find both you and the local people will feel uncomfortable as a result. It is a different matter in the hotels of Amman, Aqaba and in the Dead Sea region where it is acceptable to wear swimwear. Two-piece swimsuits are acceptable, although a one-piece is by far more appropriate. Shorts are rarely worn by either sex.

MEDICINES Other items to pack are prescribed medicines with a doctor's note explaining what they are in case you are questioned, and over-the-counter products such as painkillers, indigestion tablets, antihistamines and rehydration salts. You might like to pack antiseptic wipes and cream, plasters, bandages and safety pins for any cuts or emergency situations before you can reach a hospital. Your hotel should be able to assist in such a situation, but if you are out and about take a note of the emergency ambulance and first-aid service number. Pharmacies are dotted around the main towns and are generally well-stocked with day-to-day medicines.

Pack rehydration tablets and high factor suncream (at least factor 15) for when you are exploring, as the summer sun can be intense. You can buy bottled water easily in local shops. Follow the guidelines set out in the health section on pages 57–64, especially if you plan to spend time camping or exploring in the wilderness where dealing with hazards such as scorpions or snakes is a greater possibility.

CAMERA AND ELECTRICAL ITEMS Be sure to pack your camera as you will be spoilt for choice on what to take pictures of, and spare batteries are vital for preventing the frustration of setting up a shot only to find your batteries need replacing and you are miles from the nearest stockist. If your camera is non-digital then remember spare rolls of film. If you are taking electrical items, such as a hair dryer, razor or laptop with power lead, pack an adaptor or a transformer because they can be difficult to find once in Jordan. The electricity is 220 AC volts, 50 cycles. Sockets are the round two-prong wall style, although most modern buildings, and especially new tourist hotels, also have square three-pin-style plugs fitted.

HIKING AND TREKKING EQUIPMENT If you are planning to hike or trek in the wilderness of the nature reserves or deserts, then you will need the appropriate equipment for your trip. Having said that, you'll find it's always best to travel light because terrains and temperatures can be a challenge if weighed down with lots of heavy equipment. You'll need suitable clothing, head gear and footwear, plus you should think about carrying food and water, medicines or equipment for emergencies, a mobile phone (although always tell someone, such as the tourist police, your route, as signals can be lost in canyons), and your navigational maps. Think about taking rope and basic tools, as well as the equipment necessary for your chosen activity.

INSURANCE AND DOCUMENTS Ensure you have comprehensive medical and travel insurance before leaving for Jordan, which not only gives you adequate cover for emergency medical treatments and repatriation, but also covers you for lost luggage, cancelled or missed flights, and stolen cash, credit cards or personal property. Make sure your passport has at least six-month validity remaining and you have any visas you may need for your trip (see page 45).

If you are planning to hire a car during your stay, you'll need a driving licence valid in your country of origin, complete with a picture, which you should have held for at least a year. You may also find it useful to have an International Driving Permit (IDP) for driving in Jordan. Indeed, some car-hire companies insist on an IDP as part of their terms and conditions. An IDP is valid from the date of issue, generally inexpensive and is easy to obtain from motoring organisations. It will have an Arabic translation of your driver details, and may prove helpful if you are stopped and need to show your documents. (See also page 71.)

MONEY AND BUDGETING

The unit of currency is the **Jordanian Dinar** (officially JOD, unofficially JD), which is referred to in everyday life as the JD, pronounced *jaydee*. It is divided into 10 dirham, 100 piastres (pronounced *pee-aster*), or 1,000 fils (*fills*). The fil is the unit most commonly used, so if you see prices written as, for example, 2,500, this means JD2 and 500 fils. Depending on the exchange rate, you'll find one dinar equals around €1; a little less than £1 and about US$1.40. Banknotes come in JD50, JD20, JD10, JD5 and JD1 denominations and have Arabic one side and English on the other. Similarly, coins have their value written in English.

Banks in Jordan are open 08.30–15.00 Sunday–Thursday and can be found throughout Amman and all the other major towns. Hotels usually have money-changing facilities too. **ATM** cash machines can also be found throughout Amman and in the Queen Alia International Airport, but elsewhere you will need to find a bank in order to obtain JDs. You can do this by changing cash from your own country or with **travellers' cheques** on production of your passport, or in some cases another form of identification such as an official ID card. Commission rates in Jordan tend to be high so you may feel it worth changing at least some of your money before you depart for your visit. There are no restrictions on the amount of cash you can bring into Jordan, and as theft is rare you don't have to be unduly worried about having your cash stolen. That said, it is always wise to use hotel safes.

In hotels, restaurants and most major shopping outlets you'll find credit cards are widely accepted, although this is not always the case in the smaller towns, villages and more remote areas. **Credit cards** like Visa, MasterCard and American Express signs are much in evidence around Amman, although Diners Club less so. You can check with your credit and debit card company what establishments accept its cards before you depart.

BUDGETING Jordanians will tell you that the cost of living in their country is expensive, and it is when you learn how much the average local earns (around JD500 per month). To visitors from European countries, however, it appears to represent good value for money. The cost of getting about by public transport is cheap, dining out is inexpensive and hiring a car comparable to Europe or only a little more expensive. The biggest expense is likely to be entrance fees. Jerash will seriously dent your budget, but getting into Petra where the fees are astronomical will blow it completely.

How much?

Litre of bottled water	JD1	Postcard	200 fils
½ litre of beer	JD3	T-shirt	JD10
Loaf of bread	JD1.200	Camera film	JD4
Street snack	JD2–3	Litre of petrol	800 fils
Mars bar	600 fils	Litre of diesel	500 fils

Tipping It is good practice to round up a bill in a quality restaurant, even though a service charge of 10% will have already been added to it. Staff in budget restaurants and cafés don't generally expect a tip. If you feel you want to show your appreciation to, say, a porter or a bellboy who has helped you with your luggage then around 500 fils (JD0.500) is about right unless you are feeling generous and wish to offer JD1. If you take a short taxi ride the best option is to round up the fare, but if you have hired the driver for a day or more, and he has been particularly attentive and knowledgeable, then you could offer upwards of JD3 per day. For specialist guides consider upwards of JD5 but no more than JD10.

GETTING AROUND

BY AIR National carrier **Royal Jordanian** (✆ *03 201 8633;* f *03 201 6555;* e *aqjtbrj@ rj.com; www.rj.com*) operates scheduled, twice-daily flights (morning and early evening) between Amman and Aqaba, which makes it easy to travel between the north and the south of the country. The flight time between the two cities is just 45 minutes. Ticket prices are as little as JD23 excluding tax.

BY TAXI The public transport system in Jordan can be a little bewildering to visitors and you may find it easier and more convenient to hire one of the bright yellow **taxis** with green panels on the side doors that can be seen everywhere. Aqaba has its own fleet of lime **green taxis** that operate in the same way. Around town a journey by taxi will set you back just a few JDs. For example, from the Queen Alia International Airport in Amman a taxi will cost around JD15 for the 50-minute, 32km journey. Your taxi driver should always switch on the meter around town, which starts at JD0.15 and rises in increments. If your budget allows, you can always telephone to book one of the smart **silver radio taxis** from your hotel, although these are only available in Amman.

A cheaper option to both the yellow cabs and the silver radio cars in Amman is the *serveeces* **taxis** (service taxis), which can be a fast, convenient way to travel if you don't mind sharing the vehicle with others. This service is available in most towns. The idea is you flag a *serveeces* vehicle down, and providing your destination is one on their predetermined route they will take you there for 80 or so fils. The vehicles are easy to spot; they are usually Peugeot 504s or Mercedes, and have a sign indicating they are a *serveeces* taxi, but their destination and number are always in Arabic. If you cannot read Arabic don't despair; flag one down and ask the driver if your destination is on his route. Most drivers speak good English. The chances are you'll be planning a trip to Downtown Amman, to the Abdali bus station or to the commercial district, and you'll find that most *serveeces* taxis run between the three.

It is also possible to hire taxis for longer journeys, to the Dead Sea, Petra, Wadi Rum or Jerash from Amman or Aqaba, for instance. However, be aware that while a taxi journey around Amman or Aqaba will be inexpensive, the further afield you go the rate per kilometre rises alarmingly. In the end, you may feel a rental car is a better option if you're planning lots of long trips (see page 72). *Serveeces* **minibuses** are the cheapest option and likely to cost around JD30 for a typical trip from Amman to Petra. It will be direct, however, and you may find yourself squashed in.

An alternative is to hire one of the yellow and green taxis in Amman or the lime green taxis in Aqaba for private use for a few hours, a day or even for a few days. Be sure to negotiate or at least check the price you will be charged for such trips before embarking on them. You may be looking at over JD80 for a straightforward round day trip from Amman to Petra, or from Aqaba to Petra, but when you consider your driver will usually have a good command of English, will be knowledgeable about the sights and take pleasure in chatting to you about Jordan, and is sure to be happy to stop if you want a break or to take some photographs, then you may feel the taxi fare is worth every dinar. It's generally a comfortable way to travel, more direct and convenient, especially if you are in Jordan for just a few days and want to see as many of its fabulous sights as you can.

A word to the wise; Jordan has very few females taxi drivers, although the number is on the increase, and a local women taking a taxi would never dream of getting in the front seat with a male driver. This applies even if they are travelling with a male companion. It is simply not the done thing. Foreign women should do the same to avoid any misunderstandings.

BY BUS Jordan has a number of bus companies that provide fast and regular links between the cities in either larger minibuses or gleaming air-conditioned intercity buses. The **JETT** bus company is the largest, and its fleet of modern blue-and-white luxury buses can often be seen running up and down the Desert Highway to Aqaba in the south, or north to Irbid. It operates to a daily timetable with buses linking the major towns and the King Hussein Bridge, along with main tourist destinations like Petra and Jerash. The hub of its operation is the Abdali and Wahdat bus stations in Amman. Most destinations around Amman and to the north are served out of Abdali, but if you're planning a longer trip to, say, Aqaba, Petra, Ma'an, Karak or Madaba to the south then your JETT bus will leave from the Wahdat bus station. The destination of the bus will be clearly shown on the front; the downside is it will be in Arabic. If you don't read Arabic then you're almost sure to find the driver speaks good English and will happily point you in the right direction for your bus.

Enterprising businesses also run minibuses in competition with the large shiny air-conditioned buses. These seat around 18 people and depart when full. The advantages to travelling by minibus are that they are far cheaper than the larger buses, and, because they do not run to a timetable and are a popular mode of transport for locals, they often run more regularly on busy routes. That said, if you are travelling to a more remote region or a small town, the chances are you may have a wait for your bus to fill up and depart. It's something to consider if time is a key part of your journey. In terms of fares, to use the Amman to Petra and Aqaba to Petra example again, typically you will pay less than JD2 for a minibus, compared to around JD8 on a scheduled air-conditioned bus.

Bus companies

🚐 **Alpha Tourist Transport** 8th Circle, Amman; ☎ 06 585 0430

🚐 **JETT Tourist Transport** 7th Circle, Amman; ☎ 06 585 4679; www.jett.com

🚐 **MESK Tourist Transport** 11171 Amman; ☎ 06 439 9555

🚐 **Philadelphia Tours Transport** Madaba Bridge, 11192 Amman; ☎ 06 412 9779

🚐 **RUM Tourist Transport** Um Albasateen, Amman; ☎ 06 429 0333

🚐 **Sultan Tourist Transport** Airport Way, Amman; ☎ 06 471 4714

BY TRAIN While discussions to introduce passenger trains have been afoot for decades there is currently no service, other than the **Hejaz Railway** that runs between Amman and Damascus in Syria (see page 53). You may catch sight of the narrow track that runs south of Amman down to Aqaba, and if you're lucky you may even see one of the lovely old steam trains that ply the route. However, these only ever carry freight, especially phosphates, between the cities.

BY CAR Renting a car and touring around Jordan on your own has lots of advantages and is relatively straightforward, if a tad alarming at times. Driving is on the right, but given that many roads aren't marked with lanes, especially in rural areas, and locals tend to drive without too much thought to rights of way (which can be particularly problematic at roundabouts), it can all be a bit of a challenge for the faint-hearted. In busy areas the drama of drivers sounding their horn is all part of daily life.

Documents You will need a full driving licence valid in your country of origin, which you should have held for at least one year. Your licence should include a photo. It's a good idea to obtain an **International Driving Permit** (IDP) for driving in Jordan before you leave, because it will have an Arabic translation and make things easier if you have to show your documents. Many Jordan-based car-hire companies insist on an IDP. Most motoring organisations supply IDPs, which are valid for 12 months. You should also have at least third party insurance and be sure to keep documents with you at all times as the police often make spot checks.

Petrol stations Have some cash on you as most petrol stations do not accept credit cards and you will have to pay in JDs. Garages are plentiful in the main towns, but few and far between in the desert or more remote areas. If you can't speak Arabic just point to the petrol you need (petrol is *benzene*, 90 octane unleaded petrol is *tisaeen*, unleaded 95 octane *khamsa wa-tisaeen* and diesel is *deezel*), show your JD note or say 'full' and the petrol attendant will understand.

Regulations You should always observe traffic lights and keep to speed limits. On highways the limit is 100kph, 90kph on main roads and 60kph or 40kph in built-up areas. If you are caught exceeding these speed limits you may face a hefty on-the-spot fine of anything up to JD150. Similarly, you may face a fine, or worse, for not wearing a seatbelt or using a mobile phone, both of which are against the law. Your car-hire company should provide you with a warning triangle and a fire extinguisher, which you'll need to keep in your car.

Practical Information GETTING AROUND

2

Roads Road surfaces on the main roads are generally good, but smaller roads, especially those in less built-up areas, can be poorly maintained and unlit, so take care when driving, especially at night. In winter the more mountainous roads, such as those around Petra, can be hazardous because of snowfall. Some even get completely blocked. Driving in the desert can be equally hazardous. The sand dunes may look like the perfect photo opportunity, but if a wind gets up and whips up the sand it can make the road surface as slippery as fresh snow. If you do plan to drive in the desert it is advisable to hire a 4x4 car, and take an extra can of petrol with you and plenty of water.

It's a good idea to carry a torch too, as roads are not well lit and if you're returning after a long day walking around Petra or Wadi Rum, for example, or you're in the depth of the desert, the last thing you need is to find yourself struggling to find your road home. Road signs are plentiful and usually in Arabic and English; just not lit too well.

Accidents If you do have an accident it must be reported to the police (☏ *191*) or traffic accident reporting (☏ *190*). If you need an ambulance call ☏ 199. If your car is a rental then first telephone your hire company, which should make the call to the police for you and send someone to collect you and the car. It's wise to drive carefully because if you hit a person, or even a herd of goats or one of the camels you often see wandering in the road ahead of you, you will automatically be held liable, even if the accident wasn't your fault.

Car-hire companies

🚗 **Abdo Car Rental** ☏ 06 568 2427

🚗 **Abu Amro Car Rental** ☏ 06 560 3630

🚗 **Abu Zaid Rent a Car** ☏ 06 551 5216

🚗 **Aghreed Rent a Car** ☏ 06 461 8765

🚗 **Al-Amin Rent a Car** ☏ 06 582 7201

🚗 **Al-Anan Rent a Car** ☏ 06 535 9639

🚗 **Al-Masoud Rent a Car** ☏ 06 551 1166

🚗 **Al-Nour Rent a Car** ☏ 06 553 6632

🚗 **Al-Qilaa Car Rental** ☏ 06 562 6509

🚗 **Al-Rafedain Rent a Car** ☏ 06 582 9980

🚗 **Al-Rayyan Rent a Car** ☏ 06 581 0799

🚗 **Al-Salam Rent a Car** ☏ 06 535 8650

🚗 **Al-Salehin Rent a Car** ☏ 06 568 5737

🚗 **Al-Samer Rent a Car** ☏ 06 581 7011

🚗 **Alam Rent a Car** ☏ 06 553 3363

🚗 **Avis Rent a Car** ☏ 06 569 9420

🚗 **Budget Rent a Car** ☏ 06 569 8131

🚗 **Camel Rent a Car** ☏ 06 535 9905

🚗 **Castles Rent a Car** ☏ 06 562 6509

🚗 **Cruise Rent a Car** ☏ 06 553 0176

🚗 **Dallah Rent a Car** ☏ 06 551 1112

🚗 **Diplomat Rent a Car** ☏ 06 551 0427

🚗 **Europcar** ☏ 06 656 5581

🚗 **Hertz-Shakhshir Rent a Car** ☏ 06 553 8958

🚗 **Karnak Rent a Car** ☏ 06 533 6250

🚗 **Monte Carlo Rent a Car** ☏ 06 533 5155

🚗 **Omaish Rent a Car** ☏ 06 471 1792

🚗 **Oskar Rent a Car** ☏ 06 553 5635

🚗 **Payless Car Rental** ☏ 06 552 5180

🚗 **Petra Rent a Car** ☏ 03 215 4545

🚗 **Safari Rent a Car** ☏ 06 560 5080

🚗 **Sixt Rent a Car** ☏ 06 568 6131

🚗 **Thrifty** ☏ 06 562 2348

🚗 **U Save** ☏ 06 565 2207

ACCOMMODATION

Whether you're looking for a top-notch luxury hotel to base yourself while sightseeing or you're travelling on a budget and simply want somewhere to lay your head at night and have a cooling shower in the morning, you'll find just what you are looking for amongst Jordan's diverse range of accommodation options. Of course, you also have the option to sleep under the stars in Bedouin tents in places such as Wadi Rum, or relax and rejuvenate at the Dead Sea's collection of luxury spa resorts that are up there with the finest in the world.

HOTELS The **Jordan Hotel Association** (JHA) (*www.johotels.org*) represents around 400 hotels in the kingdom and runs regular workshops and training programmes for staff to ensure they meet the standards expected by international travellers. In turn, the association grades hotels from one to five stars, according to the level of amenities offered, and checks that standards are being met and maintained. The system isn't foolproof, however, and you may find yourself in, say, a four-star hotel that really only merits three stars if you were to judge it by similar establishments in other holiday destinations. There are five-star hotels in Amman and Petra, especially, that could do with a bit of TLC.

In the main, the **luxury hotels** that offer a health centre and spa, swimming pools, a choice of international restaurants and super-equipped guestrooms almost inevitably are graded with five stars, and certainly the super spa resorts of the Dead Sea fit into this category. Top names include Kempinski, InterContinental, Crowne Plaza, Marriott and Mövenpick. At the other end of the scale, hotels offering only basic amenities will be awarded one star. Between the two is a range of **mid-range hotels** that are well equipped, clean and can offer excellent value for money.

If you stumble upon a **budget hotel** with no classification at all, it may well still be a member of JHA but with virtually no amenities other than a sleeping area, and probably a shared bathroom. It will still be inspected but listed as unclassified. Some are geared up for travellers who want to stay just a night or two before moving on, but many are designed more with workers who have travelled here for employment in mind. It's probably better to steer clear of these establishments unless you are on the tightest of budgets.

ECO-LODGES AND CAMPSITES The other option is to stay in an **eco-lodge** on a nature reserve run by the Royal Society for the Conservation of Nature (RSCN), which is becoming an increasingly popular choice, or to camp. Jordan has very few campsites, and none at all around Amman, but those that do exist offer the most wonderful experience of sleeping under the dark night sky dotted with stars.

Most of the nature reserves run by the RSCN have **campsites**, as well as their lodges. At the Dana Nature Reserve (see page 198), located between the Dead Sea and Petra, the Rummana Campsite provides tents for up to 60 people, complete with toilets, showers and catering services. In the Shaumari Wildlife Reserve near Azraq (see page 155), the campsite is very basic, while in the Ajloun Forest Reserve north of Ajlun (see page 168) the campsite has tents with showers and toilets.

In the Wadi Rum desert, a number of privately-owned campsites have sprung up in recent years. Many are run by Bedouin families and have traditional tents made from black goats' hair with blankets on the ground to sleep on, while others are owned by companies offering their clients the 'Bedouin' experience and have canvas-style tents. Amenities vary, but most campsites nowadays have a basic toilet and shower block, and an outside cooking area. If you're planning to pitch your own tent, try to find the designated areas within campsites as random camping is largely frowned upon on the grounds of safety and preserving the environment.

RATES In terms of what you are likely to pay, the four-star and five-star hotels may list a rate that appears to be high, but because there is an oversupply of hotels at this level in Jordan at the present time you will usually be able to negotiate a much better price. We have used listed prices in the chapters of this guide. The luxury Dead Sea spa resorts, however, are popular with wealthy city folk from Amman and international conference organisers, so rates at these hotel may not be quite so flexible, and you should book well in advance. There are fewer mid-range hotels

2

so negotiation may be a tad less productive with these establishments, but it's still worth a try. Jordan is awash with budget hotels where rates are already low. Another option is to book on a package trip, which has become increasingly popular in recent years and can represent excellent value.

All hotel rates vary with the seasons. **High season** for Western visitors is regarded as being from March through to May, and September through to late October or early November, when the climate is conducive for exploring or relaxing. In the **low season** rates are reduced. Arab visitors tend to prefer July and August. The exception to the seasonal norm is Aqaba, which has an almost year-round season, but because it can experience exceptionally high temperatures in June through to September it is often quieter at these times and hotels are more inclined to negotiate in order to fill their guestrooms. Aqaba is busy in winter and you should book your accommodation as far in advance as possible.

All quoted prices will include **government sales tax** (currently 8%), but sometimes you may see an additional 10% **service charge** added to your final bill. Check when you make your booking if this will be added. The larger hotels and the establishments run by the RSCN accept credit cards in payment, but if you are staying in a small, probably unclassified city hotel then you may be asked to pay in cash.

✖ EATING AND DRINKING

Food is a serious business in Jordan and central to daily family life. Until recently, Jordanians were rarely seen eating out in restaurants. Eating in order to survive, as opposed to eating as a social event, was considered something you did in the privacy of your home with your tribe, extended family or your invited friends. The thinking stems from the Bedouin way of life, when cooking in the open air using the freshest of ingredients, and then dining with your close circle was the norm. Eating out was unnecessary and this still holds true in some areas. As a result, there is not a huge selection of restaurants once you leave the cities.

As a multi-cultural city, Amman has French, Mediterranean, Indian, Oriental and Mexican restaurants, plus lots more besides, and Aqaba has a whole host of fish restaurants, but get out into the less touristy towns and the choice becomes limited. This is even true of Wadi Musa, the town that serves the Petra Archaeological Park. In the Badia and Wadi Rum desert regions, restaurants are virtually non-existent. But this is slowly changing and more restaurants are opening.

Jordanian food is delicious, but it may come as a bit of surprise when you find you will be expected to eat your food with your fingers or use the bread as a sort of scoop. More upmarket restaurants provide cutlery, as do hotels which all have their own international and often gourmet restaurants, but traditional eateries in the middle of nowhere may put only a spoon on the table for eating soup. An age-old tradition amongst Jordanians is that eating is done with the right hand, since the left hand is used for toilet purposes. As such, eating with your left hand in a restaurant, at a Bedouin camp or if you are invited to dine with a family in their home will be met with disapproval.

BREAKFAST Most Jordanians get up at sunrise and, as such, eat breakfast early. Typically, an Arab breakfast will comprise a dish of *fuul*. A mix of brownish cooked fava beans mashed up with olive oil, lemon juice and a good helping of spices, *fuul* is perhaps an acquired taste to the Western palate more used to eggs on toast, but it is tasty and should be tried at least once. It is served ladled from a big pot with flat bread (*khubz*) and side dishes of olives (*zaytoon*), cheese (*jibneh*) or a dip made from ground chickpeas mixed with lemon juice, garlic and olive oil (*hummus*). A Jordanian will complete breakfast with a strong black tea (*shal* or *shy*), or possibly a mint tea (*shy na'na*) or a coffee (*ahwa* or *gahweh*).

In hotels, breakfast is served around 06.00/06.30–10.30. The Petra Archaeological Park opens at 06.00 and you'll find the hotels in Wadi Musa tend to start breakfast earlier than, say, the Amman hotels, but you will be told times when you check in. Breakfast in the smarter hotels is usually a buffet-style arrangement with all manner of dishes displayed for you to help yourself. It'll be the usual international assortment: juices, cereals, cheese and ham, croissants and rolls with jams, honey and marmalade, sliced bread for toasting, boiled eggs, cakes and pastries, fruit and a cooked selection that will include sausages, bacon, tomatoes and potato. Poached or fried eggs or omelettes are usually prepared to order.

You will be offered tea or coffee and may have to ask for milk (*halib*) as it isn't always brought automatically to your table (Arabs drink black tea and coffee). If you're staying in a budget hotel it's probably wise to assume the breakfast won't be quite so lavish.

LUNCH AND DINNER Jordanians tend to eat a hearty lunch around 12.00, even if they are working, and then dinner quite late in the evening. Favourite dishes include *falafel*, which is a delicious combination of ground chickpeas moulded into balls and fried. It is a staple on the menu and often served for breakfast, as a fast-food snack between meals or as a starter with salad and dips for a main meal. Jordan's national dish is the traditional Bedouin celebratory feast dish *mensaf*. Usually prepared and served in a large cast iron-style shallow pan, it comprises chunks of cooked lamb, mutton or sometimes camel on a bed of rice, smothered with spices and a creamy yoghurt sauce. It is served with potato (*batata*), flat bread (*khubez*), and dishes like *fattoush*, cubes of fried bread with parsley, and *tabbouleh*, which is a particularly flavoursome combination of chopped parsley with tomato and mint.

If you fancy trying Jordanian dishes, head for a good-quality Arabic restaurant; cheaper ones will probably have a handful of simple dishes on their menu and

RESTAURANT PRICE CODES		
Average price of main course		
Expensive	$$$$$	JD15+
Above average	$$$$	JD10–15
Mid range	$$$	JD5–10
Cheap and cheerful	$$	JD2–5
Rock bottom	$	Less than JD2

won't really give you much of a choice. If you don't know what to order, the simplest thing to do is order a *mezze*, followed by a couple of main courses for everyone in your party to share. A mezze comprises a selection of dishes on small plates, from which you can help yourself. Typically, it will have dips such as *hummus*, a tasty aubergine dip (*baba ghanouj*) or an aubergine and sesame dip (*moutabbel*), flat bread and salad, followed by *warag aynab* (vine leaves stuffed with minced meat, rice and spices), *sujuk* (spicy sausages) and a delicious spit-roasted chicken (*farooj*). The speciality of many restaurants is *magloubeh*, which translated means 'upside down'. Versions vary but it is typically a delicious dish of creamy chicken with rice and vegetables cooked with herbs. If you fancy something light try chicken with spinach (*mulukhayyeh*) or a chicken kebab (*shish tawook*). It is exceptionally rare for you to see pork on the menu, which is forbidden under Islam.

Pastries dripping with honey, milk puddings flavoured with almond (*muhallabiyyeh*), or fresh fruit like apples (*tfah*) from the south, bananas (*mooz*) and oranges (*boordan*) from the Jordan Valley or the wonderfully juicy watermelons (*batteekh*) that grow in abundance and can be seen in the green-covered fields on approach to Wadi Rum in spring and summer are the traditional ways to round off a meal.

VEGETARIAN With so many classic dishes made from vegetables, spices, chickpeas and sesame seeds, eating out in Jordan as a vegetarian is a breeze. Simply order your chosen dish or join in with everyone in a mezze and help yourself to the many meat-free dishes that will be brought to your table on tiny plates. Try *fataayir*, which is a savoury snack or light meal made of paper-thin pastry cut in triangular shapes and filled with cheese or spinach, or a tiny egg-topped pizza known as a *khubez bayd*. *Mahshi* (vegetables stuffed with rice and cooked with spices) is a good choice too. Salads, especially *tabbouleh* – made with chopped parsley, tomato and mint – and fresh fruit are always served.

DRINKS The national drink of Jordan has to be tea (*shal* or *shy*); everyone drinks it either strong and hot or flavoured with herbs or mint (*shy na'na*). Green tea (*shy akhdar*) and chamomile tea (*babunaj* or *babohbidj*) have become fashionable too. These will be served to you hot, or a refreshing alternative is to have them chilled in a tall glass. A close second in the popularity stakes is coffee (*ahwa* or *gahweh*). Every village has a local coffee shop, even two or three, which bare no resemblance whatsoever to the swish coffee houses found in the shopping malls of central Amman. Village coffee shops are rustic places where the men folk of the village meet, sip their strong Arabic coffee (*ahwa Arbeya*) or Turkish coffee (*ahwa Turkeya*), catch up with the news and join in a bit of gossip after a day's work before heading home to the family. Women (other than visitors) and children are not allowed in coffee shops; they are the preserve of the village men.

The drinking of alcohol is forbidden under Islam and in a restaurant Jordanians will order a long iced mint tea, mineral water (*mayat siha*) or a juice (*aseer*). It is acceptable for visitors to drink alcohol, but it should be done with restraint and under no circumstances venture out while intoxicated – it is considered undignified and will cause offence. Some of the more upmarket restaurants, bars and hotels will have a reasonable wine (*nibid*) list featuring local red, rosé and white Cabernet, Merlot and Chardonnay wines that are quite acceptable, plus a choice of international wines and spirits, and beer. The local beer is Amstel, which is brewed under licence, and is available in bottles, cans or draught, but is expensive.

Water (*mai as saha, my* or *mayya*) and mineral water is inexpensive and available at shops and kiosks. Water is a valuable commodity in Jordan. In recent years, most of the larger hotels have installed their own water filtering systems and the resulting water is considered safe to drink. When out and about it is safer to drink bottled water.

PUBLIC HOLIDAYS AND FESTIVALS

Jordanians love festivals and while some take the form of an Islamic religious festival, such as Ramadan (when followers fast for one month from sunrise to sunset to conform to the pillar of Islam, and which ends with the three-day feast Eid al-Fitr), others celebrate a successful crop planting or harvest, or revolve around folkloric and contemporary dance, music, theatre and art. Christmas is a festival celebrated by all Christians, and is a public holiday in Jordan, as is New Year and Independence Day on 25 May. Another big Islamic festival is Eid al-Adah, which falls 70 days after the end of Ramadan and is a time when Muslims make a pilgrimage to Makkah.

Jordan has eight public holidays when most businesses, shops and banks will be closed. New Year's Day (1 January) and His Majesty King Abdullah II's birthday (30 January) are the first two major holidays of the year. In May there are two: Labour Day (1 May) and Independence Day (25 May). Accession Day falls on 9 June, King Hussein I Remembrance Day is celebrated on 14 November and Christmas, although a Christian holiday, has been adopted as a national celebration and marked every year (25 December). In addition, there are a number of religious holidays marked annually that are variable date-wise. Mowlid an-Nabawi (the birthday of the Prophet Muhammad), Easter, Eid al-Isra wal-Miraj meaning 'Night Journey to Heaven', Ramadan and Eid al-Fitr, and the four-day feast at the end of the Hajj month of pilgrimage to Makkah known as Eid al-Adha are the main events of the year. The Islamic New Year is marked by a celebration known as the First of Muharram.

As a country with a keen eye for all things cultural, Jordan hosts an array of festivals that celebrate the arts. Performing arts festivals are part of the culture. Along with the **Amman International Theatre Festival**, the **Amman Contemporary Dance Festival** and the **Zakharef in Motion Festival** (see page 108), there's the **International Film Festival** held in the city's Royal Cultural Centre that showcases films from around the world. The largest cultural festival is the **Jordan Festival** held over several days starting around the end of June every year (✆ *06 461 3300; www.jordanfestival.com*). Celebrations centre on the Citadel in Amman where the finest talents from Jordan, the US, Europe, Asia and Arabia perform to the crowds as the sun goes down. The atmosphere is electric. You'll see jazz and pop opera, rock, classical and contemporary singers and musicians performing alongside dancers and mime artists.

Jerash, too, hosts one of the foremost events of the calendar most years. The **Jerash Festival of Culture and Arts** is one of the most well attended and respected festivals with a line-up of international singers and musicians.

Privately organised festivals are held, usually to raise funds for worthy causes. In Amman, the **Black Iris Festival**, organised by the American Women of Amman (AWA), has become an annual event. It raises much-needed funds for the work of the AWA in the realms of childcare, community-welfare issues and education. The day focuses on fun: there are bouncy castles and face painting for the little ones, raffles, a fun fair, a large food hall where local producers can display their produce and products, and in the centre of the festival ground a stage where dance

2

troupes and musicians perform for the audience. The **International Community School Food Fair** is another privately organised event that showcases the culinary expertise of Amman's schoolchildren and students. It's held at the Um al-Basateen Campus, and takes the form of areas dedicated to cuisines from around the world.

For more details on public holidays and festivals, see pages 79–80.

SHOPPING

Whether it's the smell of spice souks, authentic handicrafts or the latest designer frocks and trendiest trainers that rock your boat, you'll find Jordan offers rather a lot when it comes to shopping. Although it's probably fair to say there's nothing that quite matches the artisans' skills and extensive crafts found in the ancient souks of cities like Damascus and Cairo, Jordan does have a tradition of producing fabulous items through the craftsmanship of the Bedouins and Palestinians.

SOUKS As you stroll around the souks, such the bustling souk of Downtown Amman, you will be spoilt for choice. The waft of cinnamon (*irfeh*), cumin (*kamoun*), saffron (*zafaran*), sage (*wara'a Ghar*) and thyme (*zatar*) will draw you to the spice souks, while the beautiful hand-embroidered cushion covers and tablecloths, and fashion accessories made out of fine leather are sure to prove too much of a temptation. You'll also see brass tea and coffee pots with their beautiful etchings, marquetry jewellery boxes and hand-blown Hebron glass. Souks were once where locals bought household items and foodstuffs, but nowadays such items are more likely to be purchased on a trip to Safeway or Carrefour. Even the Bedouins of Wadi Rum shop in the big superstore in Aqaba.

At the major tourist sites of Petra and Jerash you'll see dozens of tiny stalls offering locally made souvenirs and beaded jewellery, although some items, like the stuffed camels, are kitsch to say the least. What isn't kitsch is the dazzling display of bracelets and necklaces in Amman's famous gold souk. Located in Downtown Amman's King Faisal Street, this vast space offers gold with a price tag that is surprisingly inexpensive compared to similar items in the West. Despite the price, you're still expected to haggle.

If antiques are your thing, you'll find souks have a good display. Take care though as some may be fakes and unless you yourself are an expert you may wish to seek professional opinion on their authenticity. Also be aware that it is prohibited by law to export any items from antiquity. If you fancy walking along a cobbled street full of quirky craft shops, antiques and bookstores make for Al-Rainbow Street in Amman. It's colourful in name and character.

TAX-FREE SHOPPING

As well as the huge choice of goods on display to purchase, the added bonus of shopping in Jordan is that you can claim back tax on your purchases, thereby making it an efficient tax-free way to restock your wardrobe. When you make a purchase in Jordan the price you pay includes a 16% sales tax. For locals this can make many goods, especially luxury items, expensive in relation to the average salary. Tourists visiting from outside Jordan, however, can claim back the tax. Look out for the **Premier Tax Free** sign displayed in many shops. It's a simple procedure and your sales tax will be refunded to you directly. For more information visit www.premiertaxfree.com.

SHOPPING MALLS When it comes to shopping for designer fashions, Amman has an array of glitzy new shopping malls that could almost rival those of Dubai. You'll see big names such as Versace, Gucci, Dolce & Gabbana, Jimmy Choo, Nike and Adidas in the city's huge City Mall, the Zara Centre and Al Baraka Mall. Head for Abdoun Mall in Amman and join wealthy locals and visitors buying luxury watches and jewellery. Aqaba has a handful of shopping centres, but big shiny shopping malls haven't really found their way out of Amman and into the smaller towns of Jordan just yet. No doubt they will come in time.

ARTS AND ENTERTAINMENT

From folkloric festivals and art exhibitions, theatre and films, dance and music to indigenous crafts like ceramics, pottery with unique ethnic designs, leatherwork and rugs made from goat hair, the country's cultural scene is a varied and rich mix. (See also *Culture*, page 34.)

ART Jordan has a rapidly growing arts scene that is especially prolific in Amman. The **Jordan National Gallery of Fine Arts** is one of the most prominent galleries in the Middle East and hosts more than 2000 works. The permanent exhibitions comprise impressionist and abstract paintings, prints, contemporary sculptures, photographs, weavings and ceramics that are the work of over 800 artists from developing countries. Most artists are from Jordan, with others from countries in Asia and Africa. Permanent and visiting exhibitions in Amman are also held in the **Royal Cultural Centre**, the contemporary **Nabad Gallery**, the **Darat Al Funun** gallery and the **Dar al-Anda**, along with hotel galleries including the chic **4Walls** inside the Sheraton Hotel and **The Gallery** inside the Jordan Intercontinental Hotel (see the Amman chapter, page 89). Outside Amman, exhibitions are regularly held in the libraries at Wadi Musa near Petra; the town of Madaba and cities such as Irbid and Zarqa in conjunction with the Public Department of Documents and Libraries; in the workshops of Jordan's nature reserves; and at the Jerash Festival for Culture and Arts held most years.

MUSIC The traditional music of Jordan has a distinctive rhythmic sound, and is usually played on reed pipes and the round string instrument, the *rahab*. It is still enjoyed by many Jordanians, especially the Bedouin tribes who have for centuries sat around the fire each evening, drinking herb tea, reciting stories and listening to kinfolk musicians play. The songs tell stories that have almost certainly been handed down from one generation to the next. Nowadays, popular music is heard everywhere too and Jordanians of all ages love to listen to the latest sounds on their iPods and MP3s or attend musical concerts featuring the country's top classical musicians and international pop performers. Most concerts in Amman are held at the **King Hussein Cultural Centre** (*Omar Matar St;* 06 473 9953) or the **Royal Cultural Centre** (*Al-Malekah Alia St, Shmeisani;* 06 5661026), but more and smaller venues, and venues in other towns and cities such as Aqaba, are increasingly opening their doors for musical evenings. In Amman, and to a lesser extend Aqaba, the music scene is a little more adventurous than might be found elsewhere in Jordan, especially amongst the young. Here you will hear heavy rock, indie, trance and electronic, or stumble upon a bar playing the latest live garage and hip hop sounds.

In recent years Jordan has seen a number of musicians and composers take their place on the world stage. The pop groups RUM, which plays new age sounds, and Sign of Thyme, known for the distinctive ethnic jazz mix, have built up a following in Jordan, and have played gigs in countries outside the kingdom. They are probably Jordan's best-known pop musicians. The Bedouin singer Omar al-Abdillat, composers Khalid Asad and Sameer Baghdadi, pianist Hani Naser and the popular music singer Diana Karazon are all also making a name in the international music arena.

THEATRE AND DANCE As with artistic events, Amman is leading the way for theatre and dance, both in terms of performances and tuition. The renowned **Arab Theatre Training Centre** hosts workshops designed to develop artists' creativity, technical capabilities and artistic expression, while **The National Centre for Culture and Arts of King Hussein Foundation** has its own theatre school that provides tuition to children and young people. Students go on to perform at major events throughout the city and the world. Some of the most prominent theatre and dance festivals in Jordan are held in Amman. Amongst the most famous festivals are the annual **Amman International Theatre Festival** which brings together performers from throughout the Arab world and the **Amman Contemporary Dance Festival**. Amman's **Roman Theatre** and the **Royal Cultural Centre** are popular summer venues for theatrical performances, while major dance events are held at the **King Hussein Cultural Centre** and the **Al-Balad Theatre** (see *Amman*, page 106). The most famous actors from Jordan are Jamil Awad, Shafiqa al-Till and Nadia Odeh.

CINEMA Jordan is the location for the first program of cinematic arts in the Middle East. **The Red Sea Institute of Cinematic Arts** (RSICA) (*Al-Rashid St, Aqaba;* ❧ *03 201 6201;* e *info@rsica.edu.jo; www.rsica.edu.jo*) is a joint venture between the Royal Film Commission of Jordan and the University of Southern California of Cinematic Arts that aims to provide a place of education for all those wishing to work in this specialist field. Graduates leave with the practical, creative and media skills to enter the business. The initiative was a result of His Majesty King Abdullah II's desire to give the people of Jordan and the Middle East a chance to learn the skills of filmmaking.

Jordan itself is a regular location for film-makers. Probably the most famous films to have been shot here are the 1962 British film, *Lawrence of Arabia*, starring the actor Peter O'Toole in the role of TE Lawrence and filmed at Wadi Rum; the 1989 film, *Indiana Jones and the Last Crusade*, starring Harrison Ford and filmed in Petra; and the 1977 fantasy film, *Sinbad and the Eye of the Tiger*. In more recent years, Jordan has hosted the film crew from the 2001 film, *The Mummy Returns*, starring actors Brendan Fraser and Rachel Weisz.

The latest blockbuster films are played in Jordan's cinemas. Most of the larger towns have cinemas.

SPORTS AND OTHER ACTIVITIES

Sport is a serious business in Jordan and areas are set aside with pitches for football and basketball, race tracks and tennis courts. The **Al-Hussein Gardens** in Amman, known as Sports City, the **Prince Mohammad Centre** in Zarqa and the **Al-Hassan Centre** in Irbid are just a few. Dotted throughout all the big cities are fitness centres, equestrian stables and schools, swimming pool complexes and sports clubs. Cycling, although not so much a competitive sport in Jordan, is becoming more and more popular as a way to keep fit and the formation of clubs is on the up. Diving and snorkelling is big in Aqaba, the city that hugs Jordan's only coastline in the south. There are lots of centres to choose from. The largest is arguably the **Aqaba International Dive Center** (*Corniche St;* ❧ *79 559 2095; www.aqabadivingcenter.*

com) and the **International Arab Divers Village and Diving Club** (*South Beach Rd;* ☎ *03 203 1808; www.aqaba-divevillage.com*).

Football is by far the favourite game and a regular topic of conversation is how teams are faring. Amman and Aqaba have a growing number of sport-style bars where you almost always find groups of mostly young men glued to the television watching football and basketball. Even in the smaller towns and villages everyone catches up with the latest games on television and the internet. Jordanians love to play football too, and in every village, no matter how small, there is a football pitch or an area set aside for play. Jordan has its own football association that controls its national football team, which although never having qualified for the World Cup has enjoyed significant success in other tournaments. Its home ground is the **Amman International Stadium**, just north of the city centre. The country's young are encouraged to learn football skills, and the association has pioneered the teaching of coaches and introduced leagues for children, and the Jordan League for adult players.

PHOTOGRAPHY

From the towering cliffs of Petra and the wilderness of the Wadi Rum to the bustle of Amman and the beauty of Jerash, your trip to Jordan will be full of photo opportunities. If you wish to take a photo of a local then always ask permission. Similarly, you should always check with owners if you intend taking pictures on private property. It is acceptable to take pictures at the archaeological sites. Under no circumstances take pictures near military establishments.

MEDIA AND COMMUNICATIONS

MEDIA A number of Arabic- and English-language newspapers and magazines dedicated to life in Jordan are published and are readily available from newsstands. *Ad-Dustour* (meaning 'Constitution') and *ad-Ra'i* (meaning 'Opinion') are the two largest dailies in Arabic, while the English-language newspapers are dominated by the daily *Jordan Times* and the weekly *Star* newspapers. All provide extensive coverage of the news of the day in Jordan and the world, along with listings for events taking place. International dailies such as the *Wall Street Journal, International Herald Tribune, Le Figaro, The Times* and the *South China Morning Post* are usually on sale in hotels too, albeit a few days out of date.

Living Well is a lively magazine focusing on health and wellbeing, the home, entertainment and fashion, and is one of the favourites amongst English-speaking female residents and visitors, while the more serious *Jo Magazine* and *Jordan Business* are publications that give in-depth analysis of the political arena, society and culture issues, and the business sector.

Jordan's state television, **Jordan Radio & Television** (*www.jrtv.gov.jo*), in English and Arabic, broadcasts interesting debates and international films. A wider choice of films is available on the satellite channels in most hotels. Amman has some good English-speaking stations. **Sunny** can be picked up on FM 105.1, **Mood** on FM 92, energy on FM 97.7 and **Play** on FM 99.6.

English-language newspapers and magazines
JO Magazine PO Box 17074; ☎ 06 563 0430; e qais@jo.jo; www.jo.jo

Jordan Business PO Box 3024; ☎ 06 582 0058; e info@jordan-business.net; www.jordan-business.net

The Jordan Times Jordan Press Foundation, Queen Rania al-Abdullah St; ☎06 560 0800; e editor@jordantimes.com; www.jordantimes.com

Living Well Magazine Front Row Publishing, Mohammad Baseem Khammash St, Amman 11181; ☎06 582 0058; e info@livingwell-magazine.com; www.livingwell-magazine.com

The Star www.star.com.jo.

English-language radio stations
Energy www.energyradio.jo

Jordan Radio & Television www.jrtv.gov.jo (also in Arabic)

Mood FM www.mood.fm

Play 99.6 www.play.jo

Rotana FM www.rotana.net

Sunny 105.1 www.sunny.jo

English-language television station

Jordan Radio & Television www.jrtv.gov.jo (also in Arabic)

POST Post offices can be found in all the main towns of Jordan and offer an extensive service for letters and parcels. You can buy stamps, collect parcels and send telegrams. All post offices are open ⊕ 07.00–19.00 Saturday–Thursday, 07.00–13.00 Friday, with reduced times in winter and during Ramadan. Winter times are generally 07.00–17.00 Saturday–Thursday, 07.00–13.00 Friday.

Most of the larger four- and five-star hotels provide a full range of postal services. International courier firms, like DHL Express (*www.dhl.com*), UPS (*www.ups.com*), TNT Express Worldwide (*www.tnt.com*) and FedEx (*www.fedex.com.jo*), are well represented in Amman and Aqaba.

TELEPHONE If telephoning from abroad you'll first need to dial the international code (00), followed by the country code for Jordan (962) and then the area code and the seven-digit local number. If calling within Jordan, simply dial the area code followed by the local number. Mobile numbers are eight digits long, preceded by 07. You can obtain a SIM card from any mobile phone shop to insert into your existing mobile phone for just JD10. It's easy to top up too. You'll then have your own Jordanian number and can make calls or send texts to anywhere in the world at much cheaper rates than you would if were using roaming with your existing network. Your mobile phone will need to be unlocked for you to do this, however.

To dial the emergency numbers while in Jordan simply call ☎191 for the police, ☎199 for an ambulance or the fire brigade, and ☎190 to report a traffic accident. Mobile phone signals are good in Jordan should you need to alert the emergency services. You can even get a strong signal in the wilderness of Wadi Rum, although be conscious of the fact that in places like canyons and deep valleys you may lose the connection.

Area telephone codes

Ajlun 2	Irbid 2	Madaba 5	Salt 5
Aqaba 3	Jerash 2	Mafraq 2	Tafila 3
Azraq 5	Karak 3	Petra 3	Wadi Rum 3
Amman 6	Ma'an 3	Ramtha 2	Zarqa 5

INTERNET Jordan has embraced internet technology and many homes and most businesses nowadays are connected to a fast broadband network. Around town, especially in Amman and Aqaba, and in hotel lobbies you'll see locals and visitors on their laptops surfing the net using Wi-Fi. Internet cafés are springing up, even in rural villages. They offer inexpensive, fast connection for just a few fils. If you are using your own laptop be sure to pack an adaptor as the British-style phone sockets are generally only found in new buildings, although most hotels have them in guestrooms. You can even pick up a mobile signal and log onto your email account in the Wadi Rum desert if you have roaming, although this option will be expensive.

BUSINESS

Under His Majesty King Abdullah II, Jordan has seen the development of a new business infrastructure designed for the global market. As a result, the country attracts multi-million dinar investment from major companies and is seen as a key regional business and economic hub. The strategic location of Jordan at the crossroads of Europe, Asia and the Middle East also makes it an important business centre. Amongst its main strategic investment areas are transportation, which includes upgrades of its airports and port at Aqaba, and the introduction of a railway link between Jordan and its neighbouring countries, along with sustainable energy in all its forms and tourism. One of the most successful initiatives in recent years has been the introduction of free trade zones. Jordan has a thriving phosphates industry and has become one of the largest producers and exporters of the mineral in the world. It has never lost sight of the importance of enterprise at a local level and new initiatives have been introduced for Jordanians, and significantly women, to start their own business in areas such as computing, manufacturing and tourism. For more information see *Economy*, page 28.

BUYING PROPERTY

Jordan's residential sales and leasing markets are relatively buoyant despite a world downturn and a short supply of new or good quality properties, which has been largely attributed to banks offering competitive finance packages. Interest rates in some cases have been 6–6.5% over a period of 20–25 years. The highest capital growth has been in business areas such as Amman's Abdoun district and Aqaba, both of which are locations for new build projects. Foreigners are permitted to buy property in Jordan, providing a reciprocal agreement is in place between the kingdom and the buyer's country of residence, and appropriate approval is obtained from the Council of Ministers. Resale by a foreign buyer is not permitted within five years of purchase.

CULTURAL ETIQUETTE

Jordanians are a friendly, respectful and hospitable people who you will find are almost always genuinely interested in you and your life. They will greet you with warmth and invite you to drink tea, eat dinner or visit their homes. If you are invited to someone's home you should dress conservatively and take a gift of pastries or fruit, a gift of a toy or stationery for your host's children or something from your own country, which you should give to your host on arrival. It would be inappropriate to take any form of alcohol. You will be regarded as the guest of honour, and be offered tea or coffee followed by several courses, which traditionally you would be expected to eat with your right hand. If you are dining in a hotel or restaurant rather than a private home you will find cutlery on the table more akin to the West.

Jordanians may ask you quite direct questions about your work and your family, and although this can come as a surprise to some, particularly reserved British visitors, it is not intended to be disrespectful – it is genuine interest. In turn, it is acceptable for you to reciprocate and you should show interest in your companion or host, and his or her life. Your interest will be met with beaming smiles and you will, almost without exception, be shown a picture of your host's children. However, it is considered impolite to talk at length about your or your host's marital relationship; this is considered private.

Similarly, it is considered inappropriate for a couple, even if they are married, to show affection or hold hands in public. Conversely, it is fine for same-sex friends to hold hands or touch; it is sign of their friendship, nothing more. Paying a compliment is fine and usually appreciated, but it is wise to avoid anything of a personal nature. This will be frowned upon, and may even be misunderstood if the words spoken are between a man and a woman (see *Women travellers*, page 65). Jordanians regard skimpy dress as immodest and even an insult, and you should always wear clothing that is appropriate (see *Women travellers* and *What to take*, pages 65 and 66). When visiting Jordan the rule is, quite simply, to be polite, courteous and show respect.

TRAVELLING POSITIVELY

JORDAN RIVER FOUNDATION (*www.jordanriver.jo*) Created with a mission to initiate and support sustainable social, economic and cultural programmes designed to enrich the lives and livelihoods of members of the communities, especially women and children, the JRF is a non-profit, non-government organisation chaired by Her Majesty Queen Rania al-Abdullah. You can help by becoming a member, donating your time in fundraising activities or volunteering to help with developing programmes that include the rehabilitation of victims of abuse, training and business start-ups.

ROYAL SOCIETY FOR THE CONSERVATION OF NATURE (*www.rscn.org.jo*) An independent, non-profit organisation, the RSCN aims to protect the delicate biodiversity of Jordan and to create conservation programmes that work alongside socio-economic development. It runs nature reserves designed to safeguard

STUFF YOUR RUCKSACK – AND MAKE A DIFFERENCE

The www.stuffyourrucksack.com website was set up by TV's Kate Humble to enable travellers to give direct help to small charities, schools or other organisations in the country they are visiting. Maybe a local school needs books, a map or pencils, or an orphanage needs children's clothes or toys – all things that can easily be 'stuffed in a rucksack' before departure. The charities get exactly what they need and travellers have the chance to meet local people and see how and where their gifts will be used.

The website describes organisations that would benefit from your help and lists the items they most need. Check what's required in Jordan, contact the organisation to say you're coming and bring not only the much-needed goods but an extra dimension to your travels and the knowledge that in a small way you have made a difference.

www.stuffyourrucksack.com
Responsible tourism in action

Jordan's heritage, runs breeding programmes for endangered species, enforces government laws banning illegal hunting, provides environmental education programmes and promotes initiatives that create jobs for rural communities in the fields of handicrafts and eco-tourism. You can help by visiting the reserves, buying authentic crafts or by becoming a 'friend' of the RSCN.

KING HUSSEIN CANCER FOUNDATION (*www.khcf.jo*) An independent, non-profit, non-government foundation, the KHCC was founded by Royal Degree in 1997 to help combat cancer and to offer care for sufferers in Jordan. Its mission is to educate, train and promote public awareness to aid the prevention and early detection of cancer, to supply information and research, and to provide comprehensive care. You can help KHCC by donating money online, donating through schemes operated by some hotels whereby a small sum in added to your bill, by volunteering to help patients or by donating blood.

AQABA BIRD OBSERVATORY (*www.jssd-jo.org*) Run by the Jordan Society for Sustainable Development (JSSD), this observatory in the southern city of Aqaba endeavours to preserve the natural habitat of birds. Wetlands with five ponds and dense forest areas have been created. It monitors birds and their migration patterns, and records details of Aqaba's fluctuating bird population, many of which are threatened or critically endangered species. The observatory, which is open to the public, welcomes volunteers to help with its valuable conservation work.

A world wonder
in the morning

feet up in the afternoon

The 'rose red city' of Petra was recently named as one of the new 7 Wonders of the World. Once you've experienced this extraordinary place, where history has been carved from the rock itself, you'll understand why.

Finish off a memorable day with a float in the famed Dead Sea, the lowest point on Earth, and watch the setting sun disappear over the hazy mountains.

For more information call 020 7223 1878
or visit www.visitjordan.com

visit Jordan

Part Two

THE GUIDE

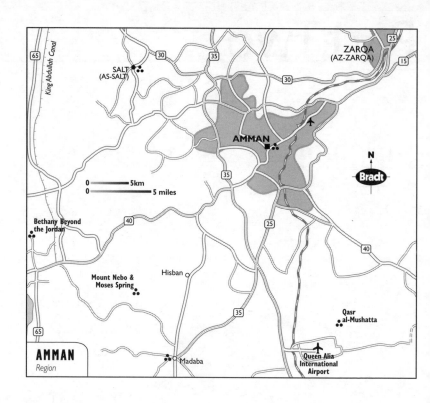

3

Amman

Telephone code: 06

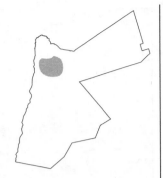

In the morning you could explore a bustling bazaar and secure a bargain Bedouin rug, then take a baguette and cappuccino lunch in a swish bistro restaurant, before spending the afternoon immersed in history at one of Amman's ancient Roman, Byzantine or Islamic sites. You might then enjoy modern art in one of the city's many galleries, and afterwards take in a literary evening or mingle with the crowds along fashionable Abu Bakr As Siddeeq Street, better known as **Rainbow Street** or Al-Rainbow Street. Later you could enjoy a gourmet meal before heading back to your ultra-modern hotel. Yes, Amman, which held the UNESCO title of Arab Cultural Capital in 2002, is a city that lives life in a 21st-century fashion, while celebrating its remarkable history extremely well.

Amman lounges over seven fertile hills, known as *jabal* or *jebel* (Arabic *jah-bahl*), that lie between the desert sands of the east and the Jordan Valley. Each quarter is named after the *jabal* on which it sits. The main thoroughfare linking one side of Amman with the other has a series of roundabouts, called Circles (*duwaar*). They give their name to the immediate area around the Circle. For example, the first roundabout you come to from the eastern side of the city is 1st Circle, which is an area of Downtown Amman; the second, 2nd Circle, is a part of Abdali, and so on. It is a busy city, but one that is surprisingly easy to navigate and most of the main sights are within easy reach of each other.

A thriving city since the time of Iron Age man, Amman can claim to be one of the oldest continuously inhabited cities in the world. It is full to the brim with archaeological sites. Most are centred around the oldest part of the city, Downtown. Here you can visit **Citadel Hill**, locally known as Jabal al-Qal'a, that towers over the city and tempts you with the remains of ancient buildings and huge defensive walls to explore. Two of the finest remains are the Umayyad Palace and the massive Temple of Hercules. In the grounds is a tiny church dated to Byzantine times, and the **Jordan Archaeological Museum**, which houses a quite remarkable collection of artefacts. At the foot of the walls of Citadel Hill is one of the major landmarks of Amman, its Roman Theatre.

Amman is the cultural centre of Jordan, with musical and theatrical venues found in the modern heart of the city alongside trendy international restaurants and luxury hotels. There are also a number of museums that celebrate its history and culture. Along with the Jordan Archaeological Museum on Citadel Hill, there is the **Jordan Folklore Museum**; the **Jordan Museum of Popular Tradition**, which give valuable insights into how life has been for dwellers of villages and the deserts over the centuries; the **Jordan National Gallery of Fine Arts** with its extensive collection of works; the **Children's Museum**; and the **Royal Automobile Museum** where recent history is told with the help of vehicle displays. Jordan's largest mosque, the 19th-century King Hussein I Mosque, can also be visited.

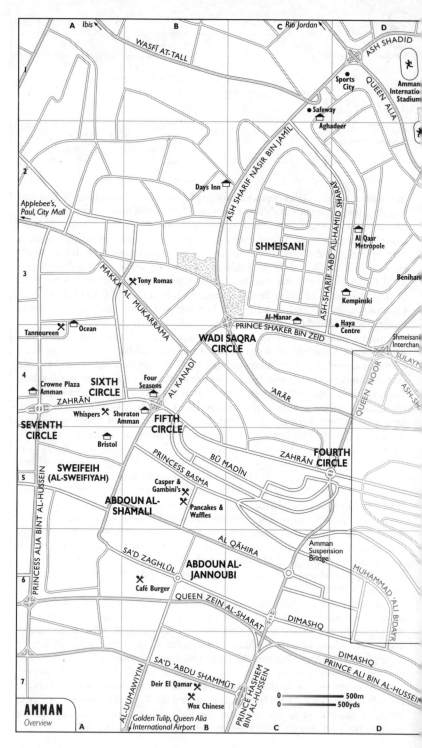

AMMAN
Overview

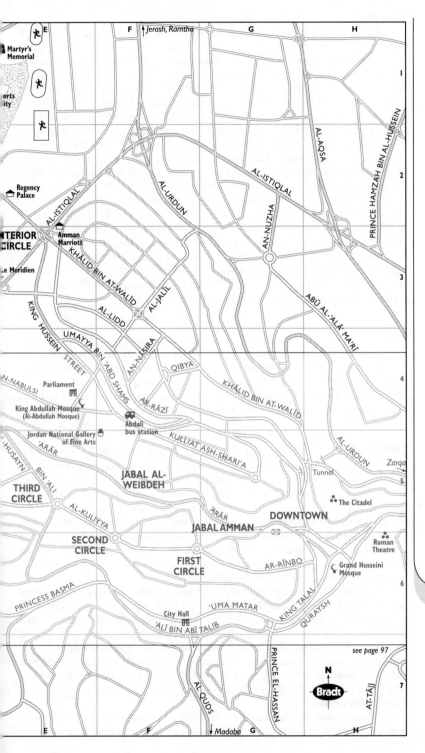

see page 97

Amman

3

Amman today is home to around 2.2 million multi-cultural people, the vast majority of whom are well-travelled, well-educated and keep the wheels of the country turning smoothly. The shiny, contemporary buildings in the commercial heart of the city testify to it being the business, political and economic hub of Jordan. Some are skyscrapers of 20 or more storeys, which is significant given the fact that until recently no building in Amman could be built more than four storeys high. A change of heart came when the powers that be decided to elevate Amman to the world stage for business, and with it the need to provide more office space of a calibre to attract major companies. Its main business districts are Abdali and the Shmeisani and Sweifieh (also known as Al-Sweifiyah) financial districts. The city's contemporary office buildings sit comfortably with artisans' workshops where potters display their skills and painters enthral you with their attention to detail.

Around three million more people live in the towns and villages that form the 27 districts of the Great Amman Municipality. Some of these suburbs are characterised by wide palm tree-lined avenues full of million-dinar houses, embassies and banks, such as seen in the Abdoun al-Shamali and Abdoun al-Jannoubi districts to the southwest of the city, while others are a mass of family homes interspersed by highways and green parks. The largest suburb outside Amman central is Zarqa, an easy 30-minute drive away and where many of the 'commuter' workers who keep Amman ticking over during working hours live.

HISTORY

Amman has a rich history that evidence suggests began in Neolithic times some 10,000 years BC. It continued to thrive during the Iron Age when it was known as Rabbath Ammon, and later took the name of Philadelphia when it became one of the Greco-Roman city-kingdoms of the Decapolis era. It became known by its present name when the Umayyad Caliphate was established in early Islamic times around AD661.

EARLY HISTORY The focal point of Neolithic inhabitation was Ain Ghazal, which lies just on the eastern outskirts of present-day Amman. This site was discovered in the 1970s when the land was being cleared and prepared for the construction of homes. Building work was halted to make way for a series of excavations that subsequently revealed Ain Ghazal to have once been a thriving community in Neolithic times. The remains of numerous homes were discovered over a site approaching 16ha in size. They have been dated to around 7,000BC. The number was so great as to suggest that these homes probably housed 2,500–3,000 people at one time. The homes would have been made of mud fashioned into bricks of various size, and painted inside with a lime plaster to reinforce the strength of the wall.

One of the most important finds at Ain Ghazal, and one that has given the world the most graphic insight into the culture of this ancient people, was the discovery of a large pit containing anthropomorphic (human-like) plaster statues. In total there were 32 figures discovered. They were made with reeds, probably bound together with twine, and then layered with lime plaster. Around 0.6–0.9m (2–3ft) in height, they appear to have a wax-like surface where the plaster has worn smooth over time. Some have features like painted hair, and eyes made from shells lined with black bitumen. The figures are now on display in the Jordan Archaeological Museum on Citadel Hill.

The countryside of Ain Ghazal in Neolithic times would have been used for farming. Neolithic culture was strong in the Levant and was a time of considerable human advancement, most notably in the realm of agriculture. Communities started to use and cultivate cereals to supplement their diet of mainly wild deer, horse meat and fruits, and although restricted to wheat species like spelt and einkorn, along with chickpeas, barley and cereal millet, it meant that these early civilisations started to enjoy a healthier way of life. Over time, this primitive form of agriculture gave rise to the farming of sheep and goats, cattle and pigs. Other than the figures of Ain Ghazal, there are no other recorded finds from the Neolithic period, but what there is gives an insight into this innovative culture and how it helped shape the history of Jordan.

IRON AGE, PERSIAN AND HELLENISTIC ERAS The Iron Age could be said to be the city's, and indeed the kingdom's, first golden era. Present-day Amman is built on the site of Rabbath Ammon, the capital of the ancient city-kingdom Ammon, which was created in the Iron Age by the Ammonites. Along with the city-kingdoms of Moab and Edom founded by the Moabites and the Edomites according to the Hebrew Bible, Ammon became a powerful entity. It was during this period that the famous King's Highway was created as a trade route between the three kingdoms and their neighbours. The route stretched from Heliopolis in Egypt, across the Sinai until it reached present-day Jordan, then through the three kingdoms to the northern cities of Gerasa (Jerash), Bosra and Damascus in Syria. It culminated in the ancient city-kingdom of Rasafa, located in present-day Syria.

Rabbath Ammon was an important stop for travelling merchants and their camels, and became wealthy as a result. According to the Old Testament, in Amos 1:14, Jeremiah 49:2 and 3, and Ezekiel 21:20 and 25:5, King David (circa b1040BC, d970BC), the ruler of the Kingdom of Israel, coveted Rabbath Ammon and attacked and conquered the city. Over the next few decades, particularly during the Persian and Hellenistic periods, Rabbath Ammon had mixed fortunes and went into decline. Today, there are no remains from the Persian period and just handful from the Greek period.

NABATEAN, ROMAN AND BYZANTINE ERAS Rabbath Ammon's fortunes changed with the arrival of the Nabateans from southern Jordan and Arabia, and the Romans from Europe. It now became known as Philadelphia after the Ptolemic ruler of Egypt, King Ptolemy II Philadelphus (309BC–246BC), an ally of the empire. During the Nabatean period (312BC–AD106) and the overlapping Roman period (63BC–AD324), Amman was extensively rebuilt in an architectural style that reflected the classical lines that had become fashionable in Europe. Streets and marketplaces were created and homes and immense temples, such as the Temple of Hercules in Amman's Citadel, were built. It was a time of great prosperity.

By the time the country entered its Byzantine period (AD324–635) the city was one of the most important in the region, so much so that when Christianity became the dominant religion of the empire, Philadelphia became the seat of a bishopric. The city would have been divided into parishes, each probably having its own place of worship and run under the direction of a bishop. The best preserved Byzantine church can be seen in the Citadel. You can clearly see its basilica-style plan and the remains of its Corinthian capitals.

UMAYYAD, ABBASID, FATIMID AND AYYUBID DYNASTIES Philadelphia continued to prosper, so when the first caliphates of the early Islamic period were established in AD661 the city became key to the new empire. It also became

RABBATH AMMON		AMMAN	
5500–4500BC	Pottery Neolithic	AD661–750	Umayyad
4500–3300BC	Chalcolithic	AD750–969	Abbasid
3300–1200BC	Bronze Age	AD968–1171	Fatimid
1200–539BC	Iron Age	1171–1263	Ayyubid
539–332BC	Persian	1250–1516	Mamluk period
332–63BC	Hellenistic	1516–1917	Ottoman period

PHILADELPHIA	
312BC–AD106	Nabatean
AD63–324	Rome
AD324–635	Byzantine

known by its present name, that of Amman. The first caliphate, the Umayyads (AD661–750), had its capital in Damascus in Syria, but it was keen to establish a military sector away from the capital and so created the district of Jund Dimashq in Amman's al-Belqa area.

The city became the seat of a provincial governor, who resided in the palace now known as the Umayyad Complex in the city's Citadel. Today, you can see the remains of the palace with its elaborate entrance, reception and throne rooms, a souk, hammam and a mosque. For a while Amman remained important to the caliphate, but gradually over time it fell into decline as the subsequent caliphates, the Abbasids (AD750–969) who had the centre of power in Baghdad, the Fatimids (AD968–1171) from Tunisia and Egypt, and the Ayyubids (1171–1263) from Egypt concentrated their efforts on their own local capital cities.

OTTOMANS Amman once again came to prominence during the Ottoman period (1516–1917) when the famous Hejaz Railway was built in 1900. Linking Damascus in Syria with Medina, the railway was the brainchild of the Ottoman Empire's Sultan Abdul Hamid II (b1842, d1918). His plan was to link his capital Constantinople, present-day Istanbul, with the holy city of Makkah so that pilgrims heading through the rugged terrain of the Midian region and Hejaz Mountains to attend Hajj could travel more quickly and easily. The railway was never completed, but important for Amman was that the track passed through the city and it became a popular stopping off point. Today the track carries trains to Damascus for passenger travel and to Aqaba in the south of Jordan for cargo.

MODERN HISTORY With the collapse of the Ottoman Empire and the kingdom becoming firstly an emirate and then the Hashemite Kingdom of Jordan in 1950 as a result of the creation of the League of Nations, the new king, King Abdullah I, declared Amman as his capital city. At the time it was little more than a provincial size town and the king immediately set about building an infrastructure worthy of a capital city. It was from Amman that he successfully conquered the West Bank and parts of Jerusalem, territories that were later annexed to Israel and their Palestinian Arab residents offered sanctuary in Jordan. His successors King Talal I, King Hussein I and the present king, His Majesty King Abdullah II, who ascended to the throne on 7 February 1999, have all ruled from Amman and presided over its growth to become one of the foremost cities of the Middle East.

BY AIR Most flights, other than a small number that fly into Aqaba's **King Hussein International Airport** in the south of the country, arrive into the Queen Alia International Airport in Amman. More than 34 airlines fly here from the Middle East and Europe, and as far afield as the USA, Canada, Hong Kong and Thailand, India, Russia and north Africa. The airport lies just off the highway that links Amman with Aqaba, around 32km south of the city centre. A 24-hour express bus service (*every 30mins 07.00–20.00 & every 60mins 20.00–07.00; journey time 30mins; 500 fils per passenger*) operates from outside the terminal to Amman's main Abdali bus station. Car-hire companies are inside the terminal if you plan to hire a car straight from the airport, and taxis are available outside. Expect to pay around JD10 for a private cab (see *Getting there and away*, page 50, for more information).

BY TRAIN Jordan has only one option for travelling into Amman by train: the **Hejaz Railway**. Using restored locomotives that trundle along the same tracks laid by the Ottomans over 100 years ago (see opposite), the Hejaz Railway runs from Damascus to Amman once a week. You can board a train at the central station in Damascus at 07.30 on a Sunday morning, and arrive in Amman at around 17.00 that afternoon. Tickets cost JD2.500 and are available from the railway station on the day of departure only (see *Getting there and away*, page 52, for more information).

BY TAXI OR BUS Arriving into Amman by taxi or bus from neighbouring countries is possible, and relatively inexpensive. Although taxis in Jordan work on the meter, you may need to check if using a local firm in Syria, Saudi Arabia or Iraq. As a guide, expect to pay around JD60 for a trip from Damascus to Amman using a Jordanian operator, and about JD30 from the King Hussein Bridge (Allenby Bridge). Shared service taxis are cheaper. Expect to pay around JD12 and JD7 per person respectively for the same journeys, but you can negotiate a price if you want the vehicle to yourself. In terms of travelling time, allow around eight hours from Damascus and about an hour from the King Hussein Bridge.

One of the main providers of long-distance buses is the **Jordan Express Tourist Transportation Company** (JETT), which runs air-conditioned buses between Damascus in Syria, the cities of Riyad, Jeddah and Dammam in Saudi Arabia, Baghdad in Iraq, Cairo in Egypt and Beirut in Lebanon into Amman's Abdali bus station [97 D1]. If you are travelling to Amman from Israel or the Palestinian Territories, you will need to take a local bus or taxis from Damascus Gate in East Jerusalem to the King Hussein Bridge (Allenby Bridge), and take a Jordanian taxi to Amman (see *Getting there and away*, page 53 for more information).

BY CAR Providing you have all your car documents, insurance, an international driving licence, observe customs and highway regulations and cross at the correct border crossings, you should be able to drive your car over the Jordanian border and into Amman without issue. Driving time into Amman from the Syrian border is around one to two hours, from Israel around one hour depending on which crossing you take, about six hours from the Iraqi border and three to six hours from Saudi Arabia. Remember not all crossings are open 24 hours (see *Border crossings*, page 47). Alternatively, there are plenty of car-hire companies in Amman should you prefer to arrive by plane, bus, taxi or train before picking up your vehicle (see *Getting around*, page 67 for more information).

BY TAXI By far the easiest way to get around Amman is by taxi. It's a relatively inexpensive way to travel, providing you stay within the city limits. Go beyond and you'll probably pay a premium. Taxis have a meter, which your driver should switch on as soon as you get in the vehicle. If they don't then request they do. The meter starts at 150 fils and you'll be able to see exactly what your fare will be at any point along your journey. Unfortunately, the driver is only obliged to switch on the meter within the city limits, so be sure to negotiate a fare if you're planning to hire the taxi for a longer journey. You'll see the bright **yellow taxis** everywhere and you can simply flag one down or have your hotel telephone for one to pick you up from your hotel.

You may see taxis parked outside hotels; apply a little caution here as often these drivers are targeting tourists and probably think they can get away with not putting the meter on and charging more than you should have to pay. Another word of caution if you are a woman: always sit in the back of the vehicle so there is no misunderstanding about your friendliness. A Jordanian woman would never dream of sitting in the front with the driver.

A cheaper option is the white *serveeces* taxis, which take set routes around the city picking up and dropping off passengers along the way. Almost all routes include Downtown Amman and the Abdali bus station [97 D1]. They are shared so don't be surprised to see other passengers already inside if you decide to hail one for your journey. *Serveeces* taxis will display their destination and route numbers, but they will be in Arabic, so prepare yourself so you know what to look out for if you're planning to use them during your stay. Typically, a fare will cost no more than 120 fils.

BY BUS Buses around Amman take the form of a shared minibus. They are comfortable, inexpensive and reliable. The downside is that they have the destination and route number in Arabic on the front so it may take a little working out as to where they are going. If you see much larger buses then these will be for longer distance travel to places like Aqaba, the Dead Sea and Irbid. Timetables for local services with route numbers are available from the Abdali bus station [97 D1]. Fares are roughly equivalent to the *serveeces* taxis so expect to pay no more than 120 fils. For a list of bus companies in Amman, see page 71.

BY CAR Although car hire in Jordan can be a little more expensive than in Europe, it is a convenient way to get around Amman and gives you the option to go further afield too. There are **car-hire** companies inside the terminal at the Queen Alia International Airport, plus a car collection area if you've booked in advance. Companies are dotted around Amman too. Rental cars have green number plates with yellow writing, whereas local privately owned vehicles have white number plates. Be sure to check the contract, in particular with regard to the number of free kilometres you can do before you are charged. The cost of the extra kilometres over and above your free ones can be exceptionally high. You should also ensure you have adequate insurance. Costs for hiring a medium-sized car for the day vary, but typically will be around JD30–40. For a little extra you can hire the services of a driver too. Driving in Amman, like the rest of Jordan, is on the right.

See page 71 for more information on car hire in Jordan.

Petrol stations

Alborj 7th Circle; ☎ 06 581 0531
Al Bayader Al-Sinna St; ☎ 06 565 0902

Khalad Al-Assaf Wasfi al-Tal St, Tla'a al-Ali; ☎ 06 552 6888

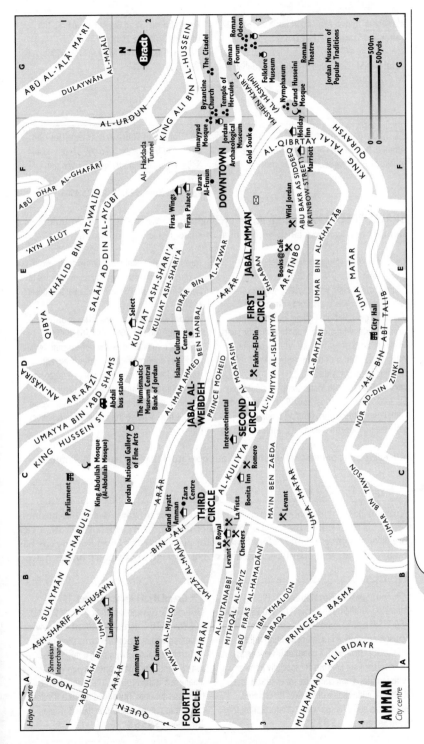

AMMAN
City centre

FOURTH CIRCLE

THIRD CIRCLE

SECOND CIRCLE

FIRST CIRCLE

JABAL AMMAN

DOWNTOWN

JABAL AL-WEIBDEH

Hoya Centre

Shmeisani Interchange

Amman West

Landmark

Cameo

Parliament

King Abdullah Mosque (Al-Abdullah Mosque)

Jordan National Gallery of Fine Arts

Abdali bus station

The Numismatics Museum Central Bank of Jordan

Al Iman Ahmed Ben Hanbal

Islamic Cultural Centre

Select

Grand Hyatt Amman

Zara Centre

Le Royal

Levant

La Vista

Chesters

Bonita Inn

Romero

Levant

Intercontinental

Fakhr-El-Din

City Hall

AR-RINBO

Books@Café

Wild Jordan

ABU BAKR AS SIDDEEQ (RAINBOW STREET)

Holiday Inn

Marriott

Firas Wings

Firas Palace

Darat Al-Funun

Umayyad Mosque

Jordan Archaeological Museum

Gold Souk

Byzantine Church

The Citadel

Temple of Hercules

Roman Forum

Roman Odeon

Folklore Museum

Nymphaeum

Grand Husseini Mosque

Roman Theatre

Jordan Museum of Popular Traditions

Al-Haddada Tunnel

N

Bradt

0   500m
0   500yds

Manaseer Queen Alia Airport Rd; 📞 06 565 0902
Taher Gas Station Prince El Hassan St, Al-Zohoor; 📞 06 477 2241
Total Gas Station Queen Rania al-Abdullah St, m 078 578 8289

Um Uthaina Sa'ad Bin Abi Waqqas St, Um Uthaina; 📞 06 552 2508
Zahran Gas Station Zahran St, Sweifieh; 📞 06 581 2539

TOURIST INFORMATION

The Jordan Tourist Board 11183 Amman; 📞 06 567 8444; f 06 567 8295; e info@visitjordan.com; www.visitjordan.com

Ministry of Tourism & Antiquities 3rd Circle, 11118 Amman; 📞 06 460 3360; f 06 464 8465; e contacts@mota.gov.jo; www.mota.gov.jo
Petra Rent a Car 📞 03 215 4545

TRAVEL SPECIALISTS From group cycling trips to wellbeing trips, Amman has a number of travel specialists who can tailor-make a package, including:

Cycling Jordan Mujama Jaber, Makka Al-Mukarrama St; m 078 555 2525; e info@cycling-jordan.com; www.cycling-jordan.com. A specialist in cycle tours from Amman over a day or longer duration, Cycling Jordan provides expert guides who are passionate about the sport to escort small groups of like-minded people through the country's countryside. Bikes & helmets can be provided.
Jordan Tours Amin Marie Complex, Boumedin St; 📞 06 593 8238; f 06 592 0704; e info@jdtours.com; www.jdtours.com. Offering tailor-made sightseeing tours from its base in Amman, this

travel specialist works with individuals as well as small groups wanting independent travel to places like Jerash, Petra & the far eastern desert castles.
Terhaal Adventures 48 Ali Nasuh al-Tahir St, Sweifieh; 📞 06 581 3061; f 06 581 2048; e team@terhaal.com; www.terhaal.com. Terhaal is a travel agency that specialises in adventure travel in Jordan. Based in Amman, it organises everything from camping trips to cycling, climbing, scuba diving, canyoning, sightseeing tours, camel & horse treks, jeep tours & balloon rides.

See *Chapter 2*, page 44 for additional tour operators that are based in Amman.

WHERE TO STAY

Amman has a wide choice when it comes to places to stay. As a major business centre of the Middle East and a location of choice for travellers either on a city break or stopping a while before heading for places like the Dead Sea, the city has establishments that offer basic amenities right through to top-notch luxury hotels.

LUXURY

Four Seasons Hotel Amman [90 B4] (192 rooms) Al-Kindi St, 5th Circle; 📞 06 550 5555; f 06 550 5556; e pabx.amm@fourseasons.com; www.fourseasons.com. A landmark building right off the 5th Circle with a panoramic view across the city, the Four Seasons is especially popular with families. From child-size robes to soft toys, it offers a wide choice of services for children. Adults can enjoy its spa where products from the Dead Sea are used. **$$$$$**

Grand Hyatt Amman Hotel [97 C2] (361 rooms) Hussein Bin Ali St; 📞 06 465 1234; f 06 465 1634; e geruschkat@hyatt.com; www.amman.grand.hyatt.com. With its sumptuous guestrooms, sauna, swimming pools, fitness suite & speciality restaurants serving Vietnamese, Milanese & Italian cuisine, the Grand Hyatt is truly international. The added bonus is it's close to Amman's shops, exhibition halls & its main attractions. **$$$$$**

🏠 **Kempinski Hotel Amman** [90 D3] (256 rooms) Abdul Hamid Shouman St, Shmeisani; ☎ 06 520 0200; f 06 520 0203; e reservations. amman@kempinski.com; www.kempinski.com. Housed in an architecturally striking building in the city centre & offering a sense of luxury, the Kempinski tempts guests with its Kempi Spa, beauty & fitness centre, eclectic bars & restaurants. There's also a bowling alley & entertainment centre. **$$$$$**

🏠 **Le Royal Hotel Amman** [97 B3] (281 rooms) Zahran St, 3rd Circle; ☎ 06 460 3000; f 06 460 3002; e info@leroyalamman.com; www.leroyalamman.com. A luxurious hotel just a few kilometres from the main attractions of Amman & its Abdali business district, the Le Royal offers beautifully presented guestrooms & lots of amenities. Its Royal Spa is on site for a spot of pampering, before choosing your dining preference from 11 different restaurants, including its Italian La Vista & its French Le Trianon. **$$$$$**

🏠 **Regency Palace** [91 E2] (251 rooms) Queen Alia St; ☎ 06 560 7000; f 06 566 0013; e info@theregencyhotel.com; www. theregencyhotel.com. Housed in a classical building that has been extensively refurbished, the Regency Palace is located in central Amman, right next to the Royal Cultural Centre. Its Le Piano Lounge & Ernesto Cigar Club are popular with locals as well as guests. Rooms are lavish & well-equipped. Its swimming pool on the 19th floor offers panoramic views. **$$$$$**

🏠 **Sheraton Amman Al Nabil Hotel & Tower** [90 B4] (425 rooms) Zahran St, 5th Circle; ☎ 06 593 4111; f 06 593 4222; e reservations.amman. jordan@starwoodhotel.scom; www.sheraton. com. A 5-star hotel, the Sheraton provides every amenity you would expect of a hotel in this class. Its guestrooms are fully equipped & have high-speed internet. Guests can enjoy cocktails & soft music in its Green Lounge & Asian food in its Sanctuary Lounge. Its 4Walls art gallery is one of the trendiest in the city. **$$$$$**

UPMARKET

🏠 **Bristol Hotel** [90 A5] (170 rooms) 5th Circle, behind Arab Medical Centre; ☎ 06 592 3400; f 06 592 3717; e bristol@bristolamman. com; www.bristolamman.com. Located close to the city's shopping & business areas, the Bristol offers accommodation in a period-style ambiance. Its richly decorated rooms & facilities, including its Luna Lounge overlooking a swimming pool & sun terrace, offer a sense of luxury. Relax in its Panacea Health Club. **$$$$**

🏠 **Crowne Plaza Amman** [90 A4] (279 rooms) King Faisal Bin Abdul Aziz St, 6th Circle; ☎ 06 551 0001; f 06 551 0003; e ammhb@ cpamman.com; www.crowneplaza.com. Occupying the highest spot in Amman, the Crowne Plaza takes full advantage of its vantage point with the rooftop Al Halabi restaurant. Dine on Jordanian & Syrian delicacies while admiring the fantastic view. Leisure time can be spent in its spa & health suite. Located mins from the shopping malls & attractions. **$$$$**

🏠 **Holiday Inn Amman** [97 F8] (200 rooms) Madina Al-Munawarah St; ☎ 06 552 8822; f 06 552 9944; e hotel@haimman.com; www. holidayinn.com. One of 2 Holiday Inns in the city, & complete with a Roman-themed restaurant, health suite, spa, business centre & swimming pool, this hotel makes a pleasing place to stay while in the city. It is near the business district & within easy reach of the Citadel. **$$$$**

🏠 **Intercontinental Hotel Amman** [97 C3] (440 rooms) Islamic College St; ☎ 06 464 1361; f 06 464 5217; e ammha@icjordan.com; www.intercontinental.com. A sprawling hotel that offers every amenity, from Wi-Fi to a spa designed as a sanctuary, 24-hr gym & a choice of restaurants, including the much-respected Cinco de Mayo, which specialises in Mexican cuisine, & the Indu, where delicious Indian food is served. The hotel is conveniently located in Downtown Amman. **$$$$**

🏠 **Landmark Hotel Amman** [97 B1] (260 rooms) Al-Hussein Bin Ali St, Shmeisani; ☎ 06 560 7100; f 06 566 5160; e info@landmarkamman. com; www.landmarkamman.com. One of Amman's newest hotels, the centrally located Landmark has a contemporary décor with amenities that include an open-air swimming pool, spa & fitness centre. Local Jordanian, European & gourmet Turkish cuisine are just some of the dining options, plus its conference facilities are considered top notch. **$$$$**

🏠 **Le Meridien Amman Hotel** [91 E3] (350 rooms) Queen Noor St, Shmeisani; ☎ 06 569 6511; f 06 567 4261; e meridien@lemeridien_ amman.com; www.lemeridien_amman.com.

Located in the modern heart of the city & just a short distance from Downtown Amman, the Le Meridian is a spacious hotel that offers excellent guest amenities. There are restaurants, including Benihana, a cosy Japanese eatery where you can see *teppanyaki* being prepared, along with a colourful health suite. On site is the Royal Convention Centre. **$$$$**

MID RANGE

🏠 **Aghadeer Hotel** [90 C1] (46 rooms) Sharif Nasir Ben Jameel St, Shmeisani; ☏06 568 3386; f 06 560 4136; e info@aghadeerhotel.com; www.agadeerhotel.com. Close to the business centre, major attractions & shopping malls, the Agadeer is a compact hotel that specialises in welcoming guests with Arabic hospitality. Its restaurant serves local dishes that have been handed down through the family. Rooms are comfortable & well equipped. **$$$**

🏠 **Al Qasr Metropole Hotel** [90 D3] (70 rooms), Al-Nakabat St, Shmeisani; ☏06 568 9671; f 06 568 9673; e alqasr@alqasrmetropole. com; www.alqasrmetropole.com. A boutique-style hotel in the Shmeisani district, the Al Qasr is popular with both leisure & business travellers. Its rooftop restaurant, Vinaigrette, has one of the best panoramic views in Amman. Rooms are cosy & have internet connection. A gym is on site. **$$$**

🏠 **Amman Marriott Hotel** [97 F3] (267 rooms) Isam Aijuni St, Shmeisani; ☏06 560 7607; f 06 567 0100; e amman@marriotthotel. com; www.marriotthotels.com. Like many of the hotels in Amman, the Marriott has full Wi-Fi in all public areas (wired in guestrooms). It offers free valet parking, a host of restaurants, including its Villa Mediterrano with an exhibition-style kitchen, plush guestrooms & a health suite. Located in central Amman. **$$$**

🏠 **Amman West Hotel** [97 A2] (51 rooms) Mahmoud Abidi St, 4th Circle; ☏06 465 7615; f 06 465 7581; e info@ammanwesthotel.com; www.ammanwesthotel.com. This welcoming hotel has undergone a complete refurbishment to provide pleasing guestrooms with amenities that include AC. Its shiny foyer leads through to the garden terrace & swimming pool. Guests can enjoy its NEWS restaurant where local & international cuisine is served, & its cosy Pizza Vino bar. **$$$**

🏠 **Days Inn Hotel** [90 B2] (112 rooms) Oman Bin Abdul Aziz St; ☏06 551 9011; f 06 551 7077; e info@daysinn.com.jo; www.daysinn. jo. Amenities at this hotel not far from Sports City include its Cali Restaurant & Bar where live Arab music is played most evenings. Guests are encouraged to dance the night away. It has its own fitness centre & an outdoor swimming pool. High-speed Wi-Fi available. **$$$**

🏠 **Golden Tulip Airport-Amman** (307 rooms) Queen Alia International Airport; ☏06 445 1000; f 06 445 1029; e info@ goldentulipairportamman.com; www. goldentulipairportamman.com. Located within the airport area & providing contemporary & well-equipped guestrooms, business facilities, a health suite & dining options, including its atmospheric Ristretto Café, the Golden Tulip is ideal for leisure or business travellers on a schedule. **$$$**

BUDGET

🏠 **Al-Manar Hotel** [90 C4] (28 rooms) Shmeisani St; ☏06 566 2186; f 06 568 4329; e info@almanarhotel.com; www.almanarhotel. com. A beautifully presented hotel, the Al-Manar offers good value for money. It is centrally located. Guestrooms have AC & private bathrooms, plus cable TV. There's free Wi-Fi in its spacious foyer & a restaurant overlooking a small pool. **$$**

🏠 **Cameo Hotel** [97 A2] (38 rooms) Mahmoud Abidi St, 4th Circle; ☏06 464 4579; f 06 462 2638; e cameohotel@yahoo; www. cameohotel.com. Relax in the 'home from home' ambiance of Cameo's apartment-style rooms furnished with contemporary furnishings & equipped with AC. Dine in its traditional styled Caravanserai restaurant where classic Jordanian dishes are served. **$$**

🏠 **Firas Palace Hotel** [97 F2] (80 rooms) Off King Hussein St, Jabal Al-Weibdeh; ☏06 465 0404; f 06 465 0122; e info@firaspalace. com; www.firaspalace.com. Facing the Citadel & the Roman Theatre, the views from most of its rooms & restaurant are good, especially when the monuments are lit up at night. The hotel has a small gym & a bazaar shop. **$$**

🏠 **Hotel Ibis** (158 rooms) 61 Mohamed Fayagh al-Assaf St; ☏06 579 9090; f 06 579 9099; e H6313@accor.com; www.ibishotel.com. This new, modern hotel has soundproofed, well-equipped guestrooms, plus a host of communal facilities & all at a budget price. Its Open Pasta & Grill Restaurant & its Café 24/7 have become firm favourites amongst locals. Located near the Amman Mall. **$$**

🏠 **Ocean Hotel** [90 B4] (24 rooms) Um Uthaina, Atetirya St; 📞06 551 7280; 📠06 551 7380; 📧 info@oceanhotel.com.jo; www. oceanhotel.com.jo. A 3-star hotel with the feel of a 5-star establishment, this super hotel has plush guestrooms & suites. It has the atmospheric Diwan Sultan Ibrahim Restaurant, where classic Lebanese dishes are served, the moody Katze Bar & a courtyard garden. **$$**

SHOESTRING

🏠 **Bonita Inn** [97 C3] (6 rooms) Queen Zain St; 📞06 461 5061; 📠06 461 5060; 📧 info@ bonitaamman.com; www.bonitaamman.com. One of the city's trendiest tapas restaurants & bars, the Bonita Inn also welcomes guests to stay. Its inexpensive rooms are equipped with Wi-Fi, satellite TV, AC & walk-in showers, & the décor is modern & tasteful. Meals are taken in its tapas restaurant overlooking a garden terrace. **$**

🏠 **Firas Wings** [97 F2] (30 rooms) Off King Hussein St, Jabal Al-Weibdeh; 📞06 465 0404;

📠 06 465 0122; 📧 info@firaspalace.com; www. firaspalace.com. Located next door to the Firas Palace Hotel & mins from the Citadel & Roman Theatre, this purpose-designed collection of studios offers convenience & good value. Studios are equipped with AC, satellite TV & private bathroom. 24-hr room service. **$**

🏠 **Rio Jordan Hotel** (50 rooms) Queen Rania al-Abdullah St; 📞06 534 3291; 📠06 534 2262; 📧 info@riojordan-hotel.com; www.riojordan-hotel.com. This welcoming hotel is a short distance from the city centre. It offers rooms that are pleasingly decorated, with AC & TV. Wi-Fi is available. Guests can enjoy Arabic cuisine in its spacious Rio Restaurant & snacks & soft drinks in its Rio Square Café. **$**

🏠 **Select Hotel** [97 D2] (25 rooms) 52 Baoniya St, Jabal Al-Weibdeh; 📞06 463 7101; 📠06 463 7102; 📧 info@select-amman.com; www.select-amman.com. This traditional hotel is 15mins or so walk from Downtown Amman in an area buzzing with restaurants. Its own restaurant is homely & serves local dishes. There's an attractive outdoor terrace where you can chill, while in the evening guests tend to congregate in its small bar. **$**

✘ WHERE TO EAT

Whether it's local dishes such as *kibbeh*, *fuul* or *falafel* served with *tabbouleh*, or it's a classic Spanish, Italian, French, Indian or Oriental dish that is tempting your tastebuds, then you are sure to find a restaurant to suit you in Amman. Its restaurants, like its people, are either traditional or ultra cosmopolitan, but all are gloriously multi-cultural.

EXPENSIVE

✘ **Benihana** [90 D3] Le Meridien Amman; Queen Noor St, Shmeisani; 📞06 569 6511; 📧 info@lemeridienamman.com; www.lemeridien. com; ⊕ 12.30–23.30 daily. Be entertained as chefs prepare sushi & cook *teppanyaki* in front of you, their audience, in this atmospheric award-winning eatery. Try the crispy *tempura*, which is recommended. The restaurant's décor is black & red in a Japanese style, with a water cascade as a focal point. **$$$$$**

✘ **Casper & Gambini's** [90 B5] Mazen Sido al-Kurdi St, Abdoun; 📞06 592 2600; www. casperandgambinis.com; ⊕ 08.00–01.00 daily. Serving a mix of classic Jordanian & international dishes prepared with careful regard to nutritional

levels, this is an elegant yet unpretentious eatery in the heart of upmarket Abdoun. Be sure to try one of its combos, a presentation of 3 dishes that include a salad, main course of rice topped with meat or seafood & a mini cheesecake or chocolate cake. **$$$$$**

✘ **Chesters** [97 B3] Zahran St, 3rd Circle; 📞06 460 3000; 📧 info@leroyalamman.com; www. leroyalamman.com; ⊕ 11.00–23.30 daily. Relax in the moody atmosphere of Chesters, a luxurious steak & cigar house that has been designed to resemble a traditional English study. Soft jazz plays in the background. Steaks with all the trimmings are served accompanied by fine wines & your choice from a selection of whiskies. **$$$$$**

✘ **La Vista** [97 C3] Zahran St, 3rd Circle; ☎06 460 3000; www.leroyalamman.com; ⊕ 11.00–23.00 daily. An Italian restaurant with dark mahogany walls & furniture, La Vista is a popular haunt of sophisticated city folk. Its freshly made pasta & pizzas, & its lengthy list of fine wines from Italy are renowned. Located inside the Le Royal Hotel. $$$$$

ABOVE AVERAGE

✘ **Applebee's** Makka Al-Mukarrama St; ☎06 554 0016; www.applebees.com; ⊕ 07.00–19.00 Mon–Fri. From its starter dishes served sizzling on a cast iron platter to the sauce-smothered steaks, spicy chicken, fresh salads, ribs, pasta & seafood, the choice at Applebee's should suit everyone. There are vegetarian & calorie-counted dishes too, plus lots of smoothies & shakes. $$$$

✘ **Deir El Qamar** [90 B7] Sa'ed Abdo Shamout St, Abdoun; ☎06 593 4666; www. deirelqamarrestaurant.com; ⊕ 18.00–23.00 daily. A Lebanese restaurant in the heart of the city, the Deir El Qamar is named after the first capital city of Lebanon. Classic dishes on the menu include *shanklish* (cheese with onions), *lebaneh* (yoghurt with garlic & mint), *makdous* (pickled eggplant) & *yalanji* (stuffed vine leaves). $$$$

✘ **Fakhr El-Din** [97 D3] Abdul Qader Koshak St, Jabal Amman; ☎06 464 1789; www. fakhreldin.com; ⊕ 18.00–23.00 daily. Try a mezze comprising dozens of small dishes topped with local delicacies, or try an authentic Arabic meal like *zagaleel hamam* (baby pigeon in a tarragon sauce) or *kastaleta Ghanam* (lamb) from Fakhr El-Din's lengthy menu. A bright Lebanese-influenced restaurant with an outside dining terrace, it is a popular choice eatery not far from Downtown. $$$$

✘ **Romero** [97 C3] Mohammed Hussein Hailkal St, Jabal Amman; ☎06 464 4227; www. romero-jordan.com; ⊕ 11.00–24.00. Inspired by the cuisine, wines & architecture of Italy, this restaurant in the heart of the business district has become known for its imaginative menu. Choose from homemade pasta with exciting sauces & dishes like its keynote *scaloppine alla rucola* (veal in a watercress & rucola sauce). $$$$

✘ **Tannoureen** [90 A4] Shat al-Arab St, Souk Um Uthaina; ☎06 551 5987; www.tannoureen. net; ⊕ 12.30–16.00 & 19.30–23.20 daily.

Housed in a period property that has been decorated to capture the look of a country villa, Tannoureen has art on the walls, a palm tree-surrounded courtyard dining space & a menu of mainly Lebanese dishes that are served with considerable artistic flair. $$$$

MID RANGE

✘ **Bonita Inn** [97 C3] Queen Zain St; ☎06 461 5061; www.bonitaamman.com; ⊕ 18.00–23.00 daily. You can listen to live music & enjoy tapas & a menu influenced by Spanish cuisine at Bonita, one of the city's favoured tapas restaurants & bars. Its menu features seafood, chicken & vegetarian paella, plus lots of tempting tapas. $$$

✘ **Levant** [97 B3] Al-Mutanabbi St, Jabal Amman; ☎06 462 8948; www.levantjo.com; ⊕ 09.00–23.00 daily. Dine informally over a lunch of skewered kebabs of chicken (*shish tawook*) or minced meat (*kebab halaby*), or enjoy an evening meal of several courses at the Levant. Homemade desserts & hubbly-bubbly water-pipes are available to round off your meal. Dine inside or on its attractive terrace. $$$

✘ **Tony Romas** [90 B3] Makka Al-Mukarrama St; ☎06 556 0608; www.tonyromas.com; ⊕ 11.00–24.00. Part of a chain of around 200 restaurants worldwide, this eatery is a bright, welcoming place that specialises in rack ribs, steaks & seafood. Try its *piccata* (salmon & shrimps in a lemon caper sauce) or a combo to experience a selection of flavours. Light bites include baked potato soup & paninis. $$$

✘ **Wild Jordan Café** [97 E3] Othman Bin Afan St, Jabal Amman; ☎06 463 3542; www. wildjordancafe.com; ⊕ 11.00–24.00 daily. One of the trendiest places to eat, read over a cup of coffee or relax with friends in the evening, this café serves organic meals, teas & shakes. See box opposite for more information. $$$

✘ **Wox Chinese** [90 B7] Mazen Sido al-Kurdi St, Abdoun; ☎06 592 2921; www.wox-chinese. com; ⊕ 11.00–23.30. One of the best Oriental restaurants in Abdoun, Wox has a long menu of Cantonese & Szechuan dishes that offers plenty of choice for chicken, beef & pork or seafood lovers. Vegetarians are well catered for too. Speciality of the house is *Siu Mei* roasted duck in a delicious soy sauce & garlic jus. $$$

With a view over the Temple of Hercules perched high on the Citadel, which is especially thrilling when it is illuminated as the sun goes down, the Wild Jordan Café is one of the trendiest eateries in Amman. Its décor is minimalist and the theme is protection of the environment. Fashionable folk gather here for a meal of organic chicken and salmon dishes served with a mouth-watering selection of salads, pasta mixes and vegetables. It serves a delicious iced mint tea with all the trimmings, and a whole raft of smoothie flavours and cocktails. Before or after your meal you can head upstairs and see interesting information boards and leaflets giving details of the work of the Royal Society for the Conservation of Nature (RSCN), to which the café is affiliated, and crafts made by local artisans under the Wild Jordan branding. The Wild Jordan Café [97 E3] (*Othman Bin Afan St, Jabal Amman;* ✆ *06 463 3542; www.wildjordancafe.com;* ⏰ *11.00–24.00*) can be found signposted from Rainbow Street.

CHEAP AND CHEERFUL

✗ **Paul** City Mall, King Abdullah II St; ✆ 06 550 2760; www.paul-international.com; ⏰ 09.00–21.00. Informality in an elegant setting could describe Paul, a popular eatery inside the mall. Lunchtime is the busiest, when diners can opt for a quick homemade savoury tart served with salad, an omelette or a quiche. A menu favourite is the savoury pancakes filled with creamy seafood. Complete your meal with a French pastry. $$

✗ **Whispers** [90 A4] Rahman Alawi St, Um Uthaina; ✆ 06 592 1850; ⏰ 09.00–18.00 daily. The salad cart at Whispers is legendary – there's everything from olives & chickpeas to dishes of corn, pasta, tomatoes & a selection of nuts. A menu features international dishes too. A great place to relax in a stylish décor with the focal point an aquarium complete with small sharks. $$

ROCK BOTTOM

✗ **Books@Café** [97 E4] Omar Ben al-Khattab St, 1st Circle, Jabal Amman; ✆ 06 465 0457; www.booksatcafé.com; ⏰ 24hr daily. Housed in a renovated Ottoman-style villa, this colourful bookshop-cum-internet café-cum-coffee shop serves a mouthwatering array of coffee blends with informal bites to eat. Choose from decaf through to dark roasted coffee blends, along with flavours including pumpkin & hazelnut. $

✗ **Café Burger** [90 B6] 17 Ahmad al-Arousy St, Abdoun; ✆ 06 592 2832; www.café-burger. com; ⏰ 11.00–23.00 daily. If you crave a homemade burger made from top-quality beef then you're unlikely to do better than Café Burger, a trendy black & white eatery in Abdoun. There are other dishes too, like grilled chicken & fish served with fries & salad. Wash it down with one of its thick creamy milkshakes made with fresh fruit. $

✗ **Pancakes & Waffles** [90 B5] Al-Isma 'eeliyah St, Abdoun; ✆ 06 593 3432; ⏰ 09.00– 18.00 daily. As its name implies, speciality of the house at this popular brunch bar is its pancakes smothered in maple syrup. Its menu has eggs cooked in every imaginable way too. Great for breakfast or an informal snack at lunchtime or in the evening. $

ENTERTAINMENT AND NIGHTLIFE

ART GALLERIES Amman shows its cultural side in the many art galleries that are dotted around the city. From colourful abstract, post modern, surrealist and contemporary pieces to impressionist paintings reminiscent of Monet, and sculptures, figurines and *objets d'art* – all are on display to purchase or simply admire. The galleries listed below are open daily and most host special evening viewing events regularly.

4 Walls [90 B4] Sheraton Amman Hotel, Zahran St, 5th Circle; 📞06 593 4111; www.sheraton.com

Broadway Gallery Salah Toukan St, Sweifieh; 📞06 581 0280; www.broadway-gallery.com

Dar al-Anda Dhirar Bin al-Azwar St, Jabal Al-Weibdeh; 📞06 462 9599; www.daralanda.com

Darat Al Funun [97 F3] Jabal Al-Weibdeh; 📞06 464 3251; e darat@daratalfunun.org; www.daratalfunun.org

Foresight Art Gallery Bin al-Roumi St, Um Uthaina; 📞06 556 0080; www.foresightartgallery.com

The Gallery [97 C3] Jordan Intercontinental Hotel, Islamic College St; 📞06 464 1361; www.intercontinental.com

Jacaranda Images Omar Bin al-Khattah St; 📞06 464 4050; www.jacarandaimages.com

Jordan National Gallery of Fine Arts Al-Muntazah, Jabal Al-Weibdeh; 📞06 463 0128; f 06 465 1119; e info@nationalgallery.org; www.nationalgallery.org

Karim Gallery Wadi Saqra St; 📞06 461 7585; www.karimgallery.com

Love On A Bike Mu'thaa Bin Jabal St, 1st Circle, Jabal Amman; 📞06 461 4288; www.loveonabike.com

Nabad Art Gallery Uthman Bin Affan St, 1st Circle, Jabal Amman; 📞06 465 5084; www.nabadartgallery.com

Orient Gallery Issam Ajlouni St, Shmeisani; 📞06 568 1303; www.orientgallery.net

Orfali Art Gallery Kufa St, Um Uthaina; 📞06 552 6932; www.orfali.net

The Studio Prince Mohammed St, Bldg 89, Downtown; 📞06 464 6367; www.thestudio-jo.com

BARS AND TEA HOUSES Amman has its share of bars, although most tend to be low key. Unless you are staying in one of the four-star or five-star international hotels where bars serve wine and spirits, you are more likely to join a group of friends and enjoy animated conversation over a refreshingly chilled mint tea or a fruit cocktail in a café. A popular way to spend an evening amongst locals is smoking tobacco in a hubbly-bubbly water pipe with a strong coffee or tea in an *argeeleh* house.

🍷**Amigo Pub** Off Abu Baker al-Seddeek, Jabal Amman; 📞06 463 3001; ⊕ 18.00–23.00 daily. The Amigo Pub is a lively place with rock providing the background music & regulars speaking loudly in conversation. You can play a game of pool here or watch sports games on big screens while enjoying drinks & informal Arabic mezze dishes or burgers.

🍷**Beerkeller Bar** [97 B3] Le Royal Amman Hotel, Zahran St, 3rd Circle; 📞06 460 3000; www.leroyalamman.com; ⊕ 11.00–24.00 daily. One of the 'in' places for both visitors & locals, the Beerkeller can be found inside the Le Royal Amman hotel. Its dark & moody décor, & big screens showing sporting events from around the world, ensures it's always popular. As its name suggests, there are lots of beers & ales, plus spirits, available.

🍷**Cantaloupe Gastro Pub** 10 Rainbow St, 1st Circle, Jabal Amman; 📞06 465 6561; www.cantaloupe.jo; ⊕ 12.00–24.00. Dine on spinach dippers, asparagus parmigiano or Indian chicken skewers, while listening to jazz & funk music at the seriously stylish Cantaloupe. Its outside terrace is transformed by evening into a fabulous viewing platform overlooking an illuminated Amman. Musical concerts are often held.

🍷**Dubliners** Comfort Hotel Suites, Ali Nahuh al-Tahir St, Sweifieh; 📞06 581 2848; www.dublinersjordan.com; ⊕ 17.00–24.00 daily. Traditional Irish ales & hearty dishes like beef & stout stew are the order of the day at Dubliners, one of Amman's own Ireland-inspired pubs. Big wooden tables & dimmed lighting give it an authentic feel. Catch up with sports events on its big screens.

🍷**JJs** [97 C2] Grand Hyatt Hotel, Hussein Bin Ali St, Jabal Amman; 📞06 465 1234; www.amman.grand.hyatt.com; ⊕ 22.00–02.00 Mon–Sat. When the city's trendy set come out to play it's usually JJs they head for. A seriously chic nightclub-style venue, it has intimate areas for quiet chats with friends, a dancefloor where louder music encourages everyone to move to the beat, & a bar space with a big screen television.

🧃**Juicebangbang** Salah al-Shaimat, Sweifieh; 📞06 551 5150; www.juicebangbang.com; ⊕ 10.00–23.00 Sat–Thu, 14.00–23.00 Fri. One of Amman's most popular bubble tea houses, JBB as it is known, is contemporary & serves a whole host of sugar-free, fat-free fruit teas &

ARGEELEH

Argeeleh has become a term used to describe smoking tobacco in a type of free-standing water pipe, known as an *argeeleh*, *argileeh*, *hookah* or hubbly-bubbly pipe. *Argeeleh* is a time-honoured tradition and all part of the culture in Amman. You will often see locals smoking on a water pipe. If you fancy giving it a try, here are a few *argeeleh* houses:

Belmondo Café Makka Al-Mukarram St; ✆06 553 3021

Berto Café Shat al-Arab St, Um Uthaina; ✆06 554 9552

Bianca Café Ahmad Fawazi St, Abdoun; ✆06 593 5234

Books@Café [97 E4] Omar Ben al-Khattab St, 1st Circle, Jabal Amman; ✆06 465 0457

Cioconat Lounge Al-Sha'ab St, Dabouq; ✆06 541 2484

Fashion Café Al-Ameer Hashem Bin al-Hussein St, Abdoun; m 077 666 5557

Jafra Café Prince Mohammed St, Downtown; ✆06 462 2551; www.jafra-group.com

Java U Al-Baranka Mall, Sa'eed al-Mufti St, Sweifieh; ✆06 592 5715

Kashmir & Al-Argeeleh Hussein Bin Ali St, Jabal Amman; ✆06 465 9520; www.kashmir-argeeleh.com

Khutter Café Irbid St, Abdoun; ✆06 593 9099

Lemon Shisha Bistro Saed Abdo Shamout St, Abdoun; ✆06 593 9371

Levant Al-Mutanabbi St, Jabal Amman; ✆06 462 8948; www.levantjo.com

Macho Picho Kurdi Center, Fawzi al-Mughrabi St, Abdoun; ✆06 593 6989; www.machopicho.com

Mijana Restaurant & Café Rainbow St, 1st Circle, Jabal Amman; ✆06 462 0744

Rejeen Rainbow St, 1st Circle, Jabal Amman; ✆06 462 5400

Rotana Café Rainbow St, 1st Circle, Jabal Amman; ✆06 461 0520

Tche Tche Café Abu Taweeleh Plaza, Makka Al-Mukarram St; ✆06 588 5837; www.tchetchecafé.com

Zoka Café Saed Abdo Shamout St, Abdoun; ✆06 592 6777

---

shakes. Ingredients such as lavender, mint, jasmine & vanilla are used, plus wheatgrass & rocca shots. ♀ **Rovers Return** Abdul Reheem al-Haj Mohammed St, Sweifieh; ✆06 581 4844; www.roversreturnjordan.com; ⊕ 11.00–23.00 daily. Looking like the set of British television's *Coronation Street* & with memorabilia from the series lining its walls, the Rovers Return feels just like a traditional pub. It's an odd sight in the middle of Amman. Everything from juices & local spirits to seafood platters are served nightly. ♀ **Tiffany Bar & Lounge** [91 E3] Le Meridien Amman; Queen Noor St, Shmeisani; ✆06 569 6511; e info@lemeridienamman.com; www.lemeridien.com; ⊕ 17.00–01.00 daily. With a chic décor & big comfy sofas that mix surprising well with walls clad in iron & vibrant art, this is both a relaxing & a fun place to spend evenings. International drinks, cocktails & upmarket brandies with cigars are served. The lounge often has live piano music & visiting musical artists. ♀ **Time Out Sports Bar** [90 D3] Kempinski Hotel Amman, Abdul Hamid Shouman St, Shmeisani; ✆06 520 0200; e reservations. amman@kempinski.com; www.kempinski.com; ⊕ 17.00–01.00 daily. Enjoy Jordanians' favourite leisure occupation (watching football on big screens) in this lively & colourful bar inside the Kempinski Hotel. You can play billiards & darts, & listen to the latest music sounds.

CINEMAS Jordanians, and in particular those who live in Amman, are well-catered for when it comes to cinemas and love to see the latest blockbuster films to have come out of Hollywood. The city's shopping malls have multiplex cinemas with up to ten screens showing different movies, many with the latest projection technology and surround sound. In contrast, don't miss the opportunity to visit the beautiful Rainbow Theatre, Amman's original cinema that has been tastefully renovated and now has lovely period features such as an old film projector on display, a foyer full of vintage film posters and plush red seats in its little one-screen cinema. Amman is a thoroughly modern city, but this charming little venue is a reminder of how cinemas used to be.

■ **Cinema City** Mecca Mall, Makka Al-Mukarrama St; ☎06 551 8611; www.meccamall.jo. A 7-screen multiplex with a City Café for refreshments on the 4th floor of the Mecca Mall.

■ **Cine Le Royal** Le Royal Hotel, Zahran St, 3rd Circle; ☎06 460 3022; www.leroyalamman.com. A high-tech 3-screen cinema in the shopping mall of the Le Royal Hotel; it shows Hollywood films.

■ **Grand Cinemas** City Mall, King Abdullah II St; ☎06 581 8808; www.grandcinemas.com. A large cineplex with 10 screens that show the latest films using RealD 3D, technology that creates a 3D effect.

■ **Grand Cinemas** Zara Centre, Wadi Saqra St; ☎06 461 3260; www.grandcinemas.com. A 5-screen cineplex that uses RealD 3D technology for a digitally enhanced view of films showing.

■ **Prime Cinemas** Al-Baraka Mall, Sa'eed al-Mufti St, Sweifieh; ☎06 580 8500; www.prime.jo. 7-screen multiplex inside the Al-Baranka shopping complex, 3 Dolby digital 3D screens.

■ **Rainbow Theatre** Rainbow St, 1st Circle, Jabal Amman; m 079 822 8830. A renovated period cinema that combines the screening of modern films with a characterful venue.

FESTIVALS
Amman enjoys a number of festivals during the course of the year, from religious events through to celebrations of theatre, music and dance.

Amman Contemporary Dance Festival The National Centre for Culture & Arts of King Hussein Foundation (NCCA), off University St, Amman; ☎06 569 0292; f 06 569 0291; e info@oac.org.jo; www.pac.org.jo. International troupes perform over several days as part of this popular spring festival.

Amman International Theatre Festival ☎06 585 7352; e aitf@nol.com.jo. An annual summer festival featuring theatrical performers from around the Arab world.

Eid al-Adha A festival that marks the end of the Hajj month of pilgrimage to Makkah. Events are held throughout Amman.

Jordan Festival Various venues; ☎06 461 3300; www.jordanfestival.com. Held over several days at the end of Jun, this festival brings together artists from the world of performing arts & music.

Ramadan A month of fasting from sunrise to sunset is marked throughout Amman, as it is throughout Jordan. It promotes patience, spirituality & humility amongst Muslims. The dates of Ramadan change every year according to the solar calendar. Eid al-Fitr is a festival to mark the end of Ramadan, held over 4 or 5 days, where families gather to celebrate & to feast.

CULTURAL CENTRES
As a city with a distinctive cultural feel, Amman has a copious number of centres and complexes dedicated to ballet and dance, music and theatrical performance, art and exhibitions.

Al-Balad Theatre Yazeed Bin Abu Sufian St, 1st Circle, Jabal Amman; ☎06 465 2005; www.al-balad.org. A purpose-built theatre designed for both community use & for staging performances of various genres from dance & mime to ballet, music & acting.

Arab Theatre Training Centre (ATTC) Zahran St, Jabal Amman; ☎06 465 2015; e info@arabttc.org; www.arabttc.org. A performing arts centre

where students take part in performances that display their creativity, technical capabilities & artistic expression.

Darat Al Funun [97 F3] Jabal Al-Weibdeh; ☎06 464 3251; e darat@daratalfunun.org; www.daratalfunun.org. Halls for exhibitions, lectures & community events form part of this large contemporary complex that also includes a much respected art gallery.

King Hussein Cultural Centre Omar Matar St, Al-Muhajareen; 06 473 9953. Regular exhibitions, festival events, concerts & plays are held in this large cultural centre made popular by locals as well as visitors.

Jordan National Gallery of Fine Arts [97 C2] Al-Muntazah, Jabal Al-Weibdeh; 06 463 0128; f 06 465 1119; e info@nationalgallery.org; www. nationalgallery.org. Temporary exhibitions are held in 2 large buildings, which complement the permanent displays of more than 2,000 pieces of fine art, sculpture & pottery.

National Centre for Culture & Arts of King Hussein Foundation (NCCA) Off University St; 06 569 0292; f 06 569 0291; e info@oac.org.jo; www.pac.org.jo. The centre regularly hosts plays & productions staged by its own Interactive Theatre Troupe.

Royal Cultural Centre Al-Malekah Alia St, Shmeisani; 06 566 1026. Primarily hosts musical concerts by classical & operatic performers, visiting international pop & rock stars, recitals & plays.

LITERARY VENUES Literary events and book signings are all part of the cultural scene in Amman. Most are held in the bookshops listed below. Call in to the shops or look in the *Life* What's On section of *The Jordan Times* for advertisements for coming events.

The Good Book Shop Rainbow St, 1st Circle, Jabal Amman; 06 461 3939

Jordan Book Center Queen Rania al-Abdullah St, Al-Jubeiha; 06 515 1882; www. jordanbookcenter.com

Philadelphia Book Gallery Al-Shahid Wasfi al-Tall St, Tla al-Ali; 06 551 5861; www. pbgjordan.com

Prime Bookstore Al-Baraka Mall, Sa'eed al-Mufti St, Sweifieh; 06 581 1204

Readers Cozmo Center, Al-Sahel Av, 7th Circle; 06 582 8488

THEATRE AND DANCE Amman hosts the annual **Amman International Theatre Festival** (06 585 7352; e aitf@nol.com.jo), which brings together performers from throughout the Arab world for several days of performances. It was during the 1999 festival that the idea for a training facility was conceived. Today, the **Arab Theatre Training Centre** (ATTC) (06 465 2015; e info@arabttc.org; www.arabttc.org) hosts a programme of workshops designed to develop artists' creativity, technical capabilities and artistic expression. Students come to the facility from Syria, Lebanon, Palestine, Tunisia and Morocco, and regularly take part in theatrical events around Jordan. Many of these are held in Amman's **Roman Theatre**, a popular venue in summer months, and the **Royal Cultural Centre** (*Al-Malekah Alia St, Shmeisani, Amman;* 06 566 1026). The ATTC works with leading groups around the Middle East and north Africa, including the High Institute for Theatre and Cultural Animation in Morocco, the Popular Art Centre in Palestine (*www.popularartcentre. org*) and the Masrah al-Madina in Lebanon (*www.almadinatheater.com*). The most famous actors from Jordan are Jamil Awad, Shafiqa al-Till and Nadia Odeh.

The **National Centre for Culture and Arts of King Hussein Foundation** (NCCA) (*off University St, Amman;* 06 569 0292; e info@oac.org.jo; www.pac. org.jo), has its own theatre school that provides tuition in creative writing, mime, movement, puppetry, voice and speech, acting and directing to children and young people. Its own Interactive Theatre Troupe is famous for the challenging plays and productions it performs locally, regionally and internationally, which centre on social issues of the day. The NCCA promotes dance too, and its Dance School provides tuition in various forms, from ballet and tap through to modern and folkloric dance. Its MISK Dance Theatre Troupe performs in Amman and at folkloric festivals throughout Jordan, and at international dance festivals, including the **Amman Contemporary Dance Festival** organised by the NCCA. It is held annually in the spring.

Another of the largest international dance festivals is also held in Amman. The **Zakharef in Motion** has a host of workshops and performances designed to attract top Jordanian and international dancers and choreographers. With all the performances, as well as the workshops, having free entry, the festival is always a must on the calendar and attracts thousands. Typically, the line-up includes ballet, synthetic and contemporary hip hop dancers from Spain, Hungary, the Scandinavian countries, Netherlands, France, the UK, Germany and the US, and of course Jordan. Most major dance events held in Jordan take place at the **King Hussein Cultural Centre** (*Omar Matar St, Amman;* ✆ *06 473 9953*), the **Al-Balad Theatre** (*Yazeed Bin Abu Sufian St, 1st Circle, Jabal Amman;* ✆ *06 465 2005; www.al-balad.org*) or the **Royal Cultural Centre** (*Al-Malekah Alia St, Shmeisani, Amman;* ✆ *06 566 1026*), but smaller venues regular host dance performances too. In Amman, there are lots of dance workshops; the **Arthur Murrey Dance Studios** (*Abdul Raheem Haj Mohammad St;* ✆ *06 586 2004; www.arthurmurrayjordan.com*), the **Elite Dance Studios** (*4 Issa Bin Salman St;* ✆ *06 583 3361; www.elitedancejo.com*) and the **Freeway Dance Studios** (*Shahroury Plaza;* ✆ *06 585 8649; www.freeway.pro*) being amongst the best. For something different try **Tango Jordan** (*2 Suleyman al-Bilbaisi St;* m *079 598 8117; www.tangojordan.com*).

SHOPPING

Amman is a shopper's delight. From its big glitzy malls full of designer fashions from big names such as Gucci, Karen Millen, Dolce & Gabbana, Jimmy Choo, Nike and Adidas and shops of CD/DVDs and gadgets, to bustling bazaars and cobbled streets full of antiques, you'll find you can purchase just about anything in the city. Jordanians will tell you the prices are high, and in a country where the average monthly salary is lower than most countries in Europe and the US, this is accurate. To the Western traveller, however, the prices are about the same as at home.

The malls of Amman offer tax-free shopping. When you make a purchase in Jordan the price you pay includes a 16% sales tax, which tourists can claim back. Look out for the **Premier Tax Free** sign (see *Tax-free shopping*, page 78).

SHOPPING MALLS The largest of the shopping malls is **City Mall** (*King Abdullah II St;* ✆ *06 586 8500;* f *06 586 8501; www.citymall.jo*). This sprawling place has four floors of shops and an atrium that floods the complex with natural light. Glass and metal give it a contemporary feel. The mall is home to more than 160 different outlets, including the country's largest supermarket, Carrefour (✆ *06 550 5800; www.carrefour.com*), and a flagship Virgin Megastore (✆ *06 550 2787; www.virginmegastore.me*). Top names in fashion found inside include Zara (✆ *06 550 2776; www.zara.com*), Reebok (✆ *06 581 9178; www.reebok.com*), Monsoon (✆ *06 585 0526; www.monsoon.co.uk*), Gap (✆ *06 585 5408; www.gap.com*) and Massimo Dutti (✆ *06 581 8227; www.massimodutti.com*).

City Mall has numerous restaurants and coffee shops for a break between shopping, an entertainment zone with an amusement arcade-style area and a cineplex with ten screens showing the latest blockbuster movies, see *Cinemas*, page 105. There's no problem with parking at City Mall; it has the country's largest undercover car park.

The landmark **Al Baraka Mall** (*Sa'eed al-Mufti St, Sweifieh;* ✆ *06 580 8888;* f *06 580 8893; www.albarakamall.com*), the largest shopping centre in Sweifieh and one of the city's iconic architectural structures, and the glossy **Mecca Mall** (*Makka Al-Mukarrama St;* ☎ *06 552 7948;* f *06 556 0703; www.meccamall.jo*) on one of the city's busiest thoroughfares, Makka Al-Mukarrama Street, are favourite places to shop for top fashions, gadgets and electrical goods, jewellery, books and cosmetics. Top names at Al Baraka Mall include Crabtree & Evelyn (☎ *06 581 8286; www.crabtree-evelyn.com*), Matalan (☎ *06 582 2300; www.matalan.co.uk*), and Versace (☎ *06 585 0132; www.versace. com*). In Mecca Mall you'll find Levis (☎ *06 585 2641; www.levis.com*) and United Colors of Benetton (☎ *06 551 7053; www.benetton.com*), PC Zone (☎ *06 556 1766; www.pczonejo.com*), Philips (☎ *06 420 1915; www.philips.com*) and Siemens (☎ *06 582 3466; www.siemens.com*). For the little ones there's Mothercare (☎ *06 581 6934; www. mothercare.com*).

Abdoun Mall, located in one of the most upmarket districts of the city, was the first purpose-designed shopping mall. Here you will find luxury goods. Be sure to visit Time Center (☎ *06 592 1601*) for an expansive collection of watches. Two of the trendiest shopping avenues, **Sweifieh Avenue** and the pedestrianised **Wakalat Street**, are both long, wide thoroughfares in Sweifieh lined with designer boutiques just begging to be explored. There is also the **Zara Centre** [97 C2] (*Wadi Saqra St;* ☎ *06 463 7315*).

SUPERMARKETS
🛒 **Carrefour** City Mall, King Abdullah II St; ☎06 550 5800; www.carrefour.com
🛒 **Cozmo** Al-Sahel Av, 7th Circle, Sweifieh; ☎06 551 0240; www.cozmocentre.com
🛒 **Miles** Mecca Mall, Makka Al-Mukarram St; ☎06 585 3444
🛒 **Safeway** 7th Circle; ☎06 568 5311; www. safeway.com.jo

TRADITIONAL SHOPPING Amman has street bazaars and souks, although these are becoming a bit of a rarity these days. Where once fabrics, household pots and pans, machinery and food – in fact just about everything – was sold from stalls that lined streets in concentrated market areas, now the people of Amman are more likely to go to the Carrefour, Safeway grocery store at 7th Circle, or Miles at Mecca Mall for food, and the malls for everything from clothing to textiles.

One of the largest remaining traditional shopping areas is the **Downtown Souk** near the Citadel, which looks rather like the markets you will see in all major Middle Eastern cities. Here you can while away hours just looking at all the goods on offer and mingle with the locals as they go about their daily lives. You'll see spice stalls that capture your attention with their aroma alone, as well as stalls selling fruit, hardware and clothes. Amongst all this will be stalls cooking the local delicacy *falafel*, the delicious patty made from ground chickpeas, and *argeeleh* tea shops where locals smoke tobacco using a traditional *argeeleh*, or *hookah*, water-pipe.

Nearby is the **Gold Souk** [97 F3] (*King Faisal St*) where you will find a dazzling display of handmade gold and silver pieces. The prices are surprisingly cheap compared to the West, but even so you will be expected to haggle with the sales people. If your purse still doesn't quite stretch to such luxuries there are plenty of authentic crafts to be found.

Jordanian women are highly skilled at embroidery and you will see pieces with designs that have been handed down through the generations. Look out for hand-woven rugs and cushions, as well as antique brass tea and coffee pots with beautiful etchings, pottery, and marquetry jewellery boxes. Hebron glass, which originates from the West Bank and is now made extensively in and around Amman from recycled glass, comes in brilliant jewel colours. Why not treat yourself to a turquoise glass goblet or a cobalt blue platter?

Amman SHOPPING

3

If you're looking for local spices then head to Downtown Amman and explore the streets near the Roman Theatre where you will find dozens of little shops selling everything from mint (*na'na*) to parsley (*ba'adoones*). You can't miss them; the aroma alone will draw you in. There's a great spice souk near the King Hussein Mosque in Subhi al-Khadhra Street too. Prices are exceptional and the choice is amazing. Look out for:

cinnamon	*irfeh*	saffron	*zafaran*
cumin	*kamoun*	sage	*wara'a Ghar*
mint	*na'na*	thyme	*zatar*
parsley	*ba'adoones*		

While in Amman don't miss the opportunity to visit **Rainbow Street**, which is also known as Al-Rainbow Street and Abu Bakr As Siddeeq Street. It's a shopping street with a real cultural edge. Head for the area between 1st and 2nd Circle and just ask for Rainbow Street; you'll be sent in the right direction. This long, partly cobbled street is open to traffic during the day, but from 20.00 on a Thursday it is pedestrianised and becomes the centre of the city for people-watching. Everyone dons their most fashionable gear to parade, stop at bars, eat with friends or enjoy a literary evening at one of its bookshops. Look out for the book signings often held at The Good Book Shop (✎ *06 461 3939*).

By day, Rainbow Street has a bohemian feel; it's one of the city's streets that leaves an impression with you. Whether it's the lovely little antiques shops where you can browse for hours, the *argeeleh* tea shops, the honey-coloured villas dating from when it was the most fashionable place in town or the quiet park at the end where you can escape the bustle of the city, it has, without doubt, a personality of its own. While you're here, look out for the brown signs to Wild Jordan (see page 123). You'll find it down some steps on your left. You can browse the authentic crafts on display, pick up some literature about the conservation work of the group and stop awhile at its trendy café. The iced mint tea is strongly recommended.

SPORTS AND OTHER ACTIVITIES

Like the rest of Jordan, the people of Amman love to watch football and basketball, and take part in these and other sports. Most of the larger hotels have their own gymnasium and spa, but even if your accommodation doesn't offer this the city is well served with sports centres and private clubs. Most will let you use the facilities just by going along, but those that have a membership system will usually issue you with visitor's pass. If you're unsure, give the centre a quick ring to check in advance.

SPORTS CENTRES

Action Target Off Queen Alia Airport Rd; ✎ 06 429 0055; www.action-target.com. Shooting club.

Amman Aikikai Aikido 33 Taqiy Al Din al-Subki St; ✎ 06 666 7467; www.ammanaikikai.com. Martial arts.

Amman Waves Aqua Park Queen Alia Airport Rd; ✎ 06 412 1704; www.ammanwaves.com. Waterpark.

Bawasel Abdoun Taekwondo Centre Cairo St, Abdoun; ✎ 06 592 7880. Martial arts.

Bowling City Athletic City, Queen Rania al-Abdullah St; ✎ 06 515 0000

Dunes Club Off Queen Alia Airport Rd; ☎ 06 412 5290; www.dunesclub.com. Swimming complex.
Istiqlal Bowling Centre Istiqlal Mall, Istiqlal St, Al-Nuzha; ☎ 06 566 4212
Jordan Bowling Centre Mecca Mall, Makka Al-Mukarram St; ☎ 06 551 2987; www.jordanbowlingcenter.com
Jordan Entertainment Centre Kempinski Hotel Amman, Abdul Hamid Shouman St, Shmeisani; ☎ 06 520 0200; www.kempinski.com. Bowling.
Jordan Speed Centre Off Queen Alia Airport Rd; ☎ 06 429 0306; www.jsc-kart.com. Karting.

EQUESTRIAN CENTRES
Annab Equestrian Centre Off Queen Alia Airport Rd; ☎ 06 412 9444
Arabian Horse Club Off Queen Alia Airport Rd; ☎ 06 429 1386
Mushatta Equestrian Centre Off Queen Alia Airport Rd; m 077 760 0110
Princess Alia Riding Centre Sports City; ☎ 06 567 5739
Saifi Stables Off Queen Alia Airport Rd; m 077 744 2222

GYMNASIUMS
Active Gym Khalda Main St, Khalda; ☎ 06 551 3031
Aline Fitness Centre 7th Circle; ☎ 06 581 1001; www.alinefitness.com
Body Design 19 Fawzi al-Qaweqji St, Abdoun; ☎ 06 592 9669
Curves for Women Abu Firas al-Hamadani St; ☎ 06 464 9049; www.curvesme.com/jordan
Fit 4 Life Al-Kurdi Bldg, Abdoun; ☎ 06 592 4499
Fitness First Mecca Mall, Makka Al-Mukarram St; ☎ 06 586 3046; www.fitnessfirst.com
Fitness One Makka Al-Mukarram St; ☎ 06 585 9924; www.fitness1club.com
Flex 7th Circle, Khalda; ☎ 06 535 6998; www.flex.com.jo
Panacea Health Club Abdelrahim Allawi St, 5th Circle; ☎ 06 592 3400
Perfect Gym Al-Hussein Complex, Abdullah Ghosheh St; ☎ 06 582 9182
Power Hut Al-Thakafe St, Shmeisani; ☎ 06 568 6672
Revolution Ladies' Gym University St, Tla'a al-Ali; ☎ 06 534 9144
Total Fitness Centre Khalaf al-Bakheet St, Swefieh; ☎ 06 585 7254; www.totalfitness.com

OTHER PRACTICALITIES

EMERGENCIES If you experience an emergency in Jordan call the **police** on ☎ 191, or the **rescue police** on ☎ 192 if you find yourself disorientated and vulnerable. Medical emergencies and **ambulances**, along with the **fire brigade**, can be contacted on ☎ 199. For **dental emergencies** contact the Speciality Hospital (☎ *06 500 1111*), the Al-Essra Hospital (☎ *06 530 0300*), the Jerusalem

FITNESS FUN FOR KIDS

Whether it's gentle exercise or just plain good fun, there are gyms and activity centres in Amman designed exclusively for children, including:

Choice Gym Al-Maha Plaza, Al-Madeenah al-Munawwareh St; ☎ 06 552 1458; www.choice-gym.com
Fun Factory Abdelrahim Allawi St, 5th Circle; ☎ 06 592 3475; www.funfactorykids.com
Funtastic 45 Damman St, Um Uthaina; ☎ 06 554 0850; www.funtasticjo.com
Fun Time Off Paris St, Sweifieh; ☎ 06 582 3975
Jingo's Jungle City Mall, King Abdullah II St; ☎ 06 582 3700; www.jingosjungle.com
Jordan Kids Club Sa'ad Zaghloul St, Abdoun; ☎ 06 592 5957
Jungle Bungle Mecca Mall, Makka Al-Mukarram St; ☎ 06 553 6511
Kids Land Al-Hijaz Towers, Makka Al-Mukarram St; ☎ 06 553 8322
My Gym Princess Basma St, Abdoun; ☎ 06 592 5113; www.mygymjordan.com

Hospital (📞 *06 438 7181*) or the University Hospital (📞 *06 535 3444*). Other **hospitals with emergency facilities** are listed below. See *Health*, page 55, for more information.

✚ **Al-Essra Hospital** Queen Rania al-Abdullah St (by Jordan University); 📞 06 530 0300; f 06 534 7888; www.essrahospital.com

✚ **Al-Jazeera Hospital** Shmeisani; 📞 06 565 7581; f 06 568 1261; www.aljazeerahospital.com

✚ **Al-Khalidi Medical Centre** 30 Bin Khaldoun St; 📞 06 464 4281; f 06 461 6801; www.kmc.jo

✚ **Arab Medical Centre** 5th Circle, Jabal Amman; 📞 06 592 1199; www.amc-hospital.com

✚ **Jordan Hospital** Queen Noor St, Shmeisani; 📞 06 560 8080; f 06 560 7575; www.jordan-hospital.com

✚ **Palestine Hospital** 11 Queen Alia St, Shmeisani; 📞 06 560 7071; f 06 568 6406; www.palestinehospital.org.jo

INTERNET Jordan, and in particular Amman, is an internet-aware society and you will see locals on their laptops picking up Wi-Fi at cafés and restaurants, and in the foyers of hotels throughout the city. For the visitor, most hotels offer at least broadband in guestrooms and Wi-Fi in the lobby areas, but an increasing number are now offering Wi-Fi throughout the establishment. If you're out and about or you prefer not to carry your laptop or any other device capable of picking up internet with you, then you might like to seek out an internet café. There are many dotted around the city, particularly near the university along University Road and in Shmeisani. See *Media and communications*, page 81.

🖥 **Al-Saha Internet Café** Al-Hashmi St, Downtown; 📱 079 960 7007; ⏲ 24 hrs

🖥 **Books @Café** [97 E4] Omar Ben al-Khattab St, 1st Circle, Jabal Amman; 📞 06 465 0457; www.booksatcafé.com; ⏲ 24hrs

🖥 **Pirate Internet Café** Al-Rabieh Ibrahim St, Al-Dabbas Bldg; 📞 06 553 6197; ⏲ 24hrs

🖥 **Saba Netcafé** Madaba St, Jabal Wehdat; 📞 06 473 3152; ⏲ 10.00–24.00

🖥 **Ur Internet Culture Café** Jordan University St; 📞 06 534 8024; ⏲ 24hrs

MEDIA Amman tends to be the focal point of the media in Jordan, and here newspapers and magazines dedicated to life in the city and further afield are published. The daily *The Jordan Times* and the weekly *Star Newspaper* are the two largest, and give coverage of the events happening in Amman. *Jo Magazine* and *Jordan Business* look at business and politics, while *Living Well* focuses on women's issues, health, the home and fashions. Amman has English-speaking radio stations: **Sunny** can be picked up on FM105.1, **Mood** on FM92.0, **Energy** on FM97.7 and **Play** on FM99.6. See *Media and communications*, page 81 for lists of newspapers, magazines and radio stations.

MONEY Banks in Amman, like the rest of the country, are open 08.30–15.00 Sunday–Thursday and can be found throughout the city. Not all have ATMs, but the number being installed is increasing fast. ATMs can be found in all the main shopping malls and at banks in the financial districts of Shmeisani and Sweifieh, and around the busy shopping area and bus station at Abdali. Hotels throughout the city generally have money-changing facilities, but the exchange rate may not always be beneficial. Check before you decide how much to change. The daily newspaper *The Jordan Times* publishes the exchange rates applicable for the day. You'll find the larger shops and restaurants are happy to take credit cards, including Visa, MasterCard and American Express, but smaller specialist stores and bazaars still prefer cash. For more information, see *Money and budgeting*, page 68.

POST The main post office can be found off 1st Circle in **Prince Mohammed Street** (*08.00–18.00 Sat–Thu, 08.00–13.00 Fri, with reduced times during Ramadan*). Here you can buy stamps, collect parcels and send telegrams. You'll find most of the larger four-star and five-star hotels provide a full range of postal services too. Amman has agents that handle parcel deliveries from international companies such as DHL Express, UPS, TNT Express Worldwide and FedEx. See *Media and communications*, page 81.

✉**Aramex** ☎06 551 5111; f 06 552 7461; www.aramex.com

✉**DHL Express** ☎06 580 0800; f 06 582 7705; www.dhl.com

✉**FedEx** ☎06 551 1460; f 06 553 1232; www.fedex.com.jo

✉**Pionex** ☎06 569 1001; f 06 569 1020; www.pionex.net

✉**TNT Express Worldwide** ☎06 593 1966; f 06 593 0884; www.tnt.com

✉**Transpost** ☎06 554 9555; f 06 554 8111; www.transpostjo.com

✉**UPS** ☎06 568 5211; f 06 560 4197; www.ups.com

WHAT TO SEE AND DO

DOWNTOWN AMMAN The oldest part of the city, Downtown Amman is a heady mix of tiny streets interspersed with busy main roads. There are traditional souks and shops, villas that cascade down the hillsides of the *jabals* that surround it, and some of the city's most iconic and ancient landmarks. Downtown is dominated by the Citadel, where you can see the remains of Roman, Byzantine and early Islamic structures. Two of the finest remains are the Umayyad Palace and the massive Temple of Hercules. In the grounds is a tiny church dated to Byzantine times, and the Jordan Archaeological Museum. Below the Citadel is the Roman Theatre. The area is dotted with museums, hotels and traditional cafés, plus parkland where you can take a quiet breather from the constant buzz of activity.

The Citadel [97 G2] (☎ 06 463 8795; f 06 461 9768; *Department of Antiquities Citadel office* f 06 465 6924; ⊕ *summer 08.00–18.00 Sat–Thu, 09.00–17.00 Fri and holidays, winter 08.00–16.00 Sat–Thu, 09.00–16.00 Fri & holidays; entry JD2*) Life in Amman, or certainly around the Downtown district, tends to revolve around the Citadel. Whether you are out exploring the souk district or dining on a salad and chilled mint tea in a café, the chances are you'll overlook the mighty defensive walls of the Citadel. At night you'll probably catch a glimpse of the city's landmark, the Roman Temple of Hercules, standing at the top of the walls illuminated in a rather eerie blue-yellow light against the night sky. It is certainly dramatic.

The Citadel is a sprawling place; an outstanding open-air museum where you can see the remains of structures from Roman, ancient Islamic and Byzantine times standing, quite majestically, together. Some are well preserved despite having withstood earthquakes and having been the scene of battles. Known locally as the Jabal al-Qala, it is an area believed to have been inhabited for more than 7,000 years from around the time when civilisations emerged in Mesopotamia (parts of present-day Iraq, Syria, Iran and Turkey) and the ancient Egyptians were becoming established in the Nile Valley. Fragments of Neolithic pottery have been found in the Citadel suggesting it was a thriving place of habitation during this period, from around 5500BC onwards. These finds make the Citadel one of the oldest continuously inhabited places in the world.

The most important and iconic archaeological site in Amman, the Citadel really shouldn't be missed on your visit. Take time to gaze at the panoramic views of the city from this high vantage point. There is little shade other than in the Jordan Archaeological Museum and under the arch of the Umayyad Monumental Gateway, so wear a hat, maybe even take a sun umbrella, and wear plenty of sunscreen. A small café is located at the entrance where you can buy refreshments, including bottles of water. An information office and toilets are here too.

The Gateway On arrival at the Citadel, you will go through The Gateway. A modern building where you can get information and maps, it is an interesting structure because of the fact that it has no foundations. It is built solely on compacted earth in order to preserve any archaeological treasures that may still be underneath, and one day may be excavated. There are three large stone pillars just beyond The Gateway: the first gives details of how Amman was called Rabbath-Ammon in ancient times, through the Bronze and Iron ages to the Persian and Hellenistic eras; the second pillar details how the city was known as Philadelphia during the Nabatean, Roman and Byzantine periods; and the third, how it took its present-day name of Amman from the Umayyad period of AD461–750.

Beyond the pillars you get your first glimpse of the Temple of Hercules, and as you make your way up the pathway you begin to understand how important a building this must have once been. It stands atop the Jabal al-Qala hill looking out over the busy Hashem Khair Street to the hillside opposite blanketed with sand-coloured houses. To your left is the **Lower Terrace of the Citadel**, where you will find the remains of a palace dated to the Ammonite period. With its thick walls that show where its rooms and courtyard would have been, the palace is regarded as confirmation that an Ammonite community thrived in the Citadel. When it was excavated numerous artefacts from the period were uncovered and they are now on display in the Jordan Archaeological Museum.

Southern Gate From your vantage point near the Temple of Hercules you can make out the remains of gates and watchtowers along the length of these great fortification walls. One of the gates, the Southern Gate, was important in antiquity due to the fact it was a control point that separated local civilians who lived in the area below the Citadel, now known as Downtown, from the leaders of the community and their staff who would reside within the city walls. It is about 4.5m (15ft) wide with pillars dated to the Umayyad period either side. The steps are clearly visible, albeit considerably worn with age.

Fortification walls The walls are believed to date from the Middle Bronze Age with later additions made during the Iron Age. Prior to this, prominent residents of the community who lived in the Citadel would have been protected by huge sloping walls of mud and gravel covered in a plaster that made it slippery and therefore too hard a challenge for any invading forces to climb. The slippery mound protected them from their own, less well off, people too. The walls were improved during the Roman period, and again when the Umayyad dynasty ruled. Today, you can still make out how they were designed to circle the entire Citadel site, and its buildings.

Temple of Hercules The Temple of Hercules is thought to have been built on the instructions of the Roman Emperor Marcus Aurelius (b121, d180) around AD161–66 and is dedicated to the hero-god Hercules. It is said to have been larger than any of the temples of Rome. The temple stood within a *temenos*, which is a piece of land

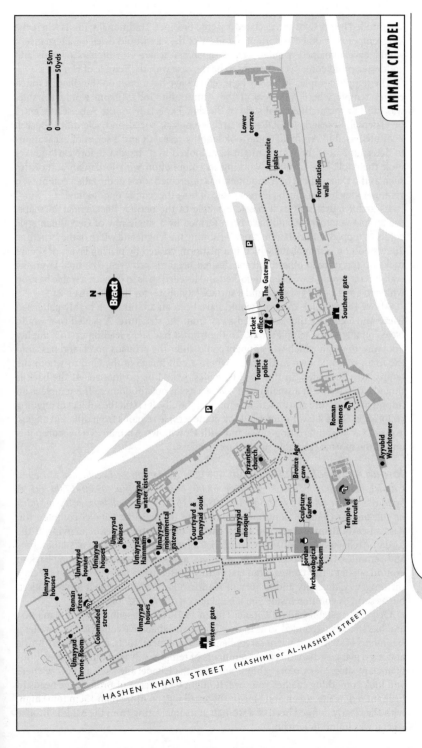

AMMAN CITADEL

0 ——— 50m
0 ——— 50yds

N Bradt

Umayyad houses
Roman street
Colonnaded street
Umayyad Throne Room
Umayyad houses
Umayyad houses
Umayyad Hammam
Umayyad houses
Umayyad water cistern
Umayyad monumental gateway
Courtyard & Umayyad souk
Byzantine church
Umayyad mosque
Bronze Age cave
Roman Temenos
Sculpture Garden
Jordan Archaeological Museum
Temple of Hercules
Ayyubid Watchtower
Western gate
Tourist police
Ticket office
The Gateway
Toilets
Southern gate
Ammonite palace
Fortification walls
Lower terrace

HASHEN KHAIR STREET (HASHIMI or AL-HASHEMI STREET)

surrounded by porticos and declared a sacred precinct. Traditionally, this is where the king, emperor or other important dignitary of the city would dwell or, alternatively, would have remained a quiet, sacred sanctuary where worshippers of gods and goddesses could come, as is thought to be the case with the Temple of Hercules.

The temple complex, which is believed to have been built on the site of a much earlier temple where followers of the Ammonite God Milkom would worship, was built to the architectural style of the day. Experts from the American Centre of Oriental Research (ACOR), an archaeological, social and scientific research institute based in Amman, undertook lengthy research and a series of excavations to determine how the temple might have looked in its heyday before earthquakes took their toll. The institute, working in conjunction with Jordanian authorities such as the Department of Antiquities, has re-erected some of the fallen columns so visitors today have a much clearer image of how the temple once looked.

Its architectural style is a classic example of the period. Rectangular in shape, the temple sanctuary would have been formed by a single row of Corinthian-style columns topped with elaborate capitals running the length and width of the structure. They stood on a stereobate, which is a platform created by placing layers of square rocks on top of each other until the desired height is achieved. The final layer, the euthynteria, would have been smoothed and levelled so as to provide a stable base on which to erect a series of steps and a surface (stylobate) for the columns.

Above the temple's columns would have been an architrave, a highly patterned frieze and a cornice that protruded away from the structure. A gabled roof would have completed the temple's look. To the front it had steps leading up to a mighty doorway, through which worshippers could enter the pronaos porch and pass into the main room, known as the cella, where a cult image of the God to whom the temple was dedicated, in this case Hercules, would be positioned. At the back is thought to have been a small room, known as an opisthodomos. The temple is an impressive structure and an iconic symbol of the city. It is still the subject of ongoing restoration. Take a few minutes to look at the temple remains from different angles. You get varying, interesting views and with Downtown Amman as a backdrop it is one of the most memorable sights the city offers.

Jordan Archaeological Museum [97 F3] (*The Jordan Archaeological Museum: Citadel;* \ *06 463 8795;* ☉ *summer 08.00–19.00 Sat–Thu, 09.00–17.00 Fri & holidays, winter 08.00–17.00 Sat–Thu, 09.00–16.00 Fri & holidays; entry included in entrance to Citadel*) Continuing your route through the Citadel complex you pass an early **Bronze Age cave** and a **garden of sculptures** before arriving at the Jordan Archaeological Museum, which has a remarkable collection of statues, pots and ceramics, fragments of ancient buildings and sarcophagi, some dating back to around 6000BC. This compact but fascinating museum is a must to really appreciate the longevity, diversity and history of Amman. From the outside it looks modest, but as soon as you step inside you'll be glad you didn't pass it by.

Originally established on Citadel Hill in 1951, the museum was Amman's first and has steadily expanded so as to now house an exhaustive collection of jewellery, fragments of statuary, ancient sarcophagi, flint and metal tools, coins, pottery bowls and jugs, glass, and architectural remnants of temples salvaged during excavations of ancient sites. Many of its exhibits are from the Citadel site itself and everywhere you look something catches your eye. It might be the case of Bronze Age beads in brilliant red, white, green and blue or the small jug, no more than 15cm (6in) high, with the clearly defined head of a woman at its lip. Dating from the Middle Bronze Age, it was found in Jericho.

Some of the museum's most prized exhibits are **plaster statues** dated to around 6000BC. These charming anthropomorphic statues, one appearing to depict a couple, others representing single figures, were discovered at Ain Ghazal in eastern Amman. Ain Ghazal is the largest Neolithic site discovered in Jordan to date, and one of the most significant due to the enormity of the artefacts uncovered. The delightful statues stand about 90cm (36in) high and are made of white plaster that has a smooth, luminous quality. You can see their noses and mouths, which appear to have a hint of a smile. Their eyes, created using cowrie shells and lined with bitumen, seem to gaze straight at you.

In a small alcove at the far end of the museum is another of its important exhibits, fragments of the **Dead Sea Scrolls**. These inscriptions on metal rather than the usual papyrus (thick paper made from the papyrus plant) are believed to be the oldest known surviving written texts from the Hebrew Bible. They date from around AD50 and were discovered during excavations at Khirbet Qumran on the shore of the Dead Sea. Four rare **Iron Age sarcophagi** can be seen in another of the museum's alcoves, while the 1.5m (5ft) tall black copy of the Mesha Stele stands prominently and can be seen from almost every viewpoint in the museum. The **Mesha Stele** is of great historical importance as its Moabite inscriptions pre-date the Bible and give an eye-witness account of life in Jordan and Palestine in the 1st Millennium BC. The original is in the Louvre Museum in Paris.

The museum's collections are displayed in chronological order starting with the earliest objects, which date from the Palaeolithic period (one million–10000BC). The second display area features Neolithic pottery with subsequent collections from the Chalcolithic period, the Bronze Ages, the Iron Age and Persian period, and the Hellenistic, Nabatean, Roman and Byzantine periods. The final areas cover the Islamic period from AD636 right through to the present, encompassing the Umayyad, Abbasid, Ayyubid and Mamluk dynasties.

There are plans to move the Jordan Archaeological Museum and its contents into a purpose-built, climate-controlled building so as to display its remarkable collection more effectively. Some of the pieces have already been moved into a new, modern building nearby that has become known as the Jordan Museum. However, the plan ultimately is to have a much larger complex that will house Jordan's national collection. At the time of publication, the original collection is still in its present building within the Citadel complex.

Umayyad Complex and Mosque

[97 F2] Continuing your visit to the Citadel, and circling round the Jordan Archaeological Museum, you come to the Umayyad Complex. The first remains you see are of dwellings that would have been occupied by staff of the governor during the Umayyad period. You have now entered the early Islamic part of the Citadel, known as the Medinah or Medina. It stretches over a considerable area and has all the essential structures of a thriving early Islamic fortified city. The complex is dominated by the remains of the Umayyad Mosque, which stands on the highest point of the hill and would have once been at the heart of the community.

The mosque would have been a considerably large building, which is clearly evident from the remains that exist today. They stand on a raised stone platform reached by a series of steps. The layout follows the popular yet simple hypostyle arrangement characterised by a cobbled courtyard containing seven rows of six columns. You can still see where the columns stood. A wall section has been placed to give an idea of how the mosque was constructed.

Umayyad Monumental Gateway As well as staff dwellings (ordinary folk would live outside the city walls as in the past), you can see the remains of a *hammam* (bath house), a souk and a palace where once the governor of the city would have lived with his family. There is little remaining of the palace today, other than the splendid restored and reconstructed Umayyad Monumental Gateway. It lies just to the north of the mosque. Visitors to the palace would have had to go through the gateway and be screened by the governor's security team before entering his home.

In its heyday, the palace would have had a reception room where the governor could receive visiting dignitaries, and a throne room. Today, you can still make out the layout of the palace, but it is the gateway that is its most prominent structure. It has a blue-grey domed roof that covers its vestibule, reached via a high arched doorway, and can be seen from most areas of the Citadel.

Umayyad Souk Between the Umayyad Mosque and the Umayyad Monumental Gateway and palace lies a *rahbah*, or a large open courtyard. It is flanked by the remains of shops and rooms. This would have been the city's Umayyad Souk. Although a peaceful place today, it would have been a hive of activity when merchants sold their wares here centuries ago.

Umayyad Water Cistern Off to the right of the Umayyad Mosque and the Umayyad Monumental Gateway is another curious structure dating from the Umayyad era. On first inspection you could be forgiven for thinking it was some type of deep pool, but then you realise it is a receptacle for holding the water supply for the Citadel's residents. This open-air circular Umayyad Water Cistern is remarkably well preserved. Built with smooth stone walls that curve around its circular shape, and with stone steps leading down to its floor, it would have collected rain water via channels carved into surrounding pavements. The walls were covered with a waterproof plaster. A discharge overflow system was incorporated into its walls, and the floor slightly sloped so as to collect silt. Known as a *birka* in Arabic, it is an outstanding structure.

Byzantine Church [97 G3] As you follow the path round towards the exit of the Citadel take a look to your right. Standing in the foreground of the Temple of Hercules is the Byzantine Church that dates to the 6th century AD. It is one of the earliest places of worship so far discovered in Jordan today, and is especially important given that it has some well-preserved mosaics on the floor of the nave. Its layout is typical of the period: a central nave leads from the entrance to the altar, flanked by aisles either side. Corinthian columns and capitals help you visualise how this church might have once looked.

The Roman Theatre Complex [97 G3] (*Off Al-Hashimi St, Al-Balad, Downtown Amman*) The Roman Theatre is carved into the side of a hill and is the centrepiece to a complex that draws visitors daily. Within this sprawling area is also the Roman Forum, which has now been turned into a park, and the Roman Odeon, situated next to gardens that are being remodelled as part of the Hashemite Plaza Project. The Jordan Folklore Museum and the Jordan Museum of Popular Traditions are also located here. It is a fascinating site in the shadow of the other great Roman structure, the Temple of Hercules in the Citadel.

Roman Theatre Amman's theatre is an imposing structure capable of holding 6,000 people, and is architecturally significant. Built in three horizontal sections, known as diazomata, and with 33 rows of auditorium seats that rise steeply to the top row, known as 'The Gods', it was positioned facing north so that its Roman audiences would be protected from the sun. It is carved deep into a hillside once used as a necropolis (graveyard) and is surrounded by a mass of houses that appear to be resting one on top of the other. The theatre's huge semi-circular void, in fact, provides a welcome break in the architectural line of the hillside.

Today, as in the past, it is one of the main venues for social gatherings, cultural performances and concerts. It has side entrances at ground level with vaulted rooms built into its foundations, known as paradoi. Traditionally, these rooms were used by actors for costume changes and by the orchestra, and even today when cultural events are held here they are often utilised for the same purposes. The side rooms also host two of Amman's finest museums. If facing the theatre, to the right is the Jordan Folklore Museum, while look to the left and you will see the sign for the slightly larger Jordan Museum of Popular Traditions.

Jordan Folklore Museum [97 G3] (✆ *06 465 1742;* f *06 461 5848;* ☉ *summer 08.00–18.00 daily, winter 09.00–16.00 daily; entry included in admission to Roman Theatre*) The Jordan Folklore Museum is an interesting museum created in the theatre's right wing. It focuses on the everyday lives of different Jordanian cultures. Through displays showing how rugs are woven using goat hair, how bread is prepared and baked, and which musical instruments were played for entertainment, it explores the communities that live in the desert and the rural villages, the Bedu and Reef cultures respectively. There are statues wearing the traditional dress of different areas of Jordan, displays of agricultural tools and a scene depicting a Bedouin way of life. In contrast, the museum also takes a look at how town folk lived a century or two ago with displays of household items and even a replica of the living space of a home.

Jordan Museum of Popular Traditions [97 G3] (✆ *06 465 1742;* f *06 461 5848;* ☉ *summer 08.00–18.00 daily, winter 09.00–16.00 daily; entry included in admission to Roman Theatre*) In the left wing of the theatre is the Jordan Museum of Popular Traditions. Founded in 1971 with the mandate to protect Jordanian and Palestinian folk heritage, it has a fascinating display of exhibits in five exhibition halls. As you enter the dark and moody atmosphere of the museum, to one side you will see a display of fine embroidery. The clothing and cushions with intricate patterns are examples of the work of women from the desert tribes of the south. In the first hall, you'll see Bedouin costumes and if you are lucky you may chance upon a local artisan giving a demonstration of how clothing was once made.

In the second hall is a fascinating collection of gold and silver antique jewellery that would have been crafted by Bedouin people and worn at special ceremonies for weddings and harvests, along with various items of cosmetic usage. Palestinian costumes are displayed in the third hall, while in the fourth are cooking pots and other household items, such as stone wheels used for grinding grain. Occasionally, you may see a demonstration of how these utensils would have been used. In the vault, which lies under the Roman Theatre and represents the fifth hall, is a collection of mosaics dating from the 6th century AD and discovered in the cities of Madaba and Jerash.

Roman Forum [97 G3] To the front of the Roman Theatre is the Roman Forum, a public square where theatre audiences would have once congregated before taking their seats inside. In more recent years the Roman Forum has been paved with a colonnaded walkway and planted with an abundance of palm trees. It is open to the public and a great place to while away some time and rest weary feet when exploring the Downtown area. Just off to one side and within the grounds is the Roman Odeon.

Roman Odeon [97 G3] A mini version of the Roman Theatre, the Roman Odeon was built around the same time as its bigger sister and holds an audience of 500. In Roman times it would have hosted small musical or poetry performances, or odes as they were then known and from which the name was derived. Amman's Roman Odeon is believed to have been covered centuries ago so that the musicians and poets were protected from the sun and rain as they performed, but is now uncovered and being restored. If you are lucky you may just catch one of the city's smaller summer cultural events which are often held in the Roman Odeon.

In 2011, the Greater Amman Municipality launched a project to transform this area of Downtown, calling it the Hashemite Plaza Project. Designed to create a contemporary space of chic cafés, shops and green spaces with the focal point of interest being the Roman Theatre and the Roman Odeon, the projects looks set to transform this area off the busy Al-Hashimi Street. The project is encompassing the remodelled Roman Forum, and includes extensive planting of trees and shrubs.

Nymphaeum [97 G3] (*Quraysh St, Downtown Amman;* ⊕ *09.00–16.00 Sat–Thu*) The monumental Nymphaeum is a landmark of the city and yet, surrounded by the constant bustle of Downtown Amman, is often overlooked by visitors. In fact, the striking fountain complex has an important place in the history books. Painstakingly built over several years to an elaborate half-hexagonal design, and completed in AD191, it was one of the main water supplies for the people who lived in the district that is now Downtown Amman. At that time the city was known by its Roman name, Philadelphia, and enjoyed much wealth; the building of a nymphaeum was only ever undertaken in prosperous cities.

The fountain is almost certainly built over underground caves and streams, which in Roman times were seen as sacred places and dedicated to the nymphs made famous in mythology, hence the name. A two-storey structure, it is believed to have once housed a 600m² pool some 3m deep, which was continuously being topped up from the underground streams that gave it a constant supply of fresh water. Despite its practical use, the fountain complex was built with mosaics and carvings, spectacular archways and statues of nymphs. You can only go into a small part of it as it is still being restored. Although much of its original decoration has been lost over time, it is a cavernous space and an interesting part of Amman's long history.

Al-Husseini Mosque [97 G3] (*Off Al-Hashimi St, Downtown Amman;* ⊕ *entry for Muslims only*) Also known as the Grand Husseini Mosque or the King Hussein Mosque (not to be confused with the King Hussein Mosque in the outskirts), the Al-Husseini Mosque is a beautiful mosque of distinctive alternating pink and white stones with two minarets from where the call to prayer is made. It is Ottoman in style, and was built here by the Emir Abdullah (later King Abdullah I) in 1924 and later restored by King Hussein in 1987. The mosque looks out over a large square that can almost always be seen animated with street vendors and pedestrians.

A plaque on the wall of the mosque suggests it is built on the site of a much earlier mosque, constructed during the second caliphate under Caliph Omar Ibn al-Khattub (b634, d644). Furthermore, it is believed to also be the site of the ancient Cathedral of Philadelphia. When visiting the mosque, why not take a look at Amman's famous **Gold Souk** (*King Faisal St*), which is just minutes away. Turn right as you leave the mosque, take the left turning into King Faisal Street and the souk is on the left. Here you'll see a vast array of gold and silver jewellery at keen prices when compared to Europe.

The Numismatics Museum Central Bank of Jordan [97 D2] (*King Hussein St, Downtown Amman;* ✆ *06 463 0301;* e *museum@cbj.gov.jo;* ⊕ *08.00–16.00 Sun–Thu; entry JD2*).

This hosts a collection of coins totalling more than 2,200, plus banknotes. It doesn't really matter if you are a keen coin collector or not, because what it provides you with, above all else, is a sense of the history of Jordan and its changing social culture. The museum opened in 1988 and its halls contain displays of coinage dating as far back as the Nabatean period. They were then quite primitive in design, and would have been made of lead, bronze or silver with a portrait of the king, or the king and his queen, on one side and a symbol, a God or an animal, on the reverse. The weight of each denomination is said to have been in line with the Greek Drachma or the Roman Denarius.

In another of the museum's halls you'll see Roman coins from the Decapolis cities, Hellenistic and Byzantine coinage with portraits of the rulers of the time stamped on one side as had been the fashion of the Nabateans. There are coins used in early and later Islamic periods too, when inscriptions of verses taken from the Holy Koran replaced portraits of rulers. In the final section of the museum are displays of coins and banknotes dedicated to more recent times when Jordan became firstly an emirate and then the Hashemite Kingdom of Transjordan, later Jordan. The first issues were of the Sharif Hussein bin Ali in Hijaz, with the collection culminating in the issues of the past few years under His Majesty King Abdullah II.

CITY CENTRE As busy as Downtown but with a more modern backdrop of shiny new office buildings, international hotels, chic art galleries and restaurants where you can dine on everything from gourmet French cuisine to Indian, Oriental and American dishes, the city centre is the commercial, financial and cultural heart of the city. Major areas to explore are around 1st Circle on Jabel Amman, the Jabel al-Weibdeh and Al-Abdali districts, home to the landmark Al-Abdullah Mosque and the Jordan National Gallery of Fine Arts, and the small lanes off Al-Rainbow.

Al-Abdullah Mosque [97 C1] (*Suleiman Al-Nabulsy St, off King Hussein St, Jabal Al Weibdeh; Mosque:* ⊕ *daily except prayer times; Islamic Museum:* ⊕ *09.00–17.00 daily except prayer times*)

If you gaze over the skyline of Amman, especially from the Citadel, there's one building in particular that will catch your eye. The Al-Abdullah Mosque has a bright blue dome covered in thousands of tiny mosaics that make it stand out from the buildings that surround it. It is a remarkable piece of exterior decoration. Two minarets stand either side. At night it is illuminated and is one of the most striking images of the city. It is the only mosque in Amman that is open to non-Muslims. Both men and women may enter, but dress should be conservative. Bare shoulders, arms and legs are not acceptable. Women will be asked to slip on an *abaya* (gown) and to cover their hair with a scarf.

It is well worth taking a look inside as the interior is exquisite. A cavernous prayer hall set right underneath the dome immediately greets you; in fact, it is one of the largest mosques in the Middle East to be unsupported by columns. Around 3,000 Muslims can pray here at any one time. The mosque's walls are decorated with bold geometric patterns that give it a subtle yet contemporary look. It is considered one of the best examples of modern Islamic architecture.

Taking around eight years to build, the mosque was completed in 1990 and dedicated to King Hussein's grandfather, King Abdullah I. It is located opposite an interesting Coptic church, and near the city's parliament buildings and the Jordan National Gallery of Fine Arts. Inside the Al-Abdullah Mosque is the Islamic Museum, which has an interesting collection of photographs taken of King Abdullah I with his family, colleagues or visiting dignitaries. There are personal items belonging to the king, and a collection of Islamic pottery and artefacts.

Darat al-Funun [97 F3] (*Off Omar al-Khayyam St, Jabal Al-Weibdeh;* ✆ *06 464 3251;* e *darat@daratalfunun.org; www.daratalfunun.org;* ⊕ *09.00–17.00 daily*) Darat al-Funun, which means 'Little House of the Arts', is just a few minutes' walk from Downtown along the Omar al-Khayyam Street (you'll need to turn right at the bend and left at the top) and although the road is steep, a visit to the gallery and its wonderfully tranquil garden is well worth the effort.

Once the home of British Major-General Frederick Peake (b1886, d1970), known in Jordan as Peake Pasha, the creator and former commander of the Jordanian Arab Legion army in the 1920s, and his staff, this elegant collection of villas standing in acres of garden is one of the finest contemporary Arab art galleries in the city. The villas have been beautifully renovated by architect and artist Ammar Khammash, who also designed the Wild Jordan centre off Rainbow Street. The décor provides a perfect backdrop to the often vivid colours of the paintings.

The richly planted gardens are used for recitals and readings in the summer months, and for displays of sculpture. In the grounds are the remains of a small **Byzantine church**, the church of St George, which would have been at the centre of the local community in the 6th century. There is also a tiny **café** housed in the porch of one of the villas, known as the Blue House. Sitting here over a tea and one of the homemade chocolate pastries, and looking out over the garden surrounded by the air of artistic talent is one of the simple rewards for exploring Amman.

While you are in a 'cultural' frame of mind, when you have completed your visit to Darat al-Funun you might like to leave by the Al-Saadi Mosque gate and walk the short distance to the **Dar al-Anda gallery** (*Dhirar Bin al-Azwar St, Jabal Al-Weibdeh;* ✆ *06 462 9599; www.daralanda.com*). This popular venue always has interesting artistic works on display, and also hosts regular events.

Jordan National Gallery of Fine Arts [97 C2] (*Al-Muntazah, off Suleiman Al-Nabulsy St, Jabal Al Weibdeh;* ✆ *06 463 0128;* f *06 465 1119;* e *info@nationalgallery.org; www.nationalgallery.org;* ⊕ *summer 09.00–19.00, winter 09.00–17.00, during Ramadan 08.30–13.30 Sat–Mon, Wed & Thu*) Founded by the Royal Society for the Fine Arts (RSFA) in 1980, this contemporary art gallery is a non-governmental, non-profit organisation with a mandate to promote cultural diversity and art from the Islamic and developing worlds. When it started it had about 50 artistic works and has steadily expanded over the past 30 or so years. Now, its display of over 2,000 works, including paintings, sculptures, prints, textiles and ceramics is considered one of the finest collections in the Middle East.

More than 800 artists from nearly 60 countries are showcased. Permanent exhibitions feature artists from counties including Algeria, Bahrain, Egypt, Morocco, Saudi Arabia, Lebanon, Denmark, the United Kingdom and France and from as far afield as the USA, Japan, Senegal, Sudan, Thailand and the Philippines. The society has, in addition, organised or been involved with well over 100 more temporary exhibitions in the gallery or in venues around Jordan and the world. The gallery, which is housed in two buildings decorated in contemporary fashion with white walls and wood flooring so as not to distract from the exhibits, hosts lectures, seminars and workshops on which visitors can reserve a place. The gallery stands in a complex full of trees and lawns dotted with sculptures, plus there is a garden designed for water conservation, a Japanese garden, a children's tactile area, and an open-air theatre where theatrical performances are held regularly. The gallery works in close co-operation with Jordan's Ministries of Culture, Education and Tourism, and many of the country's universities, including the University of Jordan (*Amman;* ✆ *06 535 5000;* e *admin@ju.edu.jo; www.ju.edu.jo*), Yarmouk University (*Irbid;* ✆ *02 721 1111;* e *yarmouk@yu.edu.jo; www.yu.edu.jo*), and the Al-Bayt University (*25113 Mafraq;* ✆ *02 629 7000;* e *info@aabu.edu.jo; www.aabu.edu.jo*). A programme of events is posted on its website and details appear regularly in *The Jordan Times.*

Haya Centre [90 D3] (*Ilya Abu Madhi St, Shmeisani;* ✆ *06 566 5195;* ⊕ *09.00–18.00 Sat–Thu*) If you're visiting the city with children then the chances are you'll be on the lookout for a venue that will both educate and keep them entertained for a few hours. The Haya Centre is ideal. A purpose-designed cultural and scientific museum, it has a whole host of interactive displays that will teach youngsters about the universe and the earth's environment and its sensitive biodiversity. One of its newest additions is a planetarium, which has a programme of shows enabling children to view the stars and planetary alignments through its high-powered telescopes.

The centre was founded in 1976 and inaugurated by King Hussein and Queen Alia al-Hussein, and has since become a major source of education and an activity centre for local as well as visiting children and their families. In addition to its interactive displays, it has a playground and a complex of rooms used for art and craft workshops. There's a library and museum, and a computer lab where children can learn all about the latest technology.

Rainbow Street Abu Bakr As Siddeeq Street, better known as Al-Rainbow Street or simply Rainbow Street, is one of the most fashionable streets in the city. It is named after the Rainbow Theatre, Amman's original cinema, which is housed in a period building partway down the street. Rainbow Street was once a narrow back street, but a municipality project saw it transformed with parkland, wide paved areas and cobbles on the roadway. Boutiques, bistro cafés and bookshops now line its length. This is where the young, not so young and the trendy folk of the city like to parade, dine on fine cuisine and be seen. It has a real café-society feel. Every Thursday at 20.00 the street is closed to traffic and becomes a great place to sit and people-watch.

Rainbow Street has its share of history, too. As you head down the street from 1st Circle, past the British Council, you'll come to an unassuming caramel-coloured **house with Art Deco balconies** behind a wall in a side street just off to the right. This was where the late King Talal lived before he ascended the throne, and where his son Hussein, who was to become King Hussein, and his brother Hassan were born. Further along Rainbow Street you'll reach an elegant villa that houses the offices, workshops and display showroom of the **Jordan River Foundation**, an initiative founded by Her Majesty Queen Rania al-Abdullah to empower local communities, especially women, to improve their handicraft skills as a socioeconomic means for a better life.

A little further on, look out for the signs at a junction to the **Royal Society for the Conservation of Nature** (RSCN) and **Wild Jordan**, which can be found a few minutes' walk from here in a modern building designed by architect and artist Ammar Khammash, who also masterminded the renovation designs at Darat al-Funun. Inside, you'll find a fascinating exhibition on the conservation work of the society at reserves around the country, such as at the Dana Biosphere Reserve in the Jordan Valley, the Mujib Nature Reserve on the Dead Sea coast and the Ajloun and Dibeen Forest Reserves. Admire the crafts of Wild Jordan and visit its café to enjoy an iced fruit tea.

ON THE OUTSKIRTS To the west and southwest of Amman's city centre lie the wealthy districts of Abdoun al-Shamali and Abdoun al-Jannoubi, where wide boulevards lined with palm trees and upmarket homes, banks and embassy buildings can be seen, and the glitzy financial district of Sweifieh. Around here are the city's swishiest shopping malls full of designer fashions and glistening gems. A little further afield are some superb museums, including the Children's Museum Jordan, that are well worth seeking out. To the north and east the feel is more traditional.

Children's Museum Jordan (*Al-Hussein National Park, off King Abdullah St;* ✆ *06 541 1479;* f *06 541 1379;* e *info@crm.jo; www.cmj.jo;* ⊕ *09.00–18.00 Sat–Thu, 10.00–19.00 Fri; entry JD3*) This super museum is designed for children of all ages, from tots to teens and their families, to learn through informal play experiences. Founded by Her Majesty Queen Rania al-Abdullah, it operates as a non-profit organisation and welcomes children who live locally as well as those visiting the city. The complex stands in the great Al-Hussein National Park, the largest green space in the city and where Ammanis come to relax, especially on Fridays.

The museum complex is packed with facilities, from the art studio and the planetarium to zones dedicated to learning about the human body and science. On site there's a colourfully decorated restaurant with a children's menu, of course, and a gift shop with lots of learning toys, books, music CDs and handicraft kits.

Royal Automobile Museum (*Al-Hussein National Park, off King Abdullah St;* ✆ *06 541 1392;* f *06 541 2270;* e *info@royalautomuseum.jo; www.royalautomuseum. jo;* ⊕ *10.00–19.00 Wed–Mon; entry JD3*) Housed in a large, modern complex that was designed by famed Jordanian architect Jafar Tukan to blend with its surroundings, the museum, like the Children's Museum Jordan, can be found in the Al-Hussein Park. It is partially submerged in the ground so that it follows the contours of the park, an illusion enhanced by its walls clad in natural untreated stone. The 5210m² complex has a mighty auditorium with four further exhibitions halls, all huge and airy, and can easily accommodate its gleaming collection of several hundred cars and motorbikes.

Most of the museum's collection has a direct connection with the royal family. Its prized exhibit is the 1916 deep red Cadillac Type 53 with V8 engine that King Abdullah I, King Talal I and King Hussein I used for official occasions. There's a 1946 Humber Super Snipe that King Abdullah I loved to drive around the kingdom, and a 1940 black Buick Super Series 56 and a 1955 Mercedes Benz 300 SL Gullwing that were among King Hussein's favourites. More recent models include a brilliant red Ferrari F40 from the 1980s, a 1990 AC Cobra V8, a 1991 BMW Z1 and a 2005 V10 Porsche Carrera GT. Even a non-car enthusiast can't help but appreciate the enormity of this collection. There is also a display of vintage and classic motorbikes.

Martyr's Memorial (*Al-Shaheed St, off Sports City;* ✆ *06 566 4240;* ⊕ *09.00–16.00 Sat–Thu*) This imposing, white, part pyramid-like structure, with two Jordanian flags flying at its entrance in respect to Jordan's military heroes, is a monument dedicated to those who lost their lives in battle for the kingdom. Dating from 1977, and designed by the respected architect Victor Adel Bisharat on instructions from King Hussein I, it stands atop a pine-covered hill reached by a series of steps. It is adorned with inscriptions taken from the Holy Koran.

Inside, a museum tells the country's military history through a chronological display of images and memorabilia, beginning with the Arab Revolt of 1916–1918 when thousands upon thousands of Arabs led by Sharif Hussein bin Ali of Makkah (b1853, d1931) fought for independence from the Ottoman Empire. It covers subsequent battles, including Israel's War of Independence, and chronicles the formation of the Arab Legion army in the 1920s by Major-General Frederick Peake, known in Jordan as Peake Pasha.

A visit to the Martyr's Memorial will be a moving experience, but one that gives you just a little more insight into how the Jordan of today was shaped in the 20th century through to present day.

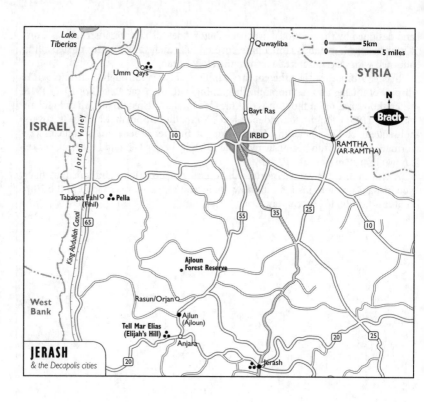

4

Jerash and the Decapolis Cities

Telephone code: 02

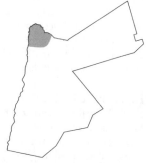

With its intricately carved marble temples and arches, great plazas, a spine-like colonnaded street and a mighty hippodrome where thousands of Romans would once have been entertained, **Jerash** was clearly an outstanding city and one that shouldn't be missed today. It has enjoyed over 6,500 years of continual occupation and is considered one of the best-preserved Roman provincial cities in the world. While Petra may be the number one visitor attraction in Jordan, Jerash certainly comes in a very close second.

Jerash is one of the famous Decapolis Cities and can trace its history back to Hellenistic and Roman times. Then the city was known as Gerasa, a prosperous place that lay on one of the most important trade routes through the country. You can wander around the ruins of what is believed to be an almost complete city and admire its Roman architecture. If your visit coincides with the summer Jordan Festival, part of which is held in Jerash, you will witness one of the best cultural experiences the country has to offer. The festival brings together numerous music, dance and theatrical artists for a programme of performances designed to tell the history of Jerash and the cities of the Decapolis.

The Decapolis – *deca* and *polis* meaning 'ten' and 'new city' respectively in Greek – formed part of a Greco-Roman initiative to create major cities on the fringes of the empire that ruled parts of Transjordan as it expanded across towards Arabia. Other than Canatha (present-day Qanawat) in Syria, and Scythopolis (present-day Beth-Shean) and Hippos (present-day Hippus or Sussita) in Israel, all the cities of the Decapolis were located in what is today the country of Jordan.

Along with Jerash, the Decapolis comprised Amman, in Roman times known as Philadelphia, along with the city of **Pella**, which lies to the west of Jerash in rolling wooded hills close to the modern town of **Tabaqat Fahl**, Capitolias on the site of present-day **Bayt Ras** and Arabella at **Irbid**. Possibly the most dramatic of all the Decapolis cities in terms of its setting is Gadara, at present-day **Umm Qays**. Here you can see the remains of its city hewn from the black basalt of the northern desert region. Umm Qays has views out over the Jordan Valley, the Golan Heights and the Sea of Galilee, and is most famous for minting its own coinage, the legend of the miracle of the Gadarene swine and for the location of the Battle of Yarmouk.

It is widely thought other cities became part of the project too; in fact as many as 18 have been identified as possibly belonging to the Decapolis. In Jordan these include Abila, the remains of which can be seen near the town of **Quwayliba, Al Husn** where it is thought the ancient city of Dion was located and a northern city known as Raphana. All the cities were designed to self-rule and to become the central point for the local communities of their region. They were large and lavish, and as you wander around their remains today, you can easily imagine the lively, prosperous Roman cities they must once have been.

The cities of the Decapolis were amongst the most impressive of the Hellenistic and Roman empires, and although in ruins today the sprawling complexes of archaeological remains dotted throughout northern Jordan give you a clear insight into how magnificent they once were.

EARLY HISTORY The Decapolis cities were located in a great swathe of land that covered northern Jordan, and although they were not built until the time of the Romans and Greeks, this territory is known to have been inhabited since the prehistoric period. Excavations have revealed evidence of Bronze Age civilisations occupying the land that became the Decapolis city of Gerasa – present-day Jerash – and Arabella – present-day Irbid – while Neolithic remains have been found around Pella near Tabaqat Fahl. The Decapolis city of Philadelphia, present-day Amman, was an important settlement in biblical times, when it was known as Rabbath Ammon.

NABATEAN, ROMAN AND BYZANTINE ERAS While much of Transjordan, which is the old name for Jordan, was being ruled by the Nabateans, the Greeks and Romans were expanding their empires across to Arabia in the north. They wanted to build new cities from where they could rule the fringes of their empire and identified key locations for them. One of the largest in Transjordan was Gerasa. This new city, where thousands of people are thought to have once lived, lay on one of the most important trade routes between the Far East, Arabia and Europe. As such, the city and its people became wealthy. Lavish temples and churches were built, as well as Roman bath complexes, shops, homes, a hippodrome for chariot races, and large theatres for drama and musical performances.

Gerasa, the remains of which can be seen alongside the modern city of Jerash, became one of the most important and cultural cities of the region. It was joined by Gadara, Philadelphia, Capitolias and Arabella, along with Abila, Al Husn where the Roman city of Dion is believed to be located, and Raphana. The aim of the Decapolis project was to introduce Greek and Roman culture to a region that until then was more used to Nabatean, Jewish and Aramean ways of life. Most of the cities were built in the years after the death of Alexander the Great in 323BC and the Roman conquest of the region in southern Syria known as Coele-Syria some three centuries later. The New Testament gospels of Matthew, Mark and Luke make reference to the cities of the Decapolis as being places where Jesus worked to spread the word of God.

Until the Coele-Syria conquest, Hellenistic culture dominated the region, but it was subsequently eclipsed by the Romans who introduced their own lifestyle. It was the Romans who developed the infrastructure of the cities by building the colonnaded streets, theatres and public buildings that can be seen today (albeit now in a ruinous state). The Romans gave each city a degree of autonomy and as a result they flourished. The fortunes of the Decapolis cities took a downward turn towards the latter years of the Roman Empire when its boundaries expanded further east into Arabia, and they were no longer needed for their original purpose of introducing Greco-Roman culture to the region. During the Byzantine period some of the cities became bishoprics, but as the early Islamic caliphates came to power so the cities began to lose their prominence in favour of other major towns and cities.

MODERN HISTORY Over the ensuing years, most of the Decapolis cities declined and were eventually abandoned and fell into disrepair. The exceptions were Gerasa and Gadara, which survived as Jerash and Umm Qays to become two of the most celebrated and visited tourist attractions in the country today. Two other Decapolis cities also survived: Arabella is now Irbid, one of Jordan's largest cities, and Philadelphia became Jordan's capital city Amman. The remains of Pella, Capitolias and Abila are now fascinating archaeological sites, and well worth a visit.

GETTING THERE AND AROUND

BY AIR The nearest and most convenient airport for visiting the Decapolis cities is the **Queen Alia International Airport** in Amman. As it lies to the south of the city, you will need to make your way to Amman, from where you can head north to visit Jerash and the other Decapolis cities (see *Getting there and away*, page 95).

BY TAXI OR BUS Amman has **taxis** and *serveeces* vehicles that you can hire for a trip to Jerash, Irbid, Pella or any of the other Decapolis sites. Depending on your destination expect to pay around JD10–50. You can negotiate much cheaper fares in a shared taxi. The journey time to Jerash is just 45 minutes or so from Amman and a good 1½ hours to Umm Qays. A cheaper option is to take a **bus**; buses run out of the Abdali bus station regularly every day to Jerash, Irbid and Umm Qays, and less frequently to Tabaqat Fahl. Expect to pay JD2–3. Remember that some of the archaeological sites are away from the main town centres and, as such, you will need to get a taxi from the town. A prime example is Pella, which lies 3km out of Tabaqat Fahl. The **Jordan Express Tourist Transport company** (JETT) (*7th Circle, Amman;* ✆ *06 585 4679;* f *06 585 4176; www.jett.com*) has the most regular timetable to these destinations from Amman. Another option is to contact companies that offer a guided tour of the Decapolis cities from Amman. There are many of them; see *Tour operators*, page 43.

BY CAR If you're travelling from or via Amman you can head north along Highway 35. The road takes you straight into Jerash after 50km, and continues on for another 38km to Irbid. From here you can head for Umm Qays, Beit Ras and Abila, which are clearly signposted. Pella, near Tabaqat Fahl, isn't quite so easy to find. From Jerash you'll need to pick up the fairly decent road (number 20), via Anjara, and keep going until you reach the T-junction with the River Jordan road (number 65). Turn right and continue for about 28km until you see signs for Tabaqat Fahl and Pella. Alternatively, you can take the road from Irbid (number 26) to the River Jordan road and left to Pella. It is advisable to ensure you fill up with petrol before you leave Amman, although both Irbid and the modern town of Jerash have plenty of petrol stations.

WHERE TO STAY

Accommodation options are limited in and around Jerash, even in the city of Irbid, as most visitors tend to stay in Amman and then head out to the archaeological sites on day trips. Of the hotels that are here, most are mid range, but welcoming, clean and in convenient locations.

⌂ **Al-Joude** (18 rooms) Yarmouk University St, Irbid; ✆ 02 727 5515; f 02 727 5517; e joude@ go.com.jo; www.aljoudehotel.com. As Irbid's best hotel, the Al-Joude can usually be found full of business & academic types. The rooms are all well presented & have amenities such as satellite TV & private bathrooms. There's a nice café-style restaurant called News Café on the ground floor, where guests & visitors can purchase sandwiches & pastries. Good room-service menu. **$$$**

⌂ **Hadrian Gate Hotel** (5 rooms) Jerash Archaeological Park; m 077 779 3907. This is Jerash's only real place to stay &, although it is a little on the expensive side given its limited amenities, it is beautifully presented & located right near Hadrian's Arch in the Jerash Archaeological Park. Room facilities include private bathrooms, & if you stay in the top floor room (number 105) you'll get your own terrace overlooking the ancient remains. It has its own little breakfast terrace. **$$$**

⌂ **Olive Branch** (33 rooms) 5km west of Jerash; ✆ 02 634 0555; f 02 634 0557; e olivekh@go.com.jo; www.olivebranch.com. jo. Set in the countryside with panoramic views over groves of olive trees & valleys, this hotel is quiet & just a short distance outside Jerash. It

offers well-equipped sgl to family rooms, & a bright, airy restaurant & bar, a swimming pool & a games room. You can camp in the grounds using the hotel's own tents or your own (from JD9). The hotel is inexpensive & good value. **$$$**

⌂ **Umm Qais Hotel** (11 rooms) Umm Qays; ✆ 02 750 0080; e info@umqaishotel.com; www. umqaishotel.com. A traditional hotel with a really welcoming feel, it is in the centre of the village & the only option for an overnight stay. There's a restaurant where guests are served local Jordanian food & a lounge with great views over the valley to where Israel meets Syria. Here you can sample local mint tea & smoke using an *argeeleh* water-pipe. **$$$**

✕ WHERE TO EAT

Apart from some seriously good places to eat at the archaeological sites themselves, the region is somewhat bereft of restaurants. You'll find stalls selling bowls of *fuul*, *falafel* and honey-soaked pastries in the souks of the towns; trendy sandwiches in the coffee shops; and American-style hamburger outlets and pizza takeaways around the university in Irbid.

✕ **Pella Resthouse** Pella; m 079 557 4145; www.romero-jordan.com; ⊕ 10.00–20.00, times can vary. A cosy restaurant that has been built & designed to reflect the architecture of the ancient site of Pella, this eatery is staffed by locals & serves a selection of grilled dishes with Arabia salads, all artfully presented. Alcohol is served here. Dine inside or outside on the terrace overlooking the Roman site & the mountains of the West Bank. **$$$$**

✕ **Umm Qays Resthouse** Umm Qays; ✆ 02 750 0555; www.romero-jordan.com; ⊕ 10.00–20.00, times can vary. Housed in an elegant hilltop stone building, this restaurant is famous as much for its views as its à la carte mezze menu. You can dine here on freshly made *sambousek* (cheese pastries) & *penne all'arrabbiata* (pasta in a spicy sauce) while looking out over the Jordan Valley, the Sea of Galilee & the Golan Heights. **$$$$**

✕ **Lebanese House** Jerash Debeen; ✆ 02 635 1301; ⊕ 11.30–22.00. One of the longest established restaurants in Jerash town, the Lebanese House is a large welcoming place that is family run. It offers a lengthy menu of authentic

dishes from the Levant, including *lebaneh* (yoghurt with garlic & mint), *zagaleel hamam* (baby pigeon in a tarragon sauce) & *Kastaleta Ghanam* (lamb). **$$$**

✕ **Olive Branch Restaurant** Olive Branch Hotel, 5km west of Jerash; ✆ 02 634 0555; f 02 634 0557; e olivekh@go.com.jo; www. olivebranch.com.jo; ⊕ 07.30–22.00. Serving local Jordanian dishes, such as a tasty version of *mensaf* (lamb with yoghurt), along with international cuisine, this bright & airy restaurant uses local produce, including olive oil from its own groves. Local wines & spirits are served. You can smoke on a water-pipe on the terrace. **$$$**

✕ **News Café** Al-Joude Hotel, Yarmouk University St, Irbid; ✆ 02 727 5515; f 02 727 5517; e joude@go.com.jo; www.aljoudehotel. com; ⊕ 09.00–19.00. Displays of sandwiches & cakes, & a menu of hot & cold pasta dishes & pizzas tempt at this lively little place on the ground floor of the Al-Joude Hotel. There's a choice of juices, beer & flavoured tea & coffee too. One of the better places to get a quick informal snack while out & about in Irbid. **$$**

OTHER PRACTICALITIES

DRESS The Decapolis archaeological sites are open spaces of ruins and as such offer little shade from the sun and desert breezes. Wear flat shoes or trainers as you'll find the ground is uneven. Depending on what route you take, you'll probably have to climb over walls or trenches.

EMERGENCIES Contact the **police** ☏ 191 or the **rescue police** ☏ 192. Medical emergencies and **ambulances**, along with the **fire brigade**, can be contacted on ☏ 199.

MONEY, POST AND INTERNET While the archaeological sites' visitor centres have limited facilities for money-changing, post and internet, you'll find all these services in the nearby modern towns. Jerash town, for example, which lies just to the east of the archaeological site, has banks and a post office off King Hussein Street, and in Irbid there are lots of banks, two main post offices and internet cafés in the downtown district near the clock tower plaza and along King Abdullah Street near Yarmouk University on the outskirts.

WHAT TO SEE AND DO

JERASH The modern city of Jerash is the largest of the Jerash Governorate, as well as its capital, and is surrounded by a number of picturesque towns and villages, including Souf, which was an important place during the Ottoman period, and Kufr Khall where most of the grapes seen in the souks around Jordan originate. The land is renowned for its fertile valleys, most of which are blanketed by fields used for agriculture. Jerash, however, is most famous for the fabulous archaeological remains of Gerasa, which was conquered by General Pompey in 63BC and went on to become one of the finest cities of the Roman Empire. Gerasa's remains lay hidden under sand for centuries until they were rediscovered, excavated and, in part, restored, and are today the country's second most visited site after Petra. Excavation work is currently underway at the site.

Jerash is easily reached by highway from central Amman; it's well signposted as you leave the city heading north. Once on the highway look out for the signposts to South Jerash and follow the route, which will take you through countryside full of olive trees until you reach the fringes of the city.

Jerash Archaeological Park (☏ *02 635 1272; ☉ summer 07.00–18.00 daily, winter 07.00–16.00 daily; entry JD8*) Widely recognised as one of the best preserved Roman provincial market towns in the world and one of the finest examples of urbanism from the period, **Gerasa**, set within what is now the Jerash Archaeological Park, is an ancient city full of treasures, surrounded by city walls. You can spend a good day exploring the park; it is huge and there are an enormous number of monumental buildings and plazas to see. However, if you only have a few hours you can easily still see its most dramatic sights. The Oval Forum is a must, as is the Cardo, and try to catch one of the chariot races in the hippodrome, which are staged most days (see *Hippodrome*, page 133).

The archaeological park is signposted; look out for the parking signs with the massive Hadrian's Arch as their backdrop. Here you'll find the ticket office and a tourist bazaar. Make your way up the stone steps just off to the right, under Hadrian's Arch and along the side of the hippodrome to the visitors' centre where

4

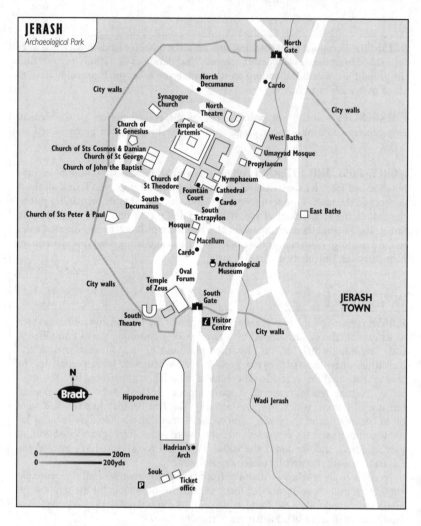

JERASH
Archaeological Park

North Gate

City walls

North Decumanus

Cardo

Synagogue Church

North Theatre

City walls

Church of St Genesius

Temple of Artemis

West Baths

Church of Sts Cosmos & Damian
Church of St George
Church of John the Baptist

Umayyad Mosque

Propylaeum

Church of St Theodore

Nymphaeum

Church of Sts Peter & Paul

Fountain Court

Cathedral

South Decumanus

Cardo

South Tetrapylon

East Baths

Mosque

Macellum

Cardo

Archaeological Museum

Oval Forum

City walls

Temple of Zeus

South Gate

JERASH TOWN

South Theatre

Visitor Centre

City walls

N
Bradt

Hippodrome

Wadi Jerash

0 ———— 200m
0 ———— 200yds

Hadrian's Arch

Souk

P

Ticket office

you can gather information on the sights you are about to see. You can also hire a guide here if you wish (*around JD20 for a tour lasting a little over an hour; languages spoken include Arabic, English, Spanish, French, Italian, Greek, Dutch and German*). There's a restaurant too, and an exhibition area that has a small but interesting display on the history of Gerasa and suggesting how it might have looked in its heyday. Although the display gives you a good insight into the city before you begin exploring, a much more detailed account can be found in the Jerash Archaeological Museum within the complex.

Hadrian's Arch This massive triumphal arch was built to commemorate a visit by the Roman Emperor Hadrian (b76, d138) to Jerash in AD129. He was a much-travelled emperor who, it is said, liked to inspect the cities of his empire and issue instructions for their development and expansion. He was doubtless impressed by the arch. A mighty structure of one huge processional arch flanked by smaller arches and columns with, unusually, capitals depicting carved acanthus leaves at their base rather than at the top, it would have stood over 20m high when it was complete. It would appear town planners intended for the arch to become a southern entry gate to the city, which suggests the emperor had sanctioned plans for an extensive southward expansion programme. However, plans to expand the city came to a stop around this time and as a result the arch became a standalone, but nonetheless impressive, structure.

Hippodrome The stadium is a remarkable sight given that it is almost complete and, newly restored in part, looks today as it might have done centuries ago. It is not a large stadium; in fact at a little over 240m long and 50m wide, it is the smallest hippodrome discovered to date in the land that once formed part of the Roman Empire. Nonetheless, it is impressive. This is where the people of Gerasa would have come to see chariot races and horse racing. The restored seating area, known as the cavea, is distinctive with 16 rows of seats, which would have held some 15,000 spectators.

The hippodrome has ten starting gates, known as carceres, through which chariots would have entered the arena. They have been restored or rebuilt from the rubble found on the site. Where stones were missing, they were quarried to blend sympathetically with the originals. The number of carceres is unusual for a hippodrome, which is probably due to its diminutive size. Normally, hippodromes of ancient Roman times would have 12 such entrances. Parts of the external structure would have held shops, and the remains of some of these can still be seen.

Regular shows performed by members of the **Jerash Heritage Company** (⟨ 02 634 2471; www.jerashchariots.com; ⊕ shows throughout the year at 11.00 & 14.00 Sat–Mon & Wed–Thu, 10.00 Fri; entry JD12, children JD2) are held in the hippodrome. The shows feature chariots competing in the classic seven lap races that were the norm in Roman times, ten fighting gladiators and 45 legionnaires in full costume demonstrating battle tactics. It is a lively show and in the setting of the hippodrome is quite spectacular.

South Gate From the hippodrome you have to follow the walkway to the visitors' centre and on towards the original entrance to the city, the South Gate. This magnificent gate is believed to date from the 2nd century. It is richly carved but almost certainly didn't stand purely as a decorative feature of the city, it would have had a practical use. Horse and carts would have passed through, as well as pedestrians, and it is probable that a market would have taken place around the gate. To the side of the gate you will see the remains of the old thick walls that surrounded the city; the present ones were added by the Byzantines.

Oval Forum From the South Gate, and past a mighty wall behind which are restored vaults that once supported the Temple of Zeus's lower terraces and, now restored, house exhibits from the site, what opens out before you is simply breathtaking: Jerash's gem, the Oval Plaza. Two gently curving sidewalks each topped by a row of elegant Ionic columns barely a metre apart enclose an inner square paved with a swirl of cobbles. The columns stand on a stylobate (platform) with a classic Greek Ionic capital at the top and an architrave epistyle that sweeps around the plaza. The two colonnades would have continued, seamlessly, heading north in a straight line along the Cardo. The Oval Forum is one of the most dramatic sights of the ancient city. It measures some 90m across and in its centre stands a column of almost the same height as the colonnades. The column hosts the flame lit at the start of the Jerash Festival.

4

Temple of Zeus The remains of the Temple of Zeus show clearly that this was once a magnificent structure, which with Gerasa's other great temple, the Temple of Artemis, almost without doubt dominated the city. It was built on the site of much earlier sacred temples, and dates from around AD162. Legend has it that a staircase led from its temenos, or sacred precinct, up the hill to its entrance, although if it still exists it is yet to be discovered. The site is still being excavated, however, so it may be revealed in the coming years. In its prime the temple would have had enormous Corinthian columns surrounding it, but these fell a long time ago, probably in an earthquake, and have lain partially buried in the hill for centuries. In their place, three columns of similar design have been added in recent years, although they are more for effect than historical accuracy. Inside, the temple is quite plain. You can find the Temple of Zeus on the hill just off to the south of the Oval Forum.

South Theatre Next to the Temple of Zeus is the South Theatre, one of the iconic images of Jerash. Here, regular cultural events, including the Jerash leg of the summer Jordan Festival, are held. The richly carved backdrop (the scaenae frons) to the lower stage (orchestra), opposite to where some 3,000 people sit in the semi-circular auditorium, provides a dramatic setting for theatrical performances. The theatre, one of two on the site (the other being the smaller North Theatre), is believed to have been built in around AD92 during the reign of Emperor Domitian (b51, d96) and is beautifully preserved. It has vaulted passageways that provide access to the orchestra, and others that lead to the auditorium and seats on different levels. Curiously, some of the front row seats still bear Greek letters that possibly indicate that they were the ones reserved for the city's most prominent citizens. The theatre has undergone an extensive restoration programme in recent years and is now one of Jerash's most magical ancient treasures.

Cardo The colonnaded stone road, known as the Cardo, begins at the Oval Forum and runs almost the entire length of the city. It is around 800m long and runs north–south through the city. Together with the South Decumanus and the North Decumanus running east–west, which meet the Cardo in a crossroads fashion at two points along its length, the Cardo would have been the main thoroughfare of the city and therefore a key part of its planning. It would have been a busy street lined with shops, the remains of which are still visible, and probably overrun with chariots. You can still see ruts in the stones from countless chariot wheels. You'll also notice a series of holes. These allowed rainwater from the Cardo to drain into an elaborate underground sewage system.

The Cardo has always been colonnaded. Originally it would have had the Ionic columns seen in the Oval Forum, but sometime during the latter part of the 2nd century Gerasa was remodelled and a row of Corinthian style columns erected either side of the then newly widened Cardo. The Corinthian columns were more lavish with heavily carved capitals on the top of the columns depicting scrolls and acanthus leaves. As you walk along the Cardo, about halfway along you will notice the columns become taller. These mark the entrance to the macellum, which was the main market place of the city. Here, shops line a courtyard with a fountain in its centre. A little further on is a mosque at the point where the Cardo meets the South Decumanus at the South Tetrapylon.

Between the South Tetrapylon and the North Tetrapylon, which are the two intersections where the South Decumanus and the North Decumanus roads from the suburbs meet the Cardo, is a wealth of archaeological treasures. The **Tetrapylon squares** are interesting too; here columns would have stood where public notices would have been placed. In this stretch you will find the striking remains of the 2nd-century **nymphaeum**; its entrance marked by four tall columns. With its gushing waters that filtered through to underground cisterns, this elaborate public fountain, which would have been finished in marble and adorned with numerous water nymph and lion head statues, would have doubtless been a focal point of the city. Even today the lavishness of the structure is impressive despite its ruinous state. Along this stretch you will also find the **Cathedral**, the remains of the west and east **Roman baths** and the extensive **Temple of Artemis** complex.

Temple of Artemis This large complex includes the remains of public buildings and courtyards, but it is the temple itself that dominates. It would have been approached by a processional way, or Sacred Way, starting deep in the residential areas on which the modern city of Jerash now stands, across the Cardo at the point marked by four huge columns and to the main gateway of the complex, known as the propylaeum. This mighty elaborate gateway was built around AD150. From here worshippers would ascend a staircase, first to the lower terrace of the temple and then to the temenos, which is a sacred precinct, before entering the temple.

In its heyday the temple would have been a sumptuous structure, heavily carved and surrounded by a colonnaded walkway. Today, a hint of its former grandeur remains. Worshippers would have passed through its portico, known as a pronaos, which today is surrounded by columns. If you visit the site with a guide, he or she may encourage you to place an item like a stick, pencil or a comb from your bag between a drum of the column to see the movement as it sways slightly. The columns are designed to sway to counteract the effects of wind and earth tremors. Worshippers would then have entered the inner cella of the temple, where a statue depicting the ancient goddess and deity Artemis would have been placed in shrine-like fashion. According to Greek mythology, Artemis was the daughter of Zeus and Leto and the sister of Apollo, and was adopted as the patron goddess of Gerasa. The cella, although exposed to the elements today, would have been built in a traditional style with a peristyle of columns on each side and walls richly decorated in marble.

Cathedral, mosque and churches On the periphery of the Temple of Artemis complex is the site of a Roman temple dedicated to Dionysus on which a church was built. It was clearly a lavish structure with intricate carvings, and is today known as the Cathedral. Inside, you'll find a shrine with an inscription dedicated to St Mary. She is seen flanked by the archangels Gabriel and Michael. Nearby, is a small mosque dating from the Umayyad period and a collection of churches. A total of 15 churches have so far been discovered on the site, but as excavations are ongoing there could be many more still buried. The largest discovered so far is the **Church of Theodore** built in the latter half of the 5th century. Little remains of the church other than its apse. It lies next to what has been dubbed **Fountain Court**, a courtyard that would have been the cathedral's atrium with a fountain in the centre.

Nearby, are the **Synagogue Church**, the **Church of St Genesius** and the well-preserved **Church of Saints Cosmos and Damian**. The latter is dedicated to twin brothers who were physicians and lived in the late 3rd century. They became famous for providing medical services to the needy free of charge and were martyred by being beheaded for their Christian beliefs. The church contains one of the finest **floor mosaics** found in Jerash and depicts animals and birds in minute detail. Here, too, is the **Church of St George**, built in AD530, and the **Church of John the Baptist** from the same period. A little further to the south the **Church of Sts Peter and Paul** can be found.

Jerash Archaeological Museum (☏ 02 635 2267; ☼ summer 08.30–18.00 daily, winter 08.30–16.00 daily) With a fascinating collection of artefacts found during excavation of the Gerasa site, including pottery, theatre tickets and ancient coinage, the museum is well worth a visit and will enhance your experience of exploring the city site. It is full of information on Gerasa's history and how the archaeological remains were discovered and are being restored. A shady garden full of sarcophagi gives a little respite from the sun. Find the museum almost opposite the macellum along the Cardo.

TABAQAT FAHL (*Pella Archaeological Site;* ☼ *summer 08.00–18.00 daily, winter 08.00–16.00 daily*) An attractive, unassuming town, Tabaqat Fahl or Fihil is set in countryside with superb views out over the northern stretch of the River Jordan valley. It is better known as **Pella**, an ancient city that, although it came to the fore as one of the Decapolis, can trace its roots back as far as prehistoric times. With remains from the Stone Age right through to medieval times unearthed, and, of course, a wealth of Roman ruins, it is considered by archaeologists to be one of the finest sites in all of Jordan. It could be argued to even surpass Jerash. The finds have included luxury items such as gold, ivory inlays, alabaster trinkets and silk, suggesting that for millennia the site was on a key trade route from Egypt.

Reference to the city was first made in ancient Egyptian inscriptions dating from the 19th century BC, and it is later thought to have been one of the main suppliers of wooden spokes for Pharaonic Egypt's chariot wheels. Around the time of Alexander the Great's conquests in the 4th century BC, Pella was becoming a thriving city and one that was key to his empire. It is widely thought that the name Pella was bestowed on the city in honour of the ruler's birthplace, Pella, the ancient capital of the kingdom of Macedonia.

In biblical times Pella is believed to have been the city of Penuel where the prophet Jacob rested on his way from Mesopotamia to Canaan and sought protection from God. He feared for his life after threats from his brother Esau, who claimed Jacob had stolen his birthright. In the Book of Genesis, Jacob is said to have wrestled with God, who took the form of a man or an angel, at Penuel (Genesis 32:24–30). Excavation work at Pella began in the 1970s and along with countless Bronze Age and Iron Age artefacts, one of the most significant finds was a Canaanite temple. It would have stood in Old Testament times. The finding has added weight to the story that the site was, indeed, that of Penuel. Furthermore, the discovery of a series of city walls dated to around 3400BC suggesting that the city was a large and important city-kingdom before and during biblical times, and the story increases in credibility even further.

The Pella site at Tabaqat Fahl today offers lots for visitors to see. As well as the ancient settlement areas that are concentrated on the hill that forms a boundary to the site, there are the remains of when it was an important city of the Byzantine era and of the Decapolis league in Roman times. It covers a huge area, and because there is no clearly defined network of roads (the roads having disappeared over time), you may find yourself wandering through the site and having to use rather a lot of imagination to visualise how it once looked. The excellent **Pella Museum** (*www.pellamuseum.org*) provides an insight into Pella's history, as well as Jordan's, and helps you to understand what you can see on the site. Displays tell you of its geology and archaeology. The museum can be found just behind the Pella Resthouse restaurant.

Among the sights are the **Great Basilica** with its mighty columns and monumental staircase. The distinctive semi-circular shape of a diminutive **Roman Theatre** can be seen, along with a **mosque**, the **Canaanite temple**, **city walls** and **churches**. The

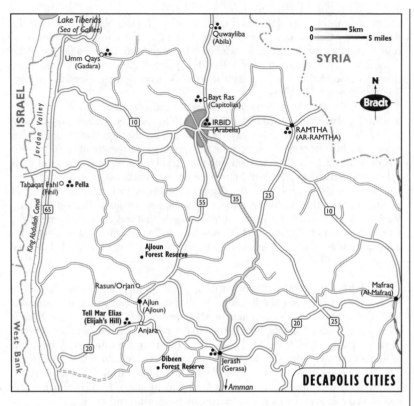

hills around Pella were believed to have been blanketed by **houses**, and the remains of these can be seen everywhere. Clearly Pella was a heavily populated place at one time. The new town of Tabaqat Fahl took its present name from a Byzantine–Arab battle that raged here in AD635, known as the Battle of Fahl. Fahl means marsh in Arabic, with Tabaqat al-Fahl, or Tabaqat Fahl, meaning Terraces of the Marsh. The site is well signposted from both Jerash and Irbid.

IRBID A large metropolis, Irbid is the capital of the Irbid Governorate, the third largest town in Jordan and the agricultural, industrial and economic hub of the north. It is home to well over 650,000 people who live and work here, and despite having been inhabited since the Bronze Age and having been the site of one of the Decapolis cities, Arabella, it has few attractions for visitors. A maze of wide avenues and streets host endless homes and shops for local people, while to the south of the downtown district, or city centre, is the vast campus of the Yarmouk University. The campus could be said to be Irbid's only real landmark, and it has given this quarter a trendy, sophisticated feel. You'll find plenty of internet cafés and chic coffee shops here, especially along the King Abdullah II Street.

Irbid is not a city on the tourist trail other than for its associations with Arabella; more it is a place that you will probably find yourself passing through *en route* to the Eastern Desert, Umm Qays or Abila. In ancient times, as Arabella, it was famous for producing some of the finest wines of the ancient world. Grapes grew in abundance here because of the rich fertile soil and temperate climate, and indeed still do. Arabella, along with its neighbouring Decapolis city of Capitolias, on the site of present-day Bayt Ras, was sprawling, although probably nowhere near the size of nearby Gerasa (Jerash) and Gadara (Umm Qays). It saw a lengthy period of construction as part of the Roman Empire, but went into decline after the Battle of Yarmouk and the start of early Arab rule. Archaeologists have unearthed many treasures around the sites, and excavation work is continuing, especially at Bayt Ras, also known as Beit Ras.

What Irbid does have, however, are some excellent museums. Arguably the best is the **Museum of Jordanian Heritage** (*Yarmouk University Campus;* ⟍ *02 721 1111;* ⊕ *10.00–17.00 Sat–Wed*). Here you can see displays that record Jordan as well as Irbid's history in a concise, orderly manner. As the site of the Decapolis city of Arabella, as well as nearby Capitolias, Irbid has seen archaeological finds aplenty unearthed as new buildings have been constructed over ancient sites, and many of these now grace the display cabinets of this museum. More can be found in the **Dar As-Saraya Museum** (*www.dam.gov.jo;* ⊕ *10.00–17.00 Sat–Wed*), which is housed in a 19th-century property that was once the home of the Ottoman governor. You can find exhibits from Pella and Umm Qays, along with a **mosaic collection** that is one of the finest outside of 'mosaic city' Madaba (see *Madaba*, page 188).

QUWAYLIBA Lying around 10km north of Irbid, Quwayliba is a peaceful village lying in the richly vegetated valley of the Wadi Quwayliba that you could easily pass by if it were not for its location next to **Abila**, one of the Decapolis cities. Abila is often referred to as Abila Raphana, although it is widely believed that the two were, in fact, separate cities of the Decapolis. The city was at one time a busy place full of Roman and Byzantine inhabitants, but is not believed to have reached anywhere near the size of Gerasa (Jerash) or Gadara (Umm Qays). It was all but destroyed by the massive earthquake that rocked north Jordan in AD747, after which it was abandoned and over the years was covered by earth, sand and grass.

It is only in recent years that the site has begun to be excavated, and as such there are only a few archaeological remains for visitors to see so far. The finest example of this once bustling city is its **Roman Theatre**, although you can clearly make out the remains of dwellings, possibly a marketplace, streets, churches, shops and a bath complex amongst the broken columns and carved stones. The most fascinating area of the site is its **Byzantine cemetery** where the tomb caves are worth a peek if you have a sense of adventure. Although they have long been relieved of the tombs themselves, they are still adorned with amazingly well-preserved frescoes on the walls and ceilings.

The Abila site is easily reached by bus from the north station in Irbid (*JD1*). It will take only 20 minutes or so, but be sure to ask the driver to let you off at the Abila ruins because the road forks just before them and you will find yourself going off in the wrong direction.

UMM QAYS Teetering on a hill overlooking the Jordan Valley to the west, the Sea of Galilee and the Golan Heights in the northwest corner of Jordan, the village of Umm Qays is a picturesque place. It is best known as being the location of the ancient Roman and biblical city of **Gadara**, and is mentioned in the New Testament as the country of the Gadarenes (Matthew 8:28). It is believed Jesus performed one of his miracles here (see box below). Like Gerasa (Jerash), Gadara underwent massive construction during the 2nd century. Long, wide colonnaded streets were built, many lined with shops, churches and mosques. Huge Roman theatres were constructed where the city's citizens could be entertained and bath complexes were introduced. One of the largest was at Al-Himma, a few kilometres north of Umm Qays, which can still be visited today.

Umm Qays has long been known as a cultural place, and here several classical philosophers and poets were born. Menippus, after whom the Menippean genre of satire is named, hailed from Gadara. He was prolific in the 3rd century BC and is often classed as one of the Cynics, a term used to describe early Greek philosophers and satirists who were known for voicing opinions and could be described as the forefathers of media commentators today. Menippus had a number of compatriots: Meleager of Gadara, a poet who became infamous as the creator of satirical prose and memorable epigrams in the 1st century BC is perhaps one of the most famous; Philodemus, who rose to fame around the same time and is credited with producing works on theology, rhetoric and music, poetry and history; and the Greek rhetoric Theodorus of Gadara who taught the then future Roman emperor, Tiberius Julius Caesar Augustus, the art of rhetoric.

In Byzantine times Gadara became a bishopric, while in AD636, during the Battle of Yarmouk between the Byzantine and Muslim Arab forces, which took place in the land surrounding Umm Qays, the city was conquered by early Islamists. In AD747 it was all but flattened by a powerful earthquake that shook the country, and for a time lay abandoned until around the latter part of the 19th century when it was rediscovered. The Ottoman Empire brought a period of reconstruction, and homes were built. The new town that emerged from the ancient ruins was referred to in records as Mkes, meaning a frontier station for collecting taxes. Today, Umm Qays has become a popular day trip destination from Amman, which is around a 90-minute drive away.

Umm Qays Archaeological Site
(☉ *summer 07.00–18.00 daily, winter 07.00–16.00 daily; entry JD3*) This ancient site is Gadara, one of the Decapolis cities that were founded and thrived during the Roman era. You can see the remains of a colonnaded terrace, a mausoleum, baths and two splendid theatres in its archaeological park, along with its museum crammed with fascinating artefacts from the site. It is not a large archaeological site and you could easily spend just a couple of hours here, which would be sufficient to do it justice. Keen archaeologists may wish to stay longer.

The approach takes you past some impressive **Roman tombs**, which look as if they may hold untold archaeological treasures inside, but are actually empty. Continue on to the car parks on your right and the visitors' ticket office. From here you can wander freely. To your right you will come to a labyrinth of streets with dwellings that are the remains of the **Ottoman village** that grew from the

4

MIRACLE OF THE GADARENE SWINE

Jesus and his disciples are said to have met a man coming out of a tomb possessed by demons on a visit to the Gadara. It is said that Jesus spoke to the demons, demanding that they depart. He sent them hurling into a herd of pigs that were grazing on the hillside (Luke 8:32). The pigs, then possessed by the demons, ran down a steep tell (hill) and into the Sea of Galilee, thus the man was cured (Matthew 8:32–33). There has been some debate as to the exact location of the miracle, but Gadara, with its hills, grazing areas, tombs and close proximity to the sea, is thought to be the place in question.

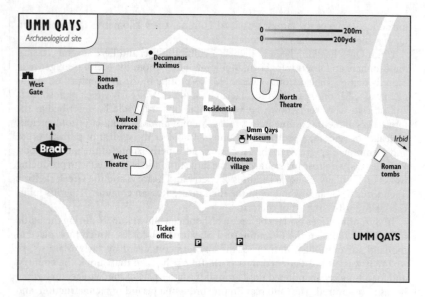

ancient ruins. Look out for the **Umm Qays Archaeological Museum** (⊕ *summer 08.00–18.00 daily, winter 08.00–16.00 daily*) housed in Biet Al-Russan, which is the former home of the Ottoman governor. It houses displays of pottery, jewellery, weapons, coins and household artefacts recovered during excavation work at the site. Beyond the museum are the ruins of the **North Theatre**, where the Romans of Gadara would have been entertained.

West of the Ottoman village are the remains of the **Roman city**. Here you can see the **Basilica Terrace**, the highlight of the Umm Qays Archaeological Site, with vaulted openings once used as shops appearing to support it. Nearby you will see the semi-circular **West Theatre**, and if you keep heading north you will come to the colonnaded paved street known as the **Decumanus Maximus**. This long wide street that follows a course east to west across the city would have been a key part of its urban planning. A series of Corinthian columns once stood along its length; some are still upright while others lie along its side walkways partially covered by earth and grass.

5

The Eastern Desert

With its endless plains of parched stony desert (*harra*) interspersed by the greenery of an odd oasis (*waha*) and imposing, if often quirky, castles and palaces (*qasr*), the Eastern Desert is one of the most barren places in Jordan. Here you will find the **Azraq Wetland Reserve** at Azraq (locally Al-Azraq al-Janubi) and the **Shaumari Wildlife Reserve**. Together with the southern deserts, the Eastern Desert forms part of the Badia region; *badia* meaning 'desert' in Arabic. If you love solitary locations you will be charmed by this massive wilderness.

The Eastern Desert extends out from the eastern fringes of Amman and apart from **Zarqa** (locally Az-Zarqa), which is a huge built-up industrial area where a large proportion of Amman's workforce live and commute from daily, the remote regional capital of **Mafraq** (locally Al-Mafraq) and the pleasing if a little dusty oasis village of **Azraq** (locally Al-Azraq al-Janubi meaning 'south Azraq', and Al-Azraq ash-Shamali, meaning 'north Azraq'), there are few towns and villages to break up the seemingly endless journey to the Iraqi border in the east, to Saudi Arabia and to the Syria border in the north.

What there is, however, is a collection of desert palaces and castles that appear as if a mirage on the horizon as you approach. Some are remote, while others lie alongside roadways or around oases. These impressive structures are among the most accessible of all those dating from the Roman and Umayyad periods found anywhere in the Israeli, Lebanese, Syrian and Jordanian desert regions. You can plot a course that takes in most, if not all, of the desert palaces by car. Alternatively, you can join an excursion; many tour operators in Amman offer trips. Some of the palaces and castles are ruins, while others have been beautifully restored and are well worth seeing. The large palace **Qasr al-Mushatta** lies just outside Amman near the airport, the mighty **Qasr al-Harrana** (also al-Kharana) with its fortress-like appearance is around 25km further on, and the largest of all the Umayyad palaces, the **Qasr at-Tuba**, lies 30km south of the Shaumari Wildlife Reserve. One of the best preserved is the UNESCO World Heritage Site of **Qusayr 'Amra** (*qusayr* meaning 'a small qasr'), which is a little over 80km away from Amman off the highway to Azraq.

At Azraq itself, the sprawling **Qasr Azraq** is a fortress that played a key role in the Arab Revolt of 1916–18, while the **Qasr al-Hallabat** was popular with the Umayyads as a place to enjoy recreational time given that it was just a few kilometres outside Amman. On the northernmost border there are the stark ruins of the Nabatean fortress **Umm al-Jimal**. *En route* you can stop at **Khirbet as-Samra** to see the ruins of what was once a fine Roman-Byzantine town. Deep in the desert a few kilometres off the road to Iraq is the **Qasr Burqu**, a sombre black castle on the edge of an oasis.

To really explore the Eastern Desert you'll need a couple of days, although the highlights can be seen in one, albeit very long, day. If you do stay overnight, bear

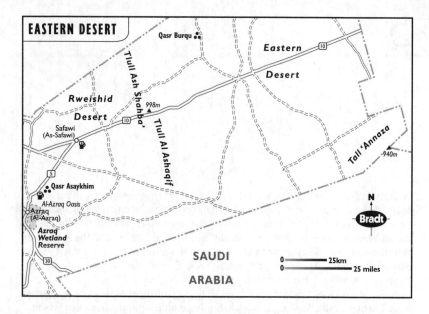

in mind that accommodation options are few. One of the best is the Azraq Lodge, an eco-lodge run by the Royal Society for the Conservation of Nature near the Azraq Wetland Reserve at Azraq or you can stay in Amman or one of the few hotels in Zarqa. A campsite with amenities is available at the Shaumari Wildlife Reserve.

HISTORY

Evidence suggests that communities have lived and thrived in the Eastern Desert for over 2.5 million years. Flint axe heads and primitive tools dating from the Palaeolithic or Stone Age and Epipalaeolithic periods have been found throughout the region, and especially around Azraq, known in antiquity as Basie. Here, a source of fresh drinking water from underground aquifers feeds into an oasis. The Nabateans, who founded the famous city of Petra around 312BC, lived, traded and farmed large areas of the Eastern Desert, focusing their efforts around Azraq.

During the Roman, Byzantine, early Islamic and Umayyad periods the desert region flourished, with existing settlements used as military bases, new communities formed and forts and palaces built in abundance. One of the most impenetrable fortresses was Azraq's own castle, the mighty Qasr Azraq, which was built by the Romans. The desert and its fortresses and palaces continued to be used during subsequent periods of power by the Ayyubids, the Mamluks and the Ottomans.

In the early 1900s, when Arab forces were increasing their efforts to thwart the rule of the Ottomans in their bid for independence, the Eastern Desert became a key location for successful campaigns. The Qasr Azraq was used by the British as its headquarters when working with the Arabs during the Arab Revolt. More recently the desert has seen an influx of Druze and Chechen communities, from Syria and the Caucasus respectively. Many joined local Bedouin tribes and settled around Azraq, while a large Chechen community stayed in Zarqa, effectively founding the city.

BY AIR The Eastern Desert does not have its own airport, but is easily reached from Amman's **Queen Alia International Airport** or Aqaba's **King Hussein International Airport** (see *Getting there*, page 48).

BY TAXI The Eastern Desert is a desolate place and understandably has few transport options. Other than at the Azraq Wetland Reserve or the campsite at Shaumari Wildlife Reserve there are few places to stay, so you'll probably begin your excursion into the desert from Amman. You can hire a private taxi in Amman but be sure to explain what you want from your trip and where you want to go so that the company can supply a vehicle that's suitable for desert driving, and calculate the fare for you. You can, if you wish, hire the services of a guide too.

BY BUS If you prefer to take a bus, first head for **Zarqa**. As home to one of the region's largest concentrations of working people who travel daily into Amman, there is never a shortage of buses from the city's Abdali bus station. Zarqa itself has two bus stations. The **New Station** is largely reserved for the intercity buses that link Zarqa with the country's other major towns, but you'll be able to catch a bus to

THE BADIA REGION

The Badia region covers around 75% of the country's total landmass. Made up of desert and desert steppes, it is part of the much larger North Arab Desert that stretches well into Syria, Iraq and Saudi Arabia. It consists of several desert areas. Northeast of Amman in the Zarqa Governorate is the Eastern Desert. It is criss-crossed by dozens of *wadis* that feed the wetlands around which the Azraq Wetland Reserve at Azraq and the Shaumari Wildlife Reserve that lies due south are located.

The northern Basalt Desert lies towards Syria and northern Saudi Arabia. Its character was formed millions of years ago when volcanic eruptions created the landscape of massive black basalt boulders after which the desert takes its name. East of the Basalt Desert is the Rweishif Desert with its unusual landscape of an endless limestone plateau dotted with lush areas of green and agricultural fields. The desert extends right to Jordan's border with Iraq. Quiet and full of endemic plants and wildlife, it is here that two new reserves, the Burqu Reserve and the Rajel Reserve, look set to be established.

To the south of Amman is the Central Desert, which you will see if driving along the Desert Highway from the city *en route* to Aqaba in the south. It is crossed by several wide *wadis* that give it an interesting appearance. At Ma'an (a large town and the closest to Petra other than Wadi Musa), if you were to take a left at the Desert Highway's junction and head out to Al-Jafr you would be in the heart of the Al-Mudawwara Desert. Crossed by broad *wadis*, it has valleys and hills, and low, rocky mountains. South of the Al-Mudawware Desert is Jordan's most famous desert, the Rum Desert, where you will find the extraordinarily landscape of Wadi Rum.

Elevations vary in the Badia region from between 600m above sea level to 900m, and as such its temperatures by day can reach well over 40°C, but by night the temperature can plummet and it can feel quite cold. Badia receives little rainfall – just 50mm a year – and is extremely dry and often windy.

places like Azraq, Qasr Hallabat and Khirbet as-Samra from the **Old Station**. Here, too, you can get a bus to Mafraq for onward buses to Umm al-Jimal on the Syrian border. Amman has a host of companies offering guided excursions by bus (see *Tour operators*, page 43).

BY CAR In a car you have the freedom to travel along any road you wish, although be sure your vehicle is suitable for the journey and that you have plenty of water, snacks and a spare container of fuel with you. Fill up with fuel before you leave. **Hire cars** are readily available in Amman (see page 72). Tell someone like the tourist police that you are intending to journey into the desert and when you plan to return.

To reach Azraq from Amman you have a choice of two routes. To go via the Zarqa Highway, take King Abdullah Street and look out for signposts to the Amman–Zarqa Highway. You'll go past the Roman Theatre. On the highway, as you approach Zarqa you'll begin to see signs for Azraq. Once on the Zarqa–Azraq road you'll pass by Qasr Hallabat and Hammam as-Srah. An alternative route is to take the Desert Highway out of Amman towards the Queen Alia International Airport until you reach the signpost for Madaba. At this junction take the road marked to Azraq. It runs in the opposite direction to Madaba. This route is ideal for visiting Qasr al-Mushatta, Qasr al-Harrana and Qusayr 'Amra. Non-stop journey time from Amman to Azraq is around 1½ hours. If you are planning to go by car to Mafraq and Umm al-Jimal, follow the instruction above for the Zarqa Highway. Once on the highway, follow the signs for Mafraq.

TOURIST INFORMATION

☑ Royal Society for the Conservation of Nature (RSCN) At the Azraq Wetland Reserve at Azraq (locally Al-Azraq al-Janubi) & the Shaumari Wildlife Reserve; ☎ 05 383 5225; f 06 463 3657; e tourism@rscn.org.jo; www.rscn.org.jo

TOUR OPERATORS

Karma House Jordan Prince Mohammad St, Amman; ☎ 06 463 1654; f 06 463 1183; e info@karma.com.jo; www.karmahousejordan.com. An excursion called Soul Searcher takes you into the desert to see the castles & palaces.
Nyazi ECO Tours Abdullah Ghosheh St, Aqaba; ☎ 06 581 5910; f 06 581 5902; e info@nyazi.com.jo; www.nyazi.com.jo. Focusing on eco-themed tours into the desert, this company is run by a team of antiquities & archaeology experts.
United Travel Agency Abdul Hameed Sharaf St, Amman; ☎ 06 566 0490; f 06 566 0269; e info@uta.com.jo; www.uta.com.jo. Also in Hamamat al-Tunisia St, Aqaba, & Taybet Zaman, Wadi Musa, near Petra. Eco-themed itineraries that cover desert trekking to the reserves & castles.

▲ WHERE TO STAY

Finding a comfortable place to stay overnight in the Eastern Desert can be a challenge. There are a handful of campsites and small hotels, the latter mostly aimed at truck drivers, or you could try the popular Azraq Lodge near the Azraq Wetland Reserve in Azraq. There are no accommodation options in Mafraq or Umm al-Jimal. Most visitors to the desert stay in Amman and follow a route around the castles by car or join a day's excursion by tour bus that returns to Amman early evening. Alternatively, they make the 100km or so journey direct to Azraq by bus via Zarqa and stay overnight.

⌂ **Azraq Lodge** (16 rooms) Near Azraq Wetland Reserve, Azraq; ☏ 05 383 5225; f 06 463 3657; e tourism@rscn.org.jo; www.rscn. org.jo; ⊕ All year. Run by the Royal Society for the Conservation of Nature (RSCN), this eco-lodge has been created in a former British field hospital on the edge of the reserve. The renovation has ensured the building's 1940s character remains. The complex, which overlooks the Azraq basin, has a terrace for mingling with other guests, a restaurant & fully equipped guestrooms with AC. There's a super little handicraft workshop too, where local women display their painted ostrich eggs & handmade textiles. **$$$$**

⌂ **Al-Azraq Rest House** (10 rooms) Al-Azraq ash-Shamali; ☏ 05 383 4006; f 05 383 5215. Other than the reserve's accommodation, this basic hotel is the only other overnight hotel option in Azraq, indeed the Eastern Desert. It is a small but pleasant hotel & set in a location that is ideal for exploring the desert. Built around a swimming pool with gardens & a sun terrace, it has its own restaurant. Guestrooms look out over the pool. **$$**

⌂ **Al-Andaleeb Hotel** (32 rooms) 151033 Zarqa; ☏ 05 398 7702; f 05 399 1440. If you're travelling on a budget then this hotel not far from the city centre may suit your requirements. It has a pleasing restaurant where local dishes are served & an intimate lounge, but other than that amenities are few. Guestrooms are a tad on the basic side, but equipped with all the essentials nonetheless. **$**

⌂ **Al-Zoubi Hotel** (12 rooms) Al-Azraq al-Janubi; ☏ 05 383 5012. This small complex of budget apartments is a little off the beaten track, but the en-suite rooms offered are presented well, & are clean. They are furnished with antique-style chairs & tables. The local family that runs the hotel is friendly & welcoming & is a mine of information on the desert. **$**

⌂ **Shaumari Camp** (10 tents) Shaumari Wildlife Reserve near Azraq; ☏ 05 383 5225; f 06 463 3657; e tourism@rscn.org.jo; www.rscn. org.jo; ⊕ All year. This basic but clean campsite is operated by the RSCN, & offer tents that accommodate 4 people. They are equipped with mattresses, sheets & pillows. Food is available & there are showers & toilets. **$**

✗ WHERE TO EAT

If you don't fancy joining the truckers who stop at street vendors along the route through Azraq for a drink and basic grilled kebab meal, or you prefer not to dine too heavily before leaving Amman, then there are only really two options where you'll find a good, wholesome and delicious meal during the day, or in the evening if staying overnight in the desert.

✗ **Azraq Lodge Restaurant** Near Azraq Wetland Reserve, Azraq; ☏ 05 383 5225; f 06 463 3657; e tourism@rscn.org.jo; www.rscn.org.jo; ⊕ 08.00–23.00. This is one of the few places in the Eastern Desert where you will get a meal, but it does come at a price. Like the eco-lodge it is run by the RSCN & focuses on local cuisine with an organic theme. Many of the fresh ingredients are grown locally. While the choice of food isn't large, the dishes that are served are artfully presented & delicious. **$$$$**

✗ **Azraq Palace Restaurant** Azraq centre; m 079 503 0356; ⊕ 12.00–16.00 & 18.00–23.00. This the best option for brunch, lunch, evening meal & supper, & any snack in between. A large restaurant, it can usually be found full of tourists who have just hopped off their bus for a break from their excursion around the desert. An extensive buffet & a lengthy beer & juice list caters for all tastes. **$$$$**

OTHER PRACTICALITIES

EMERGENCIES To contact the **police** and the **tourist police** team of the Mafraq Governorate and the Zarqa Governorate who serve the Eastern Desert and help to ensure the safety of visitors to the castles and reserves, ☏ 191 or ☏ 112. **Medical**

emergencies and **ambulances**, along with the **fire brigade**, can be contacted on ☏ 199. The nearest **hospitals** are the Zarqa Military Hospital (☏ *05 398 0621*), the government hospital in Zarqa (☏ *05 398 3323*), and the Kaser Shabib Hospital (☏ *05 398 2370*).

INTERNET Despite its remoteness, the Eastern Desert has a strong internet signal and you will find fast broadband and Wi-Fi in most of the hotels. A handful of internet cafés are springing up, most notably around the Hashemite University, the Al-Balqa Applied University and the Zarqa University in Zarqa, and in Mafraq and Azraq. The Azraq Lodge in Azraq has Wi-Fi in its reception area that is available to non-guests. You can generally get a signal on your mobile phone.

MONEY, POST AND SHOPPING You'll find banks, ATMs, shops selling day-to-day goods and post offices in Zarqa, around the area of the bus stations and downtown. Both Azraq and Mafraq have the same facilities but on a much smaller scale; head for Al-Azraq al-Janubi in Azraq and the city central square in Mafraq. Most of the hotels have money-changing facilities and a postal service for guests; ask at your reception for details.

WHAT TO SEE AND DO

DESERT PALACES AND CASTLES The palaces and castles are a curious mix; some have hints of Roman architecture, others of Syrian–Byzantine and early Islamic. As a result, historians have frequently debated their origins. The consensus is that most date from the Umayyad caliphate period when, keen to exert their authority after taking power from the Byzantines and early Arab groups, the Damascus-based Umayyads built an impressive collection of palaces, castles and monuments. One palace was built in Amman, the remains of which can be seen at the Citadel [97 G3], but the majority were built deep in the desert. The Umayyads also took over existing castles built by the Romans and renovated them to their own distinctive artistic style.

TOURING THE CASTLES

Excursions that provide tourists with a tour of the desert castles run similar routes clockwise and anticlockwise out of Amman. If you're driving then there's no reason why you shouldn't follow similar routes; they are well-trodden and have proved to be the most time efficient.

The first option leaves Amman and, via Zarqa, takes in Qasr al-Hallabat and Qasr Azraq before stopping for lunch in Azraq. It then continues on to Qusayr 'Amra and finally stops at Qasr al-Harrana. Option two takes you out of Amman on Highway 40 signposted to Azraq, stopping firstly at Qasr al-Harrana and then Qusayr 'Amra; lunch is at Azraq; then there's a visit to Qasr Azraq before making for home via Qasr al-Hallabat.

The palace ruins at Qasr al-Mushatta, near the airport, are a little off the route, but feasible to do if you spend less time at the other castles. Umm al-Jimal, too, is well worth an excursion. If you plan to visit Qasr at-Tuba or Qasr Burqu, however, you will need to hire a specialist guide and vehicle, and allow at very least a half day each to visit them in their lonely, isolated and barren desert locations.

While these structures clearly had a defensive role to play where the caliphs could, no doubt, feel safe from any potential invaders, the palaces and castles were essentially where the leaders could escape city life, relax, engage in wine and song, hunt and race their horses. They almost certainly had the air of a recreational resort. Importantly, too, they were centres where the caliphs could forge relationships with the Bedouins who lived in these remote parts of the country.

The castles and palaces were, in addition, used as trade centres. Camel caravans would stop on their long journeys through the desert from Arabia to the Levant and Syria so that the merchants and their animals could refresh. Most of the castles and palaces were built around natural springs and had water management systems with reservoirs and cisterns for storage. This meant that the caliphs not only had fresh drinking water and could grow fruit and vegetables for themselves, but could also trade in water, which was – and still is – a valuable commodity.

The remains of the fortified complexes we see today were clearly once sprawling places and had distinctive architectural designs that might have been considered progressive in their day, such as the Qusayr 'Amra with its three-vaulted roofline. Mosaics laid in intricate patterns were used to decorate floor spaces and coloured frescoes were painted to adorn the walls and ceilings. On the inner and outer façades the buildings often had intricate stone and stucco carvings. Remains of these artistic touches for which the Umayyads were famous can still be seen today. All the castles and palaces have their own distinct characteristics, and collectively they stand in testament to man's ability to build and to live in the Eastern Desert, one of the remotest, harshest places on earth.

Qasr al-Hallabat (*Off Highway 30;* ⊕ *summer 08.00–18.00 daily, winter 08.00–16.00 daily*) This attractive palace complex dating from the 2nd to 3rd century AD can be found a few kilometres outside Amman. Qasr al-Hallabat was originally a fortress built during the reign of Roman Emperor Caracella (b188, d217), one of many on the outskirts of Amman along the Roman highway via Nova Traiana that linked Damascus with Aqaba. Its purpose was to defend the empire against raiding desert tribes. The palace stands atop a high hill that was originally a Nabatean settlement, and is surrounded by thick stone walls with towers that are clear indicators of its defensive purpose. Caracella had it constructed using the stark black basalt of Jordan's northernmost desert, but when the artistic Umayyads came to power a couple of centuries later, they set about demolishing large parts of it and rebuilt using the sandy-coloured limestone that gives it the pleasing appearance it has today. They decorated it with frescoes and stucco carvings that gave it more of a grand palace feel. For a time before the remodelling, the complex was also used as a monastery by Christian monks.

In recent years an archaeological team have done an excellent job in restoring the palace. As a result it has become a popular tourist attraction and a new car park and visitors' centre, complete with refreshments, has been built. From the visitors' centre, which lies at the foot of the hill, you need to walk up the stony pathway towards the main entrance of the castle. The first building that catches your eye will be the **Umayyad mosque**, which with its carved doorways and arched vaulted interior is a fine example of 8th-century architecture. Nearby are the remains of an Umayyad-built **water management system** with dams, cisterns and channels to collect and store rainwater.

The main black and white limestone palace is a sprawling place, with towers in each corner and a central cobblestoned courtyard. As with other palaces, the ground floor would have been used for storage and the first floor, reached by the staircase, would have been where the caliph and his family and friends would have stayed. These upper rooms were clearly once lavishly decorated. From the remains you can still see finely crafted mosaics showing animals and birds bordered by geometric patterns, along with stucco carvings and ornate frescoes. It is a fascinating castle. Look out for Latin inscriptions on some of the stones; it is believed the stones originally came from Byzantine sites when the palace was constructed.

Once you have completed your tour of Qasr al-Hallabat, head a couple of kilometres east to the **Hammam al-Sarah**. This small pavilion was built by the Umayyads as a spa-cum-bathhouse. You can see the remains of the caldarium (hot bathing area) and the tepidarium (warm bathing area), complete with a hypocaust underfloor heating system. At one time, the building would have been decorated with marble and mosaics but these have long gone. The pavilion is currently undergoing restoration.

Qasr Azraq (*Near Al-Azraq ash-Shamali;* ☉ *summer 08.00–18.00 daily, winter 09.00–16.00 daily; entry JD2, inc entry to Qasr Al-Harrana & Qusayr 'Amra*) An imposing fortress, the Qasr Azraq (Qasr al-Azraq) is believed to have been built by the Romans in the 3rd century as a military base. It occupies what would have been a strategic spot for defending the Roman Empire, although key to its importance was the fact that it occupied a site adjacent to Azraq's natural spring. With water being such a scarce commodity in the desert, it was the ideal place for troops to stay. For much the same reasons, the castle continued to be used during the Byzantine and early Arab ruling periods, and when the Umayyads came to power it was extended and renovated. The progressive Umayyads also added a reservoir to store water for times of drought.

The fortress's zenith came in the Middle Ages when the Ayyubids and later the Mamluks expelled the Crusader forces from the country. The castle is said to have remained at the forefront of their defenses and underwent extensive remodelling. Much of the work involved building or rebuilding parts of the fortress using slabs of dark, often unwieldy, basalt that was quarried nearby. As a result, the fortress is distinctive in that it appears much darker and more starkly imposing than many of the other desert castles.

The fortress continued to be used throughout the time the Ottoman Turks assumed and maintained power of Jordan, or Transjordan as it was then known. When Arab forces sought independence from the Ottomans in furious battles that became known as the Arab Revolt of 1916–18, the castle became the headquarters for Lieutenant Colonel Thomas Edward Lawrence, better known as Lawrence of Arabia. He was the British Army officer who worked with Arab forces to bolster their bid for control. The little room above the gatehouse is where

AL-WALID I

Umayyad caliph Al-Walid ibn Abd al-Malik, better known as Al-Walid I (b668, d715), built the Qusayr 'Amra as a personal holiday retreat. He was a revolutionary caliph who is credited in history with masterminding some of the largest building projects ever seen under Islamic rule. These included one of the world's oldest and largest mosques: the Great Mosque of Damascus, or simply the Umayyad Mosque, in Syria. He rebuilt the Al-Masjid al-Nabawi in Medina, which is the second holiest site, in Islam, and the third holiest site the Al-Aqsa Mosque in Jerusalem. The Islamic architectural style we see today is said to have originated with Al-Walid I.

he finalised plans and gathered Arab troops before their successful assault on Damascus in 1917.

Today, the Qasr Azraq is one of a group dubbed the Desert Castles, and is a popular tourist attraction. It is a large structure with thick walls stretching for some 80m, and massive stone doors. Its entrance door alone is made from a single slab of heavy granite, which in architectural terms is a rare choice of design and must have been a feat to action. It is thought stone was used due to the shortage of hard timber.

The walls of the castle are adorned with towers in each corner and hide an inner courtyard where a small **mosque** stands in the centre. It is thought to date from the Umayyad period. Qasr Azraq is not the prettiest of castles, but it is striking and has witnessed a remarkably active past. It's easy to find; from the Al-Azraq al-Janubi junction, pass the Azraq Wetland Reserve on your right and after a little over 1km, just before you reach Al-Azraq ash-Shamali, you'll see the fortress ahead.

Qusayr 'Amra (*Off Highway 40 between Amman & Azraq; visitors' centre* ☉ *summer 07.00–19.30 daily, winter 08.00–16.30 daily; entry JD2, inc entry to Qasr Al-Harrana & Qasr Azraq*) With its soft, sandy-coloured limestone and basalt façade and its architectural design that makes it stand out against the blue sky and the flat, barren landscape, the Qusayr 'Amra is the most famous of all the Desert Castles. It was built in the 8th century AD, almost certainly in the year AD710, on the instructions of the ground-breaking Umayyad caliph Al-Walid ibn Abd al-Malik, better known as Al-Walid I, who liked to take recreational time in the desert.

While the Qusayr 'Amra, which is also known as the Quseir Amra or the Qasr Amra, is nowhere near the size of the Syrian mosque (see box opposite), it is of a progressive design. At one time it would have been part of a much larger complex that comprised a garrison, and was probably a type of hunting lodge used by the caliph. It has two-storeys, with walls constructed using square blocks of limestone and a rare and highly distinctive triple-vaulted roof over its main entrance. A single-storey section has several domes and rooms with vaulted ceilings, and in the grounds there is evidence of a water-management system.

Structurally, the Qusayr 'Amra it is one of the best preserved of all the desert fortifications, but more importantly it also has a magnificent collection of **Umayyad frescoes** that are in such good condition and of such important historical interest that the castle has been declared a UNESCO World Heritage Site. The frescoes, and indeed the architecture, are considered some of the earliest forms of Islamic art. Painted in terracotta, cream, blue and green shades, the frescoes can be seen on walls and ceilings throughout the castle.

In the main entrance hall there are frescoes depicting hunting scenes, animals, the consumption of food and wine, and of naked women, while on another wall a scene chronicles how the castle was built. The three stages of life are believed to be represented in another fresco on a ceiling. In the tepidarium (warm bathing area) the fresco shows women bathing amongst trees and plants, while another that adorns the high domed ceiling of the caldarium (hot bathing area) shows a remarkably intact and detailed picture of the astronomical ring of constellations, known as the zodiac. It is, so far, believed to be the earliest example of a painting of the night sky on a domed surface.

In a room that was possibly a dining hall, there is a significant fresco. It is said to depict the caliph with 'six kings', one of which is King Roderick of Spain (circa bAD687, dAD711). It has enabled scholars to date the castle with some accuracy.

For many years the Qusayr 'Amra was all but abandoned and open to anyone passing by. Fortunately, it escaped the attention of iconoclasts who would, no doubt, have destroyed the frescoes as happened elsewhere. In the late 19th century an Austro-Hungarian explorer and writer, Alois Musil (b1868, d1944) stumbled upon the castle and became so enthralled by the frescoes that he brought them to the attention of the world in a series of seminars and publications. The world, it seems, took notice and in the 1970s the frescoes were beautifully restored, and the castle declared a UNESCO Site in 1985.

Qasr al-Harrana (*Off Highway 40 Amman–Azraq;* ☉ *summer 08.00–18.00 daily, winter 08.00–16.00 daily; entry JD2, inc entry to Qusayr 'Amra & Qasr Azraq*) This sand-coloured castle made of rough limestone blocks may blend in with its surroundings but it is every inch a fortress. It has a distinct air of authority with impenetrable-looking walls, yet its inner layout suggests it probably wasn't a military base at all. It was possibly a palace, perhaps a caravanserai for passing merchants, although not being on a major trade route this is unlikely, or it might have been a recreational meeting place of some standing. Its exact use is unknown.

The Qasr al-Harrana, which is also often known as the Qasr al-Kharana or Kharraneh, is remarkably well preserved. An inscription on a wall of one the upper rooms suggests it was built in AD710, which would put it in the reign of the Umayyads, and yet it displays more Persian-influenced architecture, suggesting that an earlier Sassanid fort or a Byzantine temple may have stood on the site. Today, the walls are dotted with small slits that could easily have been for fighters to fire arrows through, but are considered more likely to been built to provide a discreet 'window' and give ventilation and light to the rooms inside.

From the visitors' centre, follow the pathway to the castle and enter by the main gate. You will immediately see long, vaulted rooms to your left and right that were once the stables. From here, you can explore the 60 or so rooms arranged over two floors that look out over an inner courtyard. Some of the rooms, especially those on the first floor, feature ornate protruding columns, others decorative niches. They were clearly beautifully decorated and even now, after all these years, you can still make out carvings on the rooms' walls depicting scenes of the day and patterns created with rosettes. The room directly over the entrance gateway is especially elaborate, and was probably the private quarters of the caliph.

The ground floor rooms of castles of this period tended to be used for storage and were less ornate. They provided access to the courtyard. The size of Qasr al-Harrana's courtyard comes as a bit of a surprise; somehow you expect it to be much bigger given the apparent size of the castle. As you wander around look out for the roofline; there are arches supporting vaulting ceilings and, unusually, the odd timber support beam. Timber was rarely used in the construction of these desert buildings so perhaps the Qasr al-Harrana was the project of a progressive thinking architect. Certainly, the use of timber helped it survive earthquakes, which may account for its relatively undamaged appearance today.

The castle has undergone a lengthy restoration programme since the 1970s when it was rediscovered after having been abandoned, and is today one of the most visited of all the Desert Castles. There's a little handicraft stall here near the entrance and drinks are available at the visitors' centre.

Qasr al-Mushatta (*North of Queen Alia International Airport;* ☉ *daily*) Although there are no facilities at this former palace and it's a tad difficult to reach (by skirting around the perimeter road of the airport, which may make airport personnel wonder what you're up to), the remains of the Qasr al-Mushatta are magnificent.

It is considered one of the most ambitious of all the palace complexes constructed by the Umayyads and is currently being considered for UNESCO World Heritage Site status. Everywhere there are columns topped by elaborate capitals, arches and pilaster (protruding) bases, and the remains of vaulted ceilings and carvings.

The mighty outer wall of the complex is the first thing you see when approaching. Made from fired bricks that have a distinct orange hue, this long, high wall enclosing the palace has 25 semi-circular watchtowers and one main, and rather grand, entrance. As you enter, the palace, or at least the remains of it, stretches out before you. Historical opinion concludes that this would have been the grandest of the palaces. Its carved walls depicted flowers, vines and animals, and afforded geometric patterns created by rows of rosettes, triangles and octagons. Some of these can still be seen.

The layout of the palace, which is believed to date from around AD743, suggests it had countless rooms, halls and passageways that led, axial fashion, to a throne room and the inner sanctum of the ruling caliph. Its architecture is notable. The roof of the throne roof is of a triple-barrel vaulted design, similar to that seen at another desert palace, the famous, fresco-full Qusayr 'Amra. Entry to the throne room would have been through a triple-arched arcade. The palace was never actually completed as the then ruling caliph, Walid II, died soon after instructing its construction. Foundation stones found throughout the site, however, indicate that it would have been one of the largest palaces complexes in the Eastern Desert.

Qasr at-Tuba (*Southeast of Amman;* ⊕ *daily*) Along with Qasr Burqu, the Qasr at-Tuba is the most remote of all the desert castles and palaces. It is an arduous 110km drive from Amman through the bleakest desert terrain, and as such can usually be found devoid of any visitors. It is certainly bypassed by the tour companies, which is a shame because the remains are clearly those of a once striking and extensive fortress complex. If you do plan to visit you must hire a 4x4 vehicle and a reputable guide familiar with deep desert environments. There are several routes you can take to reach it, but the most direct and the most comfortable – unless you don't mind travelling over unmade stony tracks – involves taking the road due south from Qasr al-Harrana. You can also reach it from the Amman–Aqaba highway. Dating from AD744, when the land on which it is built was on a trade route from Arabia to Syria via the spring at Azraq, the Qasr at-Tuba is constructed with architectural features that include a barrel vaulted roofline. It gives it a striking silhouette as you approach. The castle stands in a large oblong enclosure some 140m by 70m in size, which is divided in two by a long corridor with surrounding walls and towers. It is believed two buildings were earmarked for the site, but only one was ever built. The site is unfenced and always open should you wish to visit, however there are no amenities here.

Qasr Burqu (*Burqu, off Highway 10 between Al-Mafraq & the Iraqi border via As-Safawi;* ⊕ *daily*) To reach this castle at Burqu you will need specialist desert survival gear, a knowledgeable guide and a vehicle suitable to drive in the harshest of terrains. To get there you can take one of two routes: Highway 5 from Azraq to the main town and industrial centre of the eastern Badia region As-Safawi, or via Highway 10 from Al-Mafraq to As-Safawi. At As-Safawi you'll need to head east on Highway 10 until you reach signs for Burqu. The roads will be a challenge, both in terms of being dusty and monotonous. You'll find petrol, telephones and basic refreshment, although no hotels, in As-Safawi and Al-Mafraq. If you fancy a detour before continuing on to Burqu you can visit the **holy tree** of Biqya'wiyya where the Prophet Muhammad is said to have rested. It is one of Jordan's holiest sites. The tree can be found just off Highway 5 on the Azraq to As-Safawi stretch, but without any signs to point you in the right direction or any landmarks to ensure you turn off the road at the right spot you'll need to rely on your guide to take you there.

Qasr Burqu can trace its history back to the time of the Romans when it started out as a fort, was believed to have been used by Byzantine monks and was later expanded and used as a base during the period of the Umayyads. The ruins of this sturdy rectangular castle are in reasonably good shape. What sets Qasr Burqu apart from the other castles, however, and the reason why so many people make the lengthy and arduous journey to visit it, is its location. It stands, mesmerizingly, on the shores of a large lake, which because it is set deep in the desert surrounded by a flat, unsympathetic terrain comes as a complete surprise.

The lake, **Ghadeer Burqu**, provides a valuable water supply for local Bedouin communities and their camels and sheep, as it has done for centuries for passing merchants on trade routes. Countless numbers of migrating birds and wildlife are attracted to the mudflats and marshlands of the 'oasis' too, and as such it is one of Jordan's proposed new nature reserves. For now, however, it is not signposted so, like the Biqya'wiyya holy tree, you'll need to rely on your guide to find it for you.

AZRAQ *Telephone code: 05* A delightfully remote little town in the Zarqa Governorate, Azraq comprises two communities at Al-Azraq al-Janubi (south Azraq) and Al-Azraq ash-Shamali (north Azraq). Collectively they are referred to as Azraq. The town lies deep in the Eastern Desert around 100km east of Amman. Meaning 'blue' in Arabic, it has long been at the crossroads of both trading routes and bird migrations since ancient times. Evidence of dwellings and the discovery of items like primitive axe heads suggest that significant communities have lived here since the Palaeolithic period, 2.5 million years ago. The region later thrived during the time of the early Nabateans, and was colonised by the Romans, Byzantines and the Umayyads, who all recognised Azraq's strategic location.

Azraq's present population is small, but has grown and flourished because of the town's continual supply of fresh drinking water from underground aquifers, the only such resource in an otherwise barren semi-arid desert. In fact, it is the only

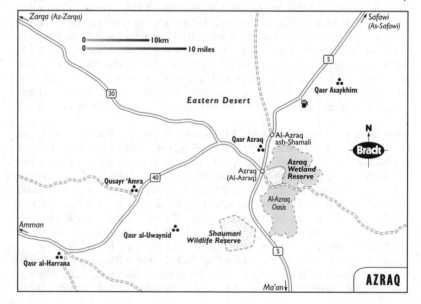

permanent source of fresh water in a desert that covers almost half the total land area of Jordan. Rainwater from the Jabal Druze is filtered and flows into a shallow basin at Azraq, while one of the longest rivers in Jordan, the Wadi Sharhan, drains north from its eastern border location straight into the oasis.

For centuries the oasis has been, and still is, an important stop on trading routes from the Middle East through to Syria and the Levant. Camel caravans carrying spices have stopped here since ancient times, attracted by the ever-present pools of fresh water. Today, as you travel on the deserted roads in and out of Azraq, seemingly in the middle of nowhere with no other cars or people to trouble you, it is not uncommon to suddenly see a convoy of trucks approach you. They may have already rested in Azraq or are about to. There could be 30 or more of them, each carrying their load to neighbouring countries, the cities or to the port at Aqaba. It's quite an experience as they thunder past, one after another after another.

The oasis lies just off to the east of the town's two main communities and is a charming stop on your travels. It is a picturesque, tranquil place and its pools, marshland and a huge mud flat known as Qa'al-Azraq provide a natural habitat for millions of migrating, breeding and wintering birds (see page 154), as well as species of plants and wildlife. The water basin is surrounded by some 60km² of silt and in turn a vast concentration of salt.

Azraq has the remains of castles speckling the landscape, including the **Qasr Asaykhim** and the **Qasr al-Uwaynid**, but is perhaps best known for its massive fortress, the Qasr Azraq (Qal'at al-Azraq), see page 148, and two of the world's finest reserves, the Azraq Wetland Reserve and the Shaumari Wildlife Reserve, run by the Royal Society for the Conservation of Nature (RSCN). Just outside the town are large Jordanian and US air force communities. Buses arrive into firstly Al-Azraq al-Janubi and then Al-Azraq ash-Shamali from Zarqa, while the roads from Zarqa (Highway 30) and Amman (Highway 40) meet here.

Azraq Wetland Reserve (\ 05 383 5017; f 05 383 5017; e *azraqtourism@rscn.org.jo; www.rscn.org.jo;* ⊕ *usually 09.00–18.00 daily but can vary; entry JD7*) Founded in 1978 to conserve the extensive pools, marshland and streams surrounding the natural oasis at Azraq, and the natural habitats they provide for flora and fauna, the Azraq Wetland Reserve covers some 12km² of the Eastern Desert. It lies between limestone and basalt desert areas and is fed by underground aquifers, rainwater that flows from the mountains, and the Wadi Sharhan, a long river that drains north from its eastern border location.

On a visit you can see several natural pools, some pools that were built by ancient civilisations, marshland that every year floods to become one massive lake and an extensive mud flat known as **Qa'al-Azraq**. It is a birdwatcher's paradise, known the world over and considered one of the finest places to see a vast number of different bird species. Thousands of migratory birds come here as a stop *en route* between Europe and Africa, while others stay to breed in the protected areas provided in the reserve or for the colder winter period. The Azraq wetland area is the only such habitat in the Arabian Desert that has a continuous and natural water supply.

Look out for the delicately coloured grey and pink Sinai rosefinch (*Carpodacus synoicus*) or the distinctive colouring of the brown, white and black Temmink's horned lark (*Eremophila bilopha*). You may also see the trumpet finch (*Rhodopechys githaginea*); the pretty sand-coloured desert lark (*Ammomanes desert*); the hoopoe lark (*Alaemon alaudipes*); the little stint (*Erolia minuta*), which travels from arctic Europe; the cute 'masked' little ringed plover; (*Charadrius dubius*); or the curious

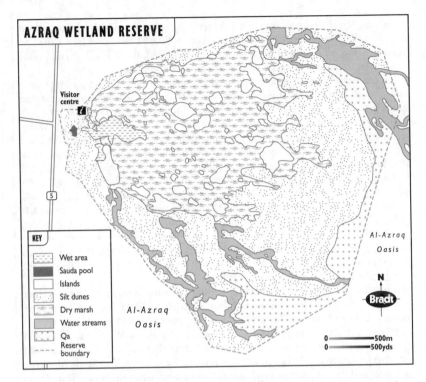

AZRAQ WETLAND RESERVE

KEY
- Wet area
- Sauda pool
- Islands
- Silt dunes
- Dry marsh
- Water streams
- Qa
- Reserve boundary

Visitor centre

Al-Azraq Oasis

Al-Azraq Oasis

0 — 500m
0 — 500yds

N

Bradt

desert wheatear (*Oenanthe desert*), which can cleverly change the look of its plumage with the seasons. In winter, scan the skies for a sighting of the mighty imperial eagle (*Aquila fasciatus*) soaring overhead.

WETLAND'S RESCUE EFFORT

In 1994, the RSCN launched a project to save the habitat of the Azraq Wetland Reserve. Where once expansive areas were covered by deep pools and lush marshland, the rapid increase in pumping out water for agricultural use and to supply the country's burgeoning population resulted in the land becoming drier. Water levels dropped significantly in the 1980s and by 1993 the underground aquifers, or springs, had all but dried up. The oasis's ecological value was on the verge of disappearing. As a result, the number of migratory birds that once was in the millions dwindled as they went to the Sea of Galilee instead, and the herds of water buffalo that once thrived here disappeared.

The RSCN's mammoth rescue effort has achieved considerable success in raising water levels, which in turn has attracted thousands of birds back to the habitat. The RSCN has built protective breeding areas, boardwalks and bird hides. A habitat restoration programme has also encouraged the return of a whole host of terrestrial and aquatic species that now thrive here, including the critically endangered Azraq killifish (*Aphanius sirhani*). This endemic fish of the Cyprinodontidae family is only found in the wetlands of Jordan and was virtually extinct in 1989, but following the launch of a captive breeding rescue programme numbers have now increased.

above left Ruined columns give a glimpse of the former splendour of the Roman Empire in Jerash (MB/A) page 127

above right Ajloun Forest Reserve is the foremost of Jordan's nature reserves, and the place to spot roe deer, striped hyena and wild boar (SS) page 168

bottom Modelled on the famous Treasury, in Petra was once used for religious events and celebrations (RM) page 220

above The majestic Crusader Castle towers above Karak and provides a panoramic view of the landscape on the King's Highway (KS) page 184

below Intricate frescos cover the walls and ceiling of Qusayr 'Amra in the Eastern Desert (RHPL/A) page 149

left   The famous mosaic map in St George's Church in Madaba which confirmed this part of the Jordan River valley as the site of Christ's baptism (RM) page 190

below   One of the most sacred places in the world, Bethany Beyond the Jordan purports to contain the baptismal site of Jesus Christ (RM) page 163

bottom   Mount Nebo, upon which Moses is said to be buried, has stunning views of the Holy Land (RM) page 187

opposite   As-Salt, Jordan's second city, was a coveted prize for the Romans, Byzantines and Mamluks over the centuries, and attracted the finest architects and masons to construct its buildings (RM) page 174

left & below left Downtown Amman's side streets and souks are the place to discover the heartbeat of daily Jordanian life (JR/A and M/A) page 78

below Jordan is no stranger to the Middle East's famously delicious desserts, including pistachios and almonds wrapped in honey-drenched puff pastry (SS) page 76

bottom Ayola Café in Madaba offers the favourite Jordanian experience of unwinding with an *argeeleh* over a puff of sweet water tobacco (YL/A) page 180

above Nubian ibex (*Capra nubiana*) herd in the Mujib Nature Reserve (DH/FLPA)

left Blue-cheeked butterflyfish (*Chaetodon semilarvatus*) and coral grouper (*Plectropomus pessuliferus*) are a common sight in the Gulf of Aqaba (RD/FLPA) page 11

below left Sinai rosefinch (*Carpodacus synoicus*) (MM/A)

below right Palestine sunbird (*Nectarinea osea*) (DH/FLPA)

Within the reserve you can go on birdwatching expeditions along the Marsh Trail – a 1.5km-long pathway that takes you through reedbeds – or take an excursion to nearby Shaumari Wildlife Reserve (see below) or head into the Eastern Desert with a group in a private 4x4 vehicle. The reserve is managed by the Royal Society for the Conservation of Nature (RSCN), which has the challenging job of preserving the habitat against the demands of the country's natural development. As a reliable source of fresh water, the oasis provides drinking water for the country's population, especially the rapidly growing city of Amman. A visit will help the work of the RSCN. On site is the extremely welcoming **Azraq Lodge** (see page 145), with its restaurant, guestrooms and gift shop.

Shaumari Wildlife Reserve *(5km southwest of the Azraq Wetland Reserve;* ☏ *05 383 5017;* f *05 383 5017;* e *azraqtourism@rscn.org.jo; www.rscn.org.jo;* ☉ *usually 09.00–18.00 daily but can vary; entry JD7; private safaris JD8. At the time of publication the reserve was closed for renovation; before making a special journey telephone ahead to check if open).* Covering a vast area of some 22km², the Shaumari Wildlife Reserve (which is also known as the Shawmari Wildlife Reserve) is one of the Middle East's, if not the world's, foremost reserves for endangered or locally extinct species. Here, if you stay alert and are fortunate, you will see some of the rarest animals on the planet, including the onager (*Equus hemionus*), which is a member of the horse family and a little larger than a donkey, and the quite magnificent white Arabian oryx (*Oryx leucoryx*), which was at one time extinct in Jordan and can now often be seen roaming happily in the desert (see box below).

You will often see rare ostriches (*Struthio camelus*) and the nibble-footed gazelle (*Gazella subgutturosa*), along with the red fox (*Vulpes velpes*), the rare striped hyena (*Hyaena hyaena*), the jackal (*Canis aureus*), the wolf (*Canis lupus*), the caracal (*Caracal caracal*) and the wild cat (*Felis sylvestris*). Look out for the reserve's

ARABIAN ORYX

The Arabian oryx (*Oryx leucoryx*) is an elegant white antelope with an appealingly mournful expression and dramatic, long, straight horns. It is indigenous to the desert and steppes of the Arabian Peninsula. It became extinct in Jordan in the 1920s, and was almost lost to the world in the 1970s when the last oryx in the wild was killed by hunters in Oman. Fortunately, in a project entitled 'Operation Oryx' organised by the Flora and Fauna Preservation Society and the World Wildlife Fund around ten years previously, a small protected herd of just nine animals was established in the US. One oryx came from London Zoo, four from Saudi Arabia, three from Oman and one from Kuwait. The project was a tremendous success as the animals thrived and the herd grew in size.

In 1978, four oryx were relocated to the Shaumari Wildlife Reserve and continued to thrive in the reserve's protected environment. In 1983, a total of 31 were released from captivity, where they had been bred and cared for, into specially prepared natural habitats within the reserve. At the time it was a major milestone in the reserve's success. There are now over 200 of these beautiful creatures in Jordan, a staggering number given that they were once almost extinct. Some were released back into the wilds of the Wadi Rum Protected Area. The oryx is still one of the most vulnerable species in the world, and Jordan, like the US before it, now supplies oryx to other countries keen to host their own reintroduction programmes.

flora; there have been over 190 different species recorded here. Bird sightings have included the mighty imperial eagle (*Aquila heliaca*), the Egyptian vulture (*Neophron percnopterus*) and the pallid harrier (*Circus macrourus*).

With its barren, dusty and flat landscape crossed by *wadis* (the largest being Wadi Shaumari after which the reserve is named), the Shaumari Wildlife Reserve comes as a sort of haven in an otherwise bleak environment. It offers visitors the chance to see these wonderful creatures in enclosures or in the wild, and helps with their protection and wellbeing. Run by the Royal Society for the Conservation of Nature, it operates programmes designed to breed and reintroduce rare and endangered species back into the wild. However, you will need a vehicle; no public transport runs to the reserve. On site is a simple campsite with ten tents and basic facilities.

MAFRAQ *Telephone code: 02* The capital of the Mafraq Governorate, Mafraq (locally Al-Mafraq) is a pleasant enough city, surrounded by agricultural fields and the black boulders typical of the northernmost desert region. As a traveller you may wish to visit the city if mingling with the locals is your thing, otherwise you will probably only visit *en route* to another destination. It's a hub for buses and *serveeces* taxis arriving into the Fellahin bus station from Amman and Zarqa, and for onward trips to Irbid and Jerash. The city also has services from the Bedouin bus station for trips to the ancient city site of Umm al-Jimal or easterly to Safawi and Burqu. There are no hotels in Mafraq and only a handful of diners that cater to the local population, as well as a few souk-style streets where they buy their everyday goods. Most are located around the Fellahin bus station. Mafraq is probably best known for the Al al-Bayt University, which is one of the finest in Jordan for Islamic studies, with schools dedicated to the sciences, law, nursing, education, the arts, business and information technology.

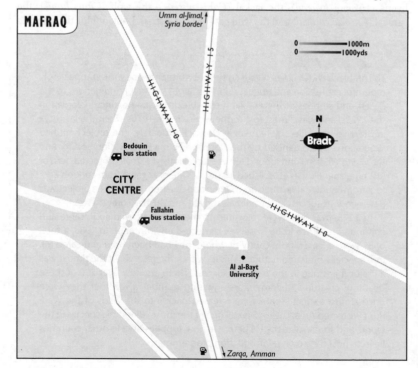

UMM AL-JIMAL Known as the Black Oasis, Umm al-Jimal is one of the country's lesser known but equally important archaeological sites. It is a monument to a lost civilisation, and lies close to Jordan's border with Syria in a desert landscape characterised by black basalt rock. Slabs of this rock have been used for centuries to create its houses, the walls that surround the town and its churches. Each structure affords a starkly imposing appearance. The somewhat sombre looking ghost town stands, oasis-fashion, surrounded by wilderness, except for a more modern village that has grown up alongside it; hence it being known as the Black Oasis.

Meaning 'Mother of Camels' in Arabic, Umm al-Jimal has a fascinating past and because it was once such an important provincial town it has been extensively excavated, so there are plenty of archaeological remains. At its peak it is thought to have been home to as many as 10,000 people. Behind the ancient city walls lie tall,

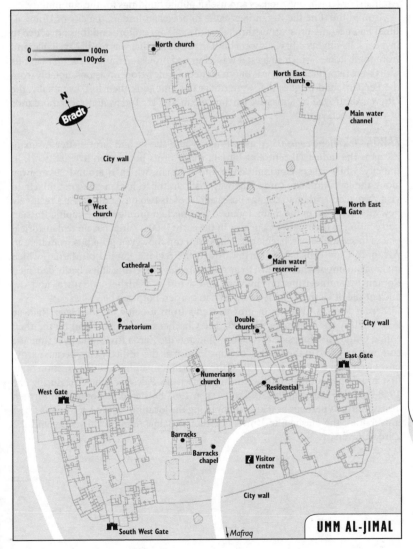

sober-looking buildings dating from the 5th century that were used as barracks, complete with their own courtyard. Look out for the remains of a tiny **chapel** and a much larger **cathedral**, a **Roman reservoir** once used to store water, lots of town gates, dwellings, shops and the outline of a **Roman fortress**.

Umm al-Jimal is believed to have been built by the Nabateans around 2,000 years ago as a purpose-built trade route town to serve the camel caravans loaded with spices that passed by on their way from Arabia to Syria. Remains of the dwellings and public buildings lay either side of a large central courtyard where camels would have been kept and refreshed before continuing their journey. In Roman times the city became a key location for defending the empire, and yet neither the Romans nor the Nabateans before them regarded this as a place worthy of being a capital city. It had no elaborate temples or palaces like those of Philadelphia (present-day Amman) or Jerash, only houses and useful public buildings for the community.

Around the time the Byzantines came to power in Jordan, the city of Umm al-Jimal had become prosperous through trade and agriculture and thus attractive to invaders. Its mighty city walls were built in the basalt that was readily available, and from tombstones, which suggest it was a hurried project. Around a century later its walls were refortified, but it was only a matter of time before invasions, notably from the Persians, and plagues that were rife at the time took their toll. Eventually, the city was destroyed by a massive earthquake in AD747. Today, it attracts thousands of visitors each year.

ZARQA *Telephone code: 05* A sprawling city and the second largest after Amman, Zarqa is the industrial centre of Jordan. Many of its population live and work in the city, while others commute daily into Amman, which is around 20km away along the fast Amman–Zarqa Highway. As a visitor to Jordan you are unlikely to visit Zarqa, other than to change buses at one of its two bus stations. As a relatively new city that was, in the main, founded by Chechen immigrants escaping Russian persecution in their native Caucasus in the early 1900s, Zarqa has no real historical places to see and no archaeological sites. You can, however, get a bus from here to Azraq, to Qasr Hallabat or northwards to the regional capital of Mafraq, which makes it an important hub. Just to its north are the interesting albeit badly damaged Roman-Byzantine ruins of churches and a fort at **Khirbet as-Samra**, and the ancient site of Umm al-Jimal on the Syrian border. Both can be visited.

Zarqa's success in terms of growth stems from it being on the Hejaz Railway line, built by the Ottomans in 1900. The Chechens were given land by the then ruling Ottomans alongside the railway line and the Zarqa River, and over time the community grew. In the 1920s it became known as the 'military city' because army bases were created here, and in 1928 the government authorised the creation of its first municipal council. Further immigrants from Palestine who fled during the 1948 Palestine War and the Six-Day War in 1967 bolstered its population further. Today, Zarqa is perhaps best known for being the location of three of Jordan's finest universities, the Hashemite University, the Al-Balqa Applied University and the Zarqa University.

6

Jordan Rift Valley and the Dead Sea

The landscape and geographical features found in the Jordan Rift Valley are some of the most dramatic anywhere on the planet. The area plunges from the great heights of the Mountain Heights Plateau to the depths of the Dead Sea, the lowest point on earth. The north has lush green fields and forests dotted with towns and villages, whereas towards the south are barren desert landscapes, mountains (*jabal*) and hills (*tell*), and huge expanses of sea and salt pans around the Dead Sea. The Jordan Rift Valley is a breathtaking landscape.

Running from Lake Tiberias, a freshwater lake also known as the Sea of Galilee that lies a few kilometres into Israel over Jordan's northernmost border, the Jordan Rift Valley continues south through the valley created by the Jordan River, known as the Ghor (meaning sunken land), to the Dead Sea. This stretch is specifically called the Jordan Valley, and follows the course of the river for about 120km until it drains into the Dead Sea. Here, forests of pine and oak trees grow, wildlife and birds flourish and because of its fertile soil and constant water supply, plus the fact that it enjoys a year-round temperate climate not unlike that of the Mediterranean, this stretch has ideal agricultural growing conditions. It supplies Jordan with the vast majority of its fresh food produce. Much is consumed by Jordanians, while exports of fruit and vegetables help to keep the country's economy buoyant.

From the Dead Sea, the valley continues its course through the Araba Valley created by the Wadi Araba. The valley is also famous in the bible as the Arabah Desert; *Arabah* meaning wilderness. Here, and for the next 155km or so, until it reaches the city of Aqaba and Jordan's only coastline at the Gulf of Aqaba and the Red Sea, the terrain is hot, dry and desert-like.

The valley has been inhabited since prehistoric times when communities were created and thrived through the cultivation of crops in this fertile region. It is part of the Great Rift Valley, which stretches from Mozambique in Africa to the south and Syria to the north. The famous trade route, the King's Highway, which linked these countries, was founded in the Iron Age. It brought fabulous wealth to the region, which continued throughout biblical times, the Nabatean and Roman periods, and early Islamic times to the present day. The highway, the remains of which lie between the Dead Sea road and the Desert Highway, attracted Bedouin tribes who created villages along its length.

Today, around 200,000 Jordanians live and work in the countryside of the valley. In the north, most derive a living from agriculture. It is the main business of the region and here the juiciest oranges (*boordan*), lemons (*laimoon*), bananas (*mooz*), peaches (*dorrag*), apples (*tfah*), watermelons (*batteekh*) and grapes (*aynab*) grow in abundance, along with olives (*zaytoon*) – used as a dish of their own or for oil – cucumbers (*kheaar*), aubergine (*badinjan*), onions (*basal*), potatoes (*batatas*) and a wide variety of cereals. The fields to the west of **Ajlun**, **Salt** and **Madaba** near

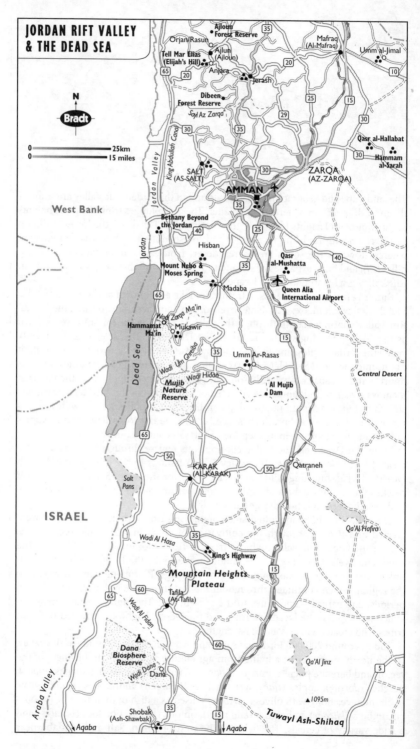

the Dead Sea are especially lush and green, while crops grow further south too, albeit more sparingly, near **Karak** (Al-Karak), and the picturesque little town of **Tafila** (At-Tafila), which you may not visit other than to change buses. In the south, in the Wadi Araba region, the population enjoys a more industrial lifestyle, with the mining of phosphates used primarily in detergents and fertilisers the greatest means of employment.

The Jordan Valley, the Dead Sea and the Wadi Araba, which together form the Jordan Rift Valley, attract thousands of visitors every year. Whether you want the moving experience of visiting its famous biblical sites such as **Bethany Beyond the Border**, **Mount Nebo** or the **Jordan River** itself, or you plan to luxuriate in the **Dead Sea**, explore Petra in the south, take in the many nature reserves or head inland to see the region's ancient towns and its desert landscape, then the valley will, without doubt, be a highlight of your holiday.

THE KING'S HIGHWAY

Dating from before the Iron Age and made famous in biblical times, the King's Highway is the world's oldest continuously used road. In ancient times it was an important trade route that linked the ancient city of Heliopolis in Egypt with Damascus and Resafa in Syria. It passed through Jordan (then Transjordan) starting at the point where the present-day modern city of Aqaba lay in the southern Arabah valley, continuing northwards through the kingdoms of Edom and Moab to Rabbath Ammon (Amman), and across the border into Syria. Along the way it passed by the cities of Petra and Ma'an, Shobak (locally Ash-Shawbak) and Karak (Al-Karak) to Madaba, and on past present-day Amman to Jerash. The people of these ancient kingdoms relied heavily on the trade route for not only goods such as spices, silks and textiles, but also for the revenue and wealth it brought.

The King's Highway at one time passed by Mount Nebo, which according to the Hebrew Bible and the Holy Koran is said to be where the biblical leader and prophet Moses is buried, along with the holy site of Bethany Beyond the Jordan where Jesus was baptized by John the Baptist. It is mentioned by name in Genesis 20:17 as the route Moses planned to take when leading the Exodus, and again in Genesis 14:5–8, when the kings of the north attacked the cities of Soddom, Gomorrah, Heshbon (Hisban), Medeba (Madaba) and Kir Moab (Karak), and attempted to take Abraham's nephew Lot hostage. As such, it has long been a Christian pilgrimage route. Muslims, too, used the highway as an early pilgrimage route to Makkah for Hajj.

The Nabateans, famous for building the extensive city of Petra, amassed much of their wealth from the King's Highway. They traded in spices and luxury goods like frankincense and gold from Arabia. When the Romans came to power in Jordan they, too, grew wealthy from the highway. The Roman Emperor Trajan (b53, d117) recognised its importance for both trade and for transporting troops of the empire, and instructed large sections of it to be rebuilt to a higher standard. He renamed the highway the Via Traiana Nova.

Today, the King's Highway may not be Jordan's main trade route, nor the route taken by visitors, who choose instead the vista afforded to them by taking the valley road past the Dead Sea, but it does pass through countryside of immeasurable beauty and some of the country's most famous ancient cities.

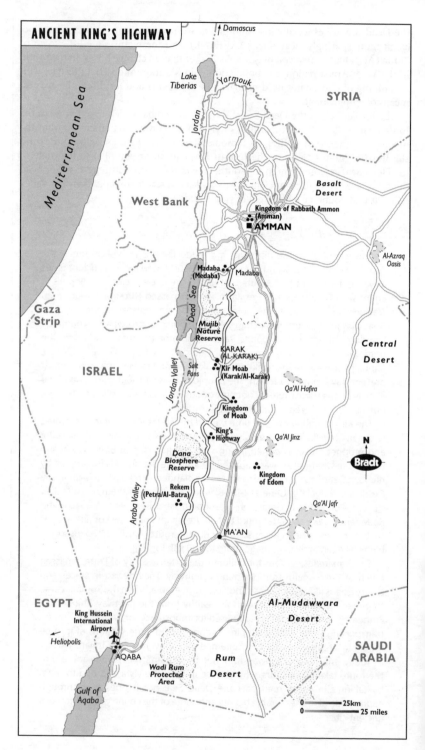

ANCIENT KING'S HIGHWAY

↑ Damascus

Mediterranean Sea

Lake Tiberias

Yarmouk

SYRIA

Jordan

Basalt Desert

West Bank

Kingdom of Rabbath Ammon (Amman)

■ AMMAN

Al-Azraq Oasis

Madaba (Medaba)

Madaba

Dead Sea

Mujib Nature Reserve

Central Desert

Gaza Strip

KARAK (AL-KARAK)

ISRAEL

Jordan Valley

Salt Pans

Kir Moab (Karak/Al-Karak)

Qa'Al Hafira

Kingdom of Moab

King's Highway

Qa'Al Jinz

N

Bradt

Dana Biosphere Reserve

Kingdom of Edom

Araba Valley

Rekem (Petra/Al-Batra)

Qa'Al Jafr

MA'AN

EGYPT

Al-Mudawwara Desert

King Hussein International Airport

← Heliopolis

SAUDI ARABIA

AQABA

Wadi Rum Protected Area

Rum Desert

Gulf of Aqaba

0 — 25km
0 — 25 miles

The Jordan Rift Valley was created many millions of years ago when, according to some findings, the Arabian tectonic plate moved northwards and then eastwards from its position off eastern Africa. An alternative version of how the valley was created cites the movement of the Red Sea Rift. The new landmass between the Mediterranean and what had become the Jordan Rift Valley was prone to flooding, but when it rose around a million years after the tectonic plate moved, it settled above sea level with some peaks reaching a height of around 1,000m. The exception is the basin of water that is now known as the Dead Sea, which at -420m is the lowest dry point on earth.

EARLY HISTORY Evidence suggests that the Jordan Rift Valley was inhabited by prehistoric man, who would have had to hunt for survival. Evidence of settlements have been discovered in the north of the valley, around the Jordan River, while in the south reaches that run along the Wadi Araba prehistoric rock carvings have been discovered. Around 10,000 years ago, Neolithic man had begun to cultivate the land in the northern reaches of the valley. Crops would have been planted and fruit trees grown. By about 3000BC, the landscape was dotted with villages, many of which had sophisticated water-channelling systems that provided a regular water supply for the community and for its agricultural fields. The volume of produce grown in the northern reaches of the valley was by this time at such a level that much of it was used to generate wealth through exports to neighbouring regions.

BIBLICAL HISTORY The River Jordan and the fertile land of the valley is well documented in the Hebrew Bible, the Christian Holy Bible and the Holy Quran, and has been associated with some of the most important events in Christian history. It was described as 'the garden of God' in the Bible's Genesis 13:10, and on the death of Moses it is said God stopped the flow of water so that Joshua could cross, leading his people to Canaan (Joshua 3:14–17). Elijah, a prophet of the Kingdom of Israel, and Elisa, who according to the bible and the Holy Koran was a prophet from north Israel, are said to have crossed the Jordan River at Beit 'Abara, meaning '*house of the crossing*'. In doing so, miracles are said to have taken place in Jordan (Book of Kings).

Famously, and for Christians the single most important event to have happened in the valley in biblical times, was the baptism of Jesus Christ. According to the New Testament's Matthew 3:13 and Mark 1:9, the Jordan River, again near Beit 'Abara, was where John the Baptist baptised Jesus. Some time later, it was at this site that Jesus is said to have sought refuge when his enemies had threatened him with capture (John 10:39). The site became known as Bethany, later Bethany Beyond the Jordan, and was where John the Baptist lived, preached and where he performed baptisms.

The Bible refers to the Dead Sea as the Valley of Salt, or the Garden of the Lord, and it is believed to be the location of the Garden of Eden (Book of Genesis). The sea is where Jesus was baptized by John the Baptist, God first spoke to Man and where he gave the Ten Commandments to Moses. Here Jacob wrestled with the angel of God, Job was rewarded for his faith and King David of Israel 'slew 18,000 Edomites' (2 Samuel 7:29). Abraham and his nephew Lot parted ways here, with Lot remaining in Jordan (Genesis 13:12). Here, five major cities thrived: Sodom, Adman, Zebouin, Gomorrah and Zoar.

In biblical times the Arabah Desert, now the Araba or Wadi Araba Valley, is often referred to. It is considered by some scholars to mean the entire stretch of the Jordan Rift Valley, from the northernmost tip of present-day Jordan to the Red

Sea. Then it would have followed a course along the present Wadi Araba River on the eastern fringes of the ancient kingdoms of Rabbath Ammon, Moab and Edom. Medaba, present-day Madaba, was one of the most influential Moabite towns (see *Madaba*, page 188).

NABATEAN, ROMAN AND BYZANTINE ERAS During the Nabatean period (312BC–AD106), the overlapping Roman period (63BC–AD324) and the Byzantine period (AD324–635), much of the country's political and religious activity was centred on Saltus, present-day Salt (locally As-Salt) and the Decapolis cities of the north (see *Jerash and the Decapolis Cities* chapter, page 127). The Jordan Rift Valley served to provide the city's inhabitants with fresh food. Meanwhile, towards the south of the Jordan Rift Valley, Petra, which lay on the exact spot where major trade routes crossed, was developing into one of the wealthiest cities of the ancient world.

EARLY ISLAMIC TO OTTOMAN PERIODS The valley had mixed fortunes during the early Islamic periods. Its towns prospered during the Umayyad caliphate (AD661–750), but when the Abbasids (AD750–969) came to power they focused their attention away from the valley and the surrounding regions to Baghdad, followed by the Fatimids (AD968–1171) from Tunisia and Egypt, and the Ayyubids (1171–1263) from Egypt, both of whom centred their empire on their own countries. Apart from when the Mamluks were in power and the valley saw several castles built to help defend their empire against the Crusaders, such as at Ajlun and Showbak, little changed in the region. During the Ottoman period much of the empire's activity revolved around its capital Constantinople. Other than its regional capital, Salt, which was now one of the wealthiest cities in the kingdom and a key trade city of the empire, Jordan and its famous valley languished until modern history saw it return to prominence.

MODERN HISTORY Following the creation of the Emirate of Transjordan in 1921, after World War I, a change of emphasis was seen in the valley. Salt, which had long been its largest and wealthiest city, was assumed to become the new capital of the emirate. However, the new emir, Emir Abdullah, recognising that Amman was better connected, chose the latter as his capital.

The Jordan Rift Valley, and in particular the stretch west of the Jordan River and alongside the Dead Sea, known as the West Bank, has a turbulent past. In 1967, the territory that had been conquered by Jordan under King Abdullah I shortly after he became king was seized by Israeli troops. The battle became known as the Six-Day War (see *History*, page 24) . As a result of this, and also the confusion arising from the 1973 Arab–Israeli War (see *History*, page 23), the Dead Sea region's population fell alarmingly. The Jordanian authorities, concerned at the turn of events, promptly invested millions in the infrastructure of the area east of the Jordan Rift Valley during the 1970s. New roads were built, villages created and modern methods of farming were introduced. The area's population grew in both number and prosperity.

In 2007, environmentalist group Friends of the Earth Middle East (FoEME) named the Jordan River as one of the top 100 most endangered ecological sites in the world. It warned that the river was close to the point of drying up completely through over channelling of water by Jordan and its neighbours Israel and Syria. Certainly the flow of water has decreased alarmingly over the decades, with the result that the Dead Sea into which it flows has less water to replenish it and is, itself, shrinking (see page 182).

BY AIR While neither the Jordan Valley nor the Araba Valley have their own airports as such, both are easily reached from Amman's **Queen Alia International Airport** or Aqaba's **King Hussein International Airport** (see *Getting there and away*, page 48). A network of fast highways and more scenic routes run from the airports to all the towns and villages in the Jordan Rift Valley region.

BY TAXI OR BUS A large number of taxi companies operate out of Amman for easy travelling to Ajlun and Salt towards the north, and Madaba, the Dead Sea and Karak towards the south. Similarly, Aqaba has taxi companies. If you're making your way to the nature reserves at Ajlun, the Mujib Nature Reserve or the Dana Biosphere Reserve then you will need to take a taxi if you don't have your own car, as there are no public transport options. As a guide, from Ajlun town centre to the nature reserve the cost of a taxi is around JD7, to the Mujib Nature Reserve or the Dana Biosphere Reserve from Amman in one of its yellow-and-green taxis, expect to pay around JD50 and JD75 respectively. If you are heading for the Dead Sea, a taxi from Amman will be around JD45. You can negotiate much cheaper fares in a shared taxi.

Buses run out of Amman and Aqaba. If you're heading for Ajlun, you'll find there are regular buses leaving Abdali bus station in Amman (*JD3*), and once you're in Ajlun you'll need to take a taxi to the castle, the reserve or to visit its houses (see page 167). If heading to Madaba, the Dead Sea or Karak, then regular buses ply these routes from both Amman and Aqaba. Expect to pay JD5–10 depending on the destination. The **Jordan Express Tourist Transport company** (JETT) (*7th Circle, Amman;* \ *06 585 4679;* f *06 585 4176; www.jett.com*) has the most regular timetable from Amman and runs fast intercity buses to the northern towns, and through to Aqaba and back, with stops along the way. If your destination is a little off the beaten track then you will need to arrange for a taxi to be waiting for you once you leave the intercity bus, unless you chance persuading a kind local to give you a lift.

BY CAR Hiring a car is a great way to explore the Jordan Rift Valley which is not always best served by public transport. If you are heading for the Dead Sea, from Amman you'll need to drive out of the city due south to the Naour Bridge, and take the turning signposted to the Dead Sea (Highway 40). Amman to the Dead Sea is a journey of approximately 65km, a little less than an hour with traffic. You can also follow this road if you're planning to visit the biblical sites of Bethany Beyond the Border and around Madaba, the Mujib Nature Reserve and the Dana Biosphere Reserve further south, or the city of Karak. You'll need to look out for signposts for Karak south of the Dead Sea. An alternative route for Karak is via the Desert Highway (Highway 15) or the old King's Highway route (Number 35). Heading north from Amman, get on the highway heading to Jerash (Highway 35), on which you'll see signs to Salt or Ajlun. From Aqaba head north on the main highway (Highway 15) until you reach Ma'an where you have the option to continue by this route to Amman or turn right towards Tafila, Karak, Madaba and the Dead Sea.

JORDAN RIFT VALLEY

WHERE TO STAY
Mid range
⌂ **The Biscuit House** (2 rooms) Orjan, Ajlun; \ 02 647 5673; e ajloun@rscn.org.jo; www.rscn.

org.jo. Housed in the same complex as The Biscuit House, one of Ajlun's working workshops (see page 169), this super B&B is quiet & surrounded by forest & countryside. It has just 2 bedrooms, the Orjan & Rasun, named after 2 villages, with a shared bathroom & a lounge. The big plus to staying here is the b/fast; it consists of traditional Jordanian goodies such as olives, white cheese, local bread, eggs & thyme & olive dips. **$$$**

Budget
🏠 **Ajlun Forest Reserve** (5 cabins, 10 tented lodges & pitch tents) Umm al-Yanabee; ☎02 647 5673; f 02 647 5673; e ajluntourism@rscn.org.jo; www.rscn.org.jo; ⏲ mid-Mar to end of Oct. Set in a large grassy spot on the edge of this forested area & surrounded by wild strawberry trees, carob trees & oaks, the reserve offers 'Africa-style' campsite accommodation in cabins with private bathrooms, along with tented lodges capable of sleeping 4 people, & rows of pitch tents on grass. Showers & toilets are available on-site, along with a restaurant & a handicraft shop. **$$**

🍴 **WHERE TO EAT**
Above average
🍴 **Ajlun Restaurant** Ajlun Forest Reserve, Umm al-Yanabee; ☎02 647 5673; e ajluntourism@rscn.org.jo; www.rscn.org.jo; ⏲ 09.00–18.00 daily. This rustic cabin-style eatery offers panoramic views out over the forested landscape around the reserve & a choice of delicious meals based on international & Arabic cuisine. Vegetarian dishes are cooked to order. Eating outside on its terrace will allow you to really appreciate your surroundings. **$$$$**

Cheap and cheerful
🍴 **Qalet al-Jabal Restaurant** Qalet al-Jabal Hotel, Al Rabad Castle St, Ajlun; ☎02 642 0202;

🏠 **Qalet al-Jabal Hotel** (20 rooms) Al Rabad Castle St, Ajlun; ☎02 642 0202; ☎02 642 0991; e contact@jabal-hotel.com; www.jabal-hotel.com. Located near the castle around 5km from the town centre, this pleasing hotel is decorated in a nostalgic style & has views of the fortress & town from most of its rooms & restaurants. A garden of exotic plants has a children's play area. **$$**

Shoestring
🏠 **Ajlun Hotel** (20 rooms) Al Rabad Castle St, Ajlun; ☎02 642 0524; f 02 642 0542; e ajloun@firstnet.com.jo. A 2-star hotel, the Ajlun offers comfortable rooms with bathrooms, AC & heating, & balconies that look out over the city. It's a little way from the centre of town so you'll need to rely on taxis to get you about. It has its own restaurant & car park. **$**

☎02 642 0991; e contact@jabal-hotel.com; www.jabal-hotel.com. A spacious restaurant where local dishes such as *mensaf* (lamb with yoghurt & spices) & *magloubeh* (chicken) are served buffet-style, the Qalet al-Jabal is decorated in a traditional manner & has a certain period charm. **$$**
🍴 **Tasali Café** The Biscuit House, Orjan; ☎02 647 5673; e ajloun@rscn.org.jo; www.rscn.org.jo; ⏲ 09.00–17.00, times can vary. Serving homemade Tasali biscuits & savoury snacks with olives from the workshop kitchen of The Biscuit House (see page 172), this rustic eatery is seriously stylish. A choice of teas include herbal flavours. Its furniture is made from recycled wood. **$$**

SHOPPING One of the best places in the Jordan Rift Valley region to buy authentic crafts is Ajlun, where there are lots of small specialist shops selling all manner of items from clothing to jewellery. The Ajlun Forest Reserve has a handicraft centre with displays of handmade biscuits, beauty products, ceramics and lots more, which have been made by mainly women who live in or around the park in villages like Rasun and Orjan. They make ideal souvenirs to take home.

SPORTS AND OTHER ACTIVITIES Outside the country's major towns there are few opportunities for the independent traveller to spend a few hours in the gym or on a tennis court, other than in the hotels. All the Dead Sea hotels have gyms with, in most cases, state-of-the-art fitness equipment and the chance to unwind afterwards in a swimming pool or spa. The hotels offer watersports and tennis. Most, such as the

Kempinski Ishtar Resort and Spa, the **Crowne Plaza Dead Sea Hotel and Resort**, the **Jordan Valley Marriott Resort and Spa**, the **Holiday Inn** and the **Mövenpick Hotel and Spa**, will allow you to use the facilities as a day visitor, for a fee.

Mountain Breeze Country Club Jala'ad, near Zai, Salt; m 077 723 4569; www. jordanadventure.com. Located in the Gilead Mountains near Zai, this club offers lots of outdoor activities such as mountaineering, archery & paintball. You can play football & volleyball or camp out overnight. Amenities include a restaurant.

OTHER PRACTICALITIES

Dress If you're heading out to the reserves ensure you have suitable clothing with you. You'll need easy-to-wear garments that cover your legs and shoulders, yet enable you to move freely. Always wear a hat. The region's reserves, including the Ajlun Forest Reserve, have shade from the trees, but you will still need to protect yourself from the sun. Good walking boots or shoes are an absolute necessity, as is a means to carry bottled water.

Emergencies If you're venturing out into the nature reserves and find you are in need of assistance, your first port of call should be to the visitors' centre. For the Ajlun Forest Reserve at Umm al-Yanabee call ☎ 02 647 5673; and for the Dibeen Forest Reserve m 079 902 9497.

Money, post and internet All the main towns of the regions including Ajlun and Salt have full money-changing and postal services in their town centres. A few internet cafés are emerging, although the best option for checking emails and surfing the internet is in the hotels or in the visitors' centres of the nature reserves.

WHAT TO SEE AND DO The Jordan Rift Valley offers an abundance of things to see and do. There's Ajlun, which has its mighty castle, endless nature trails in and around its reserve and a collection of workshops, rural villages, and the ancient city of Salt (locally As-Salt).

Ajlun *Telephone code: 02* Surrounded by mountains and dense, sweet-smelling forests of pine trees and Mediterranean oaks, and in an area dotted with nature and walking trails, reserve areas and picnic spots, Ajlun is an attractive market town and a popular place to stay when exploring the northern Jordan Valley and the towns and villages around it. With its temperate climate of sunny days, cooler evenings and warm winters, the area is renowned for its nature. Here you will find the **Ajloun Forest Reserve** and the newest reserve in Jordan, the **Dibeen Forest**.

Ajlun (or Ajloun) has been home to Jordanians for well over 1,000 years, largely because of its climate, its constant water supply and fertile lands used to grow olives, figs and cereals. The surrounding countryside is teeming with the remains of ancient villages. In the hamlet of **Zubia** on the outskirts of Ajlun, you can see the remains of a Byzantine church and centuries-old homes, while in neighbouring **Tubna** look out for the elaborate 18th-century mosque. Tubna was also the seat of the region's governor in early Islamic times. His home, known as Al'ali Shreidah, was architecturally unique in the region, for records tell us it was the first two-storey house.

Ajlun offers a lot for visitors: trails through its oak forests pass through rural villages, and there are workshops where you can see local women making soap from natural ingredients, baking biscuits and demonstrating the art of calligraphy. You can visit the tomb of the saint Al-Khadir who is reputed to have performed many miracles, and the tomb of Ikrimah bin Ali Jahal who is said to have been a companion of the Prophet Muhammed and helped spread the word of Islam before being martyred at the Battle of Yarmouth.

One of the highlights of your visit to Ajlun will be to explore the labyrinth of vaulted tunnels, huge halls and winding staircases in its medieval castle (see page 172). The town has a long history, which is linked in almost every way with its castle, the Qal'at ar-Rabad, or simply **Ajlun Castle** as it is often known. One of the finest forms of military architecture in the country, the castle was built in the 12th century by one of the commanders in the army of Salah ad-Din Yusuf ibn Ayyub, better known as Saladin (circa b1138, d1193). The Mamluks were in power during this period Ajlun's fascinating **archaeological museum** is housed within the castle, where you can see an extensive collection of ceramics, lamps, tools and fragments of buildings showing intricate drawings and inscriptions dating back to Neolithic times.

Ajlun is the capital of the Ajlun Governorate and is surrounded by more than 25 villages where the population is made up almost entirely of Bedouin tribes: the Almomani, Al-Sharee, Qudah and Alsmadi tribes amongst them. Located about 90 minutes from the capital Amman (buses are available from Abdali bus station) and less than ten minutes by car or taxi from the edge of the River Jordan, Ajlun is a historic town that embraces the present.

Ajloun Forest Reserve (*Umm al-Yanabee;* ↘ *02 647 5673;* e *ajluntourism@rscn. org.jo; www.rscn.org.jo;* ⊕ *09.00–17.00 daily, but can vary; entry JD8*) Surrounded by woodlands of evergreen oak (*Quercus calliprinos*), Aleppo pine trees, wild pistachio (*Pistacia palaestina*), carob (*Ceratonia siliqua*) and wild strawberry trees (*Arbutus andrachne*), this is one of the most beautiful nature reserves in Jordan. It lies in what is regarded as the highlands. Run by the Royal Society for the Conservation of Nature (RSCN), the reserve was founded in the Ajlun village of Umm al-Yanabee in 1987 with the mandate to help protect the evergreen oak forest ecosystem.

Here you may spot the red fox (*Vulpes vulpes*) or the striped hyena (*Hyaena hyaena*). There are wild boars and foxes, along with the rare and dainty roe deer, which became extinct in the wild in 1988 through excessive hunting. The RSCN launched a captive breeding programme to reintroduce the roe deer and it is now thriving in the reserve. It is hoped the deer will be returned to the wild in the future when their numbers have reached sustainable levels. The reserve is a woodland birdwatcher's paradise. You may see jays, which feed on the acorns dropped by the ancient oak trees.

The reserve, which covers a huge area of hilly land covering around 13km², currently has a number of designated nature trails that take in all the sections within the protected area. The trails are designed so you can follow them for just an hour or so, or spend a whole day exploring, and they are graded from easy to difficult according to the level of fitness and ability required. See box, page 176, for details about the trails on offer.

The **visitors' centre** near the entrance has details of the routes and what you will see as you make your way around. There are lodges and tents available for you to stay overnight, a restaurant and tours to nearby places of interest are available. Spring is an especially popular time to visit; you'll see countless hikers and picnickers enjoying the springtime landscape full of wildflowers.

Getting there The reserve is a little less than two hours' drive north of Amman near the picturesque Ajlun village of Umm al-Yanabee. It is easy to find by car; from Amman follow the highway heading north to Jerash, come off at the signs to Ajlun and continue until you reach the town. Once in Ajlun, Umm al-Yanabee is well

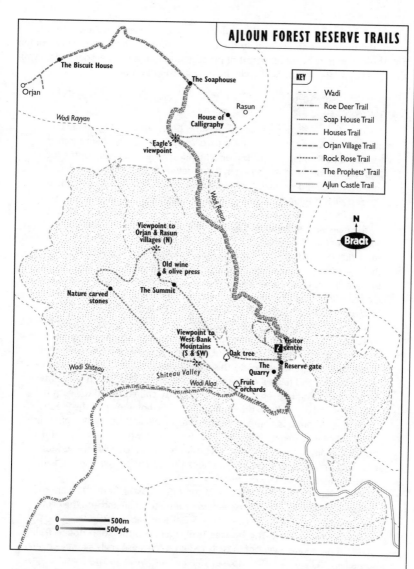

KEY

- - - -	Wadi
·—··—··—	Roe Deer Trail
············	Soap House Trail
━━━━	Houses Trail
— — —	Orjan Village Trail
·········	Rock Rose Trail
·—·—·—	The Prophets' Trail
·············	Ajlun Castle Trail

The Biscuit House

Orjan

The Soaphouse

Rasun

House of Calligraphy

Wadi Rayyan

Eagle's viewpoint

Wadi Rasun

N

Bradt

Viewpoint to Orjan & Rasun villages (N)

Old wine & olive press

Nature carved stones

The Summit

Viewpoint to West Bank Mountains (S & SW)

Visitor centre

Oak tree

Reserve gate

Wadi Shiteau

Shiteau Valley

The Quarry

Wadi Alga

Fruit orchards

0 ———— 500m
0 ———— 500yds

signposted and as you approach the village the reserve entrance comes into view. Unfortunately, there's no public transport to get you to the reserve so you'll need a car or you can take a taxi from Ajlun. It's a relatively short journey; for a taxi expect to pay around JD7.

Ajlun Houses (*Rasun & Orjan;* ✆ *02 647 5673;* e *ajloun@rscn.org.jo; www.rscn. org.jo;* ⊕ *09.00–17.00 daily, times can vary; entry free*) This collection of houses and workshops, collectively referred to as the Ajlun Houses, is part of a socioeconomic initiative established by the Royal Society for the Conservation of Nature (RSCN). The aim is to provide a sustainable income source for the people who live in and around the Ajlun Forest Reserve. The emphasis is on business management skill training and providing the opportunity and support needed to start a small business.

Ongoing marketing support is then offered once a business is up and running. In short, the initiative's aim is to help the economy of the people, especially women and those who may be under threat of poverty, and to reduce their dependency on the reserve and its resources, thereby helping its conservation.

AJLUN TRAILS

An ingenious collection of hiking trails has been organised by the RSCN in and around Ajlun. The trails not only give you a valuable insight into the town and its lush landscape, but also the lifestyle and activities of the local population. You have to pay – anything between JD8 and JD30 – but the money you spend on taking a tour or following a trail helps towards the upkeep of the Ajlun Forest Reserve and provides a sustainable means of income for the local people.

The trails vary in length and ability. The **Roe Deer Trail** (*included in the JD8 entry fee for the Ajlun Forest Reserve*) takes just half an hour or so and follows a short circular trail from the campsite, past an old stone press and the area of the reserve where the deer live; the 8km **Rockrose Trail** (*JD14*) is longer, taking three to four hours to complete. You need a certain level of ability for this trail; the first half is all uphill with some steep scrambles, but reassuringly the second half is downhill and much easier. It is guided and takes you through woodlands, orchards and farms. You'll see tiny hamlets and also presses in a building that was used in Byzantine and Roman times for winemaking and pressing olives.

The **Prophet's Trail** (*JD16*) is a much longer excursion. You'll need to allow at least five hours to complete this trail. It leaves from the forest reserve visitors' centre and takes a route to one of Jordan's oldest churches, the **Mar Elias**, which was discovered in 1999. This pretty church is said to lie on the spot identified as Tishbe in the Hebrew Bible, the hometown of the Prophet Elijah after whom it is named. It stands atop a hill and has some colourful mosaics believed to date from the Byzantine period when it was built, and a tiny chapel discovered a few years after the church, which evidence suggests probably pre-dates it. The trail continues through meadows and orchards, and includes a picnic near the ruins.

The **Orjan Village Trail** (*JD22*) and the **Ajlun Castle Trail** (*JD27*) are the longest trails and follow a course across country to Orjan and into the centre of Ajlun to spend time at its 12th-century Qal'at ar-Rabad castle.

The newest trails are **The Houses Trail** (*JD26*) and the **Soap House Trail** (*JD14*). A moderate level of fitness is required for these trails as they cover some fairly hilly terrain. The Houses Trail includes visits to The Soap House and The Biscuit House in Orjan and the House of Calligraphy in Rasun; the Soap House Trail just visits The Soap House. You can see local women making soap using natural ingredients, local homemade Tasali Jordanian biscuits and savouries, and learn some basic Arabic and how to write script (see opposite).

Other than the Roe Deer Trail, which you can join on arrival at the Ajlun Forest Reserve visitors' centre, all the trails need to be booked in advance and the leaving time from the centre checked at time of booking (\ 02 647 5673). The longer trails include lunch and a transfer back to the visitors' centre. Most are guided, although you have the option to wander freely yourself without a guide on the Roe Deer Trail and the Soap House Trail. The longest trail to Ajlun Castle is assisted part of the way by donkey.

RASUN AND ORJAN

To really get a taste of local life visit these two villages in the highlands of Jordan near Ajlun, where little has changed in centuries. Rasun and Orjan have lots of picturesque traditional houses, some brightly coloured, that line tiny narrow alleyways and lanes. Dotted around the villages are olive trees, their trunks a metre or more wide indicating that they are several hundred years old. Surrounding the villages are acres of woodland and forest. Here you will see pomegranate trees, which are easy to spot with their delicate green leaves and orange flowers that grow and develop to become delicious fruit. Pomegranate pips are used to flavour tea, for fruit juices, in cosmetics and to give a sweet taste to many desserts.

You'll see huge fig trees too, their large leaves making them distinctive as you look out over the landscape. The figs grow in abundance, changing from green to the deepest purple, and are the juiciest you're likely to taste. The villages have several streams flowing from the Wadi Zalama and Wadi Rayyan with waterside walks, which are made all the more pleasant with the scent of mint. Wild mint grows along the banks. Rasun and Orjan, location of the Ajlun Houses, see page 169, are just a few kilometres outside the boundaries of the Ajlun Forest Reserve and well worth a look.

The added benefit of the scheme is that because many of the businesses are craft orientated, they help ensure Jordan's rural traditions are not lost with the onslaught of modernism. It's a super initiative. As a visitor, the houses will afford you the chance to mingle with locals, see everyday life and observe as they demonstrate the skills that have been a key part of their lifestyles for centuries. Entry to the houses is free but, while there is no obligation at all to purchase anything, any money you spend will be helping the local economy. The three main houses are The Soap House, the House of Calligraphy and The Biscuit House.

The Soap House (*Signposted from the centre of Orjan village*) Simply walking through the door of this Orjan workshop and shop is a delight. The scent of plants used in the preparation of the soaps and other health products on display, greets you. The business is run by a team of local women from Orjan who have banded together to use their skills to make these luxurious and eco-friendly beauty products. You can tour their workshop, see the soap-making process up close and enjoy a leisurely chat over a cup of Melissa, which is a traditional brew made with lemon verbena.

The main product is Orjan soap. Made from local olive oil blended with the extracts and oils from other plants, the soap is entirely natural. It hydrates as well as cleanses the skin, and leaves it feeling soft. Other products include the refreshing smelling mint soap bar, soap flakes, soap balls, a scrub soap and bars made from honey, geranium, lavender and pomegranate. In keeping with the ethos of the RSCN initiative, the business works for the team, the consumer and uses only natural ingredients that, in turn, help the environment. The team here clearly enjoys their work.

The House of Calligraphy (*Rasun village*) This workshop, where you can see calligraphy being written and applied to clothing, cards and ornamental items for the home, and even having a go yourself, is both inspiring and educational. The team of women who run the workshop are welcoming and approachable. First, they will give you a brief introduction to Arabic and Islamic culture, and explain

Jordan Rift Valley and the Dead Sea   JORDAN RIFT VALLEY

6

how calligraphy has played a part for many years. They will explain how letters are written and what tools are used.

Next, if you fancy trying your hand at calligraphy, you will be shown through to a small workshop. You will learn how to hold the reed used to write the letters and how to form them. From here you will go through to the main silk screen area and can watch as the team demonstrate how they write the script and apply it to the items. The House of Calligraphy is a fascinating workshop and one where you will find a truly authentic souvenir to take home with you.

The Biscuit House (*Orjan village*) As its name implies, The Biscuit House is a lovely rustic little workshop that specialises in biscuits made to traditional recipes. Known as Tasali cuisine, the biscuits, plus crisps and snacks, contain only natural products, almost all of which are grown locally. You can try the molasses and Tahini sandwich cookies (a savoury snack traditionally eaten with bread), or the olive oil crisps flavoured with anise and sesame seeds. For sale, too, are delicious energy bars made with figs, honey, raisins, almonds and walnuts.

On a visit to The Biscuit House the team will first take you through to the kitchen area where the recipes are created. Most are based on recipes that have been handed down through the generations, while others offer a modern twist using ingredients available locally. You can then see biscuits, crisps and bars being made by hand and baked. The smell is divine. If you fancy sampling any of the products or just simply need a bit of a break, then head for the Tasali café located on site. Overnight bed and breakfast accommodation is also available here.

Ajlun Castle (Qal'at ar-Rabad) (*Ajlun;* \ *02 642 0956;* ⊕ *summer 08.00–17.30 daily, winter 08.00–16.00 daily; entry JD1*) The Qal'at ar-Rabad is a powerful-looking fortress, well preserved and considered one of the most important examples of medieval Arab-Islamic military architecture. It was built by Izz al-Din Usama, a commander in Saladin's army, and later enlarged after his death when a new tower and gate were added in 1214.

The castle was one of a chain of fortresses built along the country's western boundary from the Jordan Valley to the Araba Valley by the Mamluks to defend their empire from invading Crusaders. It lay at the crossroads of three main trade routes serving Jordan and passages into Syria, which had helped make both Ajlun and the Mamluks prosperous. In fact, the castle controlled the routes at this point. Ajlun had long been famous for its thriving iron mines, and although these had brought wealth to the town it had also prompted unwanted attention from invaders. The Crusaders, especially, made several unsuccessful bids to capture Ajlun and its mines. Thus the Qal'at ar-Rabad had two roles: to help protect the empire and to control and safeguard Ajlun and its valuable iron mines.

Originally the castle was surrounded by a wide, deep moat said to be around 16m wide and 15m deep. Its walls were 1m or so thick with rows of arrow slits and it had four massive watchtowers. It was, without doubt, a mighty fortress and one that successfully thwarted attacks. One of the most intriguing features of the castle is the series of pigeon lofts. This is where the Mamluks would keep the pigeons used to deliver important messages. With their capital in Cairo, it is believed the Mamluks found pigeon post, coupled with fire beacons, to be a key element in running their sprawling empire. It is said a message could be delivered from Damascus to Cairo, which is a distance of around 600km (375 miles), in just 12 hours.

The castle suffered extensive damage in 1260 when the Mamluks fought off invading Mongols, but it was fairly quickly restored and the moat, which by this time had been neglected and had become choked by debris, was cleared. Over the years the castle was used by the Ottomans, but was damaged in 1837 and 1927 when two strong earthquakes struck. In recent years the Department of Antiquities has embarked upon a restoration programme to bring the castle back to its former glory. It included rebuilding a drawbridge walkway over the moat to the main entrance.

Today, the castle is a popular attraction. The recent restoration work has meant that most of the castle is now easily accessible for visitors, although be aware that many areas are reached only by narrow, steep, winding stone staircases. You can see its now dry moat, the drawbridge and the highly decorative main gate, which has reliefs of the pigeons the Mamluks were so fond of. You can also see the towers, the remains of the stable blocks and explore the cavernous interior.

With each twist and turn you take through the network of vaulted walkways you'll come across halls probably used for dining or entertainment, rooms where the castle's inhabitants would sleep and the private quarters where the commander, or lord, of the fortress would spend his time. These rooms are the only ones with windows, but look closely and you will see how they quickly convert so they have just arrow slits for times when the castle came under attack. A well-worn series of stone steps lead, eventually, to the top of the castle, from where there is a panoramic view of the Jordan Valley.

The fortress is easy to find and a major landmark of the town. A tarmac road leads from the town centre to the castle. There is a car park outside with several refreshment stalls, toilets and a handful of souvenir shops.

Anjara (*South of Ajlun*) Anjara is a picturesque little market town surrounded by vineyards with, it is believed, a long and notable past. It was in Anjara that Jesus is said to have spoken with locals and gained followers after giving a sermon. He, with his mother Mary and his disciples, rested in a cave here on their journey across Jordan. Although there are no clear stories of this event happening in the Bible, only suggestions, the existence of a cave visited by Jesus has been sanctioned by the Vatican and it has long been a place of pilgrimage. It is considered one of the holiest places in Jordan.

A church was built here as a shrine in the 1970s, which you can visit. It is a popular place for contemplation. Known as **Our Lady of the Mountains**, or locally Sayyidat al-Jabal, the shrine has a mosaic floor and several colourful frescoes depicting scenes from the Bible. You can identify the holy people shown in the scenes by the golden haloes around their heads. To find the church, take the highway from Amman northwards towards Jerash and just before you reach the archaeological site of Jerash bear left and follow signs for Anjara. Continue for about 30 minutes until you reach the town. The Sayyidat al-Jabal has a steeple that towers over the town so you can't miss it.

DEIR 'ALLA AND MAHANAIM

The temple of Deir 'Alla, which lies atop a hill a few kilometres southwest of Ajlun, is believed to have been the biblical Succoth where Gideon is said to have chased the Midianites back to the east (Judges 8:5-16). It dates from around 1500bc. Nearby is Tulul al-Dhahab al-Gharbi, otherwise known as the biblical Mahanaim where Jacob rested on his way to meet his brother Esau (Genesis 32:1).

6

Dibeen Forest *(Jamla, south of Ajlun;* m *079 902 9497;* e *ajluntourism@rscn.org. jo; www.rscn.org.jo;* ⊕ *usually 09.00–18.00 daily but can vary)* A peaceful place of rolling hills blanketed by fragrant Aleppo pines and evergreen oak (*Quercus calliprinos*) forests sliced by valleys created by deep *wadis*, the Dibeen Forest Reserve is one of the newest and untouched of Jordan's natural parks. There are no facilities here other than parking areas and toilets for visitors (although some are planned), but a collection of short woodland trails and picnic spots have been introduced. It's a perfect place to while away a few hours and at less than an hour from Amman and around 40 minutes from Jerash, it is easily accessible, providing you have a car or take a taxi. No public transport serves the reserve at the moment.

Run by the Royal Society for the Conservation of Nature, which has pioneered a programme designed to protect its wildlife, the reserve is home to many different species of mammal, bird, reptile and plant. Around 17 of the recorded species seen here are endangered. Look out for the endemic Persian red squirrel (*Sciurus anomalus*), which thrives in the forest habitat, and the stone marten (*Martes foina*). The grey wolf (*Canis lupus*) is known to live and thrive here too. If you love orchids, the reserve is home to some of the rarest specimens. Spring is a great time to see their blazing red and yellow colours.

Salt *Telephone code: 05 (south of Ajlun)* One of Jordan's most historic towns, Salt (As-Salt locally) was at one time the country's foremost city. It largely developed from being a tiny settlement with just a handful of people to a place of considerable size during the reign of the Macedonian king, Alexander the Great (336–323BC). He considered Salt's location as being strategic to his plans to expand his kingdom by conquering the then neighbouring Persian Empire.

Over the centuries Salt grew in both size and stature to become an important trading centre and one of the most prosperous towns in Transjordan. As such, it attracted the eye of subsequent rulers. The Romans, the Byzantines who made Salt the seat of a bishopric, and the Mamluks all coveted Salt and when they had the opportunity to acquire it they apparently jumped at the chance. Although there were periods when Salt was attacked and badly damaged, most notably by the Mongols and the Egyptians, in the main it continued to flourish. In the late 19th century, Salt experienced a period of growth never seen before. Under the Ottomans, it reached its zenith.

Salt became one of the Ottoman Empire's regional capital cities and a key trading centre in its bid to expand its commercial activities eastwards from the River Jordan. As a result its population grew quickly and its infrastructure began to take on the look of a major city. The wealthy Nablus merchants who, keen to maximise on the commercial opportunities opening up in Salt, now descended on the town and ploughed vast sums of money into engaging the finest architects and masons who worked with the local honey- and gold-coloured stone to create the elegant mansions that still stand today. These had courtyards and balconies, high arched windows and domed roofs. Inside, the walls and ceilings were adorned with the most beautiful frescoes. Salt was experiencing its heyday. It had become one of the region's most affluent, influential and fashionable cities, and remained so even after the Ottoman Empire crumbled.

The city's fortunes took a downturn after World War I. In 1921, the Emirate of Transjordan was created and the formal announcement was made in the main square of Salt to much fanfare (see *History*, page 23). When the new emir, Emir Abdullah, came to power and set about organising his administration, it seemed natural for him to choose Salt as his new capital city. However, by this time the

Hejaz Railway had reached the small nearby city of Amman. The emir, recognising the potential, declared Amman to be his capital. As a result, Salt hasn't seen the investment and modernisation that has transformed Amman over the past 90 years or so, and has retained its old-world charm and architecture.

Today, Salt is a pleasure to explore. It lies in the crook of three hills with houses that line tiny streets blanketing the hillsides. You can spend hours in the labyrinth of lanes. There are souks just begging to be explored, especially the city's oldest in the Souk al-Hammam. You can sip coffee in one of its coffee houses, admire the remains of the 13th-century fortress that sits atop one of the hills, the Jabal al-Qal'a, or spend a couple of hours in the folkloric museum that celebrates the region's heritage or the archaeological museum where the story of the city's past makes interesting reading. As the capital of the Balqa Governorate, Salt has important administration buildings too, which are housed in the lovely old Ottoman buildings that so characterise this amiable city.

The land surrounding Salt is especially fertile and here the juiciest tomatoes and peaches grow, along with groves full of olives. The city's population is divided between those who make a healthy living from the land and own one of the many privately-owned farms, and those who travel into Amman for work. Also, like the rest of the world, IT is a burgeoning business in Amman and attracts youngsters fresh out of university. Salt is located around 20km northwest of Amman and the route is well signposted, taking about 20 minutes.

Citadel (*Jabal al-Qal'a*) Although in ruins today, the ancient citadel was once the buzzing centre of Salt. Here you can see the remains of the 13th-century Ayyubid fortress that once dominated the city, its heavy stone walls still punctuated by the arched windows that were so typical of the architecture of the time. Records suggest the fortress was built by al-Ma'azzam Isa, who was the nephew of Saladin, the Sultan of Egypt and Syria, in the early 1200s. You can get a great view of the town by standing on the Citadel site.

Salt Archaeological Museum (*Commercial Centre, City Centre;* \ *05 355 5651;* f *05 355 3345;* e *m.salt@doa.jo;* ⊕ *summer 08.00–19.00, winter 08.00–16.00 Wed–Mon (09.00 Fri)* Housed in an impressive Ottoman-style building with a sweeping staircase up to the entrance door protected from the sun by an arched portico, the museum has been extensively restored and comprises two bright exhibition halls. Its collection of artefacts dating back more than 6,000 years is diverse, expansive

SALT'S RELIGIOUS TOMBS

One of the most remarkable of Salt's many tombs is that of the Prophet Job, who is mentioned at length in both the Hebrew Bible and as the prophet of God in the Holy Koran. In the Bible he is the central character in the Book of Job, which is considered to be one of the oldest books and is thought to have taken place in the Early to Middle Bronze Age (around 2500–1500BC). His tomb lies in Khirbet Ayyoub.

Salt's Wadi Shu'ayb mosque is the location of the Prophet Jethro's tomb, who was the father-in-law of the Prophet Moses. The tombs of Jad and Asher, both of whom were the sons of Jacob, are here in Salt too. To the west of the city, a mosque houses the tomb of the Prophet Yasha (Joshua) who is believed to have been an apprentice of Moses.

and fascinating. All come from the Balqa region. In the main hall are pottery fragments from the important Chalcolithic archaeological site of Tuleilat Ghassul in Jordan, while the subsequent displays feature water jugs and lamps found in Salt that have been dated to the Early Bronze Age, and pottery dishes, cups and plates from the Middle and Late Bronze Ages, and the Iron Age.

Continuing your walk around the main hall of the museum you will come to the Byzantine collection of glassware, followed by pottery, jewellery and coins from the Ayyubid, Mamluk, Roman and Hellenistic periods. In the second hall, there is a display of mosaics found during excavation work at one of Salt's Byzantine churches. Also, the city's history is brought right up to date with recent photographs of its houses and streets, the bustling souks and of people at work and play. It is a lovely museum and well worth a visit. Before you leave, take a look at the building itself. Named the Beit Touqan, it is a fine example of 19th-century Saltese architecture. It was once the home of the Touqan family, a member of which was King Hussein's third wife, Queen Alia.

Salt Folkloric Museum (*Cultural Centre;* 🖐 *05 355 1781;* ⏰ *summer 08.00–19.00 daily, winter 08.00–16.00 Wed–Mon*) This super little museum shows a snapshot of traditional Bedouin and Balqa life in two main exhibition areas. You can see the heavy *jellabiyyeh* (robe) and traditional red-and-white headscarf, called a *kouffieh*, that villagers have worn for centuries, along with swords and guns, boots, jewellery and utensils used for preparing and cooking food. One of the displays is a traditional Bedouin goat-hair tent, complete with the *ash-shaq* where men would sit, drink coffee and smoke tobacco using an *argeeleh* water-pipe. Here you can see a coffee pot (*dallah*) and the pan used to roast the coffee (*mehmas*). The display also shows the other main area of a Bedouin's tent, the *al-mahram*, where the women of the tribe would congregate. Traditional Balqa village life is represented by a small house that has been carefully built using authentic stone from the region and reeds. You can see where the family would sit, sleep and eat, and where the women would cook the food. A mannequin dressed in traditional robes can be seen grinding wheat and making bread in much the same way as it would have been done in the past. The museum gives you a real feel for how life was in the past.

DEAD SEA AND AROUND

 **WHERE TO STAY**

Luxury

🏠 **Crowne Plaza Dead Sea Hotel & Resort** (420 rooms) Dead Sea Rd, Sweimeh; 🖐 05 349 4000; f 05 349 4004; e info@cprdeadsea.com; www.crowneplaza.com. A new luxury hotel that opened its doors in 2011, the Crowne Plaza is geared up for relaxation on, it appears, every level. There are sumptuous guestrooms, a top-notch spa & an outdoor tent pavilion, gourmet restaurants & swimming pools, including 'The Lake', the largest outdoor pool in Jordan at over 5,000m². **$$$$$**

🏠 **Evason Ma'in Hot Springs** (97 rooms) Ma'in, Madaba; 🖐 05 324 5500; f 05 324 5550; e reservations-main@evasonresorts.com; www.

sixsenses.com. Located in a picturesque valley next to a waterfall & built in a design that resembles local architecture, this eco-boutique hotel is 30km from Madaba. Its guestrooms are contemporary & well equipped, while leisure amenities include a luxurious spa, gym, library, daily movie & pools, plus its famous hot natural spring. **$$$$$**

🏠 **Jordan Valley Marriott Resort & Spa** (250 rooms) Dead Sea Rd, Sweimeh; 🖐 05 356 0400; f 05 356 0444; e jordanvalley@marriotthotels.com; www.marriottdeadsea.com. With its collection of top-notch guestrooms complete with climate control, fluffy feather pillows & most with views of the Dead Sea, this hotel is clearly designed with relaxation in mind. There are also superb facilities, such as a spa, which of course uses Dead Spa mud in its treatments, & gourmet restaurants. A great place to stay. **$$$$$**

🏠 **Kempinski Ishtar Resort & Spa** (220 rooms) Dead Sea Rd, Sweimeh; 📞 05 356 8888; f 05 356 8800; e sales.ishtar@kempinski.com; www.kempinski.com. For activity seekers this hotel offers tennis & a gym, while its Anantara Spa is great if you prefer a more relaxing break. Choose from body wraps & facials. The hotel has infinity pools, gardens & international restaurants, plus kids' play areas. Guestrooms are fully equipped & have AC & free internet. **$$$$$**

Upmarket

🏠 **Holiday Inn Resort Dead Sea** (202 rooms) Dead Sea Rd, Sweimeh; 📞 05 349 5555; f 05 356 0056; www.holidayinnresorts.com. An arabesque-style hotel built around 3 palm tree-fringed swimming pools, the Holiday Inn has all the amenities you would expect of this standard of accommodation. The guestrooms are beautifully presented & all have AC & free Wi-Fi, plus there are restaurants & bars, leisure activities including a gym & yoga classes, & a spa. The hotel is beside the beach with access to the Dead Sea. **$$$$**

🏠 **Mövenpick Resort & Spa Dead Sea Hotel** (346 rooms) Dead Sea Rd, Sweimeh; 📞 05 356 1111; f 05 356 1122; e resort.deadsea@ moevenpick.com; www.moevenpick.com. This hotel has been designed & built to resemble a traditional Jordanian rural village, & it works extremely well. Guestrooms are within 'mud-style' complexes & are luxuriously equipped, including having a free minibar. Walkways lead to swimming pools, spa, children's activity centre & a beach right next to the Dead Sea. **$$$$**

Mid range

🏠 **Dead Sea Spa Hotel** (272 rooms) Dead Sea; 📞 05 356 1000; f 05 356 1012; e reservations@dssh.jo; www.jordandeadsea. com. The Dead Sea Medical Centre is located within the hotel complex & is staffed by a team of medics specialising in health & relaxation therapies. Accommodation is in bungalows with AC, while on site is a range of amenities that include a tennis court, children's play & aqua

centre, restaurant & a Bedouin tent, which is used for weekly themed evening. **$$$**

🏠 **Feynan Ecolodge** (26 rooms) Near Dana Nature Reserve; 📞 06 464 5580; reservations@ feynan.com; www.feynan.com. Run by EcoHotels in conjunction with the Royal Society for the Conservation of Nature, the Feynan Ecolodge lies in a remote spot at the western entrance to the Dana Biosphere Reserve. There's no electricity; only solar energy & lighting by candles. Its guestrooms are welcoming & well equipped, & a restaurant on-site offers delicious vegetarian meals & fresh homemade bread made using local ingredients. It's cosy in winter; a fire is set using the waste from pressing olives. **$$$**

🏠 **Madaba Inn Hotel** (33 rooms) Yarmouk St, Madaba; 📞 05 325 9003; f 05 325 9008; e info@madabainn.com; www.madabainn.com. A new modern hotel, the Madaba Inn is one of the best accommodation options in Madaba. It lies opposite the St George Church, which is famous for its mosaics. The hotel offers attractive well-equipped guestrooms that echo the style of Jordan and come complete with free Wi-Fi & AC. The restaurants are also on site. **$$$**

Budget

🏠 **Dana Guesthouse** (9 rooms) Dana Biosphere Reserve; 📞 03 227 0497; e dana@ rscn.org.jo; www.rscn.org.jo. Looking out over the reserve, this simple yet pleasingly presented hotel has a welcoming feel. Its guestrooms have nice furnishings & a sun terrace, although apart from 1 suite the bathrooms are shared. Arabic food is served. What sets this hotel apart, however, is its isolated location, where you can't help but relax. **$$**

🏠 **Dana Hotel** (8 rooms) Dana Village; 📞 03 227 0537; e suleimanjarad@yahoo.com; www. danavillage.piczo.com. Housed in a charming little stone house, this hotel is run as part of the Dana Cooperative for Tourism initiative designed to give income to local families. Its guestrooms are spotless & furnished in a traditional manner complete with Bedouin rugs. Private bathrooms are available. B/fast is included & dinner can be arranged. Drinks can be taken on its rooftop Bedouin tent. **$$**

🏠 **Mariam Hotel** (57 rooms) Aisha Um Al Mumeneen St, Madaba; 📞 05 325 1529; f 05 325 1530; e reservations@mariamhotel.com;

www.mariamhotel.com. This is a gem of a hotel; a home from home. Beautifully presented guestrooms all have private bathrooms, there's a restaurant & a bar, plus a swimming pool amidst gardens full of exotic plants. It is family-run & good value. **$$**

🏠 **Salome Hotel** (34 rooms) Aisha Um Mumeneen St, Madaba; ☎ 05 3248606; f 05 3248607; e info@salonehotel.com; www.salomehotel.com. A small but beautifully presented hotel in a quiet suburb of Madaba, the Salome has its own restaurant serving homemade dishes, a lovely terrace for whiling away the evening & well-equipped rooms. A budget hotel offering good value. **$$**

Shoestring

🏠 **Chalet Village** (15 chalets) Mujib Nature Reserve, m 079 907 4960; e tourism@rscn.org.

✖ WHERE TO EAT
Expensive

✖ **Burj al-Hammam** Crowne Plaza Dead Sea Hotel & Resort, Dead Sea Rd, Sweimeh; ☎ 05 349 4000; e info@cprdeadsea.com; www.crowneplaza.com; ⊕ 12.30–14.30 & 18.00–23.30. This richly decorated restaurant specialises in Lebanese cuisine. Enjoy a buffet of delicious seafood freshly prepared with lemon & herbs, or a mezze of several dishes including *sambusac* (savoury pastries), *baba ghanoush* (a dish of aubergines & vegetables) & *yalanji* (stuffed vine leaves). **$$$$$**

✖ **The Codes** Kempinski Ishtar Resort & Spa, Dead Sea Rd, Sweimeh; ☎ 05 356 8888; f 05 356 8800; www.kempinski.com; ⊕ 19.30–23.00 Wed–Mon. Combining the flavours of Thai & Asian cuisine, this contemporary-style restaurant overlooking the Dead Sea is popular with couples looking for an elegant dining experience. Specialities include sushi & gourmet Thai green & red curries, accompanied by fine international wines. **$$$$$**

✖ **Il Terrazzo Restaurant** Jordan Valley Marriott Resort & Spa, Dead Sea Rd, Sweimeh; ☎ 05 356 0400; www.marriottdeadsea.com; ⊕ 12.30–14.00 & 18.00–23.30 daily. This elegant yet informal restaurant overlooking the Dead Sea revolves around its open kitchen where the choreography of its chefs is mesmerising. Authentic Italian pasta dishes are served, along with pizzas fresh from the oven. A full list of

jo; www.rscn.org.jo. Located on the shores of the Madash peninsula with views straight out over the Dead Sea, the campsite offers 15 dbl rooms equipped with AC & a pleasant shaded sun terrace. The concrete chalets are simple but clean & well maintained. A shower & toilet block is on site. The main entrance to the reserve & its visitors' centre are minutes away, as is the site's restaurant. **$**

▲ **Rummana Campsite** (20 tents) Dana Biosphere Reserve; ☎ 03 227 0497; e dana@rscn.org.jo; www.rscn.org.jo; ⊕ Mar–Oct. Overlooking the Wadi Dana, this campsite can accommodate 60 people in large white tents equipped with mattresses, pillows & covers. It has BBQ grills, drinking water & there are toilets & showers available for guests. There's a large Bedouin tent for community gatherings & a kitchen. **$**

Italian wines is offered. An outside terrace allows you to eat alfresco. **$$$$$**

✖ **Luigi's** Mövenpick Resort & Spa Dead Sea Hotel, Dead Sea Rd, Sweimeh; ☎ 05 356 1111; www.moevenpick-deadsea.com; ⊕ 13.00–23.00. Luigi's is an upmarket restaurant that serves truly tasty Italian dishes made with homemade pasta & sauces. Watch chefs make a pizza base & then top it with your favourite ingredients before cooking it in a traditional wood-fired pizza oven. Wines & a selection of grappa are available. Dine inside or alfresco. **$$$$$**

✖ **Panoramic Restaurant** Dead Sea Rd; ☎ 05 349 1133; ⊕ 12.00–22.30. Housed within the Dead Sea Panoramic Complex & run by Evason Ma'in Hot Springs for the RSCN, this stylish restaurant is decorated in soft neutral shades. A terrace overlooking the sea means you have the option to sit inside or dine alfresco. High-quality Arabic with a hint of Lebanese cuisine is served. Here, you can have a lunchtime snack or opt for a full hot or cold mezze. There's live acoustic music. It's popular, especially at w/ends. **$$$$$**

Above average

✖ **Below 393 Steak House** Holiday Inn Resort Dead Sea, Dead Sea Rd, Sweimeh; ☎ 05 349 5555; www.holidayinnresorts.com; ⊕ 18.00–23.00 daily. Located inside the Holiday Inn Resort Dead Sea, this chic cream & dark wood finished restaurant specialises in steak with all the trimmings. A menu of local cuisine is available if you or a member of your party fancies a dish other than a steak. It claims to have the largest selection of beers in the Dead Sea area, plus a wide choice of wines. $$$$

✗ **Chopsticks** Mövenpick Resort & Spa Dead Sea Hotel, Dead Sea Rd, Sweimeh; ☎05 356 1111; www.moevenpick-deadsea.com; ⏰ 18.30–23.00. Chopsticks gives you the chance to create your own main course from a selection of ingredients that are cooked in a personal wok. It is a tasteful restaurant with a straw & bamboo décor designed to capture a Chinese atmosphere. $$$$

✗ **Obelisk Restaurant** Kempinski Ishtar Resort & Spa Dead Sea Rd, Sweimeh; www.kempinski.com; ⏰ 06.30–11.30, 13.00–15.30 & 19.00–22.30. Affording views out over the Dead Sea, this large & neutrally decorated restaurant has live cooking demonstrations & an extensive buffet of international dishes. Dine in or alfresco on its terrace. $$$$

✗ **Olive** Evason Ma'in Hot Springs, Ma'in, Madaba; ☎05 324 5500; www.sixsenses.com; ⏰ 20.00–24.00. Housed in a Bedouin tent lit by traditional lamps, Olive has long tables or private tables amongst olive trees where authentic Bedouin dishes such as *mensaf* (lamb with yogurt) are served mezze-style. A menu of Jordanian wines is offered to accompany the meal. $$$$

Mid range

✗ **Haret Jdoudna** King Tala St, Madaba; ☎05 324 8650; e reservations@haretjdoudna.com; www.haretjdoudna.com; ⏰ 18.00–23.00. One of the best restaurants in Madaba, indeed Jordan, the Haret Jdoudna can be found within a private 19th-century food, souk & handicraft stone complex. It is remarkably good value & specialises in mezze. The cold mezze includes dips & stuffed vine leaves followed by a platter of meats fresh from the wood-burning oven, while the hot mezze features spinach pastries & stuffed mushrooms. Deserts are homemade too. $$$

✗ **Mazaien Nebo Restaurant** Between Madaba & Mount Nebo; ☎05 324 2442; m 077 940 0002; ⏰ 12.00–16.00. A large restaurant that looks out over the countryside towards Mount Nebo, the Mazaien Nebo serves a mezze menu of local Arabic & Leventine dishes. A

specialty is *sawani*, a delicious dish of chicken with thyme, & Jordan's national dish *mensaf* (lamb with yoghurt). $$$

✗ **Peace** Dead Sea Spa Hotel, Dead Sea; ☎05 356 1000; www.jordandeadsea.com; ⏰ 18.00–23.00. A bright & welcoming family-orientated restaurant, Peace serves Arabic & international dishes such as *musakhan* (chicken with lemon & pine nuts) with a *tabbouleh* (parsley & tomato salad), plus steaks & pasta, on a long buffet. An à la carte menu & a wine list is available. $$$

✗ **Roof Restaurant** Mariam Hotel, Aisha Um Al Mumeneen St, Madaba; ☎05 325 1529; www.mariamhotel.com; ⏰ 18.00–23.00. A spacious eatery with a buffet station & BBQ terrace, the Roof Restaurant offers panoramic views out over Madaba while you eat. The cuisine is classic Arabic with an international twist. A specialty is *shish tawook*, which is marinated chicken with herbs & salad (JD7). The restaurant serves alcohol; its pleasant Mount Nebo wine is great value at JD3 a glass. $$$

✗ **St George Restaurant** Madaba Inn Hotel, Yarmouk St, Madaba; ☎05 325 9003; e info@madabainn.com; www.madabainn.com; ⏰ 07.00–10.30 & 18.00–23.00. Traditional Jordanian dishes including *daoud pasha* (tasty meatballs with onions) served with *manaqesh zatar* (olive bread), & a whole raft of salads & dips that decorate its central buffet display, along with an à la carte menu offering international dishes. The team here are friendly & helpful. The restaurant has an informal yet understated elegant feel. $$$

Cheap and cheerful

✗ **Dana** Al-Nuzha St, Madaba; ☎05 324 5749; ⏰ 12.00–23.00. Located not far from the Church of the Apostles, this large restaurant decorated in a traditional Arabic style with richly coloured walls & pictures can usually be found full of tourists from an excursion bus. You can't miss it; its name is emblazoned above the entrance. A good, inexpensive buffet of local dishes is served, including *falafel* (chickpea balls), *shish tawook* (chicken kebab) & *mensaf* (lamb with yoghurt). $$

✗ **Mosaic Café** Madaba Inn Hotel; Yarmouk St, Madaba; ☎05 325 9003; e info@madabainn.com; www.madabainn.com; ⏰ 07.00–23.00. If it's sandwiches, snacks like *falafel*, salads & dips you crave while out & about exploring then you could do no better than the Mosaic Café. This bright & cheerful place is popular with locals as well as guests of the Madaba Inn. $$

Rock bottom
✗ Ayola Café Hussein bin Ali St; ☎05 325 1843; ⏲ 09.00–19.00. The Ayola is a lively little place that serves a selection of toasted sandwiches & pastries, tea, juices, coffee & cold beer. It is a popular haunt of locals smoking tobacco using a

traditional *argeeleh* water-pipe, & a good stopping off point for tourists visiting St George's Church. $
✗ Mujib Chalets Restaurant Mujib Nature Reserve; m 079 907 4960; e tourism@rscn.org. jo; www.rscn.org.jo; ⏲ 09.00–18.00 daily. This restaurant essentially provides energy-giving food for the hikers back from exploring the nature reserve, & as such has few frills. However, having said that, the food is always fresh, cooked well, based on local dishes & is generally delicious. Meals are accompanied by tea, coffee & juices. $

ENTERTAINMENT AND NIGHTLIFE
Bars, nightspots and tea houses
♀ Acacia Lounge Bar Jordan Valley Marriott Resort & Spa, Dead Sea Rd, Sweimeh; ☎05 356 0400; www.marriottdeadsea.com; ⏲ 18.00–23.30 daily. A sophisticated lounge bar with a classical décor, the Acacia serves cocktails & light bites throughout the evening accompanied by live piano music. A balcony provides fresh air & a view of the sea.
♀ Al Khayyam Bar Mövenpick Resort & Spa Dead Sea Hotel, Dead Sea Rd, Sweimeh; ☎05 356 1111; www.moevenpick-deadsea.com; ⏲ 09.00–24.00. The Al Khayyam Bar is a richly decorated lounge area that takes its theme from traditional Arabian architecture. Light snacks, pastries & drinks are served here throughout the day. In the evening it becomes a romantic place to watch the sun go down.
♀ Cellar Evason Ma'in Hot Springs, Ma'in, Madaba; ☎05 324 5500; www.sixsenses.com; ⏲ 18.00–23.00. Dark & atmospheric, Cellar hosts tastings where wine from Jordan & around the world is paired with different cheeses, mezze dishes & chocolate. An à la carte chef's menu is served.
♀ Fishing Club Beach Bar Jordan Valley Marriott Resort & Spa, Dead Sea Rd, Sweimeh; ☎05 356 0400; www.marriottdeadsea.com; ⏲ 18.00–23.30 daily. Located right beside the Dead Sea, this upmarket yet informal bar has a menu of cocktails & fine wines, & offers the chance to smoke a water-pipe. A great place to unwind.
♀ Horizon Holiday Inn Resort Dead Sea, Dead Sea Rd, Sweimeh; ☎05 349 5555; www. holidayinnresorts.com; ⏲ 11.30–14.00 & 18.00–23.30. Sip on cocktails, enjoy a chilled mint tea or smoke tobacco *argeeleh*-fashion while gazing out

over the sea in this outdoor terrace-style venue. You can sit at the bar or chill on loungers.
♀ Kish Bar Kempinski Ishtar Resort & Spa, Dead Sea Rd, Sweimeh; ☎05 356 8888; www. kempinski.com; ⏲ 17.00–01.00. A seriously chic lounge bar looking out over the sea where comfy sofas allow you to snuggle up while chatting to friends, the Kish serves a full range of fine wines & cocktails. Live music is played most evenings.
☆ Promenade Disco & Lounge Club Crowne Plaza Dead Sea Hotel & Resort, Dead Sea Rd, Sweimeh; ☎05 349 4000; e info@cprdeadsea. com; www.crowneplaza.com; ⏲ 18.00–01.00. Overlooking the hotel's 'The Lake' swimming pool, the largest in Jordan, & with views of the Dead Sea, the Promenade is a complex where you can relax over a cocktail & then dance disco-fashion into the small hours.
♀ Rawsan Mariam Hotel, Aisha Um Al Mumeneen St, Madaba; ☎05 325 1529; www. mariamhotel.com; ⏲ 11.00–23.00. With dark leather furniture & great views out over Madaba, this poolside bar offers Mount Nebo wine, beers, whisky & coffees, & the chance to smoke using an *argeeleh* water-pipe. Snacks & nibbles are served here too.
♀ Sumerian Bar Kempinski Ishtar Resort & Spa, Dead Sea Rd, Sweimeh; ☎05 356 8888; www.kempinski.com; ⏲ 08.00–23.00. A moody bar that works whether you want to play chess during the day, quietly read a book or join up with friends in the evening for drinks. It has a wide range of malt whisky, plus other spirits from around the world.
⌐ Valley Café Mövenpick Resort & Spa Dead Sea Hotel, Dead Sea Rd, Sweimeh; ☎05 356 1111; www.moevenpick-deadsea.com; ⏲ 16.00–24.00

Sun–Thu, 13.00–01.00 Fri–Sat. Live music & dancing, along with water-pipes, can be enjoyed in this café decorated like a traditional Arabian *gahwah* (coffee house). Light snacks & ice cream are served.

SHOPPING One of the best places in the Jordan Rift Valley region to buy authentic crafts is **Madaba**. Head for **Talal Street** and **Hussein bin Ali Street**. Both converge at the junction of Madaba's most famous landmark, St George's Church, so you'll find them easily. Here you will find shops specialising in the most beautiful handmade silver necklaces and bracelets, hand-woven carpets in every conceivable colour (although all hues are mixed with red), and Arabic dresses and robes. Shopping here is a delight, and you can be sure of reasonable prices.

Towns, including Karak and Ajlun, have lots of small specialist shops selling all manner of items from clothing to jewellery, plus the region's Dana Nature Reserve, Mujib Nature Reserve and the Ajlun Forest Reserve all have handicraft centres. The centres display handmade biscuits, beauty products and ceramics, plus lots more, which have been made by mainly women who live in or around the parks. They make ideal souvenirs to take home.

SPAS The Dead Sea region has a collection of spas that are up there with the finest in the world. Many are located within the hotel complexes, while others are private. There are also natural spas, such as the Hammamat Ma'in Hot Springs.

Anantara Spa Kempinski Ishtar Resort & Spa, Dead Sea Rd, Sweimeh; ☎ 05 356 8888; f 05 356 8800; www.kempinski.com. Sleek & glamorous, the Anantara Spa uses Dead Sea mud for a whole raft of treatments, from purifying body wraps to skin-tightening facials. Here you can enjoy a body scrub with sea salt & hydrating oils, traditional Thai massage or a *hammam*. Prices start from around JD50.

Dead Sea Medical Centre Dead Sea Spa Hotel, Dead Sea; ☎ 05 356 1000; f 05 356 1012; e reservations@dssh.jo; www.jordandeadsea. com. Along with offering the body wraps & beauty treatments found in most spas, this centre also has a collection of treatments aimed at using the healing properties of the Dead Sea & its products to relieve the symptoms of disorders. Various dermatological & rheumatological conditions are addressed by a team of medical experts.

Shape Up Holiday Inn Resort Dead Sea, Dead Sea Rd, Sweimeh; ☎ 05 349 5555; f 05 356 0056; www.holidayinnresorts.com. Shape Up is the contemporary spa & health suite inside the Holiday Inn. It has a sauna, steam room & gym, plus several private rooms where you can book facials & body treatments. Try its Dead Sea salt & honey scrub (JD35), its hydrating mud wrap (JD40) or a relaxing massage.

Six Senses Spa Evason Ma'in Hot Springs, Ma'in, Madaba; ☎ 05 324 5500; f 05 324 5550; www.sixsenses.com. This spa, located at the natural hot springs of Ma'in, oozes luxury. On the menu are treatments, including its zeytoun (olive) massage (JD62) & its jasmine facial (JD65). Packages are available. A wellness extras menu features a natural steam cave & spring pools.

The Spa Jordan Valley Marriott Resort & Spa, Dead Sea Rd, Sweimeh; ☎ 05 356 0400; f 05 356 0444; www.marriottdeadsea.com. One of the country's largest spas, this complex has a menu of massages, including one designed for the back that uses pouches of hot salt from the Dead Sea (JD54). Body treatments include an Arabic coffee scrub & a desert sand scrub (both JD49), a Dead Sea natural mud wrap (JD64), floatation, hot & cold stones, & facials.

Thalgo Spa Crowne Plaza Dead Sea Hotel & Resort, Dead Sea Rd, Sweimeh; ☎ 05 349 4000; f 05 349 4004; e info@cprdeadsea.com; www. crowneplaza.com. This 6,000m² spa is atmospheric, with soft lighting & candles. It offers 30 treatment rooms & tented pavilions overlooking the sea with a menu of body wraps, facials & massages that use local, organic & natural ingredients. Its whirlpool is an architectural feature. Prices start from around JD50.

Zara Spa Mövenpick Resort & Spa Dead Sea Hotel, Dead Sea Rd, Sweimeh; ☎ 05 356 1303; f 05 356 1125; www.moevenpick-deadsea. com. You can choose from packages of several days' duration or book a single treatment from a lengthy menu at this luxurious spa. Body treatments include a Serenity Dry Flotation Mud Wrap (JD82) & a Thalgo Purity Ritual Facial (JD73), plus reflexology, acupuncture & shiatsu massage.

OTHER PRACTICALITIES

Dress In the Dead Sea hotel resorts dress is smart casual and you can wear swimwear, although never lose sight of the fact that you are in a predominantly Muslim country. If you're planning to spend some time in the reserves take easy-to-wear garments that cover your legs and shoulders, yet enable you to move when climbing or negotiating the fast-flowing and steep canyons of places such as the Mujib Nature Reserve. The region's reserves, including the Dana Nature Reserve, have shade from the trees, but you will still need to protect yourself from the sun. Good walking boots and a rucksack-type bag to carry water and supplies are essential.

Emergencies If you're spending time in one of the region's nature reserves and find you are in need of assistance you should call the **visitors' centre** in the first instance. For the Mujib Nature Reserve's visitors' centre telephone m 079 720 3888 and for the Dana Biosphere Reserve ☎ 03 227 0498.

Money, post and internet The main towns of the region, including Madaba and Karak, and the Dead Sea hotels and resorts have full money-changing and postal services. A few internet cafés are emerging in the towns and villages, although the best option for checking emails and surfing the internet is in the hotels or in the visitors' centres of the nature reserves. Many hotels in the Dead Sea region offer free Wi-Fi and a fast connection.

WHAT TO SEE AND DO The iconic Dead Sea offers endless days of relaxation, while around the region is Madaba, known as the 'City of Mosaics' and home to one of the oldest views of Jerusalem and the Holy Land; the amazing biblical sites around Bethany Beyond the Jordan; nature reserves; castles; and the ancient city of Karak.

Dead Sea Your first glimpse of the Dead Sea sends a thrill of excitement through you; you just know you are somewhere really special. Famously, this large stretch of flat, impossibly still water with a view of Jerusalem on the far shore is the lowest point on the planet and one of the most religious and spiritual places on earth. Here, God is said to have first spoken to Man, Jesus was baptized by John the Baptist and Moses received his Ten Commandments. It is also believed to be the site of the Garden of Eden.

The Dead Sea is a large expanse of landlocked water fed by several rivers, including the River Jordan, but through evaporation and a slower flow of water along the river as a result of human consumption the sea is shrinking. It loses about 1m in water depth per year. As the level decreases, so a remarkable coating of salt and minerals is left behind on the rocks, which is both beautiful and also provides valuable products for medicine, beauty, agriculture and industry. However, scientists have predicted the sea could dry up over the next 40 years. At its deepest the sea currently plunges some 430m, while in contrast towards the south the sea's depth is only around 4m. It stretches southwards for some 80km from the northwest of Madaba and is, on average, 14km wide.

The sea has been an attraction for years; in fact, it is said to have been one of Egyptian Queen Cleopatra's favourite spas. Not only do people come to see this natural, peaceful phenomenon created millions of years ago, but they are also drawn by its legendary therapeutic and rejuvenating powers. Over millennia it has been one of the world's finest natural spas. Its water is incredibly salty; in fact, nine times saltier than the Mediterranean.

The sea is bursting with salts and minerals. There's magnesium, which is said to help beat stress and protect against allergies, sulphur to detoxify, calcium for the skin and potassium, which helps to balance moisture in the body. The water is also full of bromide; in fact, the sea has one of the highest concentrations of the chemical compound found anywhere in the world. It is a muscle relaxant and helps to ease muscular stiffness. There's also sodium, which is ideal for lymphatic fluid balance, and iodine for thyroid health. And don't forget the oxygen-rich air, which is created by the high barometric pressure; it helps with respiratory issues and gives you quite a lift.

You can join locals and visitors relaxing on the beach. The warm climate and diffused sun rays make it ideal for spending time here in the open air, although you will still need to use suncream and drink plenty of water. The sea and its shoreline are naturally hazy due to the lack of elevation and heat, which combine to increase the rate of evaporation. The resulting water vapour lingers in the air because the winds here are calm.

Dotted around the beach are urns full of dark brown, almost black, treacle-like mud. The intention is you cover yourself in the mud and then wash it off in the Dead Sea. The mud is full of minerals and extremely thick. You'll find it is a tad stubborn to wash off. Of course, you can bypass the mud bit, but it does leave your skin feeling extremely clean and soft when you've washed it off so it's well worth giving it a try. And it's all rather fun. You then have the opportunity you've probably dreamed of: floating effortlessly in the amazingly buoyant Dead Sea. It's said to be impossible to sink in the water because of its high salinity (saltiness).

There are several hotels on the stretch beside the Dead Sea, and all offer excellent – in fact world-class – spas that use the mud and minerals from the sea in their treatments. You can book a spa treatment or two even if you are not a guest of the hotel. The spas not only offer beauty services, but a range of health-giving treatments too, overseen by physicians and nursing staff. Among the conditions said to be relieved by the Dead Sea and its products are respiratory and circulatory conditions, and dermatological problems such as psoriasis and vitiligo. Many EU countries even provide therapeutic stays here as part of their health insurance programmes.

All the hotels have access to the Dead Sea, and providing you use their facilities, such as booking a spa treatment or even a meal in one of their restaurants, and you are happy to be screened by their security teams, then they will allow you access to their premises as a day visitor. Most also have good evening entertainment. Since there are few alternative dining and entertainment options in the area, the hotels are your best bet. The hotels are just 45 minutes or so drive from Amman, and as such have geared their services to day visitors given that many of the city's wealthiest residents come here for a day or weekend.

A little further along the Dead Sea Road towards Aqaba, on the right and signposted, you'll find the Dead Sea Panoramic Complex (see opposite), run by the Royal Society for the Conservation of Nature (RSCN). Here you can enjoy the views, follow a trail or simply relax in its restaurant. Almost opposite is a road signposted to Hammamat Ma'in springs (see page 193). The land here is the outer reaches of the RSCN's Mujib Nature Reserve, a rugged mountainous area full of deep canyons and fast-flowing rivers where some of Jordan's rarest animals and birds thrive. If you continue towards Aqaba you'll come to its entrance and reception area. Continue along the valley further and you will reach the RSCN's Dana Biosphere Reserve, which is famed for its birdwatching, see page 198.

Along with the reserves, the Dead Sea basin is an important wildlife and migrating bird haven. It has three of the most important ecosystems in the Middle East: the mountainous Mediterranean-style system towards the north, the Irano-Turasian ecosystem on the slopes of the basin's cliffs and mountains, and the desert plains of the south. Little survives in the seawater itself other than species of bacteria, hence it being known as the Dead Sea, but around its basin there are numerous species of flora and fauna, many of which are endemic.

Around the Dead Sea basin look out for sand snails hidden beneath their coiled shells and black darkling beetles, plus the rock hyrax (*Procavia capensis*), which is a rotund little creature and a distant relative of the elephant. It likes to bask in the summer sun. The birdlife is prolific and you may see the handsome black Tristram's grackle (*Onychognathus tristramii*) and the fan-tailed raven (*Corvus rhipidurus*), the sprightly sand partridge (*Ammoperdix heyi*) and the brilliant turquoise and green little green bee-eater (*Merops orientalis*). If you are lucky you will also see the Arabian rabbler (*Turdoides squamiceps*), the bar-tailed lark (*Ammomanes cinctura*) and the blackstart (*Cercomela melanura*).

Dead Sea Panoramic Complex (*Dead Sea Rd;* ✆ *05 349 1133;* e *deadsea@rscn. org.jo; www.rscn.org.jo;* ☉ *08.00–16.00; entry JD2*) Run by the RSCN, the complex is an informative place where you can learn more about the Dead Sea and the Jordan Rift Valley. In its **museum**, which you'll see just near its reception area, there are colourful displays in four main sections: geology, archaeology, ecology and conservation. It is Jordan's only specialised natural history museum and a must if you wish to know more about the Dead Sea and its surrounding areas. Two complimentary films are shown in the museum, entitled *Ecology of the Dead Sea* and the *Dead Sea in Danger*.

In the geology section, the museum looks at the creation of the Great Rift Valley, of which the Jordan Rift Valley is a part. The first display is a piece of pre-Cambrian composite rock said to be 600 million years old. In subsequent displays you'll see a collection of ancient sandstone in shades from red to black, limestone and crusted salt fragments. The wildlife and plants that thrive in the region are the subjects of the ecology section, plus the museum gives information on the conservation efforts currently in progress for the survival of the sea itself and the flora and fauna that exists in its basin.

The museum's archaeological section tells of the many civilisations that have lived here since prehistoric times, and looks at how man played a part in the look of

---

SAFETY IN THE DEAD SEA

It's a good idea to wear aqua or plastic shoes in the Dead Sea because the hard crusted salt on the sea bed and rocks is sharp and can easily scratch your feet. Where wooden steps or walkways are provided by the hotels to enable you to access the sea these, too, can get blistering hot in the summer sunshine. If you have any scratches on your body, however small, be prepared for them to sting in the salty water. There is no shade around the Dead Sea, other than in the hotel complexes, so protect yourself with suncream and a hat. Drink plenty of bottled water to prevent dehydration.

the landscape through the construction of villages. Among the displays is one that explores a palace and spa complex that was built by Herod in the 1st century AD on the site of the present-day Zara Hot Springs at Hammamat Ma'in, and copper mines constructed much earlier in around 4500BC at Wadi Feynan, which is near the Dana Nature Reserve.

The complex is built in the indigenous golden stone travertine to an Islamic-Oriental design that helps it blend in with its surroundings on the edge of the Zara mountain range. Its elevated vantage point between the Dead Sea and the Zara Hot Springs offers superb views out over the sea. There is a restaurant with a terrace, an amphitheatre where musical or cultural events are often held (details from the complex's reception), toilets and a garden. Look out for the limestone near the Rock Garden; it is 100 million years old. A **craft shop** with authentic items like ceramic plates and beauty soap supplied by the women who live in and around the nature reserves of Jordan and who work in cooperatives, is near the museum. From the complex you can take a tour of the Zara Cliffs via a special designated hiking trail.

Zara Cliff Walk One of the best ways to really appreciate the beauty of the Dead Sea and its surroundings is to take a walk along the cliff. It's a long way down, so by following the Zara Cliff Walk, which has been designed as an easy, self-guided trail by the RSCN, you will know the safest route to take. It's inadvisable to do the walk after sunset, however. A leaflet and map are available from the Dead Sea Panoramic Complex's reception and museum. The walk is broken down into four stages; each a little under a mile long. There are four stop stations along the route with boards that give you details of the area you are in, points of interest and the distance you have travelled so far. You can break off at any point along the route and make your way back.

Starting at the museum, head past the Nature Shop and the amphitheatre until you reach the start of the trail. It's clearly marked. From here, follow the signs off to your right towards the first stop station. This section of the trail will take you past rocks where you can observe black darkling beetles and sand snails. Continue on to the second, third and fourth stations, passing by valleys of date palm trees and dense Tamarix shrubs with their delicate pink-and-white flowers that thrive in the salty, moisture-rich air of the Dead Sea region. Look out for rock formations along trails that are covered in mineral deposits that make them glisten in the sunshine. Across the water on a clear day you can see Palestine and the West Bank.

Baptism Valley Bethany Beyond the Jordan and Elijah's Hill form part of the Baptism Site of Jesus Christ, which is signposted bearing right from the T-junction at the end of Highway 40 from Amman. It lies just north of the Dead Sea. At the same junction you can follow signs to your left that will take you to Mount Nebo and Moses Spring. To reach the sites of ancient Medeba (Madaba), Machaerus (present-day Mukawir) and Hammamat Ma'in, where King Herod is said to have bathed, all of which are to the east of the Dead Sea, follow the King's Highway (number 35) and the well-signposted roads (see also *Dead Sea*, page 182).

The Baptism Site of Jesus Christ (*North of the Dead Sea;* m *077 760 7036;* e *promotionunit@baptismsite.com; www.baptismsite.com;* ⊕ *summer 08.00–18.00, winter 08.00–16.00, last entry 1hr before; entry JD12, inc a shuttle bus around the site & an audio guide in 7 languages; suitable for visitors with disabilities; car parking available on site*) The site follows a 2km route along the Wadi Kharrar, locally Wadi al-Kharrar. In antiquity the area was known as Saphsaphas but, taking its name from

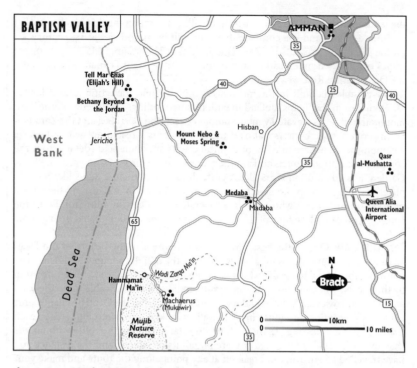

BAPTISM VALLEY

Tell Mar Elias
(Elijah's Hill)
Bethany Beyond
the Jordan
AMMAN
West
Bank
Jericho
Hisban
Mount Nebo &
Moses Spring
Qasr
al-Mushatta
Medaba
Madaba
Queen Alia
International
Airport
Dead Sea
Wadi Zarqa Ma'in
Hammamat
Ma'in
Machaerus
(Mukawir)
Mujib
Nature
Reserve
N
Bradt
0   10km
0   10 miles

the river, is now known as Wadi Kharrar. The route starts at the visitors' centre and the hill area of Tell Mar Elias (Elijah's Hill) and passes some fascinating sites until it reaches the River Jordan and the Bethany Beyond the Jordan sacred site. Along the way you will pass by the remains of Byzantine churches and a monastery, the Church of the Arch's intricate mosaic floor dating from the 4th century that has been dubbed the Prayer Hall, a series of caves where hermits once lived, and a complicated network of water channels, baptism pools, wells and a cistern hewn in rock.

One of the first points of interest is Tell Mar Elias, which translated means **Elijah's Hill**, after the Prophet Elijah who lived before Jesus Christ. Elijah appears regularly in the Hebrew Bible as Elias (Elias is Arabic for Elijah) and in the Holy Quran, where he is referred to as a 'messenger from God'. He is said to have been made known to Moses, John the Baptist and to Jesus Christ after his death. Tell Mar Elias near Bethany Beyond the Jordan is not to be confused with the Tell Mar Elias near Aljun, which lies close to the ruins of Listib, a village believed to have been Elijah's home town of Tishbi (2 Kings 17:1).

One of the biblical references to Elijah refers to God ordering Elijah to flee King Ahab and Queen Jezebel, who ruled Israel in around 869–850BC, by going to the stream 'east of Jordan'. The stream is widely believed to be Wadi al-Kharrar. At the end of his life Elijah is said to have ascended to heaven from here on a chariot of fire. Pilgrims have long been drawn to the area, and especially the hill where the remains of a sanctuary believed to be dedicated to Elijah can be seen.

Close by are the remains of the **Church of the Arch**. This large rectangular church has an elaborate mosaic floor depicting crosses, and as such is more than likely to have been one of the area's most important places of worship for visiting pilgrims from around the 5th century when it was built. A large arch has been reconstructed on the site, which makes a dramatic sight as you approach. Here, on

21 March 2000, the late Pope John Paul II blessed the baptism site, and since then the church has been renamed in his honour as the Church of John Paul II.

The discovery of **Bethany Beyond the Jordan**, one of the most sacred places on earth and where John the Baptist lived when he baptised Jesus Christ, can be attributed to the famous mosaic map in St George's Church in Madaba (see page 188). Historians and scholars had long known about the site from the Bible (John 1:28 and 10:40) and from various texts dated to the Byzantine and medieval periods, but the exact location had remained something of a mystery until the map was discovered in the 1880s and prompted a programme of excavations that resulted in confirmation that this was, indeed, the exact site.

Dating from the 6th century AD, the map is made up of millions of tiny pieces and shows the earliest known pictorial view of how the Holy Lands once looked. Its detailing is extraordinary and meant that exact sites that were significant in biblical times and mentioned in the Bible could be identified with accuracy. One of these was Bethabara, that through translation became Bethany and, in turn, Bethany Beyond the Jordan (River) to distinguish it from the Bethany that was the biblical home of Lazarus and located in the present area of the West Bank. John the Baptist lived in a cave here, which was converted to a church in the 4th century – making it one of the earliest known places of worship. It was here that Jesus Christ sought to be baptised by John, anointed by God and launched his work. He was 30 years of age. It is said there were a number of events that took place during Jesus's stay in Bethany. It was here he first assembled his disciples, Peter, Andrew, Simon, Philip and Nathaneal, and where he first prayed to God.

Bethany Beyond the Jordan has a wealth of archaeological remains, and as excavation and surveying work is ongoing the number is sure to increase over the coming years. The remains are being restored and recorded, and information gathered to present to visitors, as well as pilgrims who come to this sacred site. The area lies opposite Jericho on the West Bank and is one of the earliest known Christian pilgrimage routes across the river between Jerusalem and Mount Nebo. Bethany Beyond the Jordan and Elijah's Hill, along with the many churches and sites on the Baptism Site of Jesus Christ, are among Jordan's most visited religious sites.

Mount Nebo and Moses Spring (*Northeast of the Dead Sea;* ⊕ *summer 07.00– 19.00 daily; entry JD1*)

One of the holiest sites in all of Jordan, the top of Mount Nebo is the place where the biblical prophet Moses is said to be buried. The exact spot, however, has been disputed. With views of the Jordan Valley, the Dead Sea and across to Jericho and Jerusalem, it is here that Moses was instructed by God to look out over the Promised Land before his death (Deuteronomy 34:1). Mount Nebo has been a place of pilgrimage for centuries and even today Christians come here to experience its sense of calm.

In 1933, a small church and monastery built in the 4th century AD by early Christians were discovered and have since been enlarged into a complex in honour of Moses. It was here in 2000 that the late Pope John Paul II held a sermon. Outside, stands a high **Serpentine Cross**, known as the **Brazen Serpent Monument**. It was designed by Italian artist Giovanni Fantoni as symbolic of the brass serpent carried by Moses across the desert and the cross on which Jesus was crucified. It makes a dramatic sight alongside the complex. An information board near the foot of the cross tells you at this point you are 46km from Jerusalem, 27km from Jericho and 50km from Bethlehem.

Inside, there are inscriptions and extensive **mosaics** in both the old church, which follows a traditional basilica design, and the more modern church built when the complex was enlarged. The mosaics depict animals and birds, and are highly coloured and detailed. Look out for the mosaics in the presbytery of the new chapel built to protect them; they are the oldest and date back possibly to when the original church was built. The oldest is a panel with a braided cross. Underneath the old church a series of tombs have been discovered hollowed out in the rock.

Mount Nebo stands in an area known as Siyagha, which roughly translates as 'well-protected', and it is here you can find the Biblical Moses Spring.

Hisban (*North of Madaba*) The villagers of the unassuming modern village of Hisban, also spelt Hesban, are used to seeing visitors, although they tend not to come in the large numbers seen in nearby Madaba. The reason is the tell (hill) against which the village nestles. On top of the hill is a whole collection of archaeological treasures, but because they have only been excavated over the past 40 years or so there are still many layers to uncover and, as such, serious archaeology enthusiasts tend to pass the site by. It is a shame because the remains cover a vast history. They are currently part of the **Madaba Plains Project**, an initiative that aims to unravel Hisban's history (*visit www.madabaplains.org & www.hesban.org*).

Today, the hill has archaeological remains that have been dated to the Paleolithic Age when it is believed to have been first inhabited. In biblical times, the village is believed to have been the walled city of Heshbon. According to the Old Testament, it was here that the then Ammorite king, King Sihon, refused to let the Israelites pass through in their Exodus and where, in retaliation, they mounted a battle, killed the king and captured the city (Numbers 21:21–30). Hisban later went on to be an important Ammorite capital and hosted a fortress in Hellenistic and Roman times.

When the Byzantines came to power, Hisban assumed the role of an ecclesiastical centre. Churches and monasteries were built here and many remained in use even after the Umayyads, the Abbasids and the Mamluks came to power. Little remains of the churches today; even their mosaic floors are on display in Madaba. Finally, it became an Ottoman village, but when the Ottoman Empire collapsed Hisban was all but abandoned until it attracted the eye of a local Bedouin tribe who settled and encouraged its development. Today, you can see fragments of all these layers, together with a network of caves and underground caverns. Hisban can be found just north of Madaba, from where inexpensive buses (*300 fils*) run regularly from the centre. If driving, the hill can be seen on approach to the village and a small road leads to its summit.

Madaba *Telephone code: 05 (30km south of Amman, regular buses link the two)* Madaba is the capital of the Madaba Governorate and the country's fifth largest town. With its tree-lined streets, honey-coloured buildings and historically important sites, it is a town that shouldn't be missed. Wander around its streets and you will be greeted by one local after another keen to welcome you. They are proud of their town, and rightly so. Dubbed the 'City of Mosaics', it lay on land that has been inhabited since Neolithic times, was an important town in biblical times, was a religious centre, has world-famous Byzantine and Umayyad mosaics and is home to the earliest known surviving depiction of Jerusalem and the Holy Lands.

Here you can visit the maze of tiny streets full of Ottoman houses and churches; it is the oldest area of the town. In the Madaba Archaeological Park you'll see mosaics dating from the 6th century. Excavation work continues in and around the park, and more and more mosaics are being discovered. Madaba has a wealth of museums and churches, and is best known for the world famous mosaic in the Orthodox Church of Saint George, which lies in the heart of the town. Here you can see its 1,500-year-old mosaic map of Jerusalem and the Holy Lands. It is astonishing in its complexity and depicts villages, hills and valleys as far as the Nile Delta. It is said to have even led archaeologists to discover previously unknown sites. Bethany Beyond the Jordan is one such site.

Madaba has hotels and a handful of restaurants, and makes an ideal place to stay if you prefer a less touristy base for exploring the biblical sites around Bethany Beyond the Jordan. Mount Nebo is nearby too, along with Mukawir, Umm ar-Rasas and the Hammamat Ma'in Hot Springs, which were a popular spa centre in Roman times. A visit to these and the other sites all play a part in the rich history for which Madaba and its surrounding villages are famous. Being fairly central in the country, the town is within easy reach of Amman, the northern towns such as Jerash and Ajlun, the Eastern Desert, and southern Petra and Aqaba. Madaba is a growing, working town so you will have lots of opportunities to mingle with the locals and get a feel for everyday life. Many locals travel to Amman to work; others work in the fields, tourism or in the horse breeding industry for which the town is renowned.

Madaba is a delightful town to wander around. As well as the mosaics there are some splendid Ottoman houses dating from the 19th century, lots of lanes opening out into courtyard gardens and souks full of the quality carpets for which the town is known. For a panoramic view of this attractive town head for Madaba Hill (Tell Madaba), itself an important archaeological site where the remains of the fortified city wall can still be seen. Look out for John the Baptist Church; it towers over the town and is a landmark.

History Madaba is full to the brim with history and treasures. In fact, it is widely considered to be one of the first truly settled communities in the history of Jordan. Its history stretches back even further than Amman, the country's capital. From the Neolithic era and Bronze Age when the town saw its earliest infrastructure created and its land cultivated right through to the biblical, Roman, Byzantine and early Islamic periods, Madaba's ancient history is legendary. Its archaeological treasures and remains are among the finest in Jordan, if not the world. It came to the fore in biblical times as an important Moabite commercial town on the border of Moab and Rabbath Ammon, and was mentioned at considerable length in the Hebrew Bible's Old Testament's Book of Joshua, and the account of Moses and the Exodus (Numbers 21:30).

The town, which was then known as Medeba, lay on the King's Highway, the world's oldest continuously used route that also passed through the nearby towns of Karak (Al-Karak), Tafila (At-Tafila) and Shobak (Ash-Shawbak). It was a strategic town and as such was coveted by the Edomites from the ancient kingdom of Edom, the Ammonites from the land that is present-day Amman, and the Israelites. According to the Bible, the Moabite king, King Mesha, freed Madaba from Israelite control in around 850BC (2 Kings 3) and recorded his victories on the famous Mesha Stele. The original Mesha Stele is in the Louvre Museum in Paris, but a copy of the 1.5m (5ft) tall black granite slab is on display in the Jordan Archaeological Museum at the Citadel in Amman (see page 116). It is considered an important document in that it gives an eyewitness account of life in Jordan and Palestine in the 1st Millennium BC.

By 165BC, Madaba had been conquered by the Ammonites and then by the Nabateans. A century or so later it became a key town in the Roman Empire's Provincia Arabia, which was a province created to replace the Nabatean kingdom of Petra. It was a prosperous time for Madaba. New colonnaded streets were built and classical public buildings replaced basic dwellings. By the time the Byzantines came to power in AD324 it was an influential town.

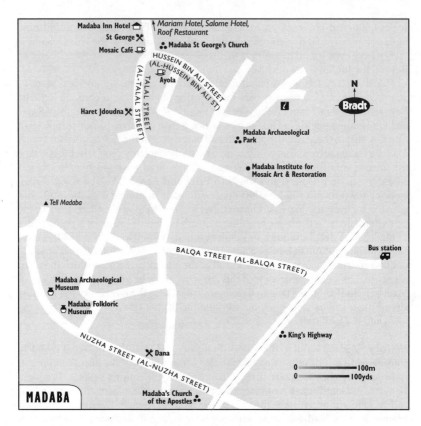

MADABA

Madaba's zenith came with the Byzantine era. It became an important ecclesiastical centre with a number of churches and cathedrals built, and Christian bishops assigned to the town. It became a centre for Christian pilgrimages. The churches, including the famous St George's Church where the world-renowned mosaic of Jerusalem and the Holy Lands can be seen, were richly decorated. Extensive remains of mosaic floors that would have once been in the churches can be seen throughout Madaba, and bear testament to its religious importance. The Byzantine period was also a time when elaborate palaces and dwellings were built, and a water-management system and reservoir were constructed to supply the growing town with a reliable water supply.

In AD747, Madaba was hit by a powerful earthquake that all but destroyed the fabulous buildings and infrastructure the Byzantines had created. While it continued to be occupied for a time, Madaba began to fall from grace as the rulers, the Umayyads, increasingly focused their efforts on their capital Damascus in Syria. Madaba was abandoned, and remained so until the 19th century when Christians from Karak settled here. In the intervening years, the mosaics that had been so carefully created by Byzantine mosaicists lay untouched and covered by debris from the earthquake-stricken buildings. As the town's new settlers began building homes, so the mosaics were rediscovered and are now one of Jordan's finest Byzantine collections.

St George's Church (*Hussein bin Ali St; ⊕ summer 07.00–19.00 daily, winter 07.00–16.00 daily, times may vary for Fri prayers; entry JD1*) This attractive little church is Madaba's top tourist spot. It dates from the 19th century and was built on the site of a Byzantine church. As you enter its heavy wooden doors and step inside to the cool sky blue and white interior you are immediately drawn to the astonishingly detailed **mosaic floor**. This is what everyone comes to Madaba to see. It dates from between AD542 and AD570. The map shows the new church of Jerusalem, which is known to have been dedicated in November AD542, but buildings built after AD570 are not shown, hence the relatively precise estimation of its age. This is the map of Jerusalem and the Holy Lands that has made the town so famous. It is the earliest known glimpse into how life was in ancient times.

The mosaic is made up of over two million pieces and at one time showed every major biblical site from the Mediterranean to the eastern desert of Jordan, and from Lebanon across to the Nile delta. It was much larger; in fact a whopping 15.6m by 6m, 94m² in size. It is damaged and parts are missing, but this in no way detracts from the enormity of its value. Villages and towns, rivers, hills and desert are shown in amazing detail, almost from a 3D prospective. You can make out the Dead Sea with fish swimming out and along the River Jordan, presumably to escape the salty waters. The unknown artist was clearly a master of his craft. As to why it was created in the somewhat remote ancient settlement of Medeba, as it was then known, remains a mystery, but one theory is that pilgrims were told of the map and used it to find their way to the Holy Lands.

Such is the detail of the mosaic that when it was discovered during the construction of a new church in 1884 it caused much excitement amongst archaeologists and historians. It showed places that were at that time unknown, and prompted excavations. One of the sites unearthed a few years later was Bethany Beyond the Jordan (see page 185). The mosaic is something of a masterpiece, and although you'll probably need to manoeuvre amongst fellow tourists in the cramped space inside the church to study it properly, it is well worth a visit.

When you leave the St George's Church, take a left out of the churchyard and continue along **Hussein bin Ali Street**, which is full of shops selling authentic crafts like painted ostrich eggs, silverware, Arabic clothing and carpets. You'll know you're in the right place because you'll see hand-woven carpets in bright reds and blues draped over walls. The weavers will tell you the sun enhances the colours.

Madaba Archaeological Park (*Abu Bakr as-Saddeeq St; visitors' centre & museum:* \05 325 3563; ☉ *08.00–17.30 daily; entry JD2 inc the Madaba Archaeological Museum & the Church of the Apostles*) Comprising a maze of churches and homes lining the old Roman streets, the park has developed around the centre of Madaba in an area covered with a profusion of **mosaics**. They show colourful pictures of birds and animals, flowers, plants and fish, as well as numerous scenes depicting mythological figures. Most visitors head for the 'map' and don't visit the other mosaics in and around the park, which is a shame because they are well preserved and very detailed. There are an amazing number of them, and the total is increasing all the time as more and more are discovered. Some are being preserved in the park's museum. Two of the best places to see the park's mosaics are in the Church of the Virgin and Hyppolytus Hall.

Church of the Virgin Climb up the little flight of stone steps and once inside you can study the quite magnificent mosaic that covers almost the entire area of the floor. It has intricate hunting scenes, flowers and geometric patterns. Outside is a courtyard with even more mosaics, most of which show animals and plants. The colours are brilliant.

6

Hyppolytus Hall You can also visit the park's Hyppolytus Hall, which is part of a 6th-century mansion that was clearly once one of the finest houses in the town. Here you will see an elaborate Byzantine mosaic that is said to tell the story of the handsome mythological Greek Hyppolytus, who fell in love with his stepmother Phaedra. There are many figures represented; some wearing bright orange robes others dressed in white or blue. The mythological goddess of love, Aphrodite, is depicted, along with Artemis and Adonis. They appear to be trying to control a handful of mischievous cupids who add a touch of humour to the scene. All the characters appear to be dancing outside amongst trees and shrubs, although Hyppolytus himself has been lost from the scene. It is a beautiful mosaic; in fact one of the prettiest in Madaba.

Madaba Institute for Mosaic Art and Restoration (*Hasimi St;* \ *05 324 0723;* f *05 324 8632; grounds & workshop* ⊕ *08.00–14.00 Sun–Thu*). Located just outside the archaeological park, this school teaches students how to create mosaic pictures, and how to repair and restore ancient mosaic works using time-honoured methods. It is the only such school in the Middle East and operates in conjunction with Jordan's Ministry of Tourism. Examples of its work can be seen in the grounds, and you can visit its workshop at certain times to see mosaics being restored.

Madaba Archaeological Museum (*Off Al-Nuzha St;* \ *05 324 4056;* ⊕ *09.00– 17.30 daily*) Housed in a period building full of tiny rooms and corridors, this museum contains dozens more examples of the mosaics found around the town. Because they are delicate or were problematic to protect in their original locations, the mosaics have been moved to the safety of the museum. Displays at one end of the museum show traditional Jordanian costumes, as well as items of jewellery and ancient pottery found during excavations around the town. A stone's throw away is the small **Madaba Folkloric Museum** (*entry free*), which contains displays of traditional costumes worn by the men and women of Madaba and Karak, along with silver jewellery, footwear, household items such as stones used to grind cereals, and platters used for eating.

Church of the Apostles (*King's Highway;* \ *05 325 3563;* ⊕ *08.00–17.30 daily; entry JD2 inc the Madaba Archaeological Park & Museum*) Dating back to the 6th century AD, this large church, built to a traditional basilica style with chapels lying either side, was once one of the finest in the area. Its **floor mosaic** is outstanding. Created in AD568, it is notable for being one of the few works to bear the name of the

---

THE ART OF MOSAICS

Around Madaba there are numerous workshops where locals continue the art of producing intricate works of art using mosaics. One of the largest, with seven workshops, is Jordan Jewel (\ *05 324 1364; www.jordanjewel.com*). With a staff totalling around 178, of which around 70% are physically handicapped, this organisation provides valuable jobs for the community. Mosaic pictures, jugs and even tabletops are beautifully made using coloured fragments of limestone, onyx, agate, moonstone and jade. Images such as the four seasons, the Tree of Life, Mount Nebo and traditional Bedouin life can take weeks of painstaking work to create. You can visit the workshops to see artisans at work and, if you wish, purchase any of the items to take home as a souvenir.

mosaicist who created it; in this instance, Salomios. The mosaic depicts numerous pigeons apparently in flight, with a border of vines and animals. You'll see a wolf and even a hen with her tiny chicks. The centrepiece is a striking circular mosaic featuring a confident-looking woman, thought to be the mythological sea goddess Thalassa. She is depicted emerging from the sea with a variety of marine life behind her. There are fish, a couple of marine creatures and even a comical octopus. The mosaic is delightful and given its age, complexity and condition it is an important example of mosaics found in Madaba. A new arched building protects it from the elements.

Hammamat Ma'in (*Inland from the Dead Sea, south of Madaba; ⊕ 06.00–16.00; entry JD10*) Known as Hammamat Ma'in and also Zarqa Ma'in, the natural hot spring waters found a little inland from the Dead Sea cascade in alarming fashion from high cliffs. They are said to have attracted visitors for centuries, including King Herod, who resided nearby at Mukawir during the time of Jesus Christ, and the Romans who had a penchant for therapeutic spas. The waters are hot; temperatures of around 40°C are not uncommon.

You can find them signposted from Madaba, the Dead Sea or from the King's Highway. You probably won't spend long here, but a dip to invigorate you between sightseeing excursions is recommended. Access to the springs is now via a new five-star hotel complex, and a small admission charge is made for non-guests to use the car park.

Mukawir (*Inland from the Dead Sea, south of Madaba*) Near Madaba is the somewhat bleak hill of Mukawir, known in biblical times as Machaerus. It is famous from biblical times as being the place where John the Baptist was imprisoned and beheaded. King Herod the Great (circa b73BC, d4BC), who ruled Judaea during the time of Jesus Christ, had a mighty stronghold built on top of the hill in around 30BC, on the site of a previous castle that had been destroyed 20 or so years earlier. He used it as a military base from where he could defend his empire. Upon Herod's death, his son Herod Antipas (circa b20BC, dAD39) inherited the castle and took up residence.

According to the New Testament, Herod Antipas had John the Baptist imprisoned after he made remarks about Herodias (circa b15BC, dAD39) with whom Herod had fallen in love. Herod was married to the daughter of King Aretus IV (circa b9BC, dAD40) at the time, and Herodias was his sister-in-law. The love triangle was opposed by John the Baptist. As the story goes, Herodias's daughter, Salome, is traditionally believed to be the female incensed by John the Baptist's remarks. She announced that she would perform the seductive dance of the seven veils for the head of John the Baptist. Herod Antipas agreed and it was at Mukawir where he gave instructions to his followers to behead John the Baptist.

Some years later in around AD36, Herod Antipas was defeated in battle by King Aretus IV. It was seen by many as divine retribution for the death of John the Baptist. Mukawir is a site often visited by pilgrims today. You can climb to the summit of this rather strange-looking, barren hill, topped by stone pillars indicating where the palace once stood. It will be a moving experience. The reward for the challenging climb is a great view out over the Dead Sea. It is an hour or so south of Madaba by car.

Mujib Nature Reserve (*Beside Dead Sea, Mujib Bridge, visitors' centre:* m *079 720 3888;* f *079 998 7448;* e *tourism@rscn.org.jo; www.rscn.org.jo; ⊕ usually 09.00– 18.00 daily but can vary; entry JD7*) With its border on the Dead Sea at 420m below sea level, the Mujib Nature Reserve has the distinction of being the lowest nature reserve on earth. It is also one of Jordan's most dramatic. It extends from the Madaba mountains in the north to Karak, with peaks that plunge into canyons and fast-flowing rivers from heights of well over 900m above sea level. The 1,300m variation in elevation, combined with the remoteness of many of its areas and the constant water supply from seven different rivers that cross its rugged terrain (including the mighty Wadi al-Mujib that drains into the Dead Sea), have given the reserve one of the finest safe natural habitats for flora and fauna in the country.

The reserve's biodiversity is exceptional. There have been at least ten species of carnivore and mammals recorded including the caracel (*Caracal caracal*) from the lynx family, the Arabian leopard (*Panthera pardus nimr*), the Eurasian badger (*Meles meles*) and the red fox (*Vulpes vulpes*), along with the rare and beautifully nimble honey-coloured Nubian ibex (*Capra ibex nubiana*). The Mujib Nature Reserve is a birdwatchers' paradise, with around 102 species of breeding and migratory birds having been recorded. Among them are black storks (*Ciconia nigra*), honey buzzards (*Pernis apivorus*) and the Levant sparrowhawks (*Accipiter brevipes*), plus the rare and distinctive brown-and-orange lesser kestrel (*Falco naumanni*), which breeds here in the spring. Birds of prey include Bonelli's eagle (*Aquila fasciatus*) and the Barbary falcon (*Falco pelegrinoides*). More than 300 different species of plants have been noted, including a vast number of aquatic plants and those that thrive in the river beds, such as palm trees and tamarix trees.

The reserve is one of Jordan's most popular places to enjoy activity sports. Five main **hiking** trails follow a course through the mountainous regions and should be tackled only by experienced climbers, while a further three follow its rivers and

LOT'S CAVE

The biblical character Lot, the nephew of Abraham, is described in the Book of Genesis as having fled the burning and destruction of the ancient city of Sodom with his wife and two daughters. God's orders were not to look back, but, famously, Lot's wife did and as a result was turned into a pillar of salt (Genesis 19:26). Lot and his daughters survived and sought refuge in a cave near the ancient town of Zoar. It was here the family is said to have lived, and where Moab and Ben-Ammi, the forefathers of the Moabites and Ammonites, were born.

Despite biblical references to a wayward lifestyle and even incest, Lot is considered to be a good man by both Christians and Muslims. In the Holy Koran he is referred to as a Prophet of Islam and in the Hebrew Bible as a 'righteous man'. Lot's Cave, as his refuge has become known, is a place of pilgrimage. It can be found at Deir ain Abata, which is a couple of kilometres north of the present-day town of Safi on the southern shores of the Dead Sea. The spot was known in the Bible as the Valley of Salt, probably because of the natural salt deposits that have for centuries covered shoreline stones and boulders and given them a fluffy white appearance. Today, the salt plain is known as the southern Ghor.

Excavation works at the site have revealed Bronze Age and Nabatean remains, and even Byzantine mosaic floors. More recently the remains of a monastery believed to have been built by early Christians to mark the spot of Lot's place of refuge have been discovered, although sited unsteadily on the edge of slope has meant that much of the structure has fallen away. The cave and monastery are signposted but no public transport goes there, only excursions, and it is a bit of a climb up some stone steps to see them.

another two cross flatter ground. These include the popular **Ibex Trail** (*JD20 with a guide*), which heads off from the Mujib Bridge into a deep gorge and takes around four hours, and the shorter **Siq Trail** (*JD12 with a guide*), which follows an easier, if wetter, route along the river through the Mujib gorge.

Most of the trails pass by the reserve's rivers: Wadi Um Ghreiba, Wadi al-Hidan, Wadi al-Mujib, Wadi Atoun, and to the north Wadi Zara and Wadi Zarqa Ma'in. Some pass by settlements, such as Raddas. If you take one of the riverside trails you should expect to cross rivers, plunge into pools and climb rocks against the powerful flow of the river, therefore being a confident swimmer is essential. You must be accompanied by a trained guide and this can be arranged through the Royal Society for the Conservation of Nature, which manages the reserve. You can book ahead of your trip or in the visitors' centre near Mujib Bridge. The reserve is signposted from the Dead Sea, and if you follow the road with the sea to your right then you will find the reserve easily. It is also signposted from Karak. Within the reserve is a campsite called Chalet Village, see page 178, and the Mujib Chalets Restaurant, see page 180.

Umm Ar-Rasas (*Southeast of Madaba; entry free, but there are plans to introduce an entry fee of JD1 when its new visitors' centre is complete*) One of the oldest places in Jordan, mentioned in both the Old and New Testaments of the Bible, and an UNESCO World Heritage Site in its entirety, Umm Ar-Rasas is a gem of an archaeological site. You can see the ruins of the city walls that would have at one time enclosed a Roman military camp (castrum), and Byzantine and early Muslim communities, and the remains of buildings and 16 churches, some of which are adorned with beautiful archways and mosaics. Look out for courtyards and a well, and staircases that are worn smooth through centuries of countless feet trampling on the stone steps. The town's ancient name was Kastron Mefa'a, which is believed to have originated from the Roman castrum.

Extensive but as yet incomplete excavation has revealed an astonishing array of artefacts. The most important find, and the one that has placed Umm Ar-Rasas firmly on the world map, is the **mosaic in the Church of St Stephen**. It is considered an artistically, technical and geographically important historical find. Dating from AD718, the almost perfectly preserved floor is made up of millions of tiny pieces and is the largest discovered to date in Jordan. In importance it ranks second only to the map of the Holy Land in Madaba. More than 25 major cities of the Old and New Testaments that lay to the west and east of the Holy Land's River Jordan are depicted in amazing detail. Their names are given in ancient Greek script.

On close inspection you can see hunting and fishing scenes, mythological figures and religious icons, and lots of panels with houses and streets that depict the Holy Land's towns, including Medeba (Madaba) and Jerusalem. The borders show geometric patterns, as was the fashion of the day. Around the site are other smaller mosaic floors. Visit the Church of Bishop Paul, the Church of the Priest Wa'il, the Church of the Lions, the Church of the Rivers, the Church of the Palm Tree and the Church of Bishop Sergius.

Nearby, you may catch sight of a **square tower**. At 15m tall, it is the highest ancient tower in Jordan, but with no doorway or staircase to enable anyone to go inside or reach the top its historical purpose is a matter of debate. Suggestion is that it was where stylites, or early Christian monks, would go to reflect. They would climb the tower using a removable ladder and then spend time in isolation in a room at the top. The tower stands amongst a complex of ruins that comprise quarries, water channels, dams and cisterns. Umm Ar-Rasas lies southeast of Madaba, pretty much central between the fast Desert Highway and the old King's Highway route.

6

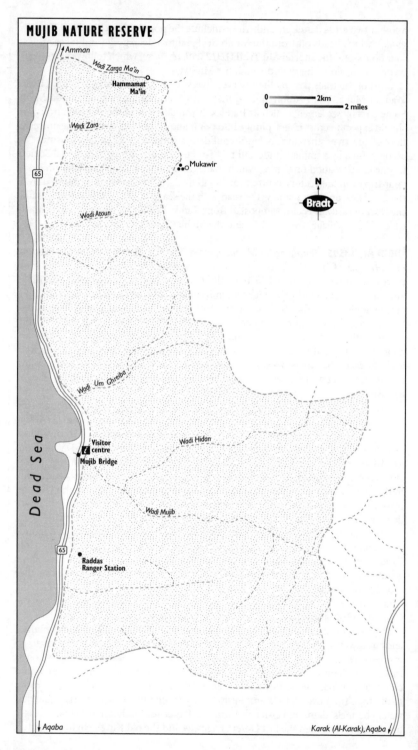

Karak *Telephone code: 03* Located on the King's Highway and with an authoritative 'I've seen it all' sort of feel, Karak, locally Al-Karak, greets the visitor in spectacular style. Its massive **Crusader castle**, surrounded by mighty city walls and perched tantalisingly on top of a hill just begging to be explored at length, is the first thing you see as you approach from the highway. You can't miss it. This is the spot that everyone who visits Karak makes a beeline for. First, head for the Castle Plaza, where you'll find a handful of okay but not very inspiring places to eat, and then make your way to the visitors' centre and the castle via a wooden drawbridge over its moat. Inside, you can visit its chapel and keep, its upper court and its lower court where you'll find the Karak Archaeological Museum (see page 198). The castle and museum tell the story of Karak. Its history is linked almost entirely, but not completely, to its castle.

Karak has been inhabited since the Iron Age and a number of tools and pottery fragments dating from the period can be seen today in its museum. In biblical times, Karak is believed to have been the Moabite stronghold city of Qir of Moab, and later the Qir (or Qer) of Harreseth referred to in the Hebrew Bible's Book of Kings and the Book of Amos. For a spell the city was occupied by the Nabateans and the Romans, and under the Byzantines it was made a bishopric. Around this period the city was known as Kharkha, which over time became Karak. It was during the crusades, however, that Karak really came into its own.

King Fulk (circa b1090, d1143), a member of the Court of Anjou who was crowned King of Jerusalem in 1131, was a supporter of King Louis VI of France and an ally of King Henry I of England. He was a passionate supporter of the Crusades (see *History*, page 20) and became affiliated with the Knights Templar. Fulk became something of a legend in the Holy Lands and became known to King Baldwin II of Jerusalem. When the king sought a husband for his daughter Melisende (he had no sons and wanted to safeguard his daughter's future as Queen) he turned to Fulk. The couple was married in 1129 and ruled Jerusalem from the time of Baldwin II's death in 1131.

As ruler, King Fulk sought to strengthen his kingdom's defenses against invaders and built a number of castles, including Karak castle. Work began in the 1140s and it became a large formidable fortress. It was known as the Crac des Moabites, meaning Karak in Moab. The ensuing years brought prosperity and power to Karak, largely because it was now central to the trade routes that existed between Egypt, Makkah and Syria. However, the city's fortunes changed when Saladin, the Sultan of Egypt, launched a series of attacks on the castle in response to Raynald de Chatillon (circa b1125, d1187), a fearsome warrior and new owner of Karak, who had launched attacks on Saladin's empire. Saladin captured the castle in 1189, but abandoned it some years later.

Apart from spells when the castle was enlarged by the Mamluks and served, in part, as a garrison during the Ottoman Empire, it remained unused and fell into disrepair through attacks and vandalism. The stones with which it was originally constructed contained saltpetre, which is a chemical compound used to make gunpower. As such, many of the stones were removed in times of battle. Today, the castle is a fascinating place to visit and one that will give you an insight into Karak's formidable past. In recent years the citadel and castle have been restored and information provided for visitors. At the foot of the hill lies the city of Karak and here you can see some fine examples of Ottoman houses. To visit Karak, head south from Amman on the King's Highway, or take the main Desert Highway, number 15, and bear right onto the road to Karak (number 50). The city is well signposted.

Citadel of Karak (*Karak;* \ *03 235 1216;* ☉ *summer 08.00–19.00 daily, winter 08.00–16.00 daily; entry JD1*) This sprawling complex dominated by its castle and surrounded by thick city walls, lies around 900m above sea level. From the Castle Plaza, head over the wooden drawbridge to the entrance. Inside, you'll find a maze of dimly lit passageways and high vaulted halls spread out over seven floors. Look out for the barracks and a ruined chapel, the ancient kitchens complete with an olive press, the eerie dungeons and the Mamluk keep, where you'll find the remains of a former palace. Some of the most amazing passageways can be found deep underground. You can reach them through a big heavy door, and then by descending a stone staircase to the depths of the castle.

Karak Archaeological Museum (*Karak Citadel; details as above; entry included in Karak Castle*) The museum can be found along the west wall of the castle within the citadel, and has an extensive collection of pottery fragments and bowls, glass vessels, weapons, coins, inscriptions and jewellery that date back to Moabite times in the first millennium BC right through to the Nabatean era, Roman, Byzantine and early Islamic times to the Crusader years. In another section, the exhibits include a skeleton believed to date from the Bronze Age from the nearby site of Bab adh-Dhra, and Iron Age tools and trinkets. The museum is housed in a huge castle vault once used as the living quarters of Mamluk soldiers; it provides both space for the exhibits and an atmosphere that makes you feel you are experiencing a real slice of history.

Mazar Islamic Museum (*Mazar, near Karak;* \ *03 237 0319;* ☉ *summer 08.00– 15.00 Wed–Mon; entry free*) This small museum can be found in the village of Mazar, locally Al-Mazar, which is a ten-minute drive or so south of Karak. It is dedicated to the early Islamic civilisations and their culture, which ruled in the region from around AD632, and has an expansive collection of sculptures, ceramics and coins. Find it in the centre of the village near the mosque.

Dana and Dana Biosphere Reserve (*South of Tafila; visitors' centre:* \ *03 227 0497;* f *03 227 0499;* e *dana@rscn.org.jo; www.rscn.org.jo;* ☉ *usually 09.00–18.00 daily but can vary; entry JD7 to reserve; guides available from JD15 per hr*) A sprawling reserve that nestles against the high mountainous plateau near Quadesiyya, south of the pleasant little town of Tafila (At-Tafila), and sweeps down in spectacular fashion to the desert plains of the Araba Valley, the Dana Biosphere Reserve is Jordan's largest protected area. The drop is an astonishing 1,200m from its highest point to 200m below sea level. Here you can explore granite-layered limestone mountains sliced by deep *wadi* gorges or hike across stony desert wildernesses. You can marvel at its sand dunes, visit villages that are the homes of the local Bedouin Ata'ta tribe, follow nature trails through dense forest and, if you are lucky, see its extraordinary mix of plants, wildlife, birds and mammals. The visitors' centre is signposted once you have travelled through the villages of Al-Qadisiyya or Al-Rashadiyya, where many of the original Dana families moved to escape the harsh winters, and into the remote Dana itself.

The reserve, which could be said to sit at the crossroads of Europe, Asia and Africa, has four distinct bio-geographical regions: the Mediterranean, Sudanian, Arabian and Irano-Turanian. When combined with the reserve's temperate climate and its constant source of water, the regions give it a biodiversity ideal for hosting an incredible mix of flora and fauna. Recent records have listed over 800 different species of plant here. You can see its landscaped blanketed with evergreen oak (*Quercus calliprinos*) and Phoenician juniper (*Juniperus phoenicea*), and it has one

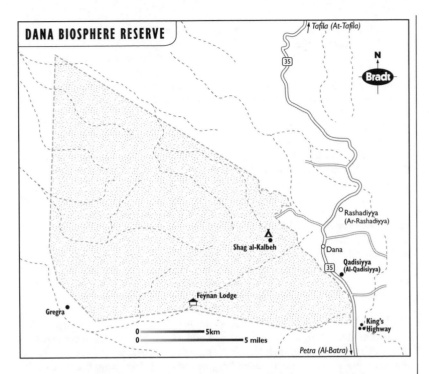

DANA BIOSPHERE RESERVE

of the only remaining forests of cypress (*Cupressus simpervirens*) in the region. Some of the plants can be found nowhere else in the world.

The Dana Biosphere Reserve is home to 38 different species of mammal and around 215 species of bird, including the beautiful and rare Nubian ibex (*Capra nubiana*), the small Blanford's fox (*Vulpes cana*), the lesser kestrel (*Falco naumanni*) and the brightly coloured Syrian serin (*Serinus syriacus*). You may catch sight of Bonelli's eagle (*Aquila fasciatus*), the barbary falcon (*Falco pelegrinoides*), and numerous bulbuls and chukars.

Half the reserve, which has won many awards for its conservation and for creating job opportunities for local people, has been designated as off-limits to goat herders and the other half is strictly controlled. The result is that its flora and fauna is thriving.

There's a choice of accommodation around the Dana Nature Reserve from campsites and small guesthouses to Feynan Ecolodge, see page 177, so it's possible to spend a few days here exploring the countryside. Archaeological remains dating from Palaeolithic times can be seen in the reserve or you could venture into Dana village itself, which is an absolute delight and unspoilt, or take some time to join a camel train or 4x4 excursions. A visitors' centre just inside the main entrance to the reserve has suggested **hiking** routes, lots of information about the reserve's conservation projects and its inhabitants, and about Dana village.

The Feynan Ecolodge, which is one of the country's newest eco-lodges, can be found on the edge of the Dana Nature Reserve on the route to Wadi Rum and Aqaba. A stay here is truly away from 21st-century living. Its ethos is to create minimal damage to the environment and it has a programme of socio-economic initiatives that have given it a ranking as being among the best eco-lodges in the world. There's no electricity, so expect everything to be powered by solar. Food waste products are used to produce fertilizer and all waste paper and plastic products are recycled.

If you enjoy walking you'll be interested to know there are a series of walks designed to take in the main areas of the reserve. Join the **Wadi Dana Trail** for a six-hour hike across the reserve, or the **Feathers Canyon Trail**, which will take you through a narrow gorge. It lasts about three hours and is a great introduction to the reserve. If you fancy more of a challenge then the **Wadi Dathneh Trail** will see you hiking through rugged mountainous terrain until you reach the oasis spot of Hammam Adethni. From here it's downhill to Feynan, following the route of the fast-flowing river.

Along with a choice of nature walks, which are guided or self-guided and can be booked at the visitors' centre, you can take a 4x4 excursion or join a camel trek (*approx JD20 for 5hrs*). Along the routes you will see numerous archaeological remains dating from Palaeolithic and Nabatean times, and disused copper mines.

Be sure to visit nearby **Dana village**, too. This enchanting little village made of earth-coloured bricks and blending, seamlessly, with the environment, has amazing views out over the Wadi Dana and the Araba Valley. The village has a thriving handicraft heritage and here you will be able to see local women making jewellery and clothing in their workshops. A good way to really get a feel for Dana is to join its two-hour **Village Tour** (*bookable at the reserve visitors' centre*). Dana, the Dana Biosphere Reserve and Feynan Ecolodge are all well signposted from Karak, Tafila and Petra.

Shobak Castle (*3km west of Shobak;* ⊕ *summer 08.00–17.30 daily, winter 08.00–16.00 daily*) Dating from the same era as Karak Castle but smaller in comparison, Shobak Castle, also often spelt Shawbak and Ash-Shawbak, is a ruined stronghold that once played a key role in defending the region. It dates from the time of the 12th-century Crusaders, and is said to have been built by Baldwin I of Jerusalem in 1115 during an expedition to Jordan. In honour of the king who partly funded the building of this mighty fortification that was once home to thousands of people, it was named the Mons Regalis or Krak de Montreal, meaning the Mont Royal or Royal Mountain.

Like Karak Castle, over the years it was the scene of many bloody battles, and eventually fell to the hands of the Ayyubid sultan Salah ad-Din Yusuf ibn Ayyub, better known as Saladin (circa b1138, d1193) who invaded the kingdom in 1187. At the Battle of Hattin, Saladin's army fought and enslaved most of the Crusaders' forces and took control of the castle. By the time the Mamluks came to power in the 13th century the castle had fallen into disrepair.

Today, although in a ruinous state, it is an interesting reminder of the period and has some architectural features that make it worth a detour of an hour or so. On approach to the castle you will see the towers and city walls; these date from the Mamluk period and are inscribed with some well-preserved calligraphic script that is believed to date from the late 13th century. Step inside, and you will notice its formidable gatehouse, the remains of a chapel and a labyrinth of dark, dank passageways, not all of which appear particularly welcoming. Around the castle are some interesting Ottoman dwellings and the remains of an Ayyubid palace.

Shobak Castle lies a few kilometres west of the small **village of Shobak**, locally Ash-Shawbak, near the southern boundaries of the Dana Nature Reserve. Buses run to the village from Wadi Musa and Amman, but there is no public transport to the castle itself so you will need a car or hire a taxi. You'll pass by orchards too, where the tastiest apples in Jordan are grown. If you see someone selling any along the way or in the village of Shobak be sure to stop for a kilo or two; they are delicious.

7

Petra

Telephone code: 03

A UNESCO World Heritage Site in its entirety since 1985 and one of the New Seven Wonders of the World, the **Petra Archaeological Park** (Al-Batra) is an astonishing 2,000-year-old city chiselled by hand with meticulous detail into the sheer, pink-hued rock face of the mountains towards southern Jordan. At its zenith there were probably thousands of buildings and an ingenious complex of dams and water channels. It is the legacy of the Nabateans, a highly creative and industrious dynasty that had immeasurable wealth and created one of the greatest survivors of the ancient world.

Petra is the stuff of legend. As the capital of the Nabatean empire, it was one of the most important cities in the ancient world, only to be later abandoned and lost hidden deep in the Wadi Araba mountains. Only a handful of Bedouins knew of its existence. It wasn't until the 19th century that Petra was rediscovered by a young Swiss traveller, Johann Ludwing Burckhardt. You'll find that nothing quite prepares you for your first visit. Its huge size, complexity and haunting beauty are such that will stagger even the most seasoned of travellers.

Known as the 'rose city' because of its buildings hewn in salmon pink sandstone sliced by kaleidoscopic shades of crimson, orange, purple, blue and yellow, Petra occupies a site covering some 264,000m^2 of mountainous terrain at **Wadi Musa** in the governorate of Ma'an. Since it was rediscovered it has been declared a national park and the Bedouin families who lived in the caves have been moved to a new settlement just outside Wadi Musa, at Umm Sayhun. Most still spend their days working in the park; some are official guides, others care for horses and camels or sell souvenirs. Tourism has given them a lucrative way to earn money.

Petra lies in a basin at the foot of Jabal Harun, the highest mountain in the Wadi Araba range that stretches from the Dead Sea to the Gulf of Aqaba. It is famous as being the believed burial place of the Prophet Aaron, brother of Moses. The word Petra means 'rock'. Even as you approach Wadi Musa you'll see a difference in the landscape. Moulded over millennia by the wind and rain into bulbous rock formations that give way to deep canyons, the mountainous space looks haunting and unnatural. Set deep in this fantasy landscape is the city of Petra.

Although some of the thousands of temples and dwellings, baths, tombs and funerary halls, arched gateways, colonnaded streets and monasteries have been lost to earthquakes and the ravages of time, the 800 or so that remain are truly awesome. It is believed that the site hasn't yet been fully excavated. Who knows how many more monuments have yet to be discovered.

You can see the **Obelisk Tomb** and **Bab as-Siq Triclinium**, curious-looking tombs built one on top of the other and displaying a fusion of Hellenistic and Roman architecture. There's the largest of the Royal Tombs to see, known as the **Urn Tomb**, along with the **Palace Tomb**, the **Sextius Florentinus Tomb** and the

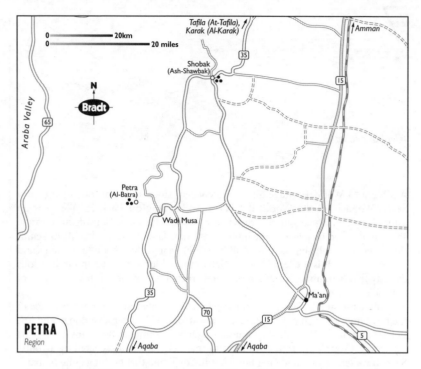

Map labels:
Tafila (At-Tafila), Karak (Al-Karak)
Amman
Shobak (Ash-Shawbak)
35
15
65
N
Brad
Araba Valley
Petra (Al-Batra)
Wadi Musa
35
70
15
Ma'an
15
5
Aqaba
Aqaba
PETRA Region
0 — 20km
0 — 20 miles

mighty temple of **Qasr al-Bint**, plus the **Ad-Deir Monastery** structure that lies on the top of a mountain, and a massive semi-circular theatre.

The most famous of all is the Al-Khazneh temple, otherwise known as **The Treasury**. To reach this astonishing tomb, with its carving so well-defined that it is bewildering to think it is more than 2,000 years old, you'll first need to experience a tantalising walk through the **Siq**. With each step the excitement mounts until, eventually, you get your first humbling glimpse of The Treasury. Petra stands as a unique tribute to the skill and unbelievable craftsmanship of a lost civilisation.

HISTORY

Although Petra is best known for its connection with the Nabateans and is today one of the Jordan's most iconic and visited tourist attractions, this ancient city lies in countryside that can trace its history back much earlier, to prehistoric and Iron Age civilisations, and to the time of the ancient Egyptian pharaohs.

EARLY HISTORY It is believed the city that was to become known as Petra, and the area surrounding it, was first settled during prehistoric times. The remains of human settlement and the use of land for agricultural purposes suggest civilisations existing here up to 10,000 years ago. Mines dating from the Chalcolithic period have been discovered at nearby Umm al-Amad, and are chronicled by UNESCO as being an exceptional example of mining structures from the period. A Neolithic settlement was also discovered at Beidha, which lies around 10km north of the city, and an Iron Age community was discovered at Umm al-Biyara.

Evidence points to the area flourishing during the time of the famous Pharaoh Tutankhamen (b1341BC, d1323BC), his father the Pharaoh Akhenaton (circa b1353BC, d1336BC) and his queen Nefertiti, and the female Pharaoh Hatshepsut (b1508BC, d1458BC) of Egypt's 18th dynasty. Ancient Egyptian texts suggest the community was then known as Sela, which means rock, Seir or Pel. In early biblical times, it is believed to have been inhabited by the Horites, a people who have been identified in similar Egyptian texts and who lived a primitive life in the mountain caves.

The Horites were the predecessors of the Edomites who, according to the Hebrew Bible, Genesis 36, founded a kingdom, Edom, in the region that now surrounds Petra. According to the Old Testament, Edom and the kingdom of Ammon, which was founded by the Ammonites north of the Dead Sea, and Moab founded by the Moabites, were fabulously rich through their trading activities. Edom, in particular, is said to have been on a major trading route from Egypt to the Levant and Mediterranean, and grew wealthy through its resources of copper.

According to ancient biblical texts found on the shores of the Dead Sea, known as the Dead Sea Scrolls, Petra was then called Rekem. Indeed, an inscription referring to the city as Rekem was discovered in a rock next to a river, the Wadi Musa, just opposite where the entrance to the Siq is located. However, this is no longer visible as it was necessary to build a bridge over the river, which meant the inscription was covered up.

THE NABATEANS (312BC–AD106) Petra's emergence as a major city and the pinnacle of its existence came with the Nabateans. This ancient Arab tribe is believed to have originated in northern Arabia some 2,500 years ago, and later travelled extensively in the Canaan region (present-day Israel, Lebanon and Palestine). One of the first known kings of the Nabateans was Aretas I (circa b200BC, d144BC). His name appears in the oldest known inscription from the Nabatean period found in Halutza, Israel.

The Nabateans arrived in Jordan in around 312BC. Although enjoying a nomadic life throughout their kingdom, which stretched from the Arabian Peninsula, known today as the Middle East, across the northern territories of Ptolemaic Egypt to the Kingdom of Judea of ancient Israel to the east, they settled in Petra and founded what was to become one of the most prosperous cities of the ancient world.

It lay on the exact spot where major trading routes crossed. Merchants from the Levant and the Mediterranean, Egypt and Syria traded in gemstones, spices, silks and textiles, animal skins and feathers with their fellow merchants from China, India and southern Arabia. Two of the most famous routes, the India to Egypt and the Arabia to Damascus routes, and the legendary Incense Route of the 3rd and 2nd centuries BC ran through southern Jordan. The Nabateans, who themselves traded in incense, frankincense, myrrh and gold, were recognised as having control of vast stretches of the routes. It brought fabulous wealth to the Nabateans who lived in splendour.

Petra became the capital of their kingdom in the 1st century BC and with their amassed wealth the Nabateans created palaces and temples, monasteries, rock-cut tombs where they buried their dead and even a theatre capable of holding 7,000 people carved into the sandstone rock. The city was like a fortress, protected from invaders by the towering mountains that surrounded it. It also had the added advantage of being fed by a constant stream of water, which contributed greatly to the wellbeing of its people and their ability to grow foodstuff.

The Nabateans, clearly an astute people, recognised that the water supply needed to be controlled and so created an ingenious network of dams, tunnels and aqueducts to channel it, and reservoirs and cisterns to store it for times of drought. As a result,

TOP TIPS FOR VISITING THE PETRA ARCHAEOLOGICAL PARK

- Allow plenty of time for your visit and take it slowly. You can see a lot in a day, but to really explore its treasures you should allow two or even three days.
- Keep to the marked trails for maximum safety and avoid cliff edges and slippery slopes. Keep a firm grip on young children.
- Petra is best seen in the early morning or late afternoon when the sun captures the intricate detailing of the treasures. The Siq and The Treasury will be in shadow from around midday until late afternoon.
- There is a restaurant inside and several refreshment stops with toilets, but other than that there are few places with shade. Bring bottled water with you and always cover your head and shoulders to protect you from the intense sun. Litter bins are available.
- Wear good walking boots or trainers as the terrain is rough and there will be rocks to climb. If you are planning to visit the Ad-Deir Monastery it will involve a climb up 800 steps. Wear light clothing and cover your head.
- If you have limited time, or don't fancy walking for exceptionally long distances, you can hire a horse-drawn carriage at the entrance to the site. It will take you along the 1,200m-long Siq to The Treasury and back. Elderly visitors or those with a disability may request a special permit at the visitors' centre that allows carriages to go beyond The Treasury to see the highlights.
- You can hire a guide from the visitors' centre, join a group or wander around the site freely on your own. There are maps and guides available at the visitors' centre.
- Photographs are permitted.
- Do not take or purchase any coloured stones, chunks of rock or shards of pottery, and remember trading in antiquities is punishable by law.
- If you are caught in a rainstorm during your visit, avoid *wadis* and flowing streams that may be subject to flash flooding. Stick to high ground.
- If you become lost or distressed for whatever reason while in the park, the recognised distress code is four repetitions of any signal, for example, four shouts, four whistles or four flashes of a torch or camera in darkness.
- For an altogether different experience of Petra, join a tour for a candlelit walk through the Siq and a presentation of storytelling and music in front of The Treasury, itself lit by candles. Tours leave at 20.30 each evening.

the city grew in size and statue. Their achievements are all the more impressive given that Petra is set in one of the most rugged and barrens places on the planet.

THE ROMANS (63BC–AD324) The Nabateans had long been an ally of the Roman Empire that dominated great swathes of land around the Mediterranean and into Arabia. Over time the Nabatean kingdom became absorbed into its hegemony, along with land that is present-day southern Syria, the Sinai Peninsula of Egypt and the northwestern outreaches of Saudi Arabia. A new division of the empire was created, which became known as the Arabia Petraea region. Petra was its capital city.

During these early years of Roman rule and the subsequent period of Byzantine influence, Petra flourished. New temples, churches and tombs were built and marble-paved colonnaded walkways lined by public buildings, such as a nymphaeum to collect spring water, were created. Around a century later, Petra's fortunes took a turn. The Romans declared that it would no longer be the centre of commerce and this, together with the growing popularity of transporting goods by ship, saw the city decline to the point that it was all but abandoned. The few people who remained were dealt another blow in AD363 when an earthquake flattened many of the buildings and severely damaged dams and cisterns. As they left so Petra was gradually forgotten.

MODERN HISTORY Although Petra appeared in explorers' chronicles over the next few centuries, it was all but lost to the world by the 7th century. There were countless stories of a 'lost city', and Petra began to take on the air of a mythical place. One explorer, overcome with the desire to find this lost city, went down in history books as the person to have rediscovered Petra.

In the early 1800s, a Swiss explorer, Johann Ludwing Burckhardt, travelled to the Levant in order to learn the Arabic language in preparation for a planned expedition to Africa. He believed he would be accepted as a Muslim if he could speak the language and have knowledge of the culture. During his travels he had heard stories of a 'lost city', and became increasingly drawn to finding it.

According to folklore, Burckhardt disguised himself as a pilgrim seeking to visit the Tomb of Aaron and in 1812, by this time fluent in Arabic, managed to convince his Bedouin guide to take him to the city. On his return, Burckhardt recounted his discoveries to the Western world, with mixed results. It seems Petra became the haunt of thieves seeking to find valuable artefacts in the tombs and temples, but in the main it was a monumental find for the world.

In 1985 it was declared an UNESCO World Heritage Site in order to preserve its legacy of outstanding ancient architectural and water engineering expertise. In 2007, it was announced that Petra had been named one of the New Seven Wonders of the World, alongside the Great Wall of China, Machu Picchu in Peru, Christ the Redeemer in Brazil, Chichen Itza in Mexico, Rome's Colosseum and the Taj

Mahal, plus honorary candidate the Great Pyramid of Giza. Today, Petra, which is twinned with ancient Plovdiv, the second-largest city in Bulgaria, is one of the most wondrous places to visit in the world. It attracts thousands of visitors from all corners of the globe.

GETTING THERE AND AWAY

BY AIR While Petra doesn't have its own airport, it is within easy reach of the **Queen Alia International Airport** south of Amman, which is around 220km away. The drive should take you about 2½ hours along the Jordan Valley road or the Desert Highway. Whichever route you choose the views are extraordinary. The **King Hussein International Airport** in Aqaba is another option, and although there are fewer flights available into this southern hub, the journey to Petra is remarkably easy. The airport lies to the north of Aqaba, and Petra is a little over 120km away on the highway. Allow about 1½ hours for your journey. If you are lucky you may catch a glimpse of the Hejaz Railway train making its way from Amman to Aqaba along the ancient tracks that lie off to your right (see *Getting there and away*, page 48).

BY TAXI AND BUS Amman and Aqaba have a large number of privately owned **taxis** and *serveeces* to hire, although be sure to check the fare to Wadi Musa before you depart. It is a lengthy journey and the price, although comparable to Western standards, may come as a bit of a shock. From Amman to Wadi Musa, for instance, you'll probably pay around JD80 in one of the yellow-and-green taxis, compared to a bus for which the fare would be around JD8 one-way, or a minibus about JD2. From Aqaba it will be about the same. Nonetheless, most taxi drivers speak good English and have lots of stories to tell about Jordan. They are almost always obliging and will stop along the way if you want a break, detour or to take a few photographs. When you weigh up the cost and convenience, you may feel a taxi is worth it for the experience.

Most of the bus companies provide excursions or run regular routes to Wadi Musa centre. The **Jordan Express Tourist Transport company** (JETT) (*7th Circle, Amman;* \ *06 585 4679;* f *06 585 4176; www.jett.com*) has the most regular timetable from Amman and runs through to Aqaba and back.

BY CAR The journey to Wadi Musa and Petra is straightforward. There are three routes you can take from Amman (where you'll almost certainly arrive into Jordan, and where you'll hire a car). Take the Dead Sea Road alongside the Jordan Valley (number 65), past the turnings to Madaba and Karak, and then take the left turning marked to Tafila (number 60) and to Petra (number 35) for one of the most scenic journeys ever. If you fancy passing through more towns and villages, take the road out of Amman to Madaba (number 19), continue onto Karak (number 35) and onto Tafila before following the signs to Petra.

Alternatively, you can take the Desert Highway out of Amman due south. This is the quickest and most straightforward route, if a bit samey in terms of sandy landscapes. On the highway, after about 180km look out for the Aneizah crossing, where you'll see signposts for Petra and Wadi Musa. Follow this road, passing the old Shawbak (Al-Shawbak) city, until you reach Wadi Musa. From Aqaba you simply need to follow the highway until you reach the signs for Petra. You'll pass Taybeh village. Something to note is that some signs may read Al-Batra, which is the local name for Petra. Once you arrive in Wadi Musa go past the Spring of Moses (Ain Musa) and the police station until you reach Shaheed roundabout, which is the centre of the town. If you continue from here, downhill, you'll reach the Petra Archaeological Park.

Meaning Valley of Moses, which is named after Moses, the prophet referred to in the Hebrew Bible, the Christian Holy Bible and the Holy Koran who is said to have passed through the region, Wadi Musa is a bustling town and the closest to Petra. On the approach road from Amman and Aqaba you will pass the **Spring of Moses** (Ain Musa). Legend has it that Moses was ordered by God to speak with a rock in order to produce water for his people in the hills of Petra (Exodus 17). However, Moses struck the rock rather then speak with it, with the result that water spurted forth and created the Spring of Moses. The Nabateans are said to have built channels to divert the spring water to Petra.

Wadi Musa has hotels and restaurants that serve the many thousands of people who visit the Petra Archaeological Park (see page 214). As part of the Ma'an Governorate, it is the administrative centre of the region that includes Petra and a handful of other tiny villages, and has a burgeoning Bedouin community who were relocated here when the Nabatean city became a national park.

The local Bedouin people are friendly and happy to talk. They come from three main tribes; the **Bdul**, who are traditionally a semi-nomadic tribe, the **Liyathna**, who claim descent from the Nabateans, and the **Ammarins**, who although not original dwellers of the Petra site have lived in Beidha, just north of the city and a short distance from Wadi Musa, for centuries. Further tribes live in Wadi Musa, including the Hassanat and the Nawafleh, while across the valley are the Fallahat and Farajat tribes. Almost all have land and grow fava beans, olives and potatoes, and have numerous fruit trees. Their fruit is considered some of the best in Jordan. The apricots, greengages and figs are simply delicious. The families own horses too, which they are authorised to take to the Petra Archaeological Park in order to offer rides to tourists, see page 215.

Wadi Musa is a traditional Jordanian town full of houses and tiny shops, where it is possible to mix with the locals. You can take a pleasing stroll around its narrow streets, albeit with difficulty in places as the terrain is exceptionally hilly. Surrounding Wadi Musa are the mountains of the Wadi Araba, and here, in winter, snowfall regularly falls and cuts off the village entirely.

GETTING AROUND

By taxi and bus Wadi Musa is a relatively compact town and while easy to navigate has steep hills and it can be something of a challenge to cover any distance **on foot**. If you're staying in the town centre, for example, the walk to the Petra Archaeological Park's main gate is all downhill, signposted and will take you about 30 minutes or so. Easy. Remember, though, you will have a return journey that will be hard going, especially after a day of walking around Petra. It will take considerably longer. There are a few local taxi companies that run the bright **yellow cabs** you'll see running about. Simply call and tell them where you want picking up and at what time in the usual way. A taxi rank can be found at the entrance to the Petra Archaeological Park. Fares are inexpensive but be sure to check the price of your journey before you depart because tourists, like in most other tourist destinations, are a bit of a target and routinely overcharged. Around JD2 for a journey around town is about right, but to get this you may have to be firm and bargain. Most of the hotels in Wadi Musa provide free guest **shuttle buses** to the main entrance of the Petra Archaeological Park. Some are run on a timetable basis so you know when your return bus will be leaving, while others can be booked ad-hoc at the hotel's reception.

Taxi companies

🚗 **Alanbat Taxi** m 077 952 2208
🚗 **Petra Taxi Service** m 077 724 4189
🚗 **Petra Taxis** m 070 531 4368

By car Driving around Wadi Musa couldn't be easier, but it is a busy place and steep in parts so be careful and take it slowly. The town has several petrol stations, the largest being on the approach road from Amman, just before you meet an intersection with the road from Aqaba signposted for Wadi Musa. **Car-hire** companies are few and far between so you'll probably find it easier to rent in Amman or Aqaba. If you want to rent in Petra, a company worth trying is **Petra Rent a Car** (✆ *03 215 4545*).

TOURIST INFORMATION

🄯 **Petra Development & Tourism Region Authority** Wadi Musa; ✆ 03 215 7093; e info@petrapark.com; www.petrapark.com

TOUR OPERATORS

Jordan Inspirational Tours Al Saad Bldg 106; ✆ 03 215 7317; f 03 215 7317; e info@jitours.com; www.jitours.com. Offering themed excursions that range from photographic & nature to trips on horseback or in a 4x4, this company prides itself on taking an eco approach to tourism.

Jordan Tours & Travel Wadi Musa 112; ✆ 03 215 4666; f 03 215 4600; e eid@jordantours-travel.com; www.jordantours-travel.com. If you wish to go on a Petra by Night tour, try your hand at a cookery workshop or fancy an excursion on horseback, camel or bicycle, this company is able to organise it for you.

La Beduina Eco-Tours & Travel Wadi Musa 80; ✆ 03 215 7099; f 03 215 6931; e beduina1@go.com.jo; www.labeduinatourscom. Specialising in tours on horseback, entitled the Lawrence of Arabia Riding Experience, this company escorts riders through the mountainous desert terrain surrounding Petra.

Petra Moon Tourism Services Wadi Musa 129; ✆ 03 215 6665; f 03 215 6666; e info@petramoon.com; www.petramoon.com. Tours of archaeological sites, cuisine- & handicraft-themed trips, accommodation in Bedouin-style tents & more.

🏠 WHERE TO STAY

As one of the world's major UNESCO World Heritage Sites, and one of Jordan's foremost tourist attractions, Petra welcomes thousands of visitors every year. As such, a blossoming number of hotels have sprung up in recent years. Whether you like a touch of luxury or you're travelling on a shoestring, your requirements are sure to be met.

Luxury

🏠 **Grand View Resort** (133 rooms) Queen Rania al-Abdullah St, Wadi Musa; ✆ 03 215 6871; f 03 215 6984; e info@grandview.com.jo; www.grandview.com.jo. Located on a hilltop with views out over Mount Hor & Aaron's Tomb, the Grand View certainly lives up to its name. Its rooms are beautifully presented in earth colours, & its magnificent lobby, lounge area, Café Royal restaurant & bars all exude a subtle sense of luxury. Sweeping views of the valley

can be enjoyed from its outdoor swimming pool terrace. **$$$$$**

🏠 **Mövenpick Resort Petra** (183 rooms) Wadi Musa; ✆ 03 215 7111; f 03 215 7112; e resort.petra@moevenpick.com; www.moevenpick.com. Located right at the entrance to the Petra Archaeological Park, this lovely hotel offers fine dining in 7 restaurants, a fitness suite & well-equipped luxurious guestrooms. Architecturally, the hotel captures the traditional Jordanian desert style, while its arabesque décor

& antiques seen the moment you step inside its large, bright reception foyer give it a discerning feel. **$$$$$**

🏠 **Taybet Zaman Hotel** (102 rooms) Taybeh, Wadi Musa; 📞 03 215 0111; f 03 215 0101; e reservation@taybetzaman.com; www. jordantourismresorts.com. Located on the outskirts of Wadi Musa, this 5-star holiday village is built around a renovated hamlet to a traditional 19th-century Jordanian style. Its guestrooms & restaurant areas are arabesque in design, plus there's a *hammam* & an outdoor swimming pool for guests to enjoy. Its sister holiday village is nearby Beit Zaman (*03 215 7401; f 03 215 7406; e reservations@beitzaman.com*). **$$$$$**

Upmarket

🏠 **Crowne Plaza Resort** (147 rooms) Wadi Musa; 📞 03 215 6266; f 03 215 6977; e ammhc@ cprpetra.com; www.crowneplaza.com. Tucked in at the foot of the Petra Mountains, this luxurious hotel is mins' walk from the entrance to the Siq. A choice of restaurants serve cuisine from the Mediterranean & Arabia, plus it runs an eatery inside the archaeological site itself. Active types can use the hotel's outdoor pool & terrace with its amazing views of the wilderness, the health suite & a tennis court (the only one around Petra for miles). **$$$$**

🏠 **King's Way Hotel** (95 rooms) Wadi Musa; 📞 03 215 6799; f 03 215 6796; e info@kingsway. com.jo; www.kingsway.com.jo. An imposing sandstone-coloured hotel that blends with its surroundings, the 4-star King's Way offers guestrooms with lots of amenities including fast internet, an old-style Al-Areesha coffee shop & à la carte restaurant. Life here revolves around its outdoor swimming pool. Located near the Spring of Moses in Wadi Musa. **$$$$**

🏠 **Mövenpick Nabatean Castle** (90 rooms) 71811 Petra; 📞 03 215 7201; f 03 215 7209; e resort.petra.nabatean@moevenpick.com; www.moevenpick-hotels.com. With panoramic views from almost every room of the hotel, the Mövenpick Nabatean Castle is perched high on a hilltop at an altitude of 1,400m, overlooking the Great Rift Valley. It's just 10mins from the archaeological site entrance. Its guestrooms are well equipped & all have AC. Exercise enthusiasts will love the indoor pool with its outdoor terrace & fitness suite, while foodies have a choice of

WADI MUSA (SKETCH MAP) Not to scale

cuisines. There's a library & a playroom for the kids. **$$$$**

🏠 **Petra Marriott Hotel** (99 rooms) Queen Rania al-Abdullah St, Wadi Musa; 📞 03 215 6407; f 03 215 7096; e petra@marriotthotels. com; www.marriott-petra.com. A central atrium several floors high around which guestrooms are located provides a bright, airy feel. There are 2 international restaurants, Dushara & L'Affresco, & its Aretas lounge bar caters for all tastes. An outdoor pool & sun terrace complement the hotel's Turkish bath complex. **$$$$**

Mid range

🏠 **Amra Palace Petra** (70 rooms) Wadi Musa; 📞 03 215 7070; f 03 215 7071; e info@

amrapalace.com; www.amrapalace.com. Owned & run by a Petra-born family, this upmarket hotel has guestrooms that are both luxurious & yet homely. The added bonus is Wi-Fi throughout the hotel. Local dishes are the speciality in its restaurant, & there's an indoor pool, jacuzzi & *hammam* complex where guests can relax. **$$$**

🏠 **Candles Hotel** (35 rooms) Wadi Musa; ☎ 03 215 6954; f 03 215 7311; e candles@nets.com. jo; www.candlespetra.com. Located in the heart of Wadi Musa, just a few mins' walk from the main entrance to the Petra Archaeological Site, this 3-star hotel has a refreshing, contemporary feel. Its guestrooms are modern & have facilities that include free Wi-Fi & AC. Its restaurant serves international dishes, plus it has a Bedouin-style terrace where guests can relax with a flavoured water-pipe. **$$$**

🏠 **Edom Hotel** (135 rooms) Wadi Musa; ☎ 03 215 6995; f 03 215 6994; e edom@go.com. jo; www.edomhotelpetra.com. A choice of restaurants – including one designed as a cave where Bedouin-style seating is arranged so visitors can sit, enjoy a water-pipe if they wish & talk into the small hours – is one of the excellent amenities of this modern hotel in the centre of town. Another is its Turkish bath & a terrace, which affords spectacular views over the town. **$$$**

🏠 **Petra Palace Hotel** (83 rooms) Wadi Musa; ☎ 03 215 6723; f 03 215 6724; e ppwnwm@go.com.jo; www.petrapalace.com. jo. A modern hotel set around a heated outdoor swimming pool & sun terraces, the Petra Palace has a commanding view of the Petra mountains that surround it. It offers pleasing guestrooms with lots of amenities. Its bar, where soft music is played, serves a full range of international drinks, while its restaurant, bathed in natural light, has an extensive international menu. **$$$**

🏠 **Petra Panorama Hotel** (130 rooms) Queen Rania al-Abdullah St, Wadi Musa; ☎ 03 215 7393; f 03 215 7389; e info@petrapanorama. com; www.petrapanorama.com. A 4-star hotel, the Petra Panorama has been designed to take advantage of the scenery, with most communal areas & AC guestrooms & suites looking out over the mountains. Modern throughout, it has an international restaurant, several bars & an outdoor swimming pool. **$$$**

Budget

🏠 **Alanbat Hotel** (80 rooms) Wadi Musa; ☎ 03 214 6265; f 03 215 6888; e info@alanbat. com; www.alanbat.com. Run by a local Wadi Musa family, the Alanbat & its 2 nearby sister hotels are located in the centre of the town. With comfortable rooms complete with AC & free Wi-Fi, a spacious restaurant with an à la carte menu & buffet of international dishes, & a small outdoor pool, this is good value for money place to stay. Staff here are multilingual. **$$**

🏠 **Petra Inn Hotel** (80 rooms) Wadi Musa; ☎ 03 215 6401; f 03 215 5401; e petra-inn@ yahoo.com; www.petrainn.20m.com. A great value & welcoming hotel, the Petra Inn has guestrooms with amenities that include AC, private bathroom & satellite TV, plus a large restaurant that caters for international taste but serves a range of Bedouin dishes, such as *mulukhayyeh* (chicken with spinach), if you want to eat like a native. The hotel often hosts themed entertainment. **$$**

🏠 **Petra Sunset Hotel** (28 rooms) Wadi Musa; ☎ 03 215 6570; f 03 215 6950; e info@ petrasunset.com; www.petrasunset.com. With its central location just a few mins' walk from the centre of town & Petra archaeological site, comfortable guestrooms & a restaurant serving international as well as Oriental dishes, this is a convenient place to stay if visiting Wadi Musa on a budget. The hotel can organise a variety of excursions, including a visit to Little Petra. **$$**

🏠 **Venus Hotel** (35 rooms) Wadi Musa; ☎ 03 215 7165; e info@petravenushotel.com; www.petravenushotel.com. This budget hotel has comfortable rooms with amenities such as satellite TV & minibar. Jordan's national dish, *mensaf* (lamb with a spicy yoghurt sauce & rice) followed by *konafa* (honey-smothered wheat & goat's cheese squares) are the specialities of the restaurant. International dishes are also served. A traditional Bedouin area with bright red cushions is available for after-dinner relaxation. **$$**

Shoestring

🏠 **Ammarin Camp** Beidha village, 10km north of Wadi Musa; m 079 975 5551; e info@ bedouincamp.net; www.bedouincamp.net. If you've ever wondered what it would be like to live the life of a Bedouin in the middle of a mountainous desert then this wonderful eco-campsite run by members of the Ammarin tribe will give you a glimpse into their lifestyle. It is a permanent Bedouin-style camp, complete with goat-hair tents & a small museum that tells their story. Nightly entertainment features local music, dances & food. Bathrooms are available at a small cost. **$**

🏠 **Musa Spring** (22 rooms, plus roof) Ain Musa, Wadi Musa; ☏ 03 215 6310; f 03 215 6910;

e musaspring_hotel@yahoo.co.uk. A favourite haunt of backpackers, this basic yet comfortable hotel is located right next to the Spring of Moses (Ain Musa) on the approach road into Wadi Musa. You can opt for a room with a private or shared bathroom, or join others sleeping under the stars on the roof. The hotel serves b/fast & will prepare picnic boxes with plenty of bottled water on request. **$**

✗ **WHERE TO EAT** Unless you are opting to dine in one of the four-star or five-star hotels, where a choice of gourmet or world restaurants are usually available, you're likely to find the restaurants in Wadi Musa more traditional than those found in the cities of Amman or Aqaba. Try a mezze to sample lots of local dishes like *falafel* (ground chickpeas moulded into balls), *fattoush* (parsley with fried bread cubes), *sujuk* (spicy sausages), *shish tawook* (chicken kebab) or the staple salad *tabbouleh* (chopped parsley with tomato and mint). Desserts are usually dripping in honey and simply divine, although a challenge on the waistline.

Expensive

✗ **Al Iwan** Mövenpick Resort Petra, Wadi Mura; ☏ 03 215 7111; e resort.petra@moevenpick.com; www.moevenpick-hotels.com; ⏱ 19.00–23.30. Tastefully decorated in honey & cream shades with a water fountain as a centrepiece, this award-winning restaurant serves a menu of Mediterranean dishes. Choose from classics like *moussaka* with olive bread & salad or grilled meat & fish in delicious sauces, accompanied by fine wine. **$$$$$**

✗ **Al-Madafa** Mövenpick Nabatean Castle; 71811 Petra; ☏ 03 215 7201; e resort.petra. nabatean@moevenpick.com; www.moevenpick-hotels.com; ⏱ 06.30–10.30 for b/fast, 12.30–15.30 for lunch & 18.30–23.30 for dinner. With its soft creamy décor & natural stone walls, this is a charming restaurant that welcomes visitors as well as its staying guests. It has its own terrace with views over the Great Rift Valley. Food is served buffet style so you can help yourself to local Jordanian dishes like delicious spit-roasted chicken, known as *farooj*, & international dishes. **$$$$$**

✗ **Aretas** Crowne Plaza Resort, Wadi Musa; ☏ 03 215 6266; e ammhc@cprpetra.com; www. crowneplaza.com; ⏱ 18.00–23.00. Whether you're dining with friends or intimately with a partner, Aretas makes an ideal setting. It is lavishly decorated with Mediterranean colours & stonework, has subtle lighting & has a menu of imaginative à la carte dishes with a strong French & Italian influence. Its delicious *tortellini con ricotta* (tortellini with cheese & spinach) is recommended. **$$$$$**

✗ **Petra Kitchen** Wadi Musa; ☏ 03 215 5900; e info@petrakitchen.com; www.petrakitchen. com; ⏱ 16.00–23.00. Be sure to make a reservation & arrive early because the price you pay includes a cookery course before you begin eating. You'll prepare soup, mezze dishes & a main Jordanian dish before taking your place in this authentically local restaurant to enjoy your meal. See box, page 213, for more information. **$$$$$**

Above average

✗ **Al-Qantarah** Wadi Musa; ☏ 03 215 5535; e info@al-qantarah.com; www.al-qantarah; ⏱ 12.30–23.00 daily. Housed in a lovely old building with arches – *alqantarah* means 'arch' in Arabic – & art on the walls, this atmospheric restaurant serves authentic dishes like *mensaf* (lamb with yoghurt) & *magloubeh* (chicken with rice). It has a salad bar with a delicious selection of dips & dishes. Try the fresh bread; it comes straight from the *taboun* old clay oven. Open for lunch, dinner & for special Arabic-themed BBQ events. **$$$$**

✗ **Basin Restaurant** Petra Archaeological Site; ☏ 03 215 6266; e ammhc@cprpetra.com; www.crowneplaza.com; ⏱ 11.00–16.00. Located inside the archaeological park surrounded by sheer mountains & ancient tombs, the Basin

Restaurant is something of an institution. Its Mediterranean-style lunchtime buffet is simply delicious. You can eat inside, but to really appreciate the enormity of your location be sure to sit on the outside terrace. Owned by the Crowne Plaza Resort. $$$$

✗ Bedha Restaurant King's Way Hotel, Wadi Musa; ☎ 03 215 6799; e info@kingsway.com.jo; www.kingsway.com.jo; ⏰ b/fast, lunch & dinner, times vary. A traditional restaurant with a terrace for dining alfresco, the Bedha has lengthy à la carte menu, plus a buffet full of international & local mezze dishes like *falafel* & *warag aynab* (stuffed vine leaves). $$$$

✗ L'Alfresco Petra Marriott Hotel, Queen Rania al-Abdullah St, Wadi Musa; ☎ 03 215 6407; e petra@marriotthotels.com; www.marriott-petra.com; ⏰ 18.00–23.00. Dine on *pasta al dente*, handmade pizzas fresh from the stone oven & steaks at this Italian restaurant inside the Marriot Hotel. Its *ravioli salmone* (salmon) served with a green onion sauce is recommended. An outside terrace offers an amazing view over the red-hued mountains that surround Petra. $$$$

Mid range

✗ Al-Deir Wadi Musa; m 079 630 4612; ⏰ 18.00–23.00. This cosy restaurant with a traditional arabesque décor is informal & a great place to while away an evening with friends. The cuisine is traditional. The speciality is the *magloubah*, which translated means upside down. It is a delicious dish of creamy chicken with rice & vegetables cooked with herbs. After your meal you will be invited to take coffee on the terrace. It rounds off the evening a treat. $$$

✗ Petra Magic Wadi Musa; ☎ 03 215 7500; www.petramagic-rest.com; ⏰ 07.00–11.00, 13.00–16.00 & 18.30–22.30. A beautifully presented family eatery, Petra Magic has an extensive menu of international à la carte dishes as well as a buffet of local salads like *tabbouleh* (parsley & tomato with cracked wheat), dips such as *hummus* & desserts so you can help yourself. It is one of the newest restaurants in Wadi Musa. $$$

Cheap and cheerful

✗ Bedouin Restaurant Amra Palace Petra; Wadi Musa; ☎ 03 215 7070; e info@amrapalace.com; www.amrapalace.com; ⏰ 18.00–24.00 summer only. This open-air restaurant revolves around its BBQ, where chefs cook chicken & lamb with all manner of spices. You can try to imagine life as a Bedouin as you sit on blankets & cushions gazing at the stars, smelling the aromas & dining on delicious exotic-tasting cuisine. $$

✗ Dushara Restaurant Wadi Musa; ☎ 03 215 6401; e petra-inn@yahoo.com; www.petrainn.20m.com; ⏰ b/fast, lunch & dinner, times vary. Located inside the Petra Inn Hotel, the Dushara is a spacious restaurant named after the son of the Nabatean God Allat. Its menu has a mix of local Bedouin dishes like *mulukhayyeh* (chicken with spinach) & *mensaf* (lamb in a spicy yoghurt sauce with rice), plus Asian & international cuisine. $$

ENTERTAINMENT AND NIGHTLIFE Other than in the hotels, which all have bars and the occasional themed music and dance evenings, the entertainment and nightlife in Wadi Musa is limited to say the least. In fact, after dark the streets are deserted. There are a few bars and restaurants, which tend to be where locals and visitors spend their evenings. At weekends local Bedouin families can usually be found at Candle Park (*entry free; parking*). Here, picnic spots and a children's playground vie for attention with its breathtaking view of Petra's entrance. The park is high on a mountainside above Wadi Musa and is one of the town's best-kept secrets. Find it on the main road out of Wadi Musa signposted to Taybeh. One after-dark event you shouldn't miss during your stay, however, is Petra by Night (see below).

Petra by Night One of the most memorable experiences in Petra is seeing the city by candlelight. There are various tours offered by enterprising small businesses in Wadi Musa, or you can join a group that leaves the Petra Archaeological Park's visitors' centre (☎ 03 215 7763) at 20.30 on Monday, Wednesday and Thursday. Leave yourself plenty of time to register for the tour. An option is to lag slightly

If you fancy learning how to cook authentic Jordanian dishes, then visit **Petra Kitchen** (*Wadi Musa;* ✆ *03 215 5900;* e *info@petrakitchen.com; www. petrakitchen.com*). You'll have a real Jordanian culinary experience. At Petra Kitchen you can cook a meal of soup, mezze dishes and a main course under the direction of the resident chef. You'll learn the secrets of regional cuisine before joining your fellow cooks to eat the meal you have prepared. This super kitchen and eatery has been decorated to an authentic style; all the furnishings, tableware and linens are local. You can opt for a one-night course or a five-night course, which includes shopping trips to local markets.

behind the group to give you a sense of being in the pitch darkness of the mile-long Siq on your own with only candlelights to guide you. It is all rather compelling, but don't let the group out of your sight in case you fall or get into difficulties. Watch your step through the Siq at night; the surface is uneven in places and, while not so much a hazard in daylight, can be a challenge in the dark.

With each twist and turn of the Siq you expect to see The Treasury come into view. Eventually, it does. It is a breathtaking sight. Lit only by hundreds of candles laid symmetrically in front of the building, and with storytellers and musicians adding to the haunting atmosphere, the mystery of how the Nabateans created such a building of immense beauty in the rock face is intensified even further. When the storyteller finishes his tales at around 21.30 you can walk towards the building and see it more closely, before beginning your walk back along the Siq. It's odd that the walk back never seems as long!

Bars and tea houses You may stumble on a handful of tiny bars in Wadi Musa, where locals go to drink tea and smoke water-pipes. They might be primitive in terms of décor but they are an authentic experience to savour. Most of the plush bars serving international alcoholic brands will be found in the hotels; they are generally open to non-residents.

☼ Al Ghadeer Roof Garden Mövenpick Resort Petra, Wadi Musa; ✆ 03 215 7111; www. moevenpick.com; ⏲ 15.00–24.00. Beautifully designed with rose-pink & white floor tiles, soft rose-coloured cushions & lavish planting of bushes & trees, this roof garden is a hidden gem. Listen to Arabic musicians playing local tunes, sip on your cocktail, smoke your water-pipe if you wish & watch the sun go down over Petra.

☼ Al Maq'aad Bar Mövenpick Resort Petra, Wadi Musa; ✆ 03 215 7111; www.moevenpick. com ⏲ 16.00–24.00. With its lavishly painted walls decorated in gold leaf to an Oriental arabesque style, & its terracotta-coloured furnishings, this is a hugely attractive bar. It is said to have been inspired by the Arabian Nights. Enjoy smoothies, juices, teas, beers & international spirits here.

☼ Al Nadeem Bar & Terrace Mövenpick Nabatean Castle, 71811 Petra; ✆ 03 215 7201; www.moevenpick.com; ⏲ 10.00–24.00 daily. Spend the evening gazing out as the sun sets over the Jordan Rift Valley from the terrace of this cosy bar. It serves a full range of international wines & spirits, plus local specialities such as chilled mint tea. Soft music plays in the background.

☼ Cave Bar Petra Archaeological Site entrance; ✆ 03 215 6266; www.crowneplaza.com; ⏲ 10.00–23.00. The Cave Bar is a landmark of Petra. Stylishly created within a 2,000-year-old tomb, the bar is a welcome sight to the thousands who visit Petra every day. Refreshing juices as well as alcoholic beverages are served from morning through to late. The Cave Bar is owned by the Crowne Plaza Resort.

SPORTS AND OTHER ACTIVITIES Sports facilities are largely confined to the larger four- and five-star hotels, but most offer a one-day pass so you can use their pools, spas and fitness suites.

Crowne Plaza Resort Health Club Wadi Musa; ☏ 03 215 6266; f 03 215 6977; e ammhc@cprpetra.com; www.crowneplaza.com. Along with running & exercise machines, a sauna, spa pool & an outdoor heated swimming pool, this health club has a tennis court, the only one in Wadi Musa.

Petra Nabatean Castle Fitness Centre Mövenpick Nabatean Castle, 71811 Petra; ☏ 03 215 7201; f 03 215 7209; e resort.petra. nabatean@moevenpick.com. This colourfully decorated complex has a 110m² heated indoor swimming pool with a large sun terrace just outside overlooking the valley, & a gym.

OTHER PRACTICALITIES

Dress When visiting the Petra Archaeological Park it is advisable to wear good sturdy walking shoes, trainers or boots as you will cover considerable ground. It will be rough and you will have steps to climb. Wear a hat or some type of head covering and good sunglasses to protect you from the sun as there is little shade, and also from the sand that at times can whip up in the Petra basin.

Emergencies Wadi Musa has its own **tourist police**, who help to ensure the safety and security of the many visitors who come here to see Petra. The tourist police can be contacted on ☏ 03 215 6441. To contact the **General Police Directorate** in the Governorate of Ma'an ☏ 191; for the **Security Directorate** in Wadi Musa ☏ 112. The nearest **hospital** is the Wadi Musa Medical Centre, ☏ 03 215 6434.

Internet Wadi Musa has a good internet connection and all of the hotels offer facilities. In the town itself there are internet cafés, including **Al-Hayek Internet Café** and **Al-Arabi Internet Café**, both near the Wadi Musa municipality office in the main town square.

Money, post and shopping You can find banks, ATMs and the main post office in the central square of Wadi Musa, plus most of the hotels have money-changing facilities and a postal service for guests; ask at your reception for details. The shops are few and far between in Wadi Musa, and those that do exist can also be found around the main square. Most are grocery stores for basic provisions, but there are a growing number of specialist artisan workshops. A small post office is also located next to the Al-Beidha Police Station on the approach to the entrance of Petra Archaeological Park.

PETRA ARCHAEOLOGICAL PARK

(Wadi Musa; ☏ 03 215 7763; Petra Development & Tourism Region Authority: ☏ 03 215 7093; e info@petrapark.com; www.petrapark.com; ⊕ summer 06.00–18.00 daily, winter 06.00–16.00 daily, evening candlelit tours 20.30–22.00 Mon, Wed & Thu; group tours in English & Arabic 07.00–15.00 daily; entry for one day JD50, two days JD55, three days JD60, inc brochure, map, horse ride from the visitors' centre to the Siq entrance and entry to museum; no credit cards accepted; free scheduled guided tours available; official private tour guides can be hired for around JD50 per day from the visitors' centre; languages spoken Arabic, English, French, Greek and Italian; horse and carriage rides from the entrance to the Siq to Al-Khazneh (the Treasury) JD20 return; camel rides

from Al-Khazneh to Qasr Al-Bint JD14) Your first port of call when visiting the park is the visitors' centre. Here you can purchase your tickets, which you should pay for in cash JDs. The charges have risen alarmingly in recent years so be sure to check the most up-to-date entrance fee before your visit to ensure you have plenty of money on you. You can join a tour if you wish, which you can organise at the visitors' centre, or explore the site on your own. Collect a map, which you will definitely need, and some literature that explains the monuments you are about to see.

If you plan to take a horse-drawn carriage through the Siq to The Treasury (at an additional cost) you can arrange this at the centre, too. Visitors with restricted mobility or those who are elderly can obtain a special pass at the centre that allows for the horse and carriage to go further, beyond The Treasury, to see the city's highlights.

Refreshments are located inside the park, and toilets can be found at the restaurants, as well as at the entrance to the Siq, next to the staircase leading to the High Place of Sacrifice, at the Siq al-Bared in Beidha, at the Ad-Deir monastery and at Qasr Al-Bint.

You'll start at the entrance and take the slow walk to the Siq, passing by the Bab al-Siq Djinn Blocks and the impressive Obelisk Tomb and Bab As-Siq Triclinium. Here, and throughout the 264,000m² park, you will see plants, birds, mammals and arthropods. It may seem like a barren environment once you are inside, but it is, in fact, home to more than 700 plants, nearly 150 different species of bird, 31 recorded species of mammal, and 185 different scorpions and insects.

OBELISK TOMB AND BAB AS-SIQ TRICLINIUM
Along the entrance to the Petra site, known as the Bab al-Siq, and just off to your left past the **Djinn Blocks**, which are three plain square crypts, lies an unusual structure. The Obelisk Tomb and Bab As-Siq Triclinium are, in fact, two tombs, one on top of the other, and are considered a fine example of a fusion of architectural styles covering several centuries.

The row of four obelisks on the upper level, and the possible remains of two others, look just like similar structures you would see on a trip to Egypt. On the ground floor, the Triclinium, which is a place where sacred feasts would have been eaten to honour the dead, dates from the time of the Nabateans. Ancient bilingual inscriptions have been found on its walls that would have been written by the hand of a Nabatean. Between the two distinct levels, the platform design is clearly Hellenistic–Roman.

A little further on and off to your right is the remains of a **dam**. The Nabateans created the dam at the entrance to the Siq to stop water flooding in and threatening to damage the city. They ingeniously bore a tunnel through sheer rock so the water could flow to another valley. The dam was later damaged in earthquakes, with the

PETRA'S HORSES

The sight of dozens of horses waiting in the baking sun to be offered as transport to waiting tourists can, to an equestrian lover, be a tad alarming. These horses, however, are well cared for. They come under the jurisdiction of the Al-Rawahel Owners Association (also known as the Horse Owners Society) and are registered and monitored. In the main, the horses are privately owned. Their owners are obliged to register them, obtain an official registration number so they can be used in the park, and take them for regular veterinary inspections. Petra's staff routinely check the owners' veterinary documents and paperwork, and can order that a horse be sent home should non-compliance be discovered.

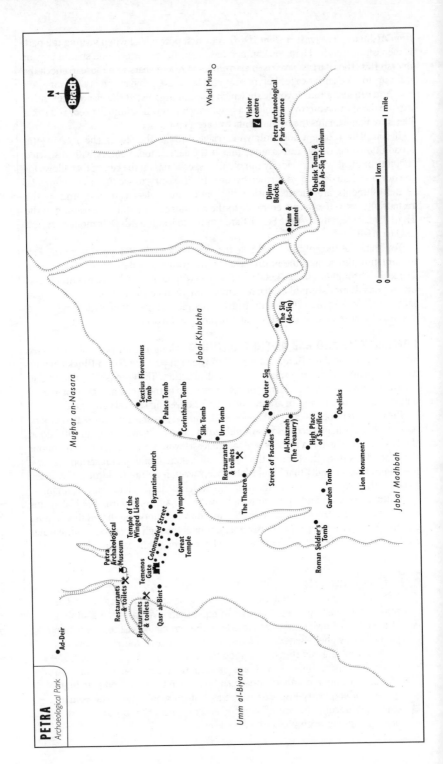

PETRA
Archaeological Park

Bradt

N

Wadi Musa

Visitor centre

Petra Archaeological Park entrance

Obelisk Tomb & Bab As-Siq Triclinium

Djinn Blocks

Dam & tunnel

The Siq (As-Siq)

Jabal-Khubtha

Sextius Florentinus Tomb

Palace Tomb

Corinthian Tomb

Silk Tomb

Urn Tomb

The Outer Siq

Restaurants & toilets

Street of Facades

Al-Khazneh (The Treasury)

High Place of Sacrifice

Obelisks

The Theatre

Mughar an-Nasara

Garden Tomb

Lion Monument

Jabal Madhbah

Roman Soldier's Tomb

Petra Archaeological Museum

Temple of the Winged Lions

Byzantine church

Nymphaeum

Colonnaded Street

Great Temple

Temenos Gate

Qasr al-Bint

Restaurants & toilets

Restaurants & toilets

Ad-Deir

Umm al-Biyara

0 1km
0 1 mile

result that for several centuries water did, indeed, flow down the Siq and flood the city. In recent times, the water-management system founded by the Nabateans was restored after a group of French visitors got caught in a flash flood inside the Siq in 1963. A total of 23 were washed away to their deaths. The system is designed for the continued protection of the Siq, the city and for all who visit the park.

THE SIQ A stunning creation of nature, the Siq (As-Siq) is breathtaking and is as awesome as the manmade city of Petra. A mile-long canyon that twists and turns through towering rock faces that almost obliterate the sun in places, it provides the main entrance into the city today. It wasn't always the main entrance; in ancient times it was the route used for ceremonial and burial processions into what was then the religious district of Petra. Votive niches along the gorge testify to this use. A triumphal arch is believed to have once spanned the entrance to the Siq, under which the procession would pass. It is long gone, but the evidence of its existence is still there.

The Siq is a natural geological feature formed by a deep split in the sandstone mountains, through which water has run to the Wadi Musa for millennia. Today, the floor of the Siq is concreted, apart from stretches that are cobbled. Although the concrete takes away a little of the romance of the place, it does make the going much easier.

With rocks in every shade of pink and orange, the Siq has some odd geological formations along its route, plus water channels hewn by hand in the rock, agricultural terraces and the niches where votive figures were placed (testifying to its use as a ceremonial route). Along the wall on one stretch is believed to be a series of what were once 4m-high camels and camel drivers carved into the rock face. Although they are quite worn now you can still make out their feet and legs. There are Nabatean sacred stones to see too, and in another stretch the remains of an ancient paved road now worn smooth over time.

AL-KHAZNEH (THE TREASURY) The Siq leads to Al-Khazneh, also referred to as the Al-Khazna, and by the Bedouins as Al-Jerrah, but better known to the world as The Treasury. Your first glimpse of this astonishing salmon-pink structure is through a narrow, dark shaft between the Siq's soaring cliffs. Tantalisingly, the view is barely 3m wide. Shrouded in brilliant sunshine, the Treasury looks unreal; like a vision at the end of the gorge. Moving closer, the Siq opens out to a large square dominated by this dazzling façade. It stands over 40m high, and almost as wide, with its intricate rock-carved friezes and statues so well-defined it is hard to believe it is so old.

The Treasury is unique in that it manages to combine Greek Hellenistic and Alexandrian Hellenistic styles effortlessly with pure Nabatean craftsmanship, something that was unusual when it was carved in the 1st century BC. Exactly why it was built is unknown, but it was probably the tomb and later a temple of a notable Nabatean. Some scholars have suggested it was the mausoleum of powerful Nabatean king, Aretas IV (9BC–AD40). A distinctive funerary cornucopia said to depict the ancient Greek mythological deity Tyche, and seen in the centre of the upper level, contains pharaoh's treasure (according, that is, to local folklore). The damaged façade indicates that numerous attempts have been made to break the urn in order to release its contents.

The Treasury is just a glimpse of what is to come. From here you can take a slight detour to see the High Place of Sacrifice, which lies to the left of The Treasury, or stroll off to its right through another short gorge, the Outer Siq, from where the hidden city of Petra with its hundreds of monuments will unfold before you. The sheer size of the city and the complexity of its tombs, temples and palaces is staggering.

HIGH PLACE OF SACRIFICE Probably once used for religious ceremonies that honoured the Nabatean gods and for funeral rites, this High Place of Sacrifice is well preserved but reached by a strenuous climb up rock-cut steps to almost the peak of the mountain Jabal Madhbah. The view looking down to the city is outstanding nonetheless, and some small reward for the long trek. You can even see the white dome of the shrine to the Prophet Aaron perched on top of Jabal Harun.

Not far from the High Place of Sacrifice is the **Lion Monument**, a huge statue of a lion carved into the solid rock that has a channel carved above its head. A spring would have once fed the channel, with the water flowing into a pool below. It was all part of the elaborate water-management network built by the Nabateans. The small **Garden Tomb** and the impressive **Roman Soldier's Tomb**, so called after a statue was found inside, are other major sights of Petra that lie near the High Place of Sacrifice. Look out for the two **obelisks** too. These 7m-high freestanding structures may have once been part of a sanctuary dedicated to the mythological Nabatean god Dushara.

STREET OF FAÇADES You'll reach the Street of Façades via the Outer Siq. It is a wall of intricate tomb façades carved into the cliff face that would have been the resting place of important Nabateans. The façades are elaborate, with details such as protruding pillars known as pilasters, decorative cavettos mouldings and corner crow-steps. Opposite are less impressive tombs, again in rows. Look beyond the Street of Façades and the awesome sight of the open plain of the city confronts you.

THE THEATRE Continue on past the Street of Facades until you reach the theatre. It was built by the Nabateans in the 1st century AD, but with its huge semi-circular shape and rows of seats, it is reminiscent of ancient Greek and Roman amphitheatre and theatre architecture. The Nabateans, who records suggest were an open-minded people and had strong bonds with the Romans, probably took a liking to the concept of a theatre where thousands could be entertained and were influenced by the architecture of similar structures that already existed.

PETRA THE FILM STAR

Petra has been the filming location for a whole host of Hollywood films. In the final scene of the 1989 film *Indiana Jones and the Last Crusade*, which was directed by Steven Spielberg, the Al-Khazneh temple (The Treasury) has a starring role. As Indiana, played by Harrison Ford, his father Professor Henry Jones (Sean Connery) and their accomplices Dr Marcus Brody (Denholm Elliott) and Sallah (John Rhys Davies) contemplate their attempt to recover the Grail and near fatal escape from the crumbling temple in which it was discovered, they are seen in front of The Treasury. As they conclude their adventure they gallop away on horseback into the Siq.

The city's ancient treasures and mystical landscape has appeared in other films too. It was one of the main filming locations for the 2009 Steven Spielberg action film *Transformers: Revenge of the Fallen*, along with the 1977 fantasy film *Sinbad and the Eye of the Tiger* starring Patrick Wayne, the 1998 film *Passion in the Desert* and the 1942 film *Arabian Nights*. Petra has been immortalised in scenes for video games and as a location in numerous novels, including the 1938 mystery *Appointment with Death* by Agatha Christie, when it was the setting for a murder.

Petra's theatre was built to seat well in excess of 3,000 people, and was later expanded so that it could accommodate up to 7,000. The theatre's auditorium comprises three sections of seating separated by walkways, with seven staircases for the unfortunates who had to climb and sit in the highest seats, then and now called 'The Gods'. The stage is central and at ground level. In the main, the theatre is carved by hand into solid rock, with only the two outer sides freestanding. It is a design that, like similar theatres of the Roman Empire, afforded it superior acoustics, which meant that everyone in the auditorium was able to hear what was being said by the performers on the stage below. Petra's theatre is remarkably well preserved.

ROYAL TOMBS The Royal Tombs lie opposite the theatre and make a spectacular sight carved as a cluster into the side of the Al-Khubtha mountain. Each displaying designs of grandiose, they are believed to have been tombs of Nabatean dignitaries rather than royals as their name suggests. The largest of the tombs and one of the most interesting is **Urn Tomb**, named after the small urn at the top of the pediment. It is a tall, narrow tomb that seems to tower over the city. You can reach it by climbing up a relatively short monumental staircase built over two rows of vaults that Bedouins believe to have been prison cells.

A large courtyard is at the top of the staircase and a high arched doorway leads through to the inner area of the tomb, a cavernous space where signs of its conversion to a church can still be seen. Up close, you can see how beautifully its façade is carved and the pink and red colours of the rock seen at this upper storey are brilliant. Urn Tomb was, it is believed, built around AD70 as a noble's tomb, and later converted to a Byzantine church in the 5th century. A series of Greek Byzantine inscriptions tells us it was reconsecrated by a bishop by the name of Jason in AD447.

A group of tombs lie to the north of the Urn Tomb, and although most are badly damaged through earthquake destruction and years of weather erosion they still make an arresting sight. The **Silk Tomb**, so called because of its unusual swirling patterns in the rock not unlike the look of the finest shot silk, is one of the most striking. It sits alongside the **Corinthian Tomb** which, although badly damaged, resembles the intricacy of the Treasury's Nabatean and classical architecture, and the magnificent, although severely damaged, **Palace Tomb**.

Completing the main group is the **Sextius Florentinus Tomb**, one of the few monuments in Petra that can be dated with any certainty. It was carved in AD126–130. A Latin inscription over the doorway tells us it was the tomb of Titus Aninius Sextius Florentinus, a Roman who was the governor of the Province of Araba in AD127, and who died circa AD130. It is an elaborately carved structure with the massive head of a fertility goddess dominating its segmented pediment, crowned by an eagle.

COLONNADED STREET Dating from the Nabatean and early Roman period, the colonnaded street runs from a plateau in front of the Royal Tombs into the heart of this ancient city. To the east where the Wadi Musa meets the Wadi al-Mataha lie the scant remains of the **Nymphaeum**, which would have been used to collect and store water. At the other end of this paved street, which would have at one time been lined with shops, artisans' workshops, temples, dwellings and public buildings, lay a monumental archway.

The road was built by the Nabateans and paved in an irregular fashion, and was later repaved uniformly in marble by the Romans, which can still be seen today. Just off to one side of the street you'll see a temple, known as the **Great Temple**. Opposite is the **Temple of the Winged Lions**. Although both are badly damaged, they were clearly impressive structures in their heyday.

Nearby is a shelter covering the remains of a **Byzantine church**. A **mosaic** that would have decorated its entire floor space features 84 medallions arranged in three columns with images of peacocks, horses, elephants, camels, human figures and baskets. The mosaic, which has been likened to the style of the famous one in Madaba depicting scenes from the Bible, is surrounded by a braided border.

QASR AL-BINT While less elaborate, but solid and imposing nonetheless, the Qasr al-Bint was probably the main temple of Petra in Nabatean times. Here, the goddess Aphrodite is believed to have been worshipped. Built in the 1st century AD, the almost square temple is unusual in that it is the only surviving freestanding building in the city. It is believed juniper wood placed between the bricks when the temple was originally constructed helped it to survive the earthquakes that claimed so many of Petra's other structures. It dominates a large paved precinct, known as a temenos, where common worshippers would have come to pray. The priests and dignitaries of the city would have prayed inside.

AD-DEIR Modelled on The Treasury, although with less detailed decoration, the Ad-Deir is Petra's second best-known attraction. Meaning monastery, the Ad-Deir is simply huge; indeed it's one of Petra's largest structures. It is carved with meticulous detail into the side of the mountain, with a similarly carved, walled and colonnaded courtyard in front. The Ad-Deir would have been used for religious events and celebrations, and has long been a place of pilgrimage. Inside the monastery, which has been dated to the 2nd century AD, you'll see an altar and crosses carved into the wall.

To reach the Ad-Deir you'll need to climb hundreds of steps, each cut with precision into the sheer rock face. They have variably been counted to total 300 to 900, but the official figure is 800. Either way it's a lot of steps to climb. If you can, try to visit the monastery in the morning when it and the steps are in shade; it makes the strenuous climb to the top just that little bit easier. Don't forget to look out over the Wadi Araba plateau before you make your descent; it is breathtaking.

PETRA ARCHAEOLOGICAL MUSEUM (*Next to the Basin Restaurant, Petra Archaeological Park;* \ *03 215 6060;* ☉ *summer 09.00–17.00, winter 09.00–16.00 daily; entry inc in Petra Archaeological Park fee*) Although a little on the small side, this museum contains a wealth of jaw-droppingly ancient artefacts found during excavations of the Petra site. There's a well-preserved statue of the god Zeus found in the Qasr al-Bint temple, along with a marble urn decorated with the heads of panthers found in Petra's cave church.

AROUND PETRA

AMMARIN MUSEUM (*Beidha village, 10km north of Wadi Musa;* m *079 975 5551;* e *info@bedouincamp.net; www.bedouincamp.net;* ☉ *times vary*) This tiny Bedouin ethnic museum inside the **Ammarin Bedouin Camp** in Beidha village celebrates the life and lifestyle of the ancient Ammarin tribe, a branch of which settled in Beidha. An ancestor of the tribe members who live and run the camp today is said to have purchased the Beidha estate for the price of ten goats and a gun. In the museum you can see primitive furnishings that would have adorned a traditional Ammarin's house, along with stones, frankincense and herbs that would have been used for healing over the centuries. Information is given against the exhibits to explain how they were used. The museum set deep in the mountainside north of Petra.

LITTLE PETRA (*Siq al-Barid;* ⊕ *summer 06.00–18.00 daily, winter 06.00–16.00 daily*) The Siq al-Barid is an archaeological site which, although bearing striking similarities to the Siq and city at Petra (hence is commonly known as Little Petra), is less well known. It lies north of Petra; the drive should take you only about 10 minutes. Here you will enter through a short gorge in the rock (the Siq) and find what was probably a suburb of Petra. There are remains of dwellings, water channels and cisterns, and tombs, all carved in the rock face.

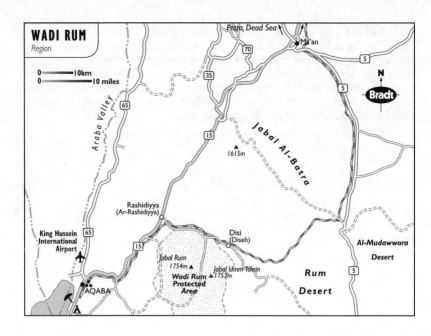

8

Wadi Rum

Telephone code: 03

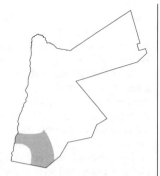

There's nothing quite like being surrounded by nature in the vast, serene desert of Wadi Rum. It is the ultimate experience if you crave getting away from it all. Here you can explore canyons on foot, climb towering mountains, such as **Jabal Rum** and **Jabal Um Ishrin**, observe wildlife or take a tour by camel caravan across the desert. You can hop on a 4x4 for a thrilling experience driving over the sand dunes or climb into a hot air balloon to see this magnificent landscape from above. Adventure, lots of fun and the experience of a lifetime – yes, Wadi Rum offers all this and rather a lot more.

Wadi Rum has towering limestone and granite mountains, deep canyons and dry, unimaginably beautiful sandy plains. On first impression you could be forgiven for thinking that animals and plants couldn't possibly survive here, but you would be wrong. It has a unique ecosystem that supports a vast number of species, some of which are endangered. If you're lucky you may catch sight of the Nubian ibex (*Capra ibex nubiana*), the grey wolf (*Canis lupus*) or the handsome Arabian oryx, which has been saved from extinction by the RSCN and released back in the wild (see page 9). They are extremely rare and if you report your sighting to the visitors' centre you will be assisting with ongoing scientific research in the desert.

The whole Wadi Rum desert was made a Protected Area in 1998 with the aim to protect and preserve the natural ecological environment, its wildlife and the lifestyle of the Bedouin communities who live here, while at the same time providing one of the most fabulous places in the world for adventure sports enthusiasts and for visitors to experience life in the desert. It covers an area of around 720km². The management team's mission is displayed near the on-site visitors' centre, and states it is committed to developing sustainable tourism, enhancing tourists' experiences, conserving the area's natural and cultural amenities, and enhancing the socio-economic status of the local communities.

There are lots of things to see: the **Seven Pillars of Wisdom**, which is a collection of natural peaks in the Um Ishrin mountain range named after the famous book by TE Lawrence, aka Lawrence of Arabia (even though he didn't actually mention the natural phenomenon in its pages); a spring, dubbed **Lawrence's Spring**; and ancient inscriptions such as those in the breathtakingly beautiful **Siq Khazali** canyon. Look out for golden sand dunes and visit **Rum** village itself, where Bedouin families now live in preference to life in the desert; although some still have a penchant for their previous nomadic lifestyle.

Wadi Rum is a wonderful place to meet and chat with the Bedouin people. Friendly and welcoming, they will tell you about their lifestyle and the many festivals they hold to celebrate births, weddings and successful harvests. You may be invited to join them for a coffee or herb tea, or you can book an overnight stay, where you will hear stories while enjoying authentic Bedouin food, and then fall asleep under the stars (literally) in the tranquillity of the desert. The Bedouin people derive much of their income from tourism and if you can use local services like guides and vehicles and pay a fair price, or you can shop in one of the craft cooperatives that have been established here, then you will be helping the local economy.

Wadi Rum is one of the key tourist attractions of Jordan, and visitors can enjoy a variety of **activities** from camel and 4x4 treks to balloon rides and mountain climbing. Accommodation options include campsites and eco-lodges. There are few eating options, but the visitors' centre and Rum village both have restaurants, along with a handful of shops. You simply must see Wadi Rum on your visit to Jordan. It is certainly one of Jordan's most important tourist destinations and attracts thousands of day trippers, hikers and climbers every year. Described by TE Lawrence as 'godlike', it is a calm and memorable place.

HISTORY

While Wadi Rum has been untouched by the development of such infrastructure as roads and major towns, it has been inhabited since ancient times and has hosted numerous communities who have lived and thrived here. The Nabateans, for example, lived and left their legacy here through the remains of a temple.

During the Arab Revolt of 1916–18, led by Sharif Hussein bin Ali of Makkah in his bid for independence from the Ottomans, Wadi Rum played a key role. It was here that TE Lawrence, the British Army officer who worked alongside the Arabs in an advisory capacity, based his operations (see *Lawrence of Arabia*, page 22).

In more recent times, His Majesty King Abdullah II and his government recognised Wadi Rum's importance to wildlife, the livelihood of its Bedouin communities and to the tourism of Jordan, and in 1998 declared it a Protected Area. With the support of the World Bank, the Royal Society for the Conservation of Nature (RSCN), which manages the park with the Aqaba Special Economic Zone Authority (ASEZA), commissioned a conservation plan that is now shaping Wadi Rum for its future protection.

GETTING THERE AND AWAY

BY AIR   The nearest airport to Wadi Rum is the **King Hussein International Airport** in Aqaba, from where you will need to hire a taxi or a car for your journey to the protected area. It can also be reached via the **Queen Alia International Airport**, located south of Amman. There are no direct public transport routes to Wadi Rum from here, so again you will need to arrange your own transport, see below.

BY TAXI   You can hire a **private taxi** to take you to Wadi Rum. If they simply drop you outside expect to pay around JD20 for the journey from Aqaba, a little more from Aqaba's ferry terminal and around JD35 from Petra. The fare from Amman will be around JD80. It's a good way to get to Wadi Rum if there are a few of you to share the cost. Once at Wadi Rum, you have the option to hire a **4x4** vehicle with a driver/guide, or join a 4x4 or camel tour.

BY BUS   **Public bus** services run from the An-Nahda Street bus station in Aqaba to Wadi Rum a couple of times a day (*JD2*). Times can vary so it's a good idea to check ahead of your journey for the most up-to-date timetable. Contact **Al-Motahedah Bus Company** (✆ *03 201 8005*) or **Trust International Transport** (✆ *03 203 2300*). Failing that, long-distance buses operated by the **Jordan Express Tourist Transport**

Company (JETT) (*Head office: 7th Circle, Amman;* ☏ *06 585 4679;* f *06 585 4176; www. jett.com.jo; in Aqaba: Al-Nahda St;* ☏ *03 201 5222*) run regularly between Amman and Aqaba, and although Wadi Rum is not on their list of stops they do pull in at the village of Rashidiyya (locally Ar-Rashidiyya). It's located on Highway 15, around 15 minutes or so from Wadi Rum. The cost from Amman to Rashidiyya is around JD8 and from Aqaba JD2, but you will need to arrange a lift to Wadi Rum from here. Locals tend to congregate at the village and are always happy to offer you a lift. If you accept, offer about JD5, although you may find yourself being expected to part with around JD8. If you are staying at a campsite in Wadi Rum ask your organiser to arrange a lift for you. Most campsite owners are happy to collect you. As with arriving at Wadi Rum by taxi, you can hire a 4x4 vehicle with a driver/guide or join a tour.

Another option is booking an excursion. Big, shiny **tour buses** operated by specialist companies leave from the main tourist towns of Aqaba and Petra almost daily; there are also trips from Amman. Prices vary enormously depending on the activities included, anything from JD30 to JD80, so shop around. Tour bus excursions can be organised through your hotel or direct with specialists (see page 43).

BY CAR One of the easiest ways to get to Wadi Rum is by car. You can **hire cars** in Aqaba, Petra and Amman. From Aqaba take Highway 15 heading north and follow signs from the Rashidiyya junction to Wadi Rum. Allow around an hour for the 58km journey. From Petra, head for Ma'an and pick up Highway 15 heading south, turning left at the same junction, and then follow the signs to Wadi Rum. Allow around 1½ hours. The quickest route from Amman is, again, along Highway 15, although you can take the Dead Sea road via Tafila (At-Tafila) or the King's Highway through towns and villages. In terms of distance, Amman to Wadi Rum is around 297km. Expect a journey time without stops to be around 3½ hours.

There's only one road into Wadi Rum so you should find it's all rather straightforward. Either side you'll see fields of watermelon. Look out for the village of Disi (also known as Diseh) and other small communities, and the freight rail track that all lie off to the left, and continue going straight until you reach the visitors' centre; car parking is found near here. If you plan to take your hire car inside the protected area, it must be a 4x4 vehicle and you must observe the regulations. The entry price per 4x4 vehicle is JD20 per day. It's far better to hire a guide; if you go off alone into the desert it's easy to get completely disorientated and you may find yourself having to contact the tourist police and be rescued from soft sand.

TOUR OPERATORS

Bedouin Adventures Wadi Rum; m 079 512 7025; f 03 202 2825; www.bedouinadventures. com. Everything from camel trekking & scrambling to camping can be arranged through this Bedouin-run business.
Bedouin Life Camp Wadi Rum; m 077 692 6907 or 078 555 1648; e yaser_zalabeh@yahoo. com; www.wadirumfullmoon.com. Organiser of

jeep safaris, camel tours, hiking experiences & camping in the desert.
Hot Air Balloon Rides Aqaba; ☏ 03 205 8050; www.royalaerosports.com. Although based in Aqaba, this specialist company can meet you at Wadi Rum & take you for a fabulous ride over the dramatic landscape of the desert in a hot air balloon.

WHERE TO STAY

Accommodation options here are few as most of the visitors who come to Wadi Rum stay for just a day and then return to their hotels in Aqaba, Petra or the Dead

Sea. The more adventurous may crave the opportunity to stay overnight, perhaps in a Bedouin tent, mingling with locals and sleeping under the stars. There are several camping sites within and around the Protected Area. Larger sites can be found in the nearby village of Disi, which is not actually part of the Wadi Rum Protected Area and often attracts weekender city-types from Amman. Some of the camps have facilities including showers, toilets and a restaurant. Price-wise, they tend to be good value and often a 'package' will include food, beverages such as herb tea or coffee, and even a tour or two. The alternative is a handful of basic bed-and-breakfast establishments in private homes in Rum village.

🏠 **Bait Ali Desert Camp** Access rd to Wadi Rum; m 079 554 8133 or 077 754 8133; f 03 202 2626; e info@baitali.com; www.baitali. com. This camp combines all the facilities of home in a Bedouin-style camp environment. Accommodation is in tents or lodges, & there are clean hot showers, toilets, a bar & a shop on-site. Bait Ali's modern kitchen specialises in local Bedouin dishes. The camp can also claim a couple of 'firsts' for Rum; it has its own amphitheatre, where cultural events are staged, & its own swimming pool. **$$**

🏠 **Bedouin Adventures Campsite** Wadi Rum; m 079 512 7025; f 03 202 2825; www. bedouinadventures.com. Located near the spectacular Um Fruth Rock Bridge with views of the Siq Burrah canyon deep inside the Protected Area, this Bedouin-style campsite has tents with mattresses & bedding. Food is cooked & served in the traditional way. It has toilets & showers. **$**

🏠 **Bedouin Life Camp** Wadi Rum; m 077 692 6907 or 078 555 1648; e yaser_zalabeh@ yahoo.com; www.wadirumfullmoon.com. You can experience a taste of Bedouin life at this camp set in the heart of the desert. Explore on a camel or jeep tour by day & chat around the campfire during the evening before falling asleep under the stars in a goat-hair tent woven by local women. **$**

🏠 **Captain's Desert Camp** Disi; \ 03 206 0710; www.captains-jo.com. Located outside the

THE BEDOUINS OF WADI RUM

Seven Bedouin tribes live in or around the Wadi Rum Protected Area, the largest of which is the Zalabia tribe. Until recent times, they all led a nomadic lifestyle, moving from place to place with their tents and living off the land and their herds of goat. As part of the conservation programme devised for Wadi Rum, a society was founded to help promote and monitor tourism and a village, known as Rum, was built and is now home to many of the tribes. Here, two schools have been built; one for girls and one for boys. There is a place of worship and a small number of shops selling basic everyday items.

Members of Zalabia tribe and others work with the society, the Rum Tourism Cooperative, to provide tourism services. They offer themselves as general guides, climbing guides and tour drivers; this is their only real source of income. They have an unmatched knowledge of the mountains and plains of Wadi Rum, and are the best possible guides. Most speak several languages. Nowadays, the majority of tribe members live in Rum and have given up the nomadic lifestyle, although some have found the transition a little difficult and return to the desert every now and then to recapture their past.

Around Wadi Rum are other Bedouin tribes, including the Sweilhieen, Dbour, Godman and Omran. The largest of the neighbouring tribes is the Zweideh who live in the village of Disi. Although they also offer tourism services, they are not wholly dependant on tourism to make a living as they have a reliable underground water supply and are able to grow fruit and vegetables to sell.

Protected Area, this camp offers large Bedouin tents that are divided into compartments for privacy. The on-site Bedouin chef prepares & cooks authentic dishes. Hiking & jeep tours can be arranged. **$**

🏠 **Captain's ECO Desert Camp** \ 03 206 0710; www.captains-jo.com. Views out over the Um Nfoos mountain set this camp apart. It comprises the traditional goat-hair tents with a central seating area where you can sit & learn all about local life. Buffets with Bedouin food is cooked & served, & a range of tours are offered. **$**

🏠 **Hillawi Camp** Wadi Rum; m 079 675 5600. The largest campsite, the Hillawi is capable of accommodating several hundred people in rows of army-style pitched tents. It offers entertainment in the form of music & dancing each evening. You don't always have the feeling of being away from it all here, but it is a lively & fun camp. Food is served from big cook pots. **$**

✗ WHERE TO EAT

There is little choice of places to eat in the Wadi Rum Protected Area, but what there is is simply delicious. Most of the camps have facilities to cook for their guests, and some welcome independent visitors. It's a great way to sample authentic local dishes. One of the best for Arabic and international dishes, complete with fresh salads, homemade bread and fruits, is in the visitors' centre's own restaurant. There are a handful of eateries in Rum village, which although on the basic side are welcoming and offer the chance to mingle with the locals.

✗ **Bait Ali Desert Camp** Access rd to Wadi Rum; m 079 554 8133 or 077 754 8133; e info@baitali.com; www.baitali.com. You don't have to be a resident camper to dine at the camp's lodge-style eatery. With its modern kitchen, zerb oven & bar facilities, plus a buffet full of tempting local dishes, this dining lodge combines atmosphere with fine cuisine. **$$**

✗ **Rum Gate Restaurant** Visitors' centre, Wadi Rum; \ 03 201 5995; www.captains-jo.com; ⊕ 08.00–16.00 daily. A large, welcoming sort of place, the Rum Gate can usually be found full of tour groups lunching on daily specials & salads from the buffet. Outdoor catering is available. What sets this restaurant apart is its fabulous view out over the desert to the Seven Pillars of Wisdom. **$$**

✗ **Wadi Rum Resthouse** Rum; \ 03 201 8867; ⊕ daily, times vary. If you fancy trying Jordan's national dish Bedouin-style then head for this restaurant on the edge of Rum. *Mensaf* is a dish of lamb that has been cooked for hours until it is tender, & is served with a delicious sauce made with yoghurt & herbs. At the Resthouse it is served on a big platter with rice. Alcohol is served here, or you could opt for tea made from local herbs. **$**

SHOPPING

As regards shopping, there are a few shops in Rum that cater for everyday needs, and also several small craft workshops at the visitors' centre complex and in the village, which are all part of the area's project to provide economic opportunities to the local Bedouin tribes. Look out for the **Nature Shop**; the **Burdah Women Cooperative Shop**, where you can find clothing and jewellery; and the **Bedouin Tattoo Arts Salhiyyah** and **Shakriyyah Cooperative**, where you can find unusual, highly artistic

SURFING

Jordan's Bedouin community has joined up to www.couchsurfing.com, a worldwide internet network site that allows travellers to log on and 'speak' to locals. In turn, local Bedouins invite their new internet friends to share a meal with them when in Jordan, and even stay with them in their home.

crafts. In Rum village you can visit the **Run Art Online** workshop where crafts are made by local women who have taken their inspiration from Wadi Rum's ancient rock artists. The inscriptions and drawing made by the ancient dwellers of the desert have been faithfully reproduced by today's women using modern techniques including sandblasting and burnishing. The shops are generally open ⊕ 08.00–17.00 daily.

OTHER PRACTICALITIES

DRESS Wear good sturdy footwear for walking or appropriate boots for hiking or mountaineering. You should also wear a hat, scarf or bandana that covers your neck; the sun can be strong in the desert and your neck and the top of your head and nose are particularly vulnerable. There is little shade other than a smattering of trees and canyons. You should always carry bottled water with you irrespective of the activity you plan to do in the desert, so a belt that can accommodate the bottle and which therefore leaves your hands free to steady yourself when, for example, exploring canyons, is a good idea too. Evening in the desert can get extremely chilly so have a jumper or shawl with you, and thicker clothing for winter excursions.

EMERGENCIES Wadi Rum has its own **tourist police** (❧ 03 196 4661) stationed in Rum who can be contacted in the event of an accident or emergency inside the Protected Area

INTERNET It may come as a surprise to see Bedouins walking around using their mobile phones or giving you their email, Facebook, Twitter or website address. However, the signals in Wadi Rum are surprisingly strong, all thanks to a high telecommunications mast. Although internet cafés have yet to come here, you will be able to connect to the internet with the right settings and provider via your mobile phone. Internet facilities are available in the visitors' centre too.

MONEY AND POST The visitors' centre can assist with changing money, although it is a far better option to visit a bank before you take the excursion to Rum. There are no ATMs or credit card facilities. You can post letters at the visitors' centre.

WHAT TO SEE AND DO

The Wadi Rum Protected Area offers many opportunities to explore the canyons and desert plateaus, whether hiking on foot, or travelling by camel or jeep. Its mountains provide an amazing variety of possibilities for mountaineering enthusiasts too, from challenging pre-marked climbs to those for the less experienced. You can camp in the protected area and spend days here soaking up the atmosphere of this vast silent wilderness.

WADI RUM PROTECTED AREA (*Aqaba Special Economic Zone Authority, Aqaba;* ❧ *03 209 0600;* f *03 203 2586; www.wadirum.jo; visitors' centre:* ⊕ *07.00–22.00*

daily; entry JD5, children free, c/vans JD5 per night, private 4x4 JD20 per day, horses JD5; fees are used to support the conservation of Wadi Rum & the economy of the local people; shops ⊕ 08.00–17.00 daily; restaurant ⊕ 08.00–16.00 daily) Before you begin your journey in the Wadi Rum Protected Area there are a few things to be considered. It is a vast area with mountains and canyons, open desert with little shade and wildlife that roams freely, and as such there are a few hazards. For your own safety, you should always leave details of your itinerary with the entrance office, especially if you are planning to climb in the mountains or trek in the desert. If following either of these pursuits, attach a copy of your itinerary to your tent too if camping overnight. Rangers ride around the area to check all is in order, and if they find you are not back at your camp at your planned time it may alert them to the fact you may have a problem.

One of the best ways to get around Wadi Rum if not hiking is by taking a tour by jeep, camel or on horseback, especially if your visit is just for a few hours or the day (see *Tours*, page 232). You can bring your own 4x4 in and you will often see tour buses operated by companies bringing large groups, usually from Aqaba, Amman, Petra or the Dead Sea region. There are lots of highlights in the Wadi Rum Protected Area for you to see, but first you might like to visit the **Interpretation Hall**. It lies just off to the left of the visitors' centre as you look at it. Here there are displays telling you about the local Bedouins and their lifestyle, the wildlife and the ongoing conservation projects of the park. A short film introduces you to Wadi Rum. It is interesting and gives you just a little insight into what you are about to see as you go out into the desert.

One highlight that cannot be missed is the **Seven Pillars of Wisdom**. This dramatic series of seven natural peaks in the **Um Ishrin** mountain range, tower over the desert landscape. They come into view behind the visitors' centre as you approach the park and have become one of the iconic images of Wadi Rum. They derived their name from the book by TE Lawrence. As you leave the visitors' centre en route to **Rum** you will pass by the peaks. The village of Rum, itself is a purpose-built place of brick and concrete houses which many of the Bedouin people who once lived in the desert now call home. Some of the Bedouins have been unable to make the full transition from their traditional way of life and although they keep a home here, they also venture back out into the desert for a few days at a

HIRING A GUIDE

Unless hiking or arriving at Wadi Rum as part of pre-arranged tour, either with a group or with your own independent guide, the chances are you'll need to hire a guide to enable you to explore the Protected Area. It is unwise to venture out in the desert in your own 4x4 vehicle. However, guides are not permitted to pick up independent visitors from the visitors' centre without a booking so you will need to do a bit of homework before your visit. You can engage a specialist operator who can organise a guide for you and have them meet you at the visitors' centre (or anywhere else you might like to be met – Rashidiyya junction, for example) or contact a freelance licensed guide yourself (see page 225). The latter will almost always work out a little cheaper. You'll need to establish what they can offer you in terms of tours and for what price, and confirm your booking. It is a good idea to reconfirm your booking a few days ahead. Take your confirmation paperwork with you. Recommended licensed freelance guides can be contacted through the Jordan Tourist Board.

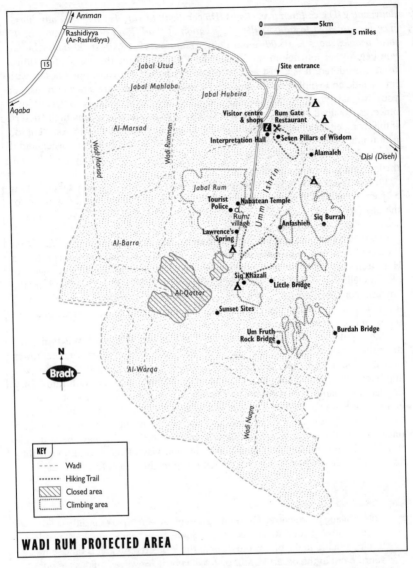

WADI RUM PROTECTED AREA

time to recapture their original lifestyle. If you are lucky and happen to visit when the villagers are celebrating a wedding or a successful harvest then you will see traditional Bedouin dancing being performed and music being played. There is a school, a handful of small shops and cafés, and the headquarters of the desert tourist police. This is a fascinating, living village.

Look out, too, for the remains of a **Nabatean Temple** just beyond the village, which is believed to date from the reign of Aretas and was used as a place of worship to the goddess Allat. Not far from here is **Lawrence's Spring**, named after TE Lawrence (see box, page 22). It is said to be where he bathed during the time of the Arab Revolt. You can see spring water at times, cascading down the mountainside. It is channeled to pools where water is stored for villagers, and for camels that come here, instinctively, to drink. When visiting the spring look out for some inscriptions on a rock face at the foot of the mountainside. They are believed to be Nabatean. The **Anfashieh** and the **Alamaleh inscriptions** and ancient **rock drawings** depicting camels, other animals, humans and plants that have been dated to around the 1st century are two further sites that clearly show how civilisations lived and thrived here, and can be seen the deeper you get into the desert.

Two further highlights of the park are deep canyons, the **Siq Burrah** and the **Siq Khazali**. Both are astonishing creations of nature. In the Siq Khazali you can see ancient **petroglyph rock drawings** and **inscriptions** clearly etched into the surface of the rock walls. They are believed to date from between the 4th and 3rd centuries BC. Watch your step in the Siq Khazali though; there are deep pools over which you must, nimbly, hop. Nearby, the area dubbed the **Sunset Sites** is designated for camping. Here you get the most amazing views as the sun sets. The Wadi Rum Protected Area also has a number of bridges to see that are, in fact, natural rock formations. There's **Little Bridge**, **Burdah Bridge** and the dramatic **Um Fruth Rock Bridge**.

Hiking and trekking If you love exploring at your own pace then hiking or trekking, either freely in the wilderness areas of the park or by following one of the trails, offers many rewards. You can cross desert plateaus, climb mountain foothills or head for the many rocky canyons just begging to be explored. Some of the canyons, known by their local name, Siq, have ancient inscriptions.

The designated hiking trails pass fascinating sites. They are marked by a series of cairns, which are small piles of stones left by Bedouins. The shortest trail leaves from the visitors' centre and takes you around the Seven Pillars of Wisdom. This remarkable natural creation can be seen from the centre and is one of the most dramatic sights in the area. You can spend a few hours hiking on this route, or a few days. Another, much longer, hiking trail leaves from Rum, which you can reach by jeep along a straight road from the entrance. The route is more challenging and follows a course that will take you past Lawrence's Spring to Khor al-Ajram and the Siq Khazali canyon, and on to Anfashieh, where you can see ancient inscriptions and sand dunes. Along the way are campsites if you plan to stay overnight.

It is possible to hire an official desert safari guide to escort you on your hiking experience. They will almost always be a local Bedouin working on a rota system who can give you first-hand knowledge of the desert. You are free to hire your own

DESERT PATROL

The desert patrol team is responsible for pioneering projects to protect the desert environment for wildlife and the local Bedouin population, and for ensuring all visitors to the vast Wadi Rum terrain are safe and accounted for. They monitor and report any damage and make sure that no hazards are present, such as litter, which can be harmful to the fragile ecosystem. You can't mistake the desert patrol team, whose governing body is the Aqaba Special Economic Zone Authority. Dressed in a long khaki *dish-dash* (light robe) tied at the waist with a bright red bandolier and a holster with a dagger, they are instantly recognisable. On their heads they wear a traditional red-and-white headscarf called a *kouffieh*. You'll meet members of the team in the visitors' centre when you arrive and see them in their jeeps with a sand cloud rising behind them as they make their way across the desert on their regular inspection trips.

independent guide, although it's a good idea to check that he or she has the relevant knowledge and experience to escort you around Wadi Rum.

Mountain climbing The mountains of the Wadi Rum region are a climber's dream, especially **Jabal Um Ishrin** and the highest peak in the protected area, **Jabal Rum**. At nearly 1,750m above sea level, Jabal Rum is the second highest mountain in Jordan. The mountains are challenging and to tackle one or more will be a memory that will last a lifetime. The concept of mountain climbing in Wadi Rum was first introduced in 1984 and quickly took off amongst the world's enthusiasts. The Bedouin people, however, have climbed here for thousands of years and have established their own network of climbing routes. Jabal Utud, Jabal Mahlaba, the Al-Warqa and the range around the Wadi Nuqra, which all lie in the Protected Area of Wadi Rum's 'wilderness zone', are popular with Bedouin climbers. Be advised that these routes, are considered dangerous for climbers unfamiliar with the terrain. If you do wish to attempt a Bedouin route it is unadvisable to do so without specialist equipment and a Bedouin climbing guide.

The main climbing areas for visitors are the mountain range of **Anfashieh**, the **Khazali** and **Um Fruth**, the vast complex of peaks at **Al-Shallaleh**, which provide the backdrop to Rum, and the Burrah peaks, which sit either side of mighty Burrah Canyon, known as the **Siq Burrah**. You can take a route followed by previous climbers or you can create your own. Either way, you should consult with the protection area office on the routes already taken or advise the team there of the route you intend to take. When you return you should report back, both so they know you are safe and do not need assistance, and to let them know if you have found a new route to be recorded.

The mountains of Wadi Rum are friable and so can easily break away. As such it is easy to lose your footing, or a route can change and you may lose your way. Climbers should be experienced before tackling Wadi Rum and capable of getting themselves out of a potential emergency situation (see box below). You should avoid using bolts and pitons as markers to minimise damage to the mountains; use natural markers instead wherever possible. Fixed protection, such as drilled placements and chains, should only be used in an emergency situation or when abseiling at designated spots.

Tours Taking a tour by **4x4 jeep** is an exhilarating, if at times bumpy, experience and you get to see most of the main sights of Wadi Rum, depending of course on what tour you take. There are two circuits that head off in different directions, with a choice of tour destinations and durations. Both circuits leave from the visitors' centre. You can bring your own 4x4 vehicle in to the park, too. If doing so it is advisable to hire a guide familiar with Wadi Rum and all it has to offer. The other option is a tour by

RESCUE AND EMERGENCY

In the event of an accident or emergency you should contact the tourist police on ☎ 03 196 4661 or alert any Bedouin guide who is in constant contact with the emergency team. Although at the time of publication there is no official rescue and emergency team at Wadi Rum, this is being addressed. The current team is made up of Bedouin climbers, guides, local volunteers and police personnel who are in touch with the Civil Defense Ambulance Service and the Royal Jordanian Helicopter Squadron.

The extensive landscape of Wadi Rum has been used as the backdrop for countless films. The most famous is the 1962 film *Lawrence of Arabia* starring Peter O'Toole, which was largely filmed in the desert plain of Khor al-Ajram in front of the Khazali mountain range. Filming, which began on 15 May 1961 and took almost 18 months to complete, involved local Bedouin tribes who acted as guides, drivers and even extras in the film itself. The Bedouins referred to Peter O'Toole as Ab al-Isfanjah, meaning 'Father of the Sponge', which refers to his liking of adding foam rubber to the saddle he used while riding the camels. It is said he found the saddle particularly uncomfortable. The practice is still in evidence today amongst the local community. Ironically, when *Lawrence of Arabia* was released it was banned in Jordan for what was considered to be an inaccurate, and at times disrespectful, portrayal of local Arab culture.

camel. Riding atop a camel is one of the experiences you simply have to try at least once, and there's no better place to do it than in the Wadi Rum desert. Camel tours leave from Rum or Alameleh on demand and can be booked at the visitors' centre. **Horseback** rides tend to be organised by private companies that have permission to operate within the Wadi Rum Protected Area (see *Tour operators*, page 225).

Tours by vehicle circuit 1 The shortest tour on the first circuit is to the Lawrence Spring via the Nabatean Temple and Rum; it takes about an hour (*JD25*). A tour to Khazali Canyon that includes the temple, Rum and the spring takes two hours (*JD35*), while a trip to the Sunset Sites via the temple, Rum, the spring and canyon takes a half hour or so longer (*JD44*). If you fancy visiting the sand dunes via the temple, Rum, the spring and canyon allow around 3½ hours (*JD51*). For a longer trip try the Um Fruth Rock Bridge tour that takes in the Nabatean Temple, Rum, the spring, Khazali Canyon, Little Bridge, the Anfashieh inscriptions and sand dunes over a four-hour period (*JD67*). The longest is a full-day excursion to Burrah Rock Bridge, when you will see the temple, Rum, the spring, Khazali Canyon, Little Bridge, the Um Fruth Rock Bridge, Burdah Rock Bridge and the Sunset Sites (*JD80*).

Tours by vehicle circuit 2 If you want a taster of the Wadi Rum experience you can opt for a tour by 4x4 jeep to the Alameleh inscriptions. It takes around an hour and covers 15km across the desert landscape (*JD25*). A slightly longer trip includes the Siq Lawrence and sand dunes (*JD35*). If you want to head off to the so-called Sunset Sites via the Siq, inscriptions and sand dunes, it will take about 2½ hours (*JD44*). A trip to the dramatic Burrah Canyon (Siq Burrah) via Alameleh, Um Ishrin, Lawrence's House and Siq Lawrence is a longer tour still, about three hours (*JD51*), or you could opt for a full day in the desert on the Burdah Rock Bridge tour, which takes in the dunes, Alameleh, Um Ishrin, Lawrence's House, Siq Lawrence, the Um Fruth Rock Bridge and the Sunset Sites (*JD80*).

Tours by camel from Rum You can take a half-hour ride to the Nabatean Temple (*JD4*), a 1½-hour ride to Lawrence Spring (*JD10*) or a five-hour ride to the sand dunes (*JD20*). If you fancy a longer ride still, with an overnight stay in a Bedouin tent, then why not opt for the Burdah Rock Bridge ride that stops awhile at the Lawrence Spring and the Khazali Canyon (*JD60*).

Wadi Rum is one of the 'must-see' places on earth, but thousands of visitors yearly have taken their toll on the fragile ecology of the desert. It is faced with a magnitude of natural environmental issues, compounded by wildlife hunters, the countless number of people hiking in the terrain and the damage caused by drivers in off-road vehicles. However, the authorities are keen for visitors to see its beauty and so have pioneered a programme of initiatives to help conserve the dwindling wildlife of the region. They have introduced organised routes for vehicles to follow so that the everyday lives of the local people are not affected and they've produced more informative publications for tourists so their knowledge of the desert, and in turn their obligations, are enhanced. In addition, the Protected Area is now patrolled by conservation rangers who ensure it is kept free from litter (a hazard for many species of animal and birdlife), and help to preserve the natural habitat needed for wildlife to thrive.

The guidelines that visitors are asked to follow for their own safety and to help protect the environment are:

• Take all litter away with you, burn toilet paper and bury human waste
• Drive your vehicle along or instruct your driver/guide to follow designated routes
• Do not hunt the animals, or remove or harm any of the fauna
• Avoid damaging trees and plants, and do not remove any of the flora
• Do not deface rock faces with graffiti, and do not remove rocks or any other artefacts
• When climbing, be sure to use the correct safety equipment but keep fixed gear to a minimum to prevent damage
• Set up camp in the designated camping area and use gas stoves or charcoal, not firewood, for fires
• Do not play loud music; it is distracting for animals, the local people who live in the desert, and for visitors keen to experience the absolute serenity of this wonderful place
• And for your safety, always follow the marked routes, take special care when descending from rock climbs, leave canyons if it rains as they may flood, take bottled water with you and inform the visitors' centre or a ranger of your plans while in the desert

Tours by camel from Alameleh From here you can take a two-hour trip to the Sunset Sites via the Alameleh inscriptions and the Siq Lawrence (*JD15*) or a longer, more leisurely ride to Siq Lawrence with a stop to see the Alameleh inscriptions (*JD20*). There's an overnight option too, with an open itinerary (*JD60*).

9

Aqaba

Telephone code: 03

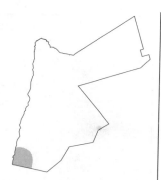

Cosmopolitan and historic, Aqaba is located along Jordan's much-prized coastline off the Gulf of Aqaba and is the country's only beach resort. As such, the many tourists who come here for the temperate climate, world-renowned diving and snorkelling, sandy beaches, historical sites, cosmopolitan restaurants and a taste of a lifestyle akin to the Mediterranean but with an Arabic twist, are joined by thousands of holidaying Jordanians. Many travel the 330km from the capital Amman. At around four hours' driving time away from the city, or a 45-minute hop by plane, it is understandable that Ammanis head south to the country's second city at every opportunity. Aqaba, which was chosen by the Arab Tourism Ministers Council as the Arab Tourism Capital in 2011 and is seen as a model world tourism city, bathes in brilliant sunshine most of the year, even in the winter months when Amman and the north is decidedly chilly. Average summer temperatures are around 39°C and in winter temperatures are around 21°C.

Aqaba is often referred to as part of the **Red Sea Oasis** with the nearby world-renowned attractions of Wadi Rum (see page 223) and the Nabatean city of Petra (see page 201). It is home to more than 103,000 people, a figure boosted by visitors from not just Jordan's cities but from around the world most months of the year. It is a popular holiday destination for visitors from the Middle East, Egypt and Europe, who can fly direct into its international airport, or fly via Amman. Along with the climate, a big attraction is its duty-free status, which makes shopping a delight. The city is referred to as the **Aqaba Special Economic Zone** (ASEZ), run by the Aqaba Special Economic Zone Authority (ASEZA). It is the capital of the Aqaba Governorate and, as the country's only seaport through which produce and goods (such as valuable phosphate) are exported, is an important Jordanian city.

Approach from the desert is via Al-Sharif Hussein bin Ali Street, which is a wide palm tree-lined dual-carriage boulevard that opens out into a huge space created by the richly planted Princess Haya Circle (roundabout) and runs beyond to meet the waterfront esplanade, King Hussein bin Talal Street (also known as the Corniche). To the right and ahead is the brand new multimillion-dinar waterfront development of Saraya al-Aqaba, with its lagoons, hotels and luxury homes. It is a welcoming access route to the city. Bright pink bougainvillea and white oleanders interspersed by olive trees, elegant public buildings, hotels and parks, plus the sea ahead, characterise your first glimpse of Aqaba city centre. Aqaba is a well-designed city, constantly lively but not overly full of cars; it has a relaxed feel. It also has one of the most idyllic views from the esplanade. From here you can see the mountains of Egypt's Sinai Peninsula ahead and the sprawling resort of Eilat in Israel off to your right.

The city is compact and easy to navigate, and offers lots for visitors to do and see. Spend time exploring the **Ayla Archaeological Park**, see the nearby 4th-century church, which is believed to be oldest known place of worship in the world, and

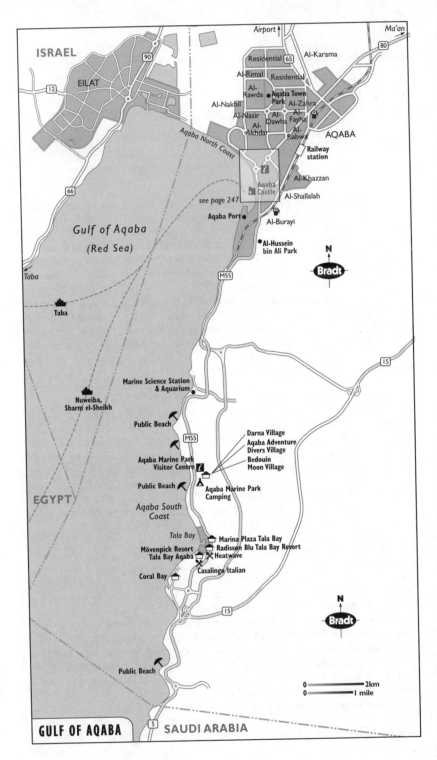

The Gulf of Aqaba is over 180km in length beginning at the Red Sea and the Straits of Tiran off Egypt's Sinai Peninsula and heading north to the point where the borders of Jordan, Egypt and Israel meet. At its widest, the gulf is 25km across. Technically, it is part of the much longer Great Rift Valley that extends from Mozambique in Africa to Syria in the north (see *Jordan Rift Valley and the Dead Sea* chapter, page 159). The gulf is a deep stretch of water rich in corals and biodiversity; in its central basin the depth plunges to over 1,850m. Its vast collection of fish and marine life, and its deep and interesting dive sites created by shipwrecks, sunken vessels and its coral ecosystem, combine to make the gulf one of the most popular diving and snorkelling destinations in the world.

Along with Jordan, Israel, Egypt and Saudi Arabia also have stretches of coastline lapped by the gulf's waters. The gulf lies to the east of Egypt's Sinai Peninsula and west of the Arabia mainland. Its northernmost coastline is dominated by the hotels and pristine beaches dotted with sun umbrellas of three cities; Eilat in Israel, Taba in Egypt and, of course, Jordan's Aqaba. A little further south lie the tourist resorts of Sharm el-Sheikh and Dahab on the Sinai Peninsula, and the quieter Haql in Saudi Arabia. The Gulf of Aqaba is one of two waterways that flow inland from the Red Sea; the other is the Gulf of Suez, which follows a course west of the Egypt's Sinai Peninsula heading north to the Egyptian city of Suez and the entrance to the Suez Canal.

head for the **Great Arab Revolt Plaza** on the other side of the city centre to really get a feel for Aqaba's history. In the plaza you'll find **Aqaba Castle**, dating from the Mamluk period, the city's fascinating archaeological museum, **Aqabawi Mosque**, the interesting **Noor al-Hussein Foundation** handicrafts centre and the **house of Sharif Hussein bin Ali**. Beyond this is the south coast, of which **Tala Bay** is one of the newest waterfront developments in Jordan with top international hotels and leisure amenities.

Aqaba is probably best known for its fantastic **diving and snorkelling**. In fact, it's a watersport enthusiast's dream. Here you can waterski, sail, fish and windsurf, as well as dive and snorkel. Aqaba is home to the world's northernmost coral reef ecosystem, which is made up of over 230 different types of soft and hard corals that teem with fish, crustaceans and mammals. Aqaba's waters are an official Protected Area (see *Aqaba Protected Area and Aqaba Marine Park*, page 263).

HISTORY

Aqaba has a turbulent past. It has been inhabited by prehistoric man, the Horites and Edomites of biblical times and the hard-working, progressive Nabateans, right through to the Romans and Byzantines, early Islamic caliphates, the Crusaders of the 12th century, the Mamluks, who built the city's landmark castle, and the Ottomans. It came under Arab control after the famous battle, the Arab Revolt of 1916–18. All have stamped their mark on Aqaba's captivating heritage.

EARLY HISTORY Extensive remains of human settlement and patches of the desert land used for agriculture, along with a whole raft of pottery fragments and primitive jewellery, have been discovered in and around Aqaba. They have been

Aqaba HISTORY

9

dated to the Chalcolithic (4500–3300BC), Bronze Age (3300–1200BC) and Iron Age (1200–539BC) periods. With its close proximity to neighbouring communities in present-day Israel and Egypt, the region was clearly considered strategic for trade and creating communities even in these early days.

In early biblical times, the coastal and inland areas are believed to have been inhabited by the Horites. They were a race of people described in length in many ancient Egyptian texts dating from as far back as around 1600BC and in the Hebrew Bible's Torah, otherwise known as the Five Books of Moses, as living in caves in southern Canaan. The historical territory of Canaan, which roughly covered the present-day southwestern regions of Jordan, along with Israel, Palestine and Lebanon, lay at the point where ancient Egypt met the Hittite Empire.

The Horites are said to have been a solitary people who survived by fishing and working the scant desert-like land, but were driven out of the region sometime before the biblical departure of the Israelites from ancient Egypt in an event known from the Hebrew Bible as the Exodus. Reference is made to Hori, who is thought to be one of the leaders of the Horites, and his and his people's departure from these lands. Where the Horites went or how long they survived is lost in time, but what is known is that they were the main predecessors of the Edomites, who established themselves in the region and founded one of the greatest kingdoms of biblical times.

According to the Old Testament's Book of Genesis (Genesis 36), the Edomites founded the kingdom of Edom, along with the biblical kingdoms of Moab and Ammon, which lay to its north. The stretch of coastline at present-day Aqaba was key to their infrastructure and was located within easy reach of the Edomite capital city Bozrah, near present-day Tafila. The port formed part of one of the busiest and most profitable trading routes of the time, which spanned from Egypt across Jordan to the Levant and Mediterranean. The Edomites traded in natural resources, which almost certainly included copper. One of their largest customers was the Egyptians, who used copper to make amulets that were routinely placed with mummified bodies in the belief that they would bring luck in the afterlife. The kingdom enjoyed fabulous wealth as a result.

Around this time the city that is now Aqaba is believed to have been called Elot – in the bible's Old Testament reference is made to King Soloman building a naval base at Ezion Geber, Elot – and then later become Ayla (which has been variously spelt as Aila or Aela). Over time the settlement was abandoned, only to be rebuilt some centuries later when the Romans came to power.

NABATEAN, ROMAN AND BYZANTINE ERAS (312BC–AD635) As the Nabateans became prominent in the land that is today southern Jordan, so the coastal port and settlement once again became a key part of their empire. This ancient Arab nomadic tribe from the Arabian Peninsula arrived in Jordan, or Transjordan as it was then known, after having established a number of ports along the gulf coast. They clearly identified what today we would describe as a niche in the market and decided to settle in the region. Petra – which lay at the exact spot where several major trading routes between Egypt, the Levant and Mediterranean, and further afield to China, India and southern Arabia, crossed – was established, with Aqaba providing access to the sea segment of the network. Most of the routes passed through the port.

The Nabateans took control of these valuable trade routes while in the Jordanian territory, and opened up Aqaba as a natural caravan stop for merchants arriving by boat or overland from Egypt. Gemstones were traded in quantity here, as were spices and silks, copper, textiles, gold, incense, frankincense and myrrh. The Nabateans, who derived phenomenal wealth as a result of controlling the port, as well as the routes, went down in history for their legacy of building public buildings, lavish palaces and tombs. Over time the Nabatean kingdom became absorbed into the Roman Empire as it expanded across to Arabia, and took control of the country.

The Romans' desire to enhance the infrastructure of the region meant that it saw a further period of development. It was during the Roman and subsequent Byzantine period that a small settlement believed to be the Ayla referred to in the Bible (1 Kings 9:26) was developed. The new city of Ayla became an important sea trading port and a caravanserai for travelling merchants along the King's Highway trade route, which by this time had been upgraded under the Roman Emperor Trajan and had become known as the Via Traiana Nova (see *King's Highway*, page 161). It stretched to Bosra in Syria, via Amman, which was a key provincial capital of the empire. The area continued to grow prosperous and in the 4th century Ayla became the garrison of the Roman legion Legio X Fretensis, otherwise known as the 'tenth legion of the sea strait'.

During Byzantine times, control of Ayla and its prosperous sea port was bestowed on Christian Arabs from south Arabia, who managed it on behalf of the country's rulers. Then it became a Byzantine bishopric and saw churches built, some of which still stand today. Over time, however, Ayla was abandoned, and either fell into ruins or became absorbed into new buildings. Parts of it can still be seen today, including, most notably, a building that because of its architecture and the fact that an altar table was discovered on the site is believed to have been a church. As it dates from the 3rd century to the early years of the 4th century, this small church is widely considered to be the world's oldest purpose-designed place of Christian worship discovered to date.

EARLY ARAB RULE, THE UMAYYAD, ABBASID AND FATIMID DYNASTIES

(AD636–1171) As the first Islamic caliphates came to power, so the port and the area surrounding it was again identified as a key facility of the empire. A period of development began, which continues to this day. In around AD650 a new city, also known as Ayla, was constructed by the early Arab caliph Uthman ibn Affan, also known as Othman (circa b579, d656), alongside the ruins of the ancient Ayla. The caliph's team of craftsmen used the ancient stones from the original settlement for much of the construction of the new city. The result was an impressive and expansive city that had the distinction of being the first to be built outside of the Arabian Peninsula's territory. The new Ayla was seen as a prosperous city. Its wealth came from the continued buoyant trade through the seaport and the fact that its reputation as a caravan stop had developed. Records also suggest that by this time Aqaba had become a stop on the pilgrimage route between Egypt and Makkah.

THE CRUSADERS, MAMLUKS AND OTTOMANS (1096–1917) The Aqaba region

was ruled by the Crusader state of the Kingdom of Jerusalem for much of the 12th century, and fortifications were constructed in abundance to defend their territories although few remain today. One of the fortresses was built on the island of Ile de Graye, which lies just off Egypt's Sinai Peninsula. Today, the island is known as Pharaoh's Island and lies in Egyptian waters. The 11th and 12th centuries were turbulent periods for Aqaba, still then Ayla. Saladin captured the region for a while (see *History*, page 20) and the fortress on the Ile de Graye became known as Saladin's Castle, but his power was short-lived after a furious battle erupted resulting in the infamous Crusader Reynald de Chatillon regaining control and seizing the stronghold.

When the Mamluks came to power in the 13th century, the whole region came under the new rulers' control and a programme of redevelopment for the coastal

For centuries Aqaba had been a thriving seaport, but under Ottoman rule and following of the opening of the Suez Canal in 1869 it was no longer the bustling place it once was. By the early 1900s it had become little more than an outpost to the Ottomans, who retained just a small military garrison presence here as a precaution against attack via the vulnerable Sinai Peninsula in Egypt. Unbeknown to the Ottomans, Arab Sharif Hussein bin Ali of Makkah (b1853, d1931), aggrieved at the increasingly nationalistic stance of the Ottoman Empire, was gathering his forces with the aim of securing independence for his people. He was backed by his sons, Ali bin Hussein, the eldest, who would become King of Hejaz (b1879, d1935); Abdullah bin al-Hussein, who would later become King Abdullah I of Jordan (b1882, d1951); and Faisal bin Hussein bin Ali al-Hashemi, who would become King Faisal I of Iraq and Syria (b1885, d1933).

By 1916 the Arab Revolt against the Ottomans was beginning. Among the first, not altogether successful, attacks on Ottoman garrisons were those in Medina and Makkah. In the meantime, French and British forces were already clearing Ottoman boats from the Red Sea. In June 1916, the French and British sent a team of officers to assist the Arabs, including Lieutenant Colonel Thomas Edward Lawrence, who was sent by the British Government in Cairo, Egypt. Lawrence, who famously became known as Lawrence of Arabia because of his writings and a subsequent film of the same name, was ordered into a liaison role. He is credited with persuading Abdullah and Faisal to redirect their forces into capturing Aqaba in line with the British strategy for conquering the Ottomans and removing the empire's forces from the region.

The first few months of 1917 saw Lawrence bring together a band of Arab Revolt forces that were mainly from the Bedouin Howeitat tribe led by Auda ibu Tayi. Abdullah and Faisal sent some of their men to assist Lawrence, who stationed themselves for a time in the Wadi Rum desert. A series of small battles between Turkish and Arab troops in the desert around Aqaba, which resulted in the deaths of several Arab soldiers, prompted Lawrence and Auda ibu Tayi to mount a full attack on the city on 6 July 1917. In the meantime, the British Royal Navy began shelling Aqaba in support of the Arab–British attack. Aqaba fell with little resistance. The Battle of Aqaba was heralded a success and meant that much-needed supplies of arms, and military support, could be transported through the seaport to the north where Faisal was still in battle with the Ottomans. Eventually, the Ottoman Empire crumbled and the region was returned to Arab rule.

port and its town began. It was around this time that Ayla became known as Aqaba, meaning 'alley', in reference to the narrow gorge created by the Wadi Yitm that was at one time a route into the city. One of the greatest projects undertaken by the Mamluks during their reign was the construction of Aqaba Castle in the 14th century on the site of a previous Crusader fortress.

When the Ottomans came to power in the 16th century, Aqaba's importance began to diminish. This was largely because the empire already had seaports of its own. The decline was compounded by the opening of the Suez Canal in 1869 when transporting goods via Aqaba's port and across land was no longer the most economical way to do things. However, nearly 400 years after the Ottomans took

Aqaba the city's fortunes changed dramatically. The Ottoman Empire's Sultan Abdul Hamid II (b1842, d1918) had decided to build a railway linking its capital Constantinople (present-day Istanbul) with the holy city of Makkah. It became known as the Hejaz Railway, and was officially opened in 1900. The plan was for it to pass through Amman, with a spur heading south to Aqaba. Although it was never completed in its entirety the spur to Aqaba was built and still carries freight across Jordan to this day.

MODERN HISTORY Ottoman rule came to an abrupt end after the Arab Revolt of 1916–18, which included the Battle of Aqaba (see box opposite). The revolt was initiated by Sharif Hussein bin Ali, and famously involved British Army officer TE Lawrence. The Arabs' success heralded a new era in Aqaba's history. It became part of the British Protectorate of Transjordan in 1925 and flourished under the Hashemite Kingdom of Transjordan, later Jordan. In 1965, the then king, King Hussein, having envisaged Aqaba to be the country's second capital city, sought a deal with neighbouring Saudi Arabia in order to facilitate expansion. In exchange for 6,000km² of desert, the Saudi Arabian authorities gave Jordan around 12km of coastline south of Aqaba. It meant that Aqaba's port and its leisure amenities could be developed.

In August 2000, His Majesty King Abdullah II declared Aqaba to be a free trade zone and vowed to invest billions of dinars in its infrastructure so as to attract foreign investment. The result has been a proliferation of new housing and industrial developments, shopping malls and the opening of new hotels and resorts. Two of its largest projects, the Tala Bay and Saraya al-Aqaba resorts, are being built to international quality standards with hotels, homes and state-of-the-art leisure amenities. The city is set to see its port moved and expanded, a brand new railway link to Jordan's major cities and its neighbouring countries of Syria, Iraq and Saudi Arabia, and a new marina. Aqaba's future looks rosy; its economic growth has surged and it now hosts major blue-chip companies from around the world. See also box, page 238.

GETTING THERE AND AWAY

BY AIR Aqaba is served by the **King Hussein International Airport** (\ *03 203 4010;* f *03 201 2397;* e *info@aac.jo; www.aac.jo*), which is somewhat compact but nonetheless receives thousands of travellers every week on flights arriving from around the Middle East, Egypt and many destinations in Europe. **Royal Jordanian** (\ *03 201 8633;* f *03 201 6555;* e *aqjtbrj@rj.com; www.rj.com*) operates scheduled, twice-daily flights (morning and early evening) between Amman and Aqaba, with a flight time of around just 45 minutes. Ticket prices can be as little as JD23 excluding tax. The airport lies around 9km to the north of the city, bordered by the Dead Sea Highway and less than ten minutes from its junction with Highway 15. You can get into the city centre in around 20 minutes by road. Taxis operate from the rank outside the terminal. Expect to pay around JD10 for a taxi journey into the centre.

AQABA'S AIRPORT

The King Hussein International Airport was opened in 1972 by King Hussein in a ceremony that heralded a new phase for the growing city of Aqaba. Then it comprised just a small apron and runway, fire station and a small passenger terminal. Although still not expansive, the airport has seen rapid development over the past 40 years and is now an important centre for the construction and maintenance of the country's light aircraft industry. Moreover, the complex includes training academies for companies such as Royal Jordanian and Ayla Aviation, and a private jet terminal. Scheduled and charter passengers passing through today will find a comfortable terminal overlooking the runway with an Aldeasea duty-free shop, a craft centre, café and banking services provided by Arab Bank Jordan. Aqaba Airport Car Rental (*www.aqabaairportcarrental.com*) can organise car hire with leading companies, including Europcar (*www.europcar.com*), Avis (*www.avis.com*), Alamo (*www.alamo.com*), National Car Rental (*www.nationalcar.com*) and Thrifty (*www.thrifty.com*), or you can contact these companies direct.

If you are making arrangements with a private taxi company, your guide and driver can wait for you right outside the terminal and you can be in Aqaba or on Highway 15 for onward travel to places such as Petra or Wadi Rum in minutes.

BY BOAT An alternative way to get to Jordan is by flying into Taba or Sharm el-Sheik on Egypt's Sinai peninsula, and then hopping aboard the **fast catamaran** from Taba's Taba Heights Marina to Aqaba's marina in Tala Bay, or the **ferries** from Nuweiba. The boat from Taba is operated by **Sindbad Xpress** (*Maysloon St, Aqaba;* \ *03 205 0077;* e *reservation1@sindbadjo.com; www.sindbadjo.com*). It leaves Taba early morning; usually around 07.00 with an immediate return from Aqaba, but check the most up-to-date departure times the day before as they can vary according to the season and the weather. Additional departure times are occasionally introduced. The boat arrives at the marina, which is around a ten-minute drive out of the city centre, some 25 minutes later. From here you can get a taxi into the centre from around JD10. The ferries between Nuweiba run several times a day and pull into the ferry terminal, which lies a few kilometres south of the city centre. Luxury fast vessels are run by **Arab Bridge Maritime Company** (*Aqaba head office:* \ *03 209 2000;* f *03 209 2001; Passenger Terminal:* \ *03 201 3236;* f *03 203 3846;* e *info@abmaritime.com.jo; www.abmaritime.com.jo*) twice daily between Aqaba and Nuweiba. For times and prices of ferries see *Practical Information* chapter, page 52. Taxis can usually be found in number right outside the terminal entrance. Expect to pay JD6; less if you're sharing. The formalities when arriving from Egypt are straightforward and you will be given a free Aqaba Special Economic Zone Authority (ASEZA) visa (see *Red Tape*, page 45). There are no sea routes from Israel or Saudi Arabia.

BY TAXI OR BUS You can hire **taxis** from the Arava border crossing with Israel into the city centre for around JD8 or *serveeces* taxis for JD1 to JD2. If you are arriving into Aqaba from Petra, which is around 113km away, expect to pay around JD35 to JD40. From Wadi Rum, which will take around 40 minutes, the taxi fare is likely to be around JD25. Amman is a four-hour drive away and so a taxi fare is likely to exceed JD100. It's a good idea to negotiate with your taxi company for the best rate ahead of your journey. **Buses** are a cheaper option, and run non-stop or with stops *en route* at major destinations, such as Petra and the highway village of Rashidiyya (locally Ar-Rashidiyya) near Wadi Rum, between the Abdali bus station in Amman and Aqaba several times a day. They tend to start at 07.00, running throughout the day until early evening. The fast buses are run by the **Jordan Express Tourist Transport Company** (JETT) (*Head office: 7th Circle, Amman;* \ *06 585 4679;* f *06 585 4176; www.jett.com.jo; in Aqaba: Al-Nahda St;* \ *03 201 5222*) and pull into the bus station between Al-Nahda Street and King Hussein bin Talal Street (also known as the Corniche) in Aqaba. Find it close to the Mövenpick Hotel. The fare from Amman to Aqaba is currently JD7.500. Local company **Al-Motahedah Bus company** (\ *03 201 8005*) runs five trips a day to Amman with a ticket cost of JD5, while **Trust International Transport** (\ *03 203 2300*) operates buses from Aqaba to Amman daily too; they pull in and out of their complex on An-Nahda Street in the city centre and cost JD7.

BY CAR Travelling to Aqaba from anywhere in Jordan is straightforward; simply follow the Dead Sea Highway if you wish to hug the valley, the Desert Highway from Amman or the King's Highway if you plan to make a few stops at towns along the way. The Desert Highway (Highway 15) has junctions along its length if you are coming from places like Petra, Wadi Rum or Karak.

On arrival at the Aqaba Special Economic Zone (ASEZ) by air, highway, border crossings or by boat into the port you need to be aware of visa and customs rules, which are quite different to the rest of Jordan. You will be given a free visa valid for one month, and should you wish to extend your stay you will need to do so at the Aqaba Special Economic Zone Authority (ASEZA) office in Aqaba (✆ 03 209 1000). Unlike ordinary visas, the ASEZ visa cannot be extended at police stations. The offices are a little difficult to find, although taxi drivers tend to know how to find them, and opening times can vary – give the office a call before making the journey. Failure to renew will result in fees and fines to pay. This is something to remember if you are arriving in Aqaba but intending to travel around Jordan for longer than a month, as you will need to return to Aqaba to renew your visa.

An alternative is to ask for a normal visa on arrival in Aqaba, which is the same as you would receive at, for example, Amman's airport. You will be charged for a normal visa (currently JD20) and these can be renewed at any police station. It is also worth remembering that the free ASEZ visa expires when you leave Jordan unlike the normal visa, which will remain valid for its duration, so if you are intending to cross borders and re-enter Jordan one or more times then you may feel a normal visa is better for you.

As regards customs rules, on arrival in Aqaba you need to declare any goods that may be subject to tax when you depart, such as electrical items, alcohol or cigarettes. This can be done at checkpoints located at arrival points. The duty-free allowance is 200 cigarettes and one litre of alcohol purchased in the zone, and anything above this should be declared.

As you approach Aqaba, you will go through a checkpoint that marks the boundary of the Aqaba Special Economic Zone. From here you simply continue along the highway and follow signs into the city centre along wide, tree-lined boulevards, such as Al-Sharif Hussein bin Ali Street. Eventually you will join King Hussein bin Talal Street, otherwise known as the Corniche, which lies alongside the Gulf of Aqaba's waters and is where most of the hotels are located. The city's North Beach will be off to your right, while the Great Arab Revolt Plaza, the port, ferry terminal and the south coast will be to your left. Aqaba has an abundance of petrol stations. There are at least two on the approach road after you have gone through the checkpoint, and many others dotted around town. Prices vary but on average are around JD0.795 a litre.

GETTING AROUND

BY TAXI You will see the lime **green taxis** with delightful pictures of camels running along their length buzzing around Aqaba at all hours. They can be flagged down easily or you can head for the taxi ranks found in King Hussein bin Talal Street opposite the marina, or at the entrance to Ayla Archaeological Park. All the hotels supply numbers and will assist you in making a taxi booking. Typically, a fare around town will be JD1 to JD2, to the ferry terminal around JD6 and to the south coast around JD7 to JD10. If you plan to take a taxi from Aqaba to Petra expect to pay around JD35 to JD40. White *serveece* taxis are the cheaper alternative and tend to congregate around the bus stations serving your destination (see below). These are shared taxis, depart when full and will cost you less than JD1 depending on your destination.

BY BUS Aqaba has several bus stations. Its central bus station, located right near the shops, is off King Hussein bin Talal Street and is used by fast **intercity** buses. The other bus stations serve specific destinations or local routes. For example, if you wish to take a bus to Petra or Wadi Rum you'll need the bus station near King Talal Street, and if you are making for Karak or Tafila then you'll need the Al-Humayma Street bus station. Local buses arrive and depart from the station next to Princess Salma Park and the one at Petra Street.

The tourist information office off Ayla Square, opposite the marina, has comprehensive timetables with details on where to board the bus appropriate for your destination. Along with the buses, another good way to get around town is by **minibus**; they run constantly during the morning then less frequently as the day progresses, and are inexpensive. They operate from the stations, as well as places of interest, such as along the south coast, North Beach and the Ayla Archaeological Park.

BY CAR Getting around Aqaba by car couldn't be easier. Its grid-like road system is easy to follow, well signposted and almost all roads lead to the sea. The city has numerous petrol stations and car parks, plus most of the hotels have their own parking facilities. If you've arrived in Aqaba by air, bus or taxi, and wish to hire a car, then most of the world's leading **car-hire** companies have offices in Aqaba city centre or in the major hotels, and there are some at the border crossing.

Car rental companies in Aqaba

🚗 **Alamo** Al-Nahda St; ✆03 205 8800; www.alamo.com

🚗 **Avis** Korneash St; ✆03 202 2883; www.avis.com

🚗 **Captain's Rent a Car** Al-Nahda St; ✆03 206 0710; www.captains.jo

🚗 **Europcar** Al-Nahda St; ✆03 203 0044; www.europcar.com

🚗 **National Car Rental** Al-Nahda St; ✆03 205 8800; www.nationalcar.com

🚗 **Thrifty** 350 Al-Rashid St; ✆03 203 0313; www.thrifty.com

BY FOOT An alternative if you don't fancy driving is to explore the city on foot. Aqaba is compact and all its main attractions and shops are located off King Hussein bin Talal Street (the Corniche). It will only take you about 30 minutes to walk from North Beach to the Great Arab Revolt Plaza and Aqaba Castle.

TOURIST INFORMATION

ℹ️ **Aqaba Special Economic Zone Authority** ✆03 209 1000; f 03 209 1052; www.aqabazone.com

ℹ️ **Aqaba Tourist Information Centre** Al-Hammamat al-Tunisyya St, Aqaba; ✆03 203 5360; f 03 209 1052; e info@aqaba.jo; www.aqaba.jo; ⏱ 08.00–18.00 daily

ℹ️ **Aqaba Visitors' Centre** Aqaba Fort, Waterfront; ✆03 201 3731; ⏱ 08.00–16.00 Wed–Mon

TOUR OPERATORS

Aqaba Sky Travel Agency Al-Rashid St; ✆03 205 0103; f 03 205 0102; e info@aqabasky.com; www.aqabasky.com. Tours around Aqaba & to places like Amman & the Dead Sea, or combination tours will allow you to see the Holy Lands in its entirety.

Nyazi ECO Tours Abdullah Ghosheh St; ✆06 581 5910; f 06 581 5902; e info@nyazi.com.jo; www.nyazi.com.jo. Organiser of tours from Aqaba to the Dead Sea, Petra, Wadi Rum & further afield, along with jeep safaris, camel caravan tours & hiking.

9

Aqaba not only attracts Jordanian visitors and tourists from around the world, but also business and conference organisers. As such, it has seen a growing number of top-name international hotels built over the last few years; and there are lots more planned. There's a mix of four- and five-star hotels with luxury features that include gourmet dining, spa and fitness centres, and leisure facilities such as watersports and tennis courts, as well as a collection of budget hotels, eco establishments and a campsite right on the beach operated by the Aqaba Marine Park (📞 *03 2032 5801*). Most can be found in the beachside areas close to the city centre, but there are further hotels being built in Tala Bay on the south coast and brand new developments just along the coast from the Ayla Archaeological Park (see page 262).

LUXURY

🏠 **Intercontinental Aqaba Resort** (250 rooms) King Hussein bin Talal St; 📞 03 209 2222; f 03 209 3320; e info@icaqaba.com; www. intercontinental.com. A 5-star hotel set around palm tree-filled gardens & with one of the longest swimming pools in Jordan, this beachside hotel oozes luxury. It is elegant & relaxed. Within the complex is a spa complex that uses Dead Sea minerals in its treatments & a fitness centre, while its rooms come complete with Wi-Fi, satellite TV & AC. **$$$$$**

🏠 **Kempinski Hotel Aqaba Red Sea** (201 rooms) King Hussein bin Talal St; 📞 03 209 0888; f 03 209 0880; e info@kempinski.com; www. kempinski.com/aqaba. This super stylish hotel sits right on the seafront with every one of its contemporary-decorated guestrooms affording great views across to Egypt. The building's design is curved, a feature you'll notice the moment you step into the lavish foyer. On site are a health centre & gym, plus a whole host of bars & restaurants. **$$$$$**

🏠 **Mövenpick Resort & Residences** (296 rooms) King Hussein bin Talal St; 📞 03 203 4020; f 03 203 4040; e resort.aqaba@moevenpick.com; www.moevenpick-hotels.com. Housed in a striking contemporary building on the shores of the Gulf of Aqaba & close to the city centre, the hotel boasts a private beach, gourmet restaurants & a health club. Children have their own Dana Club, too. Guestrooms are luxurious & well equipped with AC & Wi-Fi. A guests' shuttle bus runs between the hotel & its sister hotel in Tala Bay. **$$$$$**

UPMARKET

🏠 **Aqaba Gulf Hotel** (200 rooms) King Hussein bin Talal St; 📞 03 201 6636; e info@ aqabagulf.com; www.aqabagulf.com. A floodlit tennis court, watersports & swimming in a freshwater pool are just some of the leisure amenities offered at this landmark 4-star seafront hotel. Its pleasing guestrooms are well equipped with high-speed internet, while within the complex is a restaurant & coffee shop serving delicious local pastries. **$$$$**

🏠 **Golden Tulip Aqaba** (80 rooms) Al Saada St; 📞 03 205 1234, f 03 205 1237; e info@ goldentulipaqaba.com; www.goldentulip. com. Part of a chain & popular with families & business travellers, this contemporary hotel is a 5min walk or so from the beach in the heart of the city centre. Amenities include babysitting & a nursery, restaurant, business centre & a cosy lounge bar. Its temperature-controlled rooms are stylish & comfortable. **$$$$**

🏠 **Marina Plaza Tala Bay Hotel** (260 rooms) South Beach Rd, Tala Bay; 📞 03 206 2900; f 03 206 2904; e reservations.marina@marinaplaza. com; www.marinaplaza.com. Guestrooms at this Tala Bay hotel have a designer feel with touches like fluffy towels & quality furnishings. Views are of the hotel's pools or the bay's marina. On site are restaurants, a children's playground, gym & a centre offering most watersports from jet-skiing to banana boat rides. **$$$$**

🏠 **Mövenpick Resort Tala Bay Aqaba** (306 rooms) South Beach Rd, Tala Bay; 📞 03 209 0300; f 03 209 0301; e resort.aqaba.talabay@ moevenpick.com; www.moevenpick-hotels. com. One of the newest hotel resorts in Aqaba, this eco-friendly hotel is located in Tala Bay. It offers contemporary-styled guestrooms with all the amenities you would expect of a top-quality hotel, along with restaurants, bars & a nightclub. On site is a Zara Spa & a fitness suite, plus a

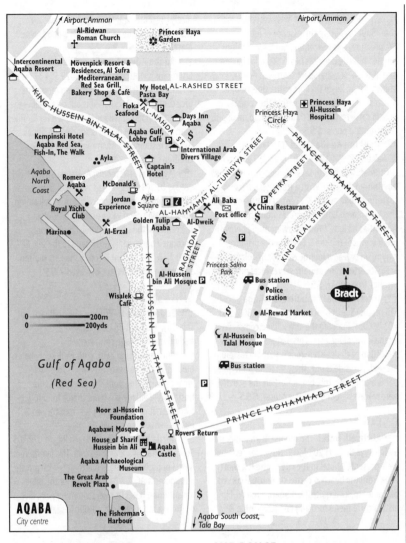

AQABA
City centre

children's activity centre. The hotel is run as a
model in sustainable tourism. **$$$$**

🏠 **Radisson Blu Tala Bay Resort** (386
rooms) South Beach Rd, Tala Bay; ☎ 03 209
0777; f 03 209 0799; e info.talabay.aqaba@
radissonblu.com; www.radissonblu.com. Located
in the new resort of Tala Bay, right on the
seafront, this top-notch hotel offers luxurious
surroundings, gourmet dining & lots of activities,
including watersports. Guestrooms are presented
in neutral colours with accents & have free Wi-Fi
& flatscreen TVs. Rooms suitable for wheelchair
users are available. **$$$$**

MID RANGE

🏠 **Captain's Hotel** Al-Nahda St; ☎ 03 206
0710; f 03 206 0717; e sales@captains.jo; www.
captains.jo. Located right in the city centre within
walking distance of the Ayla Archaeological Park &
the Corniche, this hotel is welcoming, comfortable
& good value for money. Its guestrooms have
a 'designer' feel & have Wi-Fi & AC. Within the
complex is a health suite, the Bab Al-Mandeb
rooftop café, a restaurant & an *agreeleh* terrace,
complete with Bedouin furnishings. **$$$**

🏠 **Coral Bay Hotel** (69 rooms) Aqaba South
Coast Rd; ☎ 03 201 5555; f 03 210 7097;

e reservations@coralbay.jo; www.coralbayaqaba. com. Built to capture the essence of local architecture, this welcoming hotel stands right on the water's edge. It is best known for having one of the best watersport centres in Aqaba, known as the Royal Diving Centre. Guestrooms are fresh & modern, while within the complex is an à la carte restaurant, traditional Jordanian pub & swimming pools. **$$$**

🏠 **Days Inn Aqaba Hotel** (110 rooms) Al-Sa'adeh St: 📞 03 203 1901; **f** 03 203 2982; **e** Othman.salameen@saysinn-aqaba.com; www. daysinn-aqaba.com. With a traditional décor featuring stone pillars & a central courtyard, this welcoming hotel is minutes from the beach. Amenities include a rooftop swimming pool with great views of the sea & Egypt in the distance, a gym, an *argeeleh* lounge & children's play area. Its Artemis restaurant serves local dishes & alcohol-free drinks. **$$$**

🏠 **International Arab Divers Village** (16 rooms) South Beach Rd; 📞 03 203 1808; **f** 03 203 0560; **e** info@aqaba-divevillage.com; www. aqaba-divevillage.com. This 4-star village has a collection of chalet-style rooms that are tastefully presented, inside & out. There's a restaurant, juice bar & a campsite, too, but almost all the activity here revolves around the dive centre. **$$$**

BUDGET

🏠 **Al-Dweik Hotel** (56 rooms) Al-Hammamat al-Tunisyya St; 📞 03 203 5919. This older style but well-presented hotel in the city centre is a short walk from the beach & castle. Its unusual curved balconies make it quite a landmark. Free Wi-Fi, an à la carte menu focusing on local cuisine &

nicely presented guestrooms with views across the rooftops to the sea make this a good value place to stay. **$$**

🏠 **Aqaba Adventure Divers Village** (20 rooms) South Beach Rd; **m** 079 584 3724; www.aqaba-diving.com. Revolving around its dive centre & daily excursions out on & below the water, this popular village is designed for families with an interest in diving & snorkelling. It has its own restaurant & swimming pool, bar & a children's play area. **$$**

🏠 **My Hotel** (62 rooms) Al-Nahda St; 📞 03 203 0893; **f** 03 203 0893; **e** eyad@myhotel-jordan.com; www.myhotel-jordan.com. A warm & welcoming hotel offering good value accommodation in the centre of the city, My Hotel has pleasingly decorated guestrooms with views to the sea, AC & Wi-Fi, & a restaurant & coffee shop. Its rooftop swimming pool & terrace is heavenly. **$$**

SHOESTRING

🏠 **Bedouin Moon Village** South Beach Rd, Tala Bay; 📞 03 201 5525; **e** info@ bedouinmoonvillage.com; www. bedouinmoonvillage.com. With well-kept chalets built in streets so as to resemble a Jordanian village, swimming pool & a restaurant, this hostel-style village is a good choice for budget travellers. It is located minutes from the sea & has its own diving school. **$**

🏠 **Darna Village** South Beach Rd; **m** 079 503 5696; **e** daranvillage@gmail.com. This family-run hostel opposite the beach has chalets with private bathrooms & AC, & a Bedouin tent for the more adventurous. It has its own swimming pool, dive centre & a restaurant specialising in seafood. **$**

✖ WHERE TO EAT

Whether your tastebuds are satisfied with spicy Arabic, Middle Eastern or Thai dishes, or you prefer subtle Chinese, tasty steaks, Italian pasta or a touch of à la carte French cuisine then you will be spoilt for choice in Aqaba. While the city is only bordering on being a multi-cultural place, it does attract visitors from around the world and, as such, a burgeoning number of street and hotel eateries have emerged in recent years. Many specialise in fish, as befits a coastal place, but don't be fooled into thinking that it all comes fresh out of the Red Sea. A lot of the fish offered on menus is imported from Arabia and kept frozen, but the local Jordanians do seem to have a knack of preparing and cooking it well, so you shouldn't go far wrong. The Jordanian dish *mensaf* (lamb cooked in a yoghurt sauce) and the Lebanese dish *sayyadieh* (fish cooked in a spicy fish broth) can usually be found on most menus. Both are served with rice and are tasty.

EXPENSIVE

✘ **Al Sufra Mediterranean Restaurant & Terrace** Mövenpick Resort & Residences, King Hussein bin Talal St; ☎ 03 203 4020; www.moevenpick-hotels.com; ⊕ 18.30–24.00 daily. Enjoy a tasty selection of Mediterranean-style dishes, including seafood, grills & pasta, with fine wines from the region in this elegant restaurant. Dine inside or on a covered terrace overlooking the sea. $$$$$

✘ **Casalingo Italian** Mövenpick Resort Tala Bay Aqaba, South Beach Rd, Tala Bay; ☎ 03 209 0300; www.moevenpick-hotels.com; ⊕ 18.30–23.30 daily. With a neutral décor & refined white linens, this upmarket restaurant makes dining special. It specialises in à la carte Italian cuisine. A live cooking centre complete with a wood-fired oven where fresh 'gourmet' pizzas are prepared & cooked is entertaining. Fine wines are from the regions of Italy. $$$$$

✘ **Romero Aqaba** Royal Yacht Club, King Hussein bin Talal St; ☎ 03 202 2464; www.romero-jordan.com; ⊕ 12.00–15.00 &18.00–23.00. The seafood prepared with creativity & a great use of herbs & spices is some of the best you're likely to find in Aqaba. Try the *pasta marinara*, which is creamy dish of white fish & pasta, or the risotto made with smoked salmon with a chilled bottle of Italian white wine – delicious. The view from the restaurant is fabulous & looks out over the sea. $$$$$

ABOVE AVERAGE

✘ **Ali Baba** Corner of Raghadan St & Hammamat al-Tunisyya St; ☎ 03 201 3901; ⊕ 07.00–23.30 daily. One of the landmark eateries of Aqaba, but a bit touristy, the Ali Baba specialises in fish & seafood. Look carefully & you'll see a selection of the day's catch in a tank near the bar. International-style steaks & burgers, plus a full range of Lebanese mezze dishes & *sayyadieh* are alternative options. An interesting feature are the shell-covered glass tables. $$$$

✘ **Fish-In** Kempinski Hotel Aqaba Red Sea, King Hussein bin Talal St; ☎ 03 209 0888; www.kempinski.com/aqaba; ⊕ 19.00–23.00 daily. Chic & contemporary, the Fish-In is perfect if you want to dress up for a special meal, especially if fish is your passion. Seared sea scallops with tomato salsa is among the appetizers, with the restaurant's signature dish

Hamour Clay Pot, which is a delicious mix of fish & herbs, being one of the mains. $$$$

✘ **Floka Seafood** Al-Nahda St; ☎ 03 201 0860; ⊕ 18.00–23.00 daily. A fish restaurant with silver snapper, sea bream & grouper among the dishes cooked most days, usually to perfection, Floka isn't just a place to eat but a whole dining experience. The menu is lengthy with some local dishes like *mensaf* & international-style grills & pasta. Sit indoors or dine alfresco in its garden. $$$$

✘ **Heatwave** Radisson Blu Tala Bay Resort, South Beach Rd, Tala Bay; ☎ 03 209 0777; www.radissonblu.com; ⊕ 19.00–03.00 daily. Elegant & contemporary, Heatwave serves international dishes accompanied by nightly entertainment. You can select homemade ravioli or pizzas straight from the wood-fired oven, tandoori dishes, Thai curries & fish from the wok, or a selection of grills. $$$$

✘ **Red Sea Grill** Mövenpick Resort & Residences, King Hussein bin Talal St; ☎ 03 203 4020; www.moevenpick-hotels.com; ⊕ 19.00–24.00 daily. Innovative fish & seafood dishes are served with spicy crusts & sauces inspired by Afro-Arab cuisine at this informal yet chic eatery. It is surrounded by palm trees & looks out over the Gulf. $$$$

MID RANGE

✘ **Al-Erzal Restaurant** The Gateway, Ayla Circle; ☎ 03 201 3733; ⊕ 11.00–22.00 daily. This stylish restaurant inside the entertainment complex serves authentic Lebanese dishes. Its specialty is *sayyadieh*, which it serves in highly patterned bowls. Also recommended is the *lebaneh* (yoghurt with garlic & mint), *zagaleel hamam* (pigeon in a tarragon sauce) & its BBQ meats. $$$

✘ **China Restaurant** Al-Batra St (Petra St); ☎ 03 201 4415; ⊕ 11.00–15.30 & 18.30–23.00. One of the longest established Oriental eateries in Aqaba & something of an institution, this cosy restaurant has a reputation for great authentic food prepared & cooked by its Chinese chef & his team. Vegetarian options are plentiful, plus there are around 30 different meat & seafood dishes to choose from. The tangy lemon chicken comes highly recommended. $$$

✘ **Rovers Return** King Hussein bin Talal St; ☎ 03 203 2030; www.roversreturnjordan.com. Housed in a building with a modern take on a traditional castle, this lively British pub is decorated to resemble the set of *Coronation*

Street. Memorabilia from the series line its walls. The Rovers Return serves an extensive collection of appetizers such as wedges & spring rolls, & main courses of fish platters, curries & chicken or steak with chips accompanied, of course, by chilled beer. $$$

✗ **The Walk** Kempinski Hotel Aqaba Red Sea, King Hussein bin Talal St; ☏ 03 209 0888; www. kempinski.com/aqaba; ⊕ 10.00–sunset. A stylish yet informal daytime beachside eatery, The Walk specialises in local & international salads (think Jordanian *tabbouleh*, Caesar & Greek), sandwiches, pasta dishes & pizzas, for which you can choose your own toppings. Beverages include shakers & shooters, cocktails, wines & juices. $$$

CHEAP AND CHEERFUL

✗ **Bakery Shop & Café** Mövenpick Resort & Residences, King Hussein bin Talal St; ☏ 03 203 4020; www.moevenpick-hotels.com; ⊕ 08.00–23.00 daily. Located along the busy Corniche within the Mövenpick complex, this classical-style bakery serves a raft of pastries & cakes, along with ice cream in a seemingly endless range of flavours. The creamy pistachio is recommended. You can eat in or take away. $$

✗ **Lobby Café** Aqaba Gulf Hotel, King Hussein bin Talal St; ☏ 03 201 6636; ⊕ 10.00–24.00 daily.

Elegantly decorated & offering tea, coffee, soft drinks, local wines & light snacks, this café is a popular place with locals to meet up with friends. Live piano music is played most evenings. $$

✗ **Pasta Bay** Al-Nahda St; ☏ 03 203 0893; www.myhotel-jordan.com. Contemporary with glass block walls & bright blue seating, Pasta Bar is one of the city's newest eateries. Here you can find an innovative menu of pasta dishes & pizzas with a choice of topping. It's inexpensive, informal & a fun place. $$

ROCK BOTTOM

✗ **McDonald's** The Gateway, Ayla Circle; ☏ 03 203 0330; ⊕ 10.00–24.00 daily. Known the world over for its fast, tasty & informal meals, the added benefit of the Aqaba branch of McDonald's inside the Gateway entertainment complex is the Arabic twist it applies to its burgers. $

✗ **Wisalek Café** King Hussein bin Talal St; ☏ 03 202 2600; ⊕ 12.00–23.00 daily. This is one of several small, lively cafés found along the waterfront stretch where you can get an inexpensive regular or fruit tea, coffee or milkshake. Sandwiches & toasties are served, & if you fancy trying some of the local elastic non-melting ice cream here's the place to do it. $

ENTERTAINMENT AND NIGHTLIFE

BARS AND TEA HOUSES Aqaba has a handful of smaller tea houses and coffee shops, but in the main these are located within the shopping malls or hotels. Some are hugely successful in creating a traditional Jordanian feel, complete with Bedouin-style seating and water-pipes. In Aqaba, smoking on *argeeleh* water-pipes has acquired a modern twist; here tobacco is often flavoured with fruits, such as cherry or apple.

♀ **Abu Nawwas Fun Pub** Mövenpick Resort & Residences, King Hussein bin Talal St; ☏ 03 203 4020; www.moevenpick-hotels.com; ⊕ 20.00–24.00 daily. A popular haunt of locals as well as guests of the hotel, this lively nightspot has live music & belly dancing shows every evening. Pub-style drinks & snacks are served, plus there's a lengthy menu of cocktails.

♀ **Black Pearl Fish-In** Kempinski Hotel Aqaba Red Sea, King Hussein bin Talal St; ☏ 03 209 0888; f 03 209 0880; ⊕ 18.00–01.00. You can while the evening away in this stylish bar lounge with its big comfy sofas & a dancefloor

for the energetic. A menu of cocktails will tempt you with mojitos & martinis, or try some local chardonnay or shiraz wine, beer or juices.

♀ **Coral Bay** Coral Bay Hotel, Aqaba South Coast Rd; ☏ 03 201 5555; www.coralbayaqaba.com; ⊕ 18.00–23.00 daily. Styled on a traditional Jordanian pub with alcoves & dark furniture & furnishings, this lounge bar is full of atmosphere. A range of teas & coffees are served, along with juices, local wines, spirits & snacks.

♀ **Kenzi Lounge** Radisson Blu Tala Bay Resort, South Beach Rd, Tala Bay; ☏ 03 209 0777; www. radissonblu.com; ⊕ 08.00–01.00 daily. With a reputation as a local meeting place, the Kenzi Lounge has a good range of blended & mint teas & coffees, juices, cognacs & exclusive cigars. Snacks & salads are served. The cocktail menu tempts with offerings like Caramel Martini.

♀ **Mello Chill Out Bar** Mövenpick Resort Tala Bay Aqaba, South Beach Rd; ☎ 03 209 0300; www.moevenpick-hotels.com; ⊕ 17.00–01.00 daily. Pre-dinner drinks or a relaxing evening with friends can be achieved rather effortlessly in this bar. It is dark & moody with rich purple walls & soft furnishings. Wines & champagnes are served, along with a collection of cognacs. You can watch as entertaining bartenders mix cocktails.

♀ **Rum Bar** Aqaba Gulf Hotel, King Hussein bin Talal St; ☎ 03 201 6636; www.aqabagulf.com; ⊕ 17.00–24.00 daily. With its deep wooden bar & wall panels, & accent red for seating & carpet, this is a cosy bar within the seafront Aqaba Gulf Hotel. A cocktail menu with a nightly special is available, along with wines, spirits, soft drinks & light snacks.

♀ **Siraj Arguilah Terrace & Lounge** Mövenpick Resort Tala Bay Aqaba, South Beach Rd; ☎ 03 209 0300; www.moevenpick-hotels. com; ⊕ 17.00–01.00 daily. Live music & belly dancing shows, & an assortment of finger foods, teas & colourful cocktails are served up nightly in this lively lounge bar. The décor is a vibrant burnt orange & there's a terrace overlooking the sea.

NIGHTLIFE Most of Aqaba's nightlife revolves around its hotels and resorts, where you'll find a choice of nightclubs, bars and discos. For more authentic Jordanian music and traditional folkloric dances performed by local dance troupes head for the Souk by the Sea or look out for special events that happen periodically in and around the city.

Souk by the Sea Al-Nahda St. Every Fri evening a terrace beside the Captain's Hotel is transformed into a lively souk from 18.00 onwards. You just have time to browse the stalls full of handicrafts before a troupe of local dancers accompanied by musicians take to the inner 'stage' & perform time-honoured traditional dances at 19.30. Children's activities are provided. The outdoor market, which continues on to around 23.00, is a community development project founded to generate revenue for the Aqaba people.

SHOPPING

Aqaba enjoys a duty-free status and as such prices are considerably lower than elsewhere in Jordan. People from Wadi Rum and Petra, and even Amman, come here to shop for electrical items, fashions and consumables such as alcohol and food, but strictly speaking you are obliged to pay the duty if you are leaving the Aqaba region through the checkpoints that exist on the highways. It is fair to say that if your purchases are clearly for your own use, and you are not buying large quantities for resale, then you will probably not be asked to pay any duty. The exception is electrical items, which you will almost certainly be charged duty on.

One of the best ways to find authentic local goods is to visit a souk. The best and busiest is the **Aqaba Souk** and the **Al-Hamaymah Street Souk**, which can be found just inland from the seafront along Zahran Street. Here, locals and visitors mingle and haggle for anything from Aqaba blankets, which are much sought-after throughout the country, to rugs and Bedouin jewellery at stalls that line the street. You can usually find stallholders setting up early in the morning, and packing up around 21.00 in winter or midnight in the summer months. Here, too, you will see craftspeople at work filling little bottles with coloured sand, and creating pictures from it and even your name. For more traditional handicrafts that have been carefully made by local craftspeople head to the Great Arab Revolt Plaza where you'll find the **Noor al-Hussein Foundation** (see *Noor al-Hussein Foundation*, page 262).

The **Gateway** entertainment centre (*Ayla Circle, next to the Royal Yacht Club;* ☏ *03 201 2200*) is the city's largest retail and leisure complex. Here you will find stores selling everything from jewellery and the latest fashions to household items, along with restaurants, coffee shops and a large multimedia experience-style cinema. On Saturdays you can join locals in visiting the Gateway centre's **bazaar** (☏ *03 202 2200;* ⊕ *11.00–21.00*). It's a real experience, and as Jordanians are such a friendly people you'll be sure to have lots of conversations.

Artisans and artists come to the Gateway bazaar every week; most are from Aqaba, others from further afield places such as Wadi Rum. You will see brightly coloured ceramic bowls and jugs, glass lamps, water-pipes, jewellery steeped in Bedouin tradition, antiques and paintings. You could easily spend a day here browsing and, as there's a nice little restaurant where you can get a *falafel* or two and salad, or fast food like donuts at Spongy Donuts or burgers at McDonalds, it's a great way to spend a Saturday.

Aqaba has a growing number of shopping malls where you'll find several floors of fashions, household items and electronic goods. The **Zena Mall** (☏ *03 201 5000*) can be found in the city centre on the corner of Raghadan Street and Hammamat al-Tunisyya Street, while the **Dream Mall** (☏ *03 205 1711*) is at the Princess Haya Circle and the **Shweikh Mall** (☏ *03 201 3051*) can be found in Tareq ben Ziad Street. Most have a supermarket for day-to-day essentials, or you could try the **Safeway** (☏ *03 203 4950*) complex in Iben Zaidoun Street. All the malls have a selection of coffee and snack bars.

SPORTS AND OTHER ACTIVITIES

Aqaba is a sports enthusiast's dream. Whether your thing is action sports like skydiving or your visit to Aqaba is planned to revolve solely around its fabulous diving and snorkelling opportunities, then the city will not disappoint.

SPAS As Aqaba sees a growing number of luxury hotels and resorts opening up, the number of spas is steadily increasing too. Almost all are inside the resort complexes and are generally open to both guests and non-guests. Around town though, a handful of traditional *hammam*-style spas still exist.

Aqaba Turkish Bath King Hussein bin Talal St; ☏ 03 203 1605. Housed in a lovely period building, this traditional *hammam* spa is open to both men & women (women must reserve in advance & are given an appointment). Here, you can relax in the steam bath followed by a scrub & massage.

Hammam Bab al-Hara Ayla Shopping Centre, Al-Rashid St; 📱 079 966 3800. A traditional *hammam*-style of spa for men only, yet being located in a shopping centre it has a modern feel. Offers a Turkish bath, steam room, sauna & massage suite. It is popular with local men as well as visitors.

Interfit Spa Intercontinental Aqaba Resort, King Hussein bin Talal St; ☏ 03 209 2222; 🖷 03 209 3320; www.intercontinental.com. Enjoy Dead

Sea mud wraps & scrubs, marine detoxifying & revitalizing treatments, facials & massage in this candle-lit spa with an exotic Oriental-style décor. Sauna, hydrotherapy bath, jacuzzi & steam room complete the spa experience, while the centre's fitness suite offers a gym, aerobic classes & squash courts.

Janna Spa Ayla Shopping Center, Al-Rashid St; ☏ 03 205 1991. With a welcoming feel & contemporary décor, this spa focuses on health & beauty for women only. Its menu is lengthy; you can choose from a Moroccan bath followed by a massage, a spell in the steam room, sauna or jacuzzi, or have a facial. The spa has its own hair salon & fitness suite, too.

Kempinski The Spa Kempinski Hotel Aqaba Red Sea, King Hussein bin Talal St; ☏ 03 209 0888;

f 03 209 0880; www.kempinski.com/aqaba. Facials, wraps, scrubs, massage & body stones are on the menu of this elegant, subtly lit spa that uses herbs, plants & flowers in all its treatments. A cell renewal scrub that uses salt from the Dead Sea combined with lime is also available.
Zara Spa Mövenpick Resort Tala Bay Aqaba, South Beach Rd, Tala Bay; ✆ 03 209 0300; f 03 209 0301; www.moevenpick-hotels.com.

Following the success of the Zara Spa at the Movenpick's hotel beside the Dead Sea, the hotel decided to open a spa in its new Aqaba hotel. The result is a place of utter tranquillity. You can enjoy a steam bath, hydropool & jacuzzi, plus take a sauna & then be cooled down by being covered in snow from the spa's crushed ice fountain. It's an interesting experience & is recommended.

ADVENTURE SPORTS Specialist companies in and around Aqaba offer several different flying experiences – you can take flying lessons or simply enjoy a piloted flight over the Aqaba landscape for an hour or so; go hot air ballooning over the city or to places like the dramatic Wadi Rum desert; or you could experience the thrill of skydiving.

Flying schools

Ayla Aviation Academy King Hussein International Airport; ✆ 03 206 4777; www. aylaaviation.com. Based at Aqaba's airport, the academy is a training school for pilots. A choice of training courses are designed for students wishing to learn to fly for both recreational purposes & as a career, & to achieve the qualifications needed for a commercial pilot licence or a private pilot licence. Facilities include simulator rooms & accommodation. Prices vary according to course & duration.

Royal Aero Sports Club of Jordan King Hussein International Airport; ✆ 03 205 8050; m 079 730 0299; www.royalaerosports.com. Enjoy hot air ballooning (JD130); microlight flying (JD30 for 10min flight to JD150 for a flight lasting 60mins) over nearby Wadi Rum; ultralight flying (from JD75); parachuting & skydiving with the members of this club based at Aqaba's airport. Book 24hrs in advance.

WATERSPORTS Aqaba offers a vast number of opportunities for enjoying the water. Whether you like to take things steady on a glass-bottomed boat, fancy a submarine trip or riding on a yacht with the wind catching the sails, enjoy windsurfing or waterskiing, or prefer an exhilarating jet-ski or speedboat trip, there are companies offering services for novices right through to experienced watersports enthusiasts. Most offer trips of a few hours to a day or more.

Watersport centres and boat trips

Neptune Submarine Vision South Beach Rd, Tala Bay; m 077 943 0969; www.aqababoat. com; JD26. This hour-long excursion on board an AC submarine observatory allows you see the fantastic array of fish & marine life of the Red Sea without getting wet. It travels along the coast

JORDAN EXPERIENCE

One of Aqaba's newest tourist attractions, the Jordan Experience (*The Gateway, Ayla Circle, next to the Royal Yacht Club;* ✆ *03 201 2200. At the time of writing this attraction is being upgraded and is due to reopen in 2012. Check for show times and entry fee.*) is an interesting 25-minute show, which takes you through the country's history and brings you right up to date with its natural and cultural treasures supposedly while you are flying over the country. In reality, you are sitting comfortably in a motion seat, of course. Find the cinema in the courtyard of The Gateway retail and entertainment complex.

to popular dive sites, including the New Canyon, which until now had only been viewed by divers. Access is from the beach.

Sindbad Marine Transportation & Water Sports Maysloon St, Zuhair Basha Bldg; 03 205 0077; f 03 205 0008; e aqaba@sindbadjo. com; www.sindbadjo.com. Along with running ferries between Aqaba & Egypt, this company runs yacht safaris & cruises around the Gulf, trips to Pharaoh Island, glass-bottomed excursions for 3–4hrs, dinner trips & private yacht charters (from JD20). The company offers jet-skiing, waterskiing, banana boat rides, parasailing & windsurfing, too.

Sunset Cruises Sinai Divers Diving Centre, Mövenpick Resort Tala Bay Aqaba, South Beach Rd, Tala Bay; 03 209 0300; f 03 209 0301; www.sinaidivers.com; JD20–45. You can take a cruise from the harbour on board the *MY Harmattan* & see the coastline of Aqaba as the sun sets, or enjoy a glass-bottomed boat trip during the day with this specialist company.

DIVING AND SNORKELLING Aqaba's waters are officially protected and are recognised as having one of the world's finest collections of dive sites. There are also opportunities for snorkellers. Here you can see a natural fringing coral reef system covered by shallow water that extends to well over 25km along the coastline, with deep water just metres from the shoreline teeming with fish and marine life. Its backslide reaches depths of some 50m. There are natural sheer dive sites with walls, drop-offs, canyons, gardens and pinnacles, and the wrecks of fishing boats, a barge and ships, including the famous Lebanese freighter the *Cedar Pride*. One site, the New Canyon, even has a vintage 40m-long tank that was deliberately sunk to create an underwater habitat and dive site. Most are ideal for beginners, right through to experienced divers. The waters are clear so visibility is almost always excellent (usually around 20–50m) and the warm waters make it a pleasurable experience.

Dive sites The dive sites lie close to the shore and are easily reached by boat; in fact, some you can even swim to if you are strong swimmer. Even the deepest dives can take place just 100m or so from the shore. Aqaba currently has a total of 23 official dive sites, 21 of which are within the boundaries of the Aqaba Marine Park (see *Aqaba Protected Area and Aqaba Marine Park*, page 263). Confusingly, some dive centres list more than 23 dive sites, and some of those are called by different names than the ones we list below. We have taken the official number and name. Only the **Power Station**, which is a heart-pounding sheer wall dive often made in the company of whale sharks or Moray eels, and the southernmost dive site, the **Saudi Border Wall**, which is famed for its cabbage-like corals and turtles, lie outside the park's designated area.

The most northerly dive site within the Aqaba Marine Park is the **First Bay North**. To begin this dive you first descend a reef that slopes from 12m down to 30m and then swim past outstanding coral pinnacles covered in red soft corals. The next dive heading south is the **First Bay South**, which is popular for its colourful collection of coral bushes and its sandy gulley, along with the straightforward 5m dive site **Ras al-Yamanya**, where beginners can practice in safety, and the **King Abdullah Reef**, which extends some distance along the shoreline and where you can see a rare fan-like coral formation. Large shoals of fish can be seen at all these sites. Look out for species of fusiliers and Torpedo Rays.

Black Rock, with its steep slopes and hard coral-crusted pinnacles, and **Rainbow Reef**, which has a coral colony shaped like a rainbow and is a popular night-dive site, are the next sites heading south. Until now, the sites have been characterised by their natural formations, whereas the next dive along the shoreline is one of the most dramatic of all. The **Cedar Pride** dive plunges to a depth of around 30m where a cargo vessel of more than 70m in length rests on a sandy bed (see box, page 257). The wreck of the *Cedar Pride* lies just 150m or so off-shore from the King Abdullah Beach and can be reached easily by small boat. If you are a strong swimmer you can reach it by swimming.

The wreck of a barge that sunk in 1996 and a fishing boat lie close to the *Cedar Pride* at a dive site dubbed **Tarmac Five**, while a little further on is **Japanese Garden**, a shallow dive site so called because of its varied collection of flora and fauna. It is popular because shoals of brilliantly coloured sergeant majors and species of fusilier are often seen here, along with the added bonus of occasionally seeing turtles gliding majestically through the waters. Still heading south, the next dive sites are **Gorgone I**, with its three prominent pinnacles, table corals and a large Gorgonian fan coral after which the site is named, along with **Gorgone II**, which has a smaller coral fan, and the **Seven Sisters** dive, so called because of its unusual formations. All are shallow dives and popular with both novices and experienced divers who want, or need, a change from deep diving.

The **New Canyon** dive is one of the most characterful and revolves around a sunken anti-aircraft canon tank said to have once been used by the Jordanian Army. It was sunk as an artificial reef in the late 1990s and having lain on the seabed ever since is now covered in coral. Next up is the dive site dubbed **Eel Canyon** because of the many eels that live here in the reef's crevices. **Yellowstone Reef** is next along the coast and is a combination dive of shallows and deep waters with an abundance of yellow-hued corals that have given it its name. Similarly, **Blue Coral** takes its name from the blue-hued corals that cover its pinnacles. The dive descends in three sections from 10m to 50m and features sandy and grassy plateaus.

Kiwi Reef is one of the most beautiful sites and a popular one with underwater photographers, while further along the coast are **Moon Valley**, which drops steeply,

UNDERWATER CAMERAS

If you are planning to take an underwater photography course then you might like to visit some of the duty-free shops in the Aqaba city centre; the prices for underwater cameras are generally low when compared to European prices and probably cheaper than you might have to pay at your dive centre (see *Shopping*, page 251).

Aqaba SPORTS AND OTHER ACTIVITIES

9

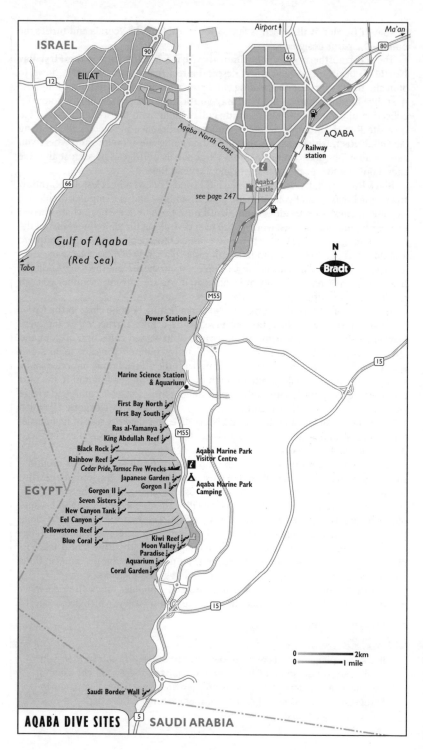

AQABA DIVE SITES

and the sites of **Paradise** and **Aquarium**, where red soft coral has covered their interesting formations. The penultimate dive site in Aqaba is the **Coral Garden**, a deep dive that has a collection of corals so beautiful that they often appear in photographs and videos. The final site and the closest to Jordan's border with Saudi Arabia, is the **Saudi Border Wall** dive, which lays just metres from the shore. Currently the diving experts in Aqaba are exploring more sites and evaluating them for future use.

Practicalities If you are planning to dive while in Aqaba be sure to contact some of the centres before you depart for your holiday to firstly check that they offer the course or dive you are interested in and secondly to find out what documentation they need you to bring, such as a diving certificate and log book to prove you have received diving tuition issued by associations such as PADI. If you do not have a certificate or are a first-time diver, then you can discuss the courses available to you. Almost all of the centres below offer tuition for beginners or refreshers and you can gain sufficient experience in just a day or so to equip you with the knowledge to tackle an open-water dive.

You will also need to check what clothing or equipment you need to bring. Again, the centres below will be able to provide equipment like tanks and probably wetsuits. If you are planning to use your own wetsuit, the general advice is to ensure it is at least 3mm thick for summer use (short suits are fine), and 5mm to 7mm thickness in spring and autumn. Drysuits are generally recommended for winter use. This information should be taken as a guide only; always check with your dive school tutor and consider his or her recommendations.

You should also think about your holiday plans for immediately after you have dived. It is dangerous to fly or even to drive or walk to higher altitudes soon after you have dived, and this affects travel almost everywhere from Aqaba, which lies at sea level. If you are planning to travel to Wadi Rum for example, you need to bear in mind that, while only a few kilometres away, it is actually well over 900m above sea level. Similarly, Petra or Amman are around 1,200m above sea level. As to how many hours you should stay in Aqaba to allow your body to adjust after surfacing from your dive, this depends largely on the depth you have dived and can be as much as six to seven hours. Always discuss this with your dive school instructor.

It is also advisable to leave a sufficient length of time between your last dive and your return home by plane, which is generally accepted to be around 18 hours. The

THE *CEDAR PRIDE*

This once formidable freighter arrived in Aqaba in 1982, but while in port a fire broke out and spread throughout most of her body except the hull. Damaged beyond repair but still afloat, the vessel caught the eye of King Hussein I, a keen diver himself, who proposed that the ship be sunk and become part of the reef ecosystem. The project to sink the ship became a mammoth task, but once a site had been found and the ship prepared, she was taken a little way out to sea and allowed to sink to the seabed. That was on 16 November 1985, and now, nearly 30 years later, the *Cedar Pride* is one of the most famous of all Aqaba's dive sites and the one that almost every diver who comes to the city wants to enjoy. The ship lies on her port side with her masts still intact and is now covered in an amazing growth of soft coral. You can circle the wreck with ease, and experienced divers can even explore her interior in safety.

National Oceanographic and Atmospheric Association (*NOAA; www.noaa.gov*) and the **Professional Association of Diving Instructors** (*PADI; www.padi.com*) provide tables detailing the time needed between diving and ascending to altitude, and detailed decompression advice.

Diving is only permitted in the park through registered agencies and dive centres, which will run through the rules and regulations. You will be told never to walk or place your equipment on the corals, for instance, as this can cause extensive damage. You should not torment the fish or marine animals, some of which are dangerous, and you should not attempt to break off coral or collect marine life. Prices for diving experiences vary enormously, but typically for a two-dive trip expect to pay around JD250 and more for certification, plus the hire of diving gear. If you simply want to hire snorkelling gear you'll find prices vary but are around the JD25-a-day mark.

Diving and snorkelling centres

Aqaba Adventure Divers South Beach Rd, south coast; m 079 584 3724; www.aqaba-diving.com. You can stay at its dive centre & then join the team on board its dive boat for daily diving trips to some of the most interesting sites in the Gulf. Specialist courses include night diving, deep water diving & reef diving.

Aqaba International Dive Centre King Hussein bin Talal St, near city centre; m 079 694 9082; e diveaqaba@yahoo.com; www.aqabadivingcenter.com. Certified diving instructors form part of the team at this dive centre, which offers a range of snorkelling excursions to explore the shallow reefs or heads out to slightly deeper water for dives. Tuition & guide available.

Aquamarina Dive Centre Al-Nahda St, city centre; ☎ 03 201 6250; f 03 203 2630; e aquama@go.com.jo; www.aquamarinadc.com. A 5-star PADI dive centre, the Aquamarina

offers the chance for beginners to try a dive & for novices & more experienced divers to learn all aspects of the sport through to professional level. Training materials are available in several languages including English, French & Swedish.

Barracuda Diving Club South Beach Rd, Tala Bay; ☎ 03 206 0501; e info@goaqabadive.com; www.goaqabadive.com. Proud of its high safety & technical standards, this club offers dive training & guided tours around sites that include the amazing *Cedar Pride* wreck. Qualification courses are available.

Bedouin Moon Village South Beach Rd, Tala Bay; m 03 201 5525; e info@bedouinmoonvillage.com; www.bedouinmoonvillage.com. One of the largest dive centres in Aqaba, the Bedouin Moon Village offers dive courses from 2–5 days duration, Dive Master courses, rescue training, courses to learn about underwater photography & cartography, & fish identification, along with diving & snorkelling trips.

YAMANIEH CORAL REEF

In 1965, King Hussein traded a huge swathe of Jordanian desert of some 6,000km² in size with Saudi Arabia in return for a further 12km of coastline in the Gulf of Aqaba lying to the south of Aqaba city. The acquisition meant that Aqaba could increase the number of hotels, dive sites and amenities it provided for visitors, as well being able to expand its port (see *Looking to the future*, page 238). Significantly, the deal included the Yamanieh Coral Reef which is one of the largest and most intricate such systems on the planet, and lies at the point where Jordan meets Saudi Arabia. The reef attracts a multitude of fish and marine life, including turtles, hunting jacks and humphead wrasses, and has contributed to Aqaba becoming regarded as one of the best places to dive and snorkel in the world.

Dive Aqaba Al Saada St, near city centre; m 079 660 0701; www.diveaqaba.com. Established in 2002 with the emphasis on fun, safe dive & educational courses to instructor level, this club operates when out on the water from its own purpose-built dive boat, *Laila One*. It takes enthusiasts to all the best dive & snorkelling sites.

Extra Divers South Beach Rd, Tala Bay; m 079 973 9318; e aqaba@extradivers.info; www.extradivers-worldwide.com. The full range of daily dive trips to the reef are offered, along with courses to experience the best of Aqaba's diving. You can find this dive centre within the Radisson Blu Tala Bay Resort complex.

International Arab Divers Village South Beach Rd, Tala Bay; \ 03 203 1808; f 03 203 0560; e info@aqaba-divevillage.com; www.aqaba-divevillage.com. This club's team of guides escort certified divers to as many as 22 dive sites along the coast daily, along with offering beginners the chance to try a dive or take a course, & professionals to obtain dive qualifications. The club has its own 4-star dive village.

Jordan Frogman Diving Centre King Hussein bin Talal St, near city centre; m 079 553 0916; e hashim@jordanfrogman.com; www.jordanfrogman.com. Part of a long-established commercial dive company, this centre offers daily diving trips & courses. You can opt for try dives or learn about & experience diving off the coast or in open water. Specialist courses include first-aid & rescue.

Red Sea Dive Centre South Beach, south coast; \ 03 202 2323; e info@aqabascubadiving.com; www.aqabascubadiving.com. With its own hotel complete with well-equipped rooms, adults' & children's swimming pools & restaurant, this dive centre is family-friendly. Its dive school has courses to suit beginners through to experienced divers, & includes wreck, deep & night dive programmes.

Royal Diving Centre (RDC) Coral Bay Hotel, Aqaba South Coast Rd; \ 03 201 5555; f 03 210 7097; e reservations@coralbay.jo; www.coralbayaqaba.com, www.rdc.jo. A PADI-registered dive centre, the RDC offers no less than 14 sites to visit for diving or snorkelling. Novices as well as experienced divers are welcome. The centre supports environmental & sustainable tourism projects.

SeaStar Water Sports Al Saada St, south coast; \ 03 201 8335; f 03 201 8339; e info@aqabadivingseastar.com; www.aqabadivingseastar.com. Boat diving, shore diving & full-guided technical dives are among the options offered by this specialist company, along with a full range of PADI courses for beginners right through to instructor level. Sample holiday dives can be arranged too.

Sinai Divers Diving Centre Mövenpick Resort Tala Bay Aqaba, South Beach Rd, Tala Bay; \ 03 209 0300; f 03 209 0301; www.sinaidivers.com. Daily snorkelling safaris (JD45) & diving excursions to Kiwi Reef (JD30–75) from a luxurious dive vessel, the *MY Harmattan*, are offered. Also available are cruises, yacht charters & a submarine observatory trip.

OTHER PRACTICALITIES

EMERGENCIES Aqaba has three **hospitals**, the Aqaba Modern Hospital in Quds Street (\ *03 201 6677*), the Islamic Hospital in Sharif Shaker ben Zeid Street (\ *03 201 8444*) and the Princess Haya Hospital (\ *03 201 4111*) off the approach road into Aqaba at the Princess Haya Circle, which are modern and well equipped. Doctors and pharmacists almost always speak excellent English and you can go to any one of them for an emergency or simply to purchase medicines from the pharmacy. Opening times of the **pharmacies** can vary though, so it is best to telephone to check. All are well signposted throughout the city.

INTERNET As a lively university city, Aqaba has an abundance of internet cafés. You only have to walk along Al-Rashid Street or take the right fork into Al-Nahda Street to see six or more in as many minutes. Most of the hotels have Wi-Fi in their business centres or foyers, and a growing number are now offering the facility as standard in rooms. Mobile connections are supported by Mada (*Al-Rashid St*, \ *06*

400 0000), Orange (*Zahran St,* ☏ *03 201 3333*), Zain (☏ *079 606 3117*) and Umniah (*Sa-ada St;* ☏ *078 800 2268*).

MONEY AND POST Head for the city centre around Ayla Circle and along Al-Nahda Street off Al-Hammamat al-Tunisyya Street where you'll find numerous banks and ATMs. The main post office (*Jordan Post Company,* ☏ *03 201 3909*) can be found in Yarmuk Street, near Al-Hammamat al-Tunisyya Street.

WHAT TO SEE AND DO

GREAT ARAB REVOLT PLAZA (*Off King Hussein bin Talal St*) This huge paved square dominates the southern end of the city centre beach and seafront, which has less to do with its size and more to do with the fact that in its centre is a mighty 132m-high flagpole from which one of the largest flags in the world sashays with the wind. The 30m by 60m black, red, green and white flag, although similar to that of Jordan, is the flag of the Arab Revolt of 1916–18. The freestanding pole was erected in 2003 to commemorate the successful outcome of Arab forces ousting the Ottomans from Aqaba, and for a time had a place in the *Guinness Book of Records* as the tallest in the world. It is capped with a 2m diameter gold-painted crown in honour of the kingdom's Royal Hashemite family. The Great Arab Revolt Plaza is home to Aqaba Castle, the fascinating Aqaba Archaeological Museum, the Aqabawi Mosque, Sharif Hussein bin Ali's house, Noor al-Hussein Foundation handicraft centre and the picturesque fisherman's harbour.

Aqaba Castle (*Great Arab Revolt Plaza, off King Hussein bin Talal St;* ⊕ *summer 08.00–18.00 daily, winter 08.00–16.00 daily; entry JD1, inc entry to the Aqaba Archaeological Museum & the House of Sharif Hussein bin Ali*) Originally the site of a Crusader fortress, this fascinating fort dates from the time of the last Mumluk sultan, Qansah al-Ghouri (b1446, d1516) who ruled in the 16th century. Arabic relief inscriptions adorning its walls and the impressive entrance gate date from the late Islamic period and attest to al-Ghouri's role in the castle's construction. They record that he had victories in battle and give an insight into the period. Further inscriptions inside one of the many rooms that lie off an inner courtyard tell of Ottoman occupation and a period of expansion for the castle. Square in shape, the castle has thick stone walls flanked by semi-circular towers, and has been altered, expanded or repaired as a result of being attacked and damaged many times since it was first built.

Over the years the castle has seen quiet times too. For what is believed to have been centuries, the castle was used as a caravanserai where pilgrims from Egypt could relax and refresh on their way to Makkah, as well as a base for military forces.

AQABA'S UNIVERSITIES

The Red Sea Institute of Cinematic Arts (RSICA) (*www.rsica.edu.jo*) is the only such school in the Middle East and north Africa to offer a MFA (Master of Fine Arts) degree qualification, and is based in Aqaba. Students learn the art of interactive media, animation and post production, digital and print processes and video production for film and television. The city's other universities include the University of Jordan at Aqaba (*www.ju.edu.jo*), the Aqaba University of Technology, the British University of Aqaba and the American University of Aqaba, along with the Institute of Banking Studies.

The small rooms around the central courtyard are where pilgrims and soldiers at different points in history would have rested. Some have been restored while others have been left largely untouched and remain as they were almost 100 years ago. Directly above the entrance gate is the Hashemite Coat of Arms, which was placed here after the successful conclusion of the Arab Revolt in 1916 (see page 241). The castle was in the thick of the action and received extensive damage from shells fired from boats anchored in the Gulf by the British Royal Navy, who were fighting as allies of the Arab forces. You can see the result of the shelling today in a battle-scarred section of the castle that lies just off to the right of the central courtyard.

Although some areas of the castle remain badly damaged, you can walk around most of it with ease. See the prison just beyond the high cross-vaulted entrance hall before heading off down a dark passageway that leads to a huge domed space with access to the central courtyard. Here you will find the caravanserai rooms. You can then explore the rest of the castle. Look out for the gloomy execution chamber, the high vaulted dining hall and the horse stables, along with the chamber where pigeons would have been fitted with messages to deliver to far-flung areas of the empire. Look out too for the stone staircases that will take you up to the second floor. Here, you can see across Aqaba's rooftops in one direction and its coastal panorama in the other. The climb and walk at this level is not for the faint-hearted however, as no guard rails are currently in place to stop you falling to the level below. Within the complex is a mosque, which is today used as offices.

House of Sharif Hussein bin Ali (*Great Arab Revolt Plaza, off King Hussein bin Talal St; ☉ summer 08.00–18.00 daily, winter 08.00–16.00 daily; entry JD1, inc entry to Aqaba Castle & the Aqaba Archaeological Museum*) This attractive stone-built mansion was once the home of Sharif Hussein bin Ali (b1853, d1931), who was the father of the first king of the Hashemite Kingdom of Transjordan, King Abdullah I, and the great-great-grandfather of Jordan's present king, His Majesty King Abdullah II. He lived here in the months after World War I. The sharif is best known as being the last Hashemite sharifian to have ruled over Makkah, Medina and Hejaz, and for launching the Arab Revolt against Ottoman rule in June 1916 in a fight that was to become known as the Battle of Aqaba (see page 241).

Today, the mansion is a museum dedicated to his time spent in Aqaba, with collections of his rifles, camel saddles, silverware, copper bowls and coffee mills and pots on display. A particularly striking display in the museum is one of *mensaf* platters; these large trays are designed to present Jordan's traditional dish of lamb in a yoghurt sauce with rice to guests in time-honoured fashion. *Mensaf* is still presented on big platters in the same manner today. Part of the mansion contains the Aqaba Archaeological Museum (see below).

Aqaba Archaeological Museum (*Great Arab Revolt Plaza, off King Hussein bin Talal St; ☏ 03 201 9063; f 03 202 2023; ☉ summer 08.00–18.00 daily, winter 08.00–16.00 daily; entry JD1, inc entry to Aqaba Castle & the House of Sharif Hussein bin Ali*) Compact but bursting with interesting artefacts, this little museum occupies part of the mansion built for Sharif Hussein bin Ali (see above). It opened in 1990 to celebrate Aqaba's history and to tell visitors about the city's often turbulent, but nonetheless fascinating, story. Most of the exhibits date from between the 7th and 12th centuries, and focus on the ancient Islamic city of Ayla and its fortunes during the Umayyad, Abbasid and Fatimid eras. There are exhibits from Egypt, Iraq, Ethiopia and even from China, all of which play their part in the make-up of modern Aqaba.

A large Kufic inscription of *Ayat Al-Kursi* from the Holy Koran that hung from the city's eastern gate in the 9th century makes a striking exhibit in one of the main halls of the museum, as does the collection of Fatimid gold dinar coins minted in Sajilmasa in Morocco, some early Islamic frescoes and a striking group of Chinese ceramics that have been dated to the 10th century. One of the most historic exhibits is the first milestone of the Roman Via Traiana Nova highway (see box, *The King's Highway*, page 161). Its inscription is still clear and reads that the Emperor Trajan opened the road from Syria to the Red Sea.

Noor al-Hussein Foundation (*Great Arab Revolt Plaza, off King Hussein bin Talal St;* \ *03 201 2641;* e *nhf_aqaba@yahoo.com; www.nooralhusseinfoundation. org;* ⊕ *summer 08.00–18.00 daily, winter 08.00–16.00 daily*) This gift shop is far more than a place to buy souvenirs or to see local handicrafts being created; it is a place where unemployed students, women and other disadvantaged members of the local population are given jobs. The centre was set up in 1986 under the auspices of the Noor al-Hussein Foundation with the aim to help the economic, social and cultural needs of families who live in Aqaba. Since then it has helped more than 50,000 individuals.

Visitors to the centre, which is housed in a lovely period building near the Aqaba Castle and the Aqaba Archaeological Museum, can see the workshop where three production areas have been established. One line handles sewing, the second is where tie-dye fabric and clothing is created, and the third is where tapestry patchwork is made and fashioned into souvenirs. Next to the workshop is the showroom, where all these items are displayed along with items produced by other workshops within the Noor al-Hussein Foundation network. The centre has been a lifeline to the people of Aqaba, not just as a result of the income created by selling the handicraft items in the showroom, but also because the complex offers them training opportunities. A children's library and Information Technology Centre provide valuable resources for learning new skills.

AYLA ARCHAEOLOGICAL SITE (*Islamic Ayla off King Hussein bin Talal St, and ancient Ayla off Al-Rashid St;* ⊕ *24 hrs daily; entry free*) The remains of this medieval city date from early Islamic times, but are thought to lie next to an even older city that was referred to in the Bible (1 Kings 9:26). This ancient city is believed to have been a caravan stop along the King's Highway, which later became the Roman Via Traiana Nova. At one time, the Islamic Ayla was the first city to be built outside the territories of the Arabian Peninsula, and as such became a strategic, and probably much welcomed, place for Egyptian pilgrims to rest and refresh on their way to Makkah. In Ottoman times, the city became a store for the Hejaz Railway, which ran from Damascus to Medina with a spur to the coast.

The remains of both settlements were discovered in the mid 1980s by an American–Jordanian archaeological team. Here you can see the world's oldest church (see below), along with the medieval city's walls, gates, a collection of public buildings and a large mosque. Information panels are provided for visitors that explain each ruin as you make your way around the site. Excavation works are ongoing and new finds are being unearthed all the time, much to the delight of archaeologists and the country's Ministry of Tourism and Antiquities; however a large part of the ancient city lies underneath the present modern city of Aqaba. You can find the remains of medieval Ayla just a few minutes' walk from the marina along the waterfront opposite the Mövenpick Hotel and Miramar Hotel. You'll need to walk a little further to Al-Rashid Street to visit its ancient namesake.

Ayla Church (*Off Al-Rashid St*) Historians and archaeologists alike, plus the *Guinness Book of Records*, consider Ayla Church to be the world's oldest known purpose-built Christian place of worship. Its architectural configuration and the discovery of religious artefacts and an altar table nearby when it was unearthed in the 1980s have lead experts to date this two-storey mudbrick church to between AD293 and AD303. The church predates even the Church of the Nativity in Bethlehem and the Church of the Holy Sepulchre in Jerusalem, both of which are believed to have been constructed in the AD320s. Ayla Church measures just 26m by 16m in size. It is an amazing find. To get there look out for the signposts from the King Hussein bin Talal Street waterfront just off North Beach.

AQABA PROTECTED AREA AND AQABA MARINE PARK (📞 03 203 5801; f 03 203 0912; e info@aseza.jo; www.aqabamarinepark.jo) Aqaba hosts the country's southernmost protected area which, unlike the country's other nature reserves created in desert and forest landscapes, comprises a stretch of shoreline some 25km long, including the coastal waters and the outstanding coral reef ecosystem of the Gulf of Aqaba. The Aqaba Protected Area is managed by the **Royal Marine Conservation Society of Jordan** (JREDS) (📞 06 567 6173; f 06 567 6183; e information@jreds.org; www.jreds.org), which aims to protect marine life and the biodiversity of the region, while working for sustainable development. Jordan's 2010–15 Tourism Marketing Strategy includes new projects, including a coral planting programme for the Red Sea.

The Aqaba Marine Park works in conjunction with the society, and manages a stretch of shoreline and its coastal waters that run along almost the entire length of the south coast for 7km. It stretches from the passenger terminal lying just south of the city centre, heading southwards towards Jordan's boundary with Saudi Arabia, and covers areas of land as well as the water itself. Aqaba is Jordan's only coastline and, as such, is a magnet for visitors keen to experience another side to the country away from its desert plateaus and cities, and enjoy its sparkling waters and marine life.

Founded in 1997, the Aqaba Marine Park offers visitors the chance to learn more about the ecosystems created by the coral reef and how to protect them, while enjoying the many activities that the shoreline, reef and waters provide. The park has its own **Marine Science Station**, where you can find the **Aqaba Marine Aquarium**. The park has a visitors' centre and a multi-purpose auditorium and exhibition hall where special events are held. It also has a library, shell museum, restaurant and gift shop. There are diving centres and campgrounds within the park's boundaries. The park's aim is to help protect the vulnerable coral reef system and marine habitats of the Gulf from the impact of the city's development and its perceived growth, while ensuring visitors can enjoy all the area has to offer. One way it does this is to manage zones.

Strict zoning is in place within the park to provide areas for specific purposes. On land there are scientific research and administration centres that manage and study the park's biodiversity, plus zones for beach relaxation, swimming, boating and a zone for diving and snorkelling. All are managed in such a way as to provide sustainable use for visitors' enjoyment without fear of damaging the fragile ecosystem. The park is managed by a team of park officers and rangers who keep a watch for the safety of tourists as well as ensuring the beaches are always kept clean and free from litter, and that all the park's regulations are upheld.

The park is one of the most densely populated stretches of water in the world in terms of its marine life, much of which can be seen simply by swimming out from the beach to a reef. The most popular dive sites and the coral reef system lie just metres from the shoreline. The waters are calm and warm with temperatures averaging around 27°C in summer, slightly cooler at around 20°C in winter, and are considered safe. They have unusual vertical currents, which when combined with the warmth of the water and the calm sea breezes make swimming, snorkelling and diving off the coastline a pleasurable and memorable experience.

The protected area is home to around 230 different species of hard and soft coral, including fungia, montipora and the archelia, which is an extremely rare specimen resembling a black spindly tree. It is only found at great depths. The Gulf of Aqaba's archelia is said to have been discovered by keen diver King Hussein I himself on an expedition. Coral reef is made up of millions of tiny animals from the aquatic cnidaria group that colonise and form structures (see box opposite). The Gulf's own reef has been formed over millennia and takes the form of a flat plateau near the shore, which has pockets of sand. Although the tidal range in Aqaba is barely 1m, at low water the reef plateau is often exposed. Teeming with fish, the plateau is a snorkeller's dream. The plateau falls off sharply at its seaward side (known as the reef crust) to provide the steep drop-offs that have made this a world famous dive site.

Around 1,000 different species of reef and deep-water fish and mammals, and a seemingly endless number of molluscs, algae, amphipods and other crustaceans have been recorded in the waters. Some are endemic to the region. If you are lucky you may see the bright yellow and black masked butterfly fish (*Chaetodon semilarvatus*), the picasso triggerfish (*Rhinecanthus aculeatus*) or the delightful clownfish (*Amphiprion ocellaris*) darting amongst the corals, or species of the squirrelfish, the boxfish or parrotfish. Look out for shoals of brilliant blue sergeant majors (*Abudefduf saxatilis*) and species of fusiliers, damsels and the larger groupers, angelfish and batfish, and even octopuses. Dramatic orangey brown scorpion fish (*Scorpaenidae*), stonefish (*Synanceia*) and lionfish (*Pterois*), and species of moray eel, all of which can be dangerous if touched or provoked, swim in the waters of the reef too. If you touch one of the fish's venomous tentacles or are bitten by an eel you should seek medical attention immediately.

The reef has a fascinating landscape of sea grasses too, which provide a habitat for a whole raft of creatures. Here you may catch sight of delicate seahorses, turtles or garden eels, which often swim undetected amongst the greenery, while on the sandy seabed look out for starfish and sea urchins. The urchin (*Tripneustes gratilla*) actually feeds on the sea grasses, along with a few species of fish, such as the surgeon fish (*Zebrasoma xanthurum*). The deeper waters of the Gulf attract a few pelagic species, such as the harmless plankton-eating whale shark (*Rhincodon typus*) or a passing manta ray. There are species of barracuda, jacks and jellyfish too.

In the Aqaba Marine Park you can enjoy all sorts of pursuits from windsurfing and jet-skiing to sailing, banana boat rides and waterskiing. Diving and snorkelling are the top ways to spend your time here, or if you don't fancy getting wet but still want to see the underwater world of Aqaba then you take a glass-bottomed boat trip or try the submarine observatory. See pages 253–4.

Aqaba Marine Aquarium (*Marine Science Station, Aqaba Marine Park;* ✆ *03 201 5144;* e *info@aseza.jo; www.aqabamarinepark.jo;* ☉ *08.00–16.00 Sun–Thu, 08.00– 17.00 Fri–Sat*) This museum has a huge tank that has been designed to resemble the underwater coral reef world of the Gulf of Aqaba. Here, the displays comprise numerous species of hard and soft coral in a whole variety of colours and shapes, along with 30 invertebrates and around 45 different species of reef fish.

The coral reef structure found in the Gulf of Aqaba is thousands of years old. It is a living organism formed by millions of tiny animals, known as polyps, from the aquatic cnidaria group that live together as a colony. Each minute animal secretes a calcium carbonate that forms a hard exoskeleton within which its body lives. When the polyps die naturally what remains is a hard, stony coral created by its exoskeleton. Aqaba's coral reef has been gauged to grow in thickness at the rate of around 1cm a year.

The warm waters of the gulf, combined with mild water currents and calm weather help these tiny animals thrive. They live on the algae zooxanthellae and the microscopic marine plant life found in the deep waters, and multiply in great numbers. However, polyps are also a food source for many of the different species of fish, turtles and sea slugs that live in the waters of the gulf. As such, the waters teem with all sorts of marine life attracted to the coral reef.

Aqaba's reef is described as fringing, which means it hugs the shoreline with lagoons and then falls to great depths just a few metres from the shore. Barrier reefs, which tend to be created over millennia further away from the shore, and atolls, which form an island, are the other two types of coral reef systems formed in tropical waters around the world. The ecosystem of all reefs is very fragile and in Aqaba visitors are asked not to break off pieces or touch the living coral, not to stand on the reef, which could cause extensive damage, and not to feed the fish. You are also asked not to leave litter on the beaches as it could be washed up into the gulf's waters and cause harm to its marine life.

AQABA BIRD OBSERVATORY (*Jordan Society for Sustainable Development (JSSD), Peace Forest, Al-Ma'abar;* ☏ *03 201 4052;* e *aqaba@jssd-jo.org;* ⊕ *08.00–17.00 daily; permit required, available from the JSSD*) Aqaba is a major stopover area for migrating birds to and from Africa and, as such, has become a popular place for birdwatchers to catch a glimpse of different species, particularly in spring and autumn each year. With this in mind the Jordan Society for Sustainable Development acquired a disused wastewater treatment plant a few years ago and transformed it into a manmade wetland reserve and haven for migrating birds, and an observatory for visitors. The aim of the observatory is to maintain and preserve the habitats for birds, monitor the birds and their migration, and to educate visitors on environmental issues associated with Aqaba and its fluctuating bird population. It is a great centre, the first of its kind in Jordan and well worth a visit.

The observatory complex comprises two main zones. The first is a huge expanse of wetland formed by five water ponds full of aquatic plants and separated by natural sand walkways, while the second area is given over to the dense vegetated forest, known as Peace Forest. Here trees native to Jordan stand, some up to 10m high. Throughout the complex are walkways, marked trails and tracks, and bird hides for you to observe the birds and wildlife up close. The conservation status of many of the birds is threatened or even critically endangered, and it is a pleasure to see them thriving in the habitat created by the observatory.

Some of the birds you are likely to see are the Madagascar little grebe (*Tachybaptus pelzelnii*), the corncrake (*Crex crex*), the vulnerable marbled teal (*Marmaronetta angustirostris*) and the lesser white-fronted goose (*Anser erythropus*). Highly

Aqaba WHAT TO SEE AND DO

9

distinctive but threatened, the falcate duck (*Anas falcata*) thrives in the wetlands too. You may catch sight of the endangered white-headed duck (*Oxyura leucocephala*), the near-threatened ferruginous duck (*Aythya nyroca*), the beautifully striking white Audouin's gull (*Ichthyaetus audouinii*), the great snipe (*Gallinago media*), the black-tailed godwit (*Limosa limosa*), the white-eyed gull (*Ichthyaetus leucophthalmus*) and the black-winged pratincole (*Glareola nordmanni*). Some species you may be fortunate to see in the reserve are critically endangered, including the striking long-legged black stilt (*Himantopus novaezelandiae*) and the attractive sociable lapwing (*Vanellus gregarius*).

You can find the Aqaba Bird Observatory at the southernmost end of the Araba Valley, around 2km north of the city centre. Head for the airport and look out for signs to the Peace Forest and the observatory. On site you'll find a visitors' centre where information on the project is displayed, along with a research centre for the study of birds, a library facility and an indigenous tree nursery and botanical garden. The observatory is often looking for volunteers to help with its valuable conservation work in protecting and raising awareness of different bird species and their habitats. Contact the centre if you feel this is something that you may be interested in.

PHARAOH ISLAND You can visit this picturesque island, that lies in Egyptian waters just off the Sinai Peninsula, to see its fairytale Crusader castle, known as the **Castle of Saladin**. It was built in the 12th century by King Baldwin's army, but when

Saladin captured Aqaba and its region (see *History*, page 240) he assumed control of the island, which was at that time known as the Ile de Graye, and took over the castle. However, the notorious Crusader Reynald de Chatillon, displeased at having one of his favourite castles taken away from him, mounted a furious reprisal and regained control of the stronghold. Over the years the castle weathered a little, but a recent restoration programme has breathed new life into this glorious place and now it is a popular day excursion. You can explore its passageways and towers, and gaze at the view of the Egyptian coastline.

Once you've finished being absorbed in its history don't leave without enjoying a spot of **snorkelling or diving**. The reefs that lie around the island are outstanding, and regularly attract enthusiasts.

You can't travel to the island unaccompanied; you need to book on an organised excursion, which can be done via almost all the hotels or dive centres. You'll need to book at least a day in advance because the organiser will need to arrange a temporary Egyptian visa for you. When you make your booking be sure to have your passport with you. One company that organises daily trips to the island is **Sindbad Marine Transportation and Water Sports** (see under *Watersport centres and boat trips*, page 253). Trips usually depart at 10.00 and return at 14.00, with lunch and time for snorkelling and swimming included. Expect to pay around JD50 per person.